CONTEMPORARY LATINA/O MEDIA

Contemporary Latina/o Media

Production, Circulation, Politics

Edited by
Arlene Dávila and Yeidy M. Rivero

NEW YORK UNIVERSITY PRESS
New York and London

NEW YORK UNIVERSITY PRESS
New York and London
www.nyupress.org

References to Internet websites (URLs) were accurate at the time of writing.
Neither the author nor New York University Press is responsible for URLs that
may have expired or changed since the manuscript was prepared.

LIBRARY OF CONGRESS CATALOGING-IN-PUBLICATION DATA
Contemporary Latina/o media : production, circulation, politics / edited by Arlene Dávila
and Yeidy M. Rivero.
pages cm
Includes bibliographical references and index.
ISBN 978-1-4798-2891-3 (hardback) -- ISBN 978-1-4798-6058-6 (pb)
1. Hispanic American mass media. 2. Hispanic Americans and mass media. I. Dávila,
Arlene M., 1965- II. Rivero, Yeidy M., 1967-
P94.5.H58C66 2014
302.23089'68073--dc23
2014012224

New York University Press books are printed on acid-free paper,
and their binding materials are chosen for strength and durability.
We strive to use environmentally responsible suppliers and materials
to the greatest extent possible in publishing our books.

Manufactured in the United States of America
10 9 8 7 6 5 4 3 2 1

Also available as an ebook

CONTENTS

Introduction

ARLENE DÁVILA

If you have been reading the business news headlines, you would think that Latin@s are being showered with an unbounded selection of new media choices. Just ten years ago, talk of Latino media could be safely reduced to a handful of TV channels (dominated by Univision and Telemundo), a larger number of radio networks, a variety of more localized venues such as cable stations, and print news. Today, however, there's a dizzying discussion of new TV channels, booming celebration of Latin@s as the "new" media market, and the entry of big media players anticipated to "transform" what we understand as "Latino media." Yet neither communications nor media scholarship has kept up with these transformations, leaving us with few answers to overarching questions in the field of Latino media and communications. We know little about what really may be "new" about current media proposals, about whether Latin@s are being offered more varied representations and opportunities for jobs and access to media markets, and about the ways they are consuming and mobilizing new media for political aims. These are exactly some of the questions that this volume seeks to answer by calling attention to issues of production, circulation, distribution, and consumption. It does so by going beyond debates over images and representation that, while important, have tended to dominate discussions of Latino media to explore a more uncharted terrain involving the larger political economic dynamics at play.

The volume focuses on Latino/Latin American media flows because what we regularly define as "Latino media" has historically been the product of transnational processes involving ownership and the importation and circulation of talent and content from Latin America. It has also been dominated by the importation and translation of programming ideas (from the United States to Latin America, particularly from the 1940s to the 1960s), the buying and selling of scripts across the region (beginning in the 1940s and continuing into the present), and, more recently, the selling of programming formats, all intended to sustain a larger and hence more profitable hemispheric market (Rivero 2009; Oren and Shahaf 2011). In other words, addressing "Latino media" means analyzing at least two industries: one with roots in Latin America and the other with roots in Hollywood, not to mention two industries that are also linked to at least three distinct language media worlds in Spanish, in English, and in Portuguese (translated into Spanish) (Rivero 2009).

Traditionally media scholars have tended to split Latin American and Latino media industries in their analyses, clearly separating the two regions and populations in their studies in ways that have tended to downplay the intricate connections between Latino and Latin America media at the level of production, circulation, and consumption. Instead, our analysis adopts a transnational focus to place these dynamics at the foreground of any contemporary analysis. The volume's focus, however, is US Latin@s and how they are being inserted into these processes, and affected by the continued Latin Americanization of genres, products, and audiences, as well as by the whitewashing of "mainstream" Hollywood media, where Latin@s, like most racially diverse communities, have been consistently bypassed. Beyond this common emphasis, the volume is purposefully broad. It focuses primarily on Spanish-language television and radio, which are the two dominant nationwide marketing and media outlets for US Latin@s, but it also touches on the state of Latin@s in mainstream prime-time TV, and to a lesser extent on regional, digital, and alternative media that have been generally more accessible to locally based communities.

At the same time, we are very aware of the limitations of this project, and present it as a start of a larger and much-needed debate. In particular, the anthology reflects a continued dominance of Mexican and Mexican American media, a product of Latino demographics, but also of the continued dominance of Mexican exports in Latino media. We were surprised by the continued scarcity of analyses looking at Cubans in Miami, notwithstanding the key role that Cuban Americans have played in the development of transnational Spanish-language media and the rising role of Miami as a "Latin Hollywood."[1] The lack of research on the involvement of Dominicans and other Latin@ groups in the development of alternative media is also another important void in the current scholarship, which we hope our volume helps to fill by inspiring more work in the future. Then there is the fact that while Latin@s are close to 16 percent of the total US population and mass media imbricate every single aspect of Americans' lives, it is impossible for this or any single volume to provide a fully comprehensive treatment of contemporary "Latino media" or Latin@s and the media. For this, we need to escape the very category of "Latino media" that has historically constrained analysis, limiting it to media that are supposedly marketed and packaged to Latin@s, in isolation from all the different media to which they are exposed and which they consume on a daily basis, from mainstream network TV, to video games, to outdoor media, to the Internet, and so on. In fact, some chapters provide glimpses of this larger media landscape that remains largely understudied, though as a general rule our focus remains on media marketed, packaged, and circulated as "Latino media." We chose this focus because it assists our analysis of the Latino media landscape at a time when new investments and developments pose questions about what may be some of the social, cultural, and political implications of these supposedly "new" media investments. This emphasis also facilitates an exploration of the problems and limits of "Latino"-specific media and of most of the corporate-driven productions and representations of Latinidad at a moment when, despite their invisibility in most media venues, Latin@s and most racial "majorities" are no longer numerical "minorities." In sum, our intention is to have more attention paid to the political economy and cultural politics of Latino media within media, communication, and cultural studies while encouraging more work to fill the enormous voids in these growing fields of study.

Likewise, we focus on the traditional rubrics of production, circulation, and cultural politics, well aware that politics embeds all stages of media production and circulation and that, as Stuart Hall's famous encoding/decoding essay once noted, these "separate" dynamics are ultimately intertwined. Matters of circulation, distribution, and policies affect decisions about production, while production processes are decisive in what is ultimately consumed and circulated as "Latino media." Our use of these rubrics is, then, strategic. Specifically, we seek to think through the transnational trends fueling the growth of "Latino" media initiatives in the United States; issues of policy and political economy that constrain the circulation of media products; and the everyday cultural politics related to all facets of media use and how they affect matters of representation, democracy, and the creation of new Latin@ publics and politics.

To this end, our contributors include a diverse group of stellar scholars working in the field of Latino media, cultural studies, and communications, who place different emphases on these issues in their analyses, but who nevertheless position matters of politics and the market at the heart of their discussion.

Indeed, the past decade has seen dramatic changes in the global political economy and the landscape of Latino media. There has been an unparalleled level of media consolidations and major new media ventures for Latin@s, as everyone seems to want a piece of the Latin@ media market. Not surprisingly, these developments have been accompanied by a rise in anti-immigration discourse and anti-Latino sentiment—a situation that reminds us of the limits of equating visibility with political empowerment. Some key initiatives include Murdoch's MundoFox, a new Spanish channel that will draw supposedly more "sophisticated" programming from Colombia, and Univision/Disney's twenty-four-hour cable news channel that will be directed at English-dominant Latin@s for the first time. Granted, there is a lot of boosterism, anticipation, and spin around these new developments, which, history warns us, merit more skepticism than optimism and praise. I recall the enormous fear and excitement provoked by Telemundo's supposed "revamping" after its purchase by Sony Pictures Entertainment, with other major corporate investors in 1998. The entry of a major entertainment giant into the Latino market was interpreted as a sign of coming of age, while the network's announcement of new revamped programming that would rely less on imports and more on Latino-specific content led many observers and enthusiasts to speak liberally of a new "Latin Hollywood" on the make (Dávila 2001).

In hindsight, we know the buzz was highly overrated. Telemundo never developed any breakthrough bilingual programming. It did increase its US-based productions, but did so by lightly tweaking the dominant Spanish-language formula that remained largely unchanged. More recently, instead of solely importing Latin American soap operas, the network has focused on importing actors and writers from Latin America and producing in Miami. This "new" formula, however, has done little to increase access to the "Latin Hollywood" for US-based, English-language–dominant Latin@s, who continue to be bypassed in favor of Latin American actors and actresses with supposedly "generic" Spanish-language fluency and name recognition in the United States through their previous participation in their countries' soap opera productions back home. Puerto Rican actors have had to migrate to Miami to find jobs in television upon Univision's purchase of one of the island's most important TV channels—another example of the types of labor inequities generated by the Spanish-only media world that increasingly have hemispheric ramifications (Rivero 2005). In turn, the growth of Miami's production industry has not represented an improvement in working conditions for US Latin@ actors and writers. Importing performers and writers has shielded the major networks from the union contracts that would lead to improved and more secure working conditions for actors and media workers in the US Latino/a media landscape (Chozick 2012). The end result is that instead of hiring US Latin@ performers, Hollywood talent agencies are going to Miami in search of "Latino talent" who are mostly from Latin America and who are sought after for their overt signs of Latinness, consisting primarily of their accents. The rise of light-skinned Spanish-language soap opera stars like William Levy and Sofia Vergara is part and parcel of this penchant for "Latin" stars who "sound" Latino, and of the tendency for language to trump race and look as the primary defining element of "Latinidad" within mainstream media representations of US Latinos (Rosa 2010).

A continued problem is the essentialized ideas about language that continue to be promoted by most "Latino-oriented" media, a situation that the rise of English-language and bilingual choices for Latin@s has not challenged. These media primarily consist of news or cheaply produced reality TV that have done little to expand opportunities for more diverse creative offerings. In fact, Christopher Joseph Westgate's contribution in this volume argues that English-language media function the way Spanish-language media historically have: both contribute to essentialist associations between Latin@s and language that are more informed by economic considerations—specifically by the need to assure exportability of content, whether it be English-language news or Spanish-language *novelas*—than by the linguistic practices of contemporary Latin@s. I also worry about the ensuing typecasting of English as the language of news and information and Spanish as the language of entertainment that may follow from the ongoing split between English-language news channels and regular entertainment programming channels.

In this context, reality TV becomes one of the few spaces where diverse linguistic practices and sounds are heard. MTV's show *Washington Heights*, featuring a multiracial Dominican cast, speaking Dominican-accented Spanish and English, was especially noteworthy. Unfortunately, reality TV remains an undependable genre and a contradictory space for anyone to attain representation and achieve access to media. These shows are cheap to produce, and while some characters may rocket into fame, most are exploited and discarded. Further, while most reality TV shows revolve around neoliberal citizenship formulations of transformation and uplift that erase everyday people's complex realities, Latin@ and Black reality TV participants tend to be concentrated in urban/ghetto exposés that are embroiled in contradictory stereotypes.[2] Other recent developments include the rise in transnational genres like narcocorridos, the pan-Latinamericanization of novelas with actors recruited from all over Latin America, and finally, the development of new media. As we will see, each of these developments represents particular openings for inclusion and representation alongside unique challenges.

In particular, transborder cultural networks that bypass national concerns and limitations in creating "Latino" products represent new types of challenges for theorizing inequalities in the flows of investment and production across the United States and Latin America. As Juan Piñón's contribution to this volume notes, processes of deregulation, privatization, and liberalization have blurred the line between the "national" and the "foreign" in the US/Latin American television landscape, while national distinctions remain very much in place. Moreover, we are in the midst of more and new types of transnationalization within the dominant Spanish-language US Latino/Latin American media market. No wonder that the Ibero-American Fiction Television Observatory (OBITEL)—which publishes annual reviews on the industry through research teams in each of its eleven member countries in Latin America alongside the United States and Spain—made the transnationalization of television fiction the topic of 2012. Among other issues, OBITEL's annual yearbook pointed to key internationalizing trends from

> 1) the adaptation of successful scripts from other countries, in particular the role played by Argentina and Colombia as producers of stories for the Spanish-speaking countries and increasingly so by Brazil and also as regards Portugal; 2) to the constitution of multinational casts as a commercial hook; 3) to the establishment of co-production models to produce or adapt fictional shows; and 4) to financing and creating production centers in countries other than their own. (Orozco and Vasallo 2012: 80)

Similarly, as Juan Piñón's contribution attests, global media companies are increasingly bypassing traditional limits on foreign investment in Latin American media, fostering new types of US and global investments, whether it is through legal loopholes, the stock exchange market, or investments in production and content-providing companies.

These global investments are not often visible. The resulting programming products may appear "local," while distinctions and hierarchies are reproduced in ways that favor global media industry over nationally based producers, who are often relegated to production processes rather than the most profitable aspects—creating and distributing media content. And here we must qualify the meaning of "local" content and "global investment" with an eye to the many ways transnational media are reconstituting what localized audiences are exposed to as "local" programming, or what they recognize as such, as well as the ways "global" investments take place. Because "local" programming has long included transcultural products (such as a Brazilian soap opera dubbed by Mexican actors exported to Chile or to the US Hispanic market), Latin American and US Latin@ audiences may not recognize that behind the new imported soap opera from Mexico or Brazil lies a Disney, HBO, or Nickelodeon (OBITEL 2012). We see similar processes at play in Hollywood's investments in India's film industry, with Sony and Warner Brothers coproducing and codistributing with Indian filmmakers as a way of entering this growing market. Ironically, while Indian studios see these investments as their opportunity to become "global," "global" partners are most interested in going "local" in India as a strategy to gain new markets (Ganti 2011: 361). In other words, it is Sony and Warner Brothers that benefit most from these investments (which allow them to tap into new markets and audiences in the developing world where they would otherwise be shunned), not Indian filmmakers or Mexican TV producers, of whom only a minority are afforded access to global audiences and recognition through these arrangements. The whitewashing of global cinema has led critics to point out that "Bollywood may make more films than Hollywood, but it shows no sign of gaining global traction. . . . Instead, both India and China are hiring more and more western actors" (Cox 2013).

Indeed, as attested to by Piñón, as well as by Rodrigo Gómez, Toby Miller, and André Dorcé in their coauthored chapter, the new transnational circuits of television production linking the US and Latin American markets are characterized by growing inequalities in the flows of television production. The United States still "reigns supreme" in production and circulation of content throughout the region; Mexico remains the primary content exporter for the entire Ibero-American market, including the US Latino market, while new investments in "Latino" programming have not produced greater or significant choices for Latin@ audiences. There are also winners and losers in the Spanish-dominant media market, countries that take the lead in production and exporting like Mexico, Colombia, and Brazil, and countries like Ecuador and Uruguay that are primarily recipients and importers, while the US Latin@ market is especially predetermined by the successful formula of importing content from Latin America. Moreover, "local" productions that are created in partnerships with global media corporations, whether produced in Latin America or in the United States for the US Hispanic market, are increasingly mainstreamed and less tied to localities, or to political, social, or culturally specific issues, as they are increasingly produced with an eye to greater exportability and marketability across nations and regions.

In other words, what we are seeing is the casualty of the "local" in favor of neutral themes and formats that can have greater exportability at the cost of diversity at all levels, in terms of media content, but also in terms of what countries, regions, actors, writers, and workers get access to these transnationalized media markets and who are shut out. Media pundits may point to a new pan–Latin American telenovela with a multinational cast of actors or to the emergence of Latin global music idols like Shakira as evidence of the existence of a diverse transnational media space. Our contributors, however, challenge these types of naive assessments by exposing the erasures and inequalities that are consistently reproduced. In all, they remind us that behind every corporately packaged new media product, new types of exclusions and erasures can be found; that in fact, every new project that targets new types of Latin@s (the bilingual, the young, the immigrant, the upwardly mobile, the Afro-Latino, the regional music lover, the growing Dominican market, and so forth) demands attention to the many differences that are contained by and through these new Latino/a marketing niches.

One recurrent issue that concerns this volume is the unparalleled levels of media ownership and concentration that have accompanied these transnational developments. The National Hispanic Media Coalition notes that in 2011 "Latinos owned a mere 2.9 percent of all commercial TV stations and only 2.7 percent of FM radio outlets. Latin@s didn't fare much better in AM radio, once thought to be a key entry point for people of color, owning only 172 AM radio stations out of 3,830, or 4.5 percent" (National Hispanic Media Coalition 2012a). Latin@s also hold less than 6.5 percent of all media jobs, both in front of and behind cameras as executives, writers, and producers, even though they now make up over 16 percent of the US population (see Frances Negrón-Muntaner's essay in this volume). This underrepresentation is especially severe in mainstream journalism, and is especially worrisome given the news' key role in shaping public opinion. Debates around immigration in the news have long been defined by stereotypes and racist tropes, in ways that dehumanize Latin@s and present them as inherently foreign threats (Santa Ana 2002, 2012). Words and representations have political implications, and when Latin@s are nowhere to be found in the newsroom, the likelihood that diverse and politically sensitive perspectives are included is dramatically lessened, as attested by the difficulty of banning the use in major newsrooms of "illegal" to refer to undocumented immigrants. Drawing from key reports on this issue, Elizabeth Méndez Berry points out that in 2010 only 1.3 percent of total news stories focused in a substantial way on Latin@s; while Latinos made up about 4 percent of total newsroom employees in 2011, 0.5 percent of op-ed articles in major newspapers around the country are written by Latinos; and only 2.6 percent of radio news staffers and 7.3 percent of TV news staffers are Latinos (Méndez Berry 2012).[3]

This lack of representation has significant implications in the current context of increasing anti-immigrant sentiment and the rise of anti-immigrant legislations, because it feeds into the misperception that Latin@s are always "foreign" or a threat. This was the predictable conclusion of a major report issued by Latino Decisions with the National Hispanic Media Coalition that circulated widely during the 2012 elections, documenting how a majority of Americans buy into dominant stereotypes of Latin@s in the news and the media that represent them as immigrant, foreign, and criminal (National Hispanic Media Coalition 2012b). Sadly, the findings from this poll were not surprising. What is striking is the persistence of stereotypes and practices of othering despite the overwhelming growth and residential diversification of Latin@ populations. Liberal racial thinking would tell us that racially based stereotypes would lessen, as racial "minorities" are everywhere present. But the continued othering of Latin@s in the media suggests that their racialization continues apace. In fact, in the current so-called post-racial context, Latin@s' racialization is accompanied by a general unwillingness to address issues of racial diversity, representation, and parity in the media and at all levels of society, especially within the Federal Communications Commission. At the height of the civil rights movement, the fight over media space was paramount; Chicanos and Nuyoricans fought for equal time on the airwaves and for policies and funding to create TV and radio programs and films that would help counter their negative portrayal in mainstream media. The rise of Chicano cinema and of Latino-specific ethnic media and media activism and advocacy in the 1970s is part and parcel of struggles for federal legislation and funding opportunities to increase Black people's and Latin@s' access to media (Bodroghkozy 2012; Classen 2004; Noriega 2000). Unfortunately, since the passing of the 1996 Telecommunications Act, which deregulated the telecommunications industry, racial minority populations have faced steeper challenges when media advocacy and activism are concerned. Not only do they face media monopolies and institutions that have exponentially grown in size and power, but also they do so with little to no resources and policies for addressing inequalities.

Overall, there is a scarcity of forums in which to analyze these transformations, given that, as a general rule, works on Latino media remain focused on textual and cultural studies analyses of representations, isolated from any examination of issues of global circulation and the structural transformations of global media or their effects on media employment and markets. One reason for this void is that communication scholars seldom produce book-length monographs, because their discipline encourages publication in peer-reviewed journals, while cultural studies scholars are not always concerned with or trained to look at matters of political economy. As a result, discussions surrounding Latino media still revolve around issues of representations and stereotypes, whose importance is evidenced by the above-mentioned study attesting to their prevalence in the American imaginary. Yet this approach does not provide us with the entire story of what's happening with Latin@s and the media. For that we need to go behind the scenes, and look at issues of production, political economy, and politics.[4] In doing so, we seek to fill a void in the field of Latino media, which has been historically devoid of analyses of political economy. We follow recent works on some of the global political economic trends behind the foundation of Hispanic marketing and important newer works on Latino media and the music industry, examining Latin@ music and performers in light of the growth of a generic "Latino" market (Cepeda 2010; Dávila 2012; Paredez 2009; Piñón 2011; Rivero 2005).

Works on the music industry have especially shown the exclusions and the violences experienced by performers as they pass through what Cepeda describes as the "Miami sound machine," the corporate-fueled institutionalized music industry behind the "Latin" music boom of the

1990s. Latin@ performers have always been subject to corporate demands to make their music more palatable to wider audiences, but Cepeda shows how investments by major transnational corporations facilitated the development of truly global stars like Ricky Martin and Shakira, performers who despite (or perhaps because of) having only a "Latin tinge" in their music, became marketed as global icons of Latinidad. Cepeda bemoans this machine because it "perpetuates a belief in Latin America as the geographic and artistic center of Latin(o) musical 'authenticity'" (Cepeda 2010: 48), not unlike what has happened with other sectors of the media industry, most notably television. But what's clear is that once again, the concerning issue is not only one of representation, the very narrow type of Latin@ idol who becomes authenticated by the industry. The issue is also about the inequalities that are sustained and reproduced through these types of authentications that make it so difficult for Latin@ musicians to access both the mainstream and the "Latino" music industry.

Indeed, since their inception in 2000, the Latin Grammys have been criticized for highlighting corporate-favored styles and rhythms in Spanish over most regionally based performers, independent recording musicians, and Latin@s performing in English. Consequently, we remain surprised when tragedies like the early deaths of Selena and, more recently, Jenni Rivera bring attention to the existence of large numbers of Latin@s who remain "untapped," such as those following regional music genres or bilingual performers and those who are not otherwise listening to the Colombian Juanes, the Mexican pop-rock duo Jesse and Joy, or other Latin American performers favored by the Latin Grammys. The sudden "discoveries" of artists like Jenni and Selena point to the existence of alternative communities and networks of distribution that bypass and challenge the limits imposed by the dominant "Latino" music establishment. A good example is provided by Hector Amaya's discussion of *narcocorridos*, a genre that was popularized through online distribution across the US/Mexico border. As he notes, notions of authenticity harbored by the music industry don't work for narcocorridos because this music is not nation-bound, while both the mainstream and the Latin@ music industries are regularly marketed in this manner. Similarly essentialist and nationalist precepts are behind Puerto Ricans' erasure from the history of hip-hop because of its marketing as a solely "Black" cultural product. Puerto Rican performers were pressed to shed their "Latinness" to fit into the dominant marketing model by an industry that could not understand the multiracial/multicultural milieu that was at the center of this new cultural expression (Rivera 2003).

This edited collection seeks to tackle wounding erasures like these that impact on Latin@s' ability to participate as media creators and stakeholders. Foremost, our collection seeks to think through the new cultural politics involving Latin@s and media by going beyond the spin around Latinos as the "new hot market," or the uncritical celebration unleashed by the announcement of one more "Latino" media station or channel in the works. These myopic, market-driven perspectives lose sight of the fact that Latin@s remain largely underserved by all media, whether or not meant specifically for "them," and that they are still largely excluded or at the bottom of the media labor market. Recall here the omission of Lupe Ontiveros from the 2013 Oscars "In Memoriam" section, which led to the revelation that Latino membership in the Academy of Motion Picture Arts and Sciences is less than 2 percent. The *Los Angeles Times* reports that Ontiveros herself was denied membership when she applied. Foremost, these market perspectives ignore the fact that community voices and local and regional-based culture and products are consistently bypassed by most current corporate-driven Latino media proposals.

This is one of the reasons social media have become such key spaces for Latin@ activism, as described, for example, by Cristina Beltrán's essay on Dreamers. These media are the one space that remains considerably more accessible to communities, even when their reach and impact remain quite limited, and they bring up additional issues around privacy and surveillance. Indeed, issues of reception and the politics of media use are especially important terrains for investigation when racially diverse communities are concerned as the last bastion through which to document alternative voices and rescue the type of differences that are consistently bypassed by mainstream representations. In particular, ethnographic analyses provide an especially useful tool to counter "overarching" narratives of Latinidad by providing fine-tuned observations of the limits of marketable formulas for reaching Latin@ constituencies and viewers. In all, many of our contributors turn to viewers, listeners, and audiences of all types to inquire about the multiple differences between popular media representations and the everyday uses of Latinidad.

*   *   *

Part 1 of this collection addresses issues of production, looking at matters of political economy and changes in production processes, the development of new hemispheric initiatives, and the reorganization of media work around old and new ethnic- and language-based hierarchies. This section includes essays that provide macro perspectives on some of the most significant new initiatives, such as Disney's ABC News and NuvoTV, as well as the politics involved in their production. Juan Piñón provides an important look at current transnationalization strategies in Latino/Latin American television, exploring some of the factors, at the local and national levels, that have facilitated the ongoing corporate consolidation of the media and led to changing levels of foreign involvement and ownership. In their chapter, Rodrigo Gómez, Toby Miller, and André Dorcé point to some of the strategies that are helping to consolidate Mexico's continued dominance in the US Latino market. Special attention is paid to the linguistic politics involved in creating media content for Latin@s, who have been historically defined as a linguistically homogeneous market to the detriment of US-born, English-dominant Latino producers and productions. These essays also examine the different types of "transnationalism" at play in Univision and Telemundo and more recent initiatives. Essays by Christopher Joseph Westgate and Henry Puente examine this key issue by looking at the linguistic politics involved in producing NuvoTV, a bilingual and English-language channel, and the new Latin@-specific English news sites developed by Fox, NBC, and Univision. Frances Negrón-Muntaner's contribution then turns us to a discussion of the current state of Latin@s' involvement in the contemporary media industries through an analysis of their participation both in front of and behind the camera. Her rich statistical data more than prove the exclusive world of mainstream media and the difficulties activists seeking to transform it must face. Vanessa Díaz's chapter, in turn, touches on the politics of work and labor through a case study of paparazzi image sales that speaks to larger trends that position Latinos at the bottom of the ethnic/racial divisions and hierarchies of cultural work in the media industry. Díaz focuses on Latinos working in mainstream celebrity culture, but similar dynamics have been documented elsewhere, showing how Latinos' incorporation in the "Latino" media sector is consistently mediated by their race, language, ethnicity, and nationality in ways that exclude some Latinos (Afro-Latinos, English-dominant Latinos) from some of the most profitable sectors of the industry (Dávila 2001; Piñón and Rojas 2011).

Part 2, on circulation, distribution, and media policies, looks more closely at some of the major local and national communications policies that have affected Latino media, as well as new patterns for distribution and circulation of media products. The essays in part 2 examine how new players and initiatives are redefining the field of circulation and distribution of "Latino" media products. Omar Rincón and María Paula Martínez explore the rise of Colombia as a new venue for production and how new patterns of circulation may be redefining ethnic and national boundaries and creating new publics, as is the case with the new "pan-Latino novelas." The cultural politics and debates around representation are a special concern of this section, debates that our contributors show are suggestive of the transnational dynamics involved. These issues are especially relevant in regard to the exportation of formats when the politics of race, ethnicity, and nationality in the United States and Latin America come to the forefront. This is evident in Yeidy M. Rivero's discussion of the debates over the Colombian adaptation of the US series *Grey's Anatomy*, coproduced by Disney Media Networks Latin America, Vista Productions, and RCN, when several Afro-Colombian organizations accused RCN of racism because the adaptation excluded the Black characters featured in the original series. Essays by Mari Castañeda and Dolores Inés Casillas examine how marketing measures such as those used for measuring audiences and ratings have historically helped shape dominant census and marketing categories that have both missed and misrecognized Latino/as. A key lesson is the overwhelming ignorance that prevents corporate America from understanding Latin@s and their needs, and the stereotypes that lead them to treat Latin@s as second-class audiences and citizens. Casillas, in particular, shows how supposedly "objective" audience evaluation companies such as Arbitron are riddled with linguistic and racial oversights that underrepresent Spanish-language radio audiences, who remain "lost in translation." Altogether, these essays expose the wide-ranging types of cultural politics unleashed by the circulation and distribution of contemporary Latino/a media.

Lastly, part 3, on consumption, reception, and politics, examines how Latinos and Latinas are consuming, using, and reshaping the media that are being targeted to them, with an eye to the new public spheres and definitions of Latinidad that may be in the works. Essays address how DREAM activists are using social media (Cristina Beltrán), some of the different reading and consuming practices of Latino/a audiences (Jillian Báez), as well as some of the differences around region, race, ethnicity, language, and gender that are consistently elided by most "Latino" media content (María Elena Cepeda, Deborah R. Vargas). In particular, Báez shows how audiences are constantly gauging their and others' identities through media, and how television viewing is a racially charged process for debating issues of citizenship, belonging, and race. Vargas, for her part, highlights the important role that Jenni Rivera played as an immigrant activist and the ways this regional music diva challenged the Miami music machine to embrace and reinstate a more working-class and queered position and identity. This section concludes with two pieces by long-standing media professionals, Juan González and Ed Morales. Morales shares his perspectives on the current state of alternative media, while González shares insights on some historical trends that have affected the current modern news media system, as well as some thoughts on media activism in the contemporary moment.

In all, we hope that even if we end up raising more questions than we can answer, we provide a necessary intervention in the field of Latino/ Latin American media. Foremost, we hope these essays impel others to seek answers and to ask new and, hopefully, different questions.

NOTES

1. See, for instance, Sinclair 2003 and Yúdice 2003.
2. See Laurie Oulette and James Hays (2008) on the role of reality TV in promoting neoliberal types of citizenship around uplift, and Eva Hageman (2013).
3. Elizabeth Méndez Berry's unpublished report draws from studies by the Pew Research Center on Excellence in Journalism, the American Society of Newspaper Editors, Fairness and Accuracy in Reporting, and the Radio Television Digital News Association.
4. We point readers to some recent anthologies (Aldama, Sandoval, and García 2012; Valdivia and Garcia 2012; Beltrán and Forjas 2008; Valdivia 2010) that, although focusing on popular culture more generally, include essays that touch on the political economy of media production. Similarly, a volume on *Ugly Betty* brings

attention to the globalization of this production across regional and national borders and the negotiations involved in remaking it as a national and global product (McCabe and Akass 2013). Our goal here, however, is to foreground and place issues of production-circulation-reception at the center of discussion.

REFERENCES

Aldama, Arturo, Chela Sandoval, and Peter García, eds. 2012. *Performing the US Latina and Latino Borderlands*. Indiana University Press

Beltrán, Mary, and Camila Forjas, eds. 2008. *Mixed Race Hollywood*. New York University Press.

Bodroghkozy, Aniko. 2012. *Equal Time: Television and the Civil Rights Movement*. University of Illinois Press.

Cepeda, María Elena. 2010. *Musical ImagiNation: U.S.-Colombian Identity and the Latin Music Boom*. New York University Press.

Chozick, Amy. 2012. "Spanish-Language TV Dramas Heat Up Miami." *New York Times*, March 8.

Classen, Steven. 2004. *Watching Jim Crow: The Struggles over Mississippi TV, 1955–1969*. Duke University Press.

Cox, David. 2013. "Attempting the Impossible: Why Does Western Cinema Whitewash Asian Stories?" *Guardian*, January 2.

Dávila, Arlene. 2001. *Latinos, Inc.: Marketing and the Making of a People*. University of California Press.

Ganti, Tejaswini. 2011. *Producing Bollywood: Inside the Contemporary Hindi Film Industry*. Duke University Press.

Hageman, Eva. 2013. "From Foreclosure to the Amazon: Lifestyle and Debt in Reality TV." Paper presented at the American Studies Association conference, Washington, DC, November 24.

Latino Decisions. "How Media Stereotypes about Latinos Fuel Negative Attitudes towards Latinos." September 18. http://www.latinodecisions.com/blog/2012/09/18/how-media-stereotypes-about-latinos-fuel-negative-attitudes-towards-latinos/.

"Lights, Camera, Acción!" 2012. *Economist*, December 15.

McCabe, Janet, and Kim Akass, eds. 2013. *TV's Betty Goes Global*. I. B. Tauris.

Méndez Berry, Elizabeth. 2012. "Latino Media Fund." Unpublished report on funding for Latino media.

Miller, Toby, Nitil Govil, John McMurria, Tina Wang, and Richard Maxwell. 2008. *Global Hollywood: No. 2*. British Film Institute.

National Hispanic Media Coalition. 2012a. "FCC Report Shows That Latino Media Ownership Remains Extremely Low." November 16. http://www.nhmc.org/content/fcc-report-shows-latino-media-ownership-remains-extremely-low/.

———. 2012b. "The Impact of Media Stereotypes on Opinions and Attitudes towards Latinos." September. http://www.latinodecisions.com/blog/wp-content/uploads/2012/09/RevisedNHMC.Aug2012.pdf.

Noriega, Chon. 2000. *Shot in America: Television, the State, and the Rise of Chicano Cinema.* University of Minnesota Press.

OBITEL. 2012. *Transnationalization of Television Fiction in Ibero-American Countries.* Edited by G. Orozco and M. Vasallo de Lopes. Porto Alegre, Brazil: Universidade Globo and Editora Sulina.

Oren, Tasha, and Sharon Shahaf. 2011. "Introduction: Television Formats—A Global Framework for TV Studies." In *Global Television Formats: Understanding Television across Borders*, edited by Tasha Oren and Sharon Shahaf, 1–20. Routledge.

Orozco Gómez, Guillermo, and Maria Immacolata Vassallo de Lopes, eds. 2012. *Transnationalization of Television Fiction in Ibero-American Countries.* Ibero-American Observatory of Television Fiction (OBITEL).

Oullette, Laurie, and James Hay. 2008. *Better Living through Reality TV: Television and Post-Welfare Citizenship.* Wiley Blackwell.

Paredez, Deborah. 2009. *Selenidad: Selena, Latinos, and the Performance of Memory.* Duke University Press.

Pew Research Center Project on Excellence in Journalism. 2010. "Media, Race and Obama's First Year." http://www.journalism.org/analysis_report/media_race_and_obama%E2%80%99s_first_year.

Piñón, Juan, and Viviana Rojas. 2011. "Language and Cultural Identity in the New Configuration of the US Latino TV Industry." *Global Media and Communication* 7: 129.

Rivera, Raquel. 2003. *New York Puerto Ricans in the Hip Hop Zone.* Palgrave.

Rivero, Yeidy M. 2005. *Tuning Out Blackness: Race and Nation in the History of Puerto Rican Television.* Duke University Press.

——. 2009. "Havana as a 1940s-1950s Latin American Media Capital." *Critical Studies in Media Communication* 26 (3): 275–93.

Rosa, Jonathan. 2010. "Looking Like a Language, Sounding Like a Race: Making Latina/o Panethnicity and Managing American Anxieties." PhD diss., University of Chicago. ProQuest/UMI (AAT3419689).

Santa Ana, Otto. 2002. *Brown Tide Rising: Metaphors of Latinos in Contemporary American Public Discourse.* University of Texas Press.

——. 2012. *Juan in a Hundred: The Representation of Latinos on Network News.* University of Texas Press.

Sinclair, John. 2003. "'The Hollywood of Latin America': Miami as Regional Center in Television Trade." *Television and New Media* 4 (3): 211–29.

Valdivia, Angharad. 2010. *Latino/as in the Media.* Polity.

Valdivia, Angharad, and Matt Garcia, eds. 2012. *Mapping Latina/o Studies.* Peter Lang.

Vargas, Deborah. 2012. *Dissonant Divas in Chicana Music: The Limits of La Onda.* University of Minnesota Press.

Yúdice, George. 2003. *The Expediency of Culture.* Duke University Press.

PART I

Production

1

Corporate Transnationalism

The US Hispanic and Latin American Television Industries

JUAN PIÑÓN

The transnational as a concept has gained increasing attention from scholars to reflect the complex and hybrid flows of populations, finances, corporations, technologies, and cultures that provide the context for media expansion across borders. Such expansion results from the intensification of globalization processes in the last decades. The transnational, in contrast to the notion of "international," was born out of the necessity to defy binary oppositions between the national and the foreign, the local and the global (Georgiou, 2006), by underscoring the porous character of national borders, borders that the notion of international seems to reify. The transnational also underscores the multispatial, multilayered, hybrid identities and cultures that coexist at cross-border, regional, and global levels. While a new set of media-related, differentiated socioeconomic-cultural processes is felt at global levels, upon an expanding financial, legal, communicational, and technological infrastructure worldwide, we can understand their articulations and speed only by taking into account the specific historical conditions of the geographies in which they are taking place.

In the case of the Americas, the relationship between the US media and Latin America has long been characterized by the increasing penetration of the US media, as a foreign corporate and cultural force, into the region (Schiller, 1991; Miller et al., 2005). At the same time, the increasing transnational relevance of evolving hybrid and complex corporate relationships between US Hispanic media and Latin American media requires us to pay attention to new institutional media modalities that are simultaneously shaping and blurring the notion of the national and forging a new industrial television character that rests mostly on the televisual constructed as culturally proximate for the region. The national broadcasting television industries in the Latin American region were born in a close relationship with US broadcasting technologies, media corporations, financial institutions, sponsors, and advertising companies. These relationships were rooted in the transnational corporate relationships that had been forged during the hemispheric expansion of the radio broadcasting industry (Fox, 1997; Sinclair, 1999). The launch of television in the region was made possible initially by imported technological flows, capital, programming, production schemes, and industrial television routines, mostly from the United States. Several Latin American nations, however, mainly the ones with the largest domestic markets, such as Brazil, Mexico, and Venezuela, were able to develop strong national television industries with very specific cultural and industrial characteristics. Brazilian TV Globo, Mexican Televisa, and Venezuelan Venevision benefited from both the relative sociopolitical stability enjoyed by these nations and the close relationship of these dominant corporations with their national governments, which favored these television networks through the establishment of monopolistic and duopolistic market structures (Fox and Waisbord, 2002). Due to these market conditions, these corporations were able to flourish as programming producers with regional impact and gain an important presence in the world television marketplace. Through their participation as owners and investors in US Hispanic-oriented media corporations, these Latin American corporations were able to make historically strong inroads into the US Latino television market with their programming and audience preferences.

The notion of programming counterflows revealed the robust and dynamic performance of the Latin American television industry and its penetration of the US and global markets (Straubhaar, 1991, 2007). But the new industrial US television landscape (Lotz, 2007) and the increasingly interwoven corporate relationship across the hemisphere require us to revisit the definition of these flows as interregional (Keane, 2006; Thussu, 2007). The purpose of this essay is to understand the new ways the transnational takes shape in the relationships between US and Latin American media corporations, particularly in the national broadcasting industries.

I argue that the line between the national and the foreign in US Hispanic and Latin American television has become blurry because of the increasing presence of transnational capital, productions, and formats. Further, the products passing as local/national are made possible through the strategic arrangement of these foreign media companies with national-local players. I complicate the well-established notion of cultural proximity, in which audiences tend "to prefer and select local or national cultural content that is more proximate and relevant to them" (Straubhaar, 1991: 43), by illuminating the industrial dynamics in which cultural proximity is pursued and constructed through television programming strategies devised by transnational corporations in order to succeed in national and regional markets. By examining some recent changes in transnational production arrangements, this essay reveals a manufactured condition of cultural proximity. Furthermore, the power of these manufactured televisual proximities is felt within a programming *circuit of exhibition* in which certain television networks establish programming agreements with other television networks across the whole hemisphere. These arrangements mirror domestic rivalries at transnational levels while also ensuring the visibility of their production styles and narrative strategies overseas. Structuring the programming offer within the region is an important outcome of this distribution strategy, by securing screens for exhibition for hegemonic players while cementing the familiarity of their particular foreign-produced content, marking it as culturally proximate at regional levels.

The region's integration into the global economy has resulted in increased forms of transnational presence within a television industry that needs capital flows to be competitive at national and regional levels, but is still tied to the legal limitations on foreign ownership imposed by specific broadcasting media regulations. Frequently the legal framework that limits foreign ownership has been defied by legal loopholes, corporate joint ventures, partial investments, stock market shares, and the increasing push of ownership deregulation. Also, transnational capital and global media are gaining more of a presence in national settings, not as foreign cultural forces, but through the faces of local-national production houses with access to distribution screens in national networks. As a result, transnational corporate agreements have not only secured the transnational circulation of programming in specific screens, but also cemented the power of certain media players to become the main sources of production and distribution across the hemisphere, reinforcing the privileged position of media corporations with transnational reach.

The main questions guiding my analysis are the following: How has the new industrial television landscape reshaped the relationship between US Hispanic television corporations and Latin American television industries? What are the specific ways the transnational is deployed within the industrial space of the US Hispanic and Latin American television landscape? Finally, how is a new form of foreign presence and participation changing common ways of thinking about transnationalism within the region?

For that purpose, I underscore two dimensions that uniquely reveal the new transnational configuration of the broadcasting television industry: transnational media ownership and investment and corporate agreements for hemispheric programming flows. First, I trace media ownership and the kind of transnational production strategies that resulted from the specific legal-industrial configuration that allows the production of a *manufactured cultural proximity*. Second, I highlight the programming flows that resulted from corporate hemispheric programming agreements. These particular programming flows, which I call *circuits of exhibition*, reveal the hidden dynamics that fuel distribution flows.

Television Corporate Ownership and Investment within a New Media Landscape

Through the combined processes of deregulation, privatization, and liberalization, the landscape of US Latino and Latin American television industries has dramatically changed (Fox and Waisbord, 2002). These industrial changes have resulted in the rising visibility of new television network competitors, the growing relevance of national independent house productions, the intensifying financial processes of foreign investments, and the active participation of global media players through the launching of localized television networks within the region. These developments have allowed the number of national media players to increase while also creating heightened production-programming-distribution relationships with regional and global media counterparts.

In contrast to the sweeping trend of deregulation in telecommunications, cable, and satellite television, the broadcasting industry is still widely protected from transnational participation, mainly on the basis of its strategic character, expressed by "the idea of 'home,' of a bond between the nation and broadcasting" (Monroe, 2000: 12). In the United States, for instance, the 310 provision mandates that television station licenses be granted only to US citizens while also imposing a 25 percent limit on foreign ownership and investment in broadcasting TV stations (Carter, 2000, 431). This scheme of limited foreign participation in media ownership is practiced in Argentina with up to 30 percent foreign ownership, Brazil with 30 percent, and Colombia with 40 percent. In Mexico, Venezuela, and Uruguay, however, foreign participation in this sector is explicitly excluded. Chile is the only country with a major media industry in the region with no limits on foreign participation and ownership (Investment Development Agency, n.d.). Yet media industries require capital for growth, so applying strict limits to foreign ownership seems to pose particular challenges to an industry that wants to benefit from access to global financial flows through stock markets. For instance, in the case of Mexico, where the law explicitly forbids foreign ownership in broadcasting media, since 1989 new regulations from the National Commission of Foreign Investment classified foreign investment originating from the Mexican Stock Market as "neutral" (Robles, 1999). Such neutral investments are not considered "ownership" and do not count in defining foreign investment (38). In the case of Argentina, the 30 percent limit on foreign ownership can be lifted in a reciprocal relationship with other nations offering more opportunities for foreign investment in media communication corporations. For Colombia, control of the company should remain in national hands, and the nation from where the foreign investment originates should offer the

Table 1.1. Ownership of National Television Broadcasting Networks and Production Houses

Country	Television Networks		Production Companies	
	National	Foreign Participation	National	Foreign Participation
Argentina	America 2 Televisión Pública*	El Trece Canal 9 Telefe	100 Bares El Árbol Ideas del Sur Cris Morena RGB Ent. Pol-ka	Telefe Contenidos Dori Media Underground Endemol-Argentina
Brazil	Globo TV Bandeirantes Rede Record SBT TV Brazil*		Globo TV Bandeirantes Rede Record SBT TV Brazil*	
Chile	Canal 13 Mega UCV TVN*	TV Canal La Red Chilevisión	UCTV TVN Mega Wood Valcine Promo Chile Ltda My Friend Cristian Galaz Buen Puerto	Chilevisión
Colombia	RCN Caracol TV Canal Uno* Señal Colombia* Canal Institucional*		RCN Vista Producciones Colombiana de Televisión Video Base	Caracol TV RTI-Colombia Fox Telecolombia Teleset
Mexico	TV Azteca Cadena 3 Once TV* Canal 22*	Televisa	Azteca Argos Canana Films El Mall Adicta Films Once TV* Canal 22*	
U.S. Hispanic	Estrella TV Telemundo	Azteca America MundoFox UniMás Univision Vme	Telemundo	Azteca Univision Venevision-Miami Plural Imagina MundoFox

Table 1.1. (continued)

| Country | Television Networks | | Production Companies | |
	National	Foreign Participation	National	Foreign Participation
Venezuela	Canal I Globovisión La Tele Meridiano TV Televen TV Familia Vale TV ANTV* TVES* TeleSur* CAVT* Vive TV*	Venevision	Radio Caracas Televen Latina Prod. Quimera Visión TVES La Celula La Villa del Cine Eduardo Gadea Montesacro Films Juan Manuel Díaz	Venevision

Source: Ibero-American Observatory of Television Fiction (Obitel 2012).
*State-owned, non-for-profit public networks.

same opportunities to Colombian investors (Investment Development Agency, n.d.).

Due to this regulation, the broadcasting television industry remains largely a national endeavor with very few exceptions, while foreign participation through partial investment or as neutral investments seems to be rising. In 2011, there were forty-seven national broadcasting television networks in the seven main Latin American markets of Argentina, Brazil, Chile, Colombia, Mexico, Venezuela, and the US Hispanic market (table 1.1). There are thirty-four national private broadcasting networks and thirteen nonprofit public national broadcasting networks (Obitel, 2012). Out of the forty-seven national television networks, twelve have a foreign presence. Some of these television networks have foreign participation through the stock exchange market (SEM) or from direct investment, and a few from takeovers by foreign entities. In Argentina, El Trece, owned by the Clarín Group Argentina, with a presence in the Argentinean and London SEMs, has 8.75 percent ownership by the Booth American Company. Twenty percent of Canal 9 is owned by the Argentinean Daniel Haddad and 80 percent by Mexican-owned Albavisión. Telefe is 100 percent owned by Spanish-owned Telefónica. In Chile, where there is no restriction on foreign ownership, Telecanal was sold to the Mexican entrepreneur Guillermo Cañedo (a former

Televisa executive). La Red was sold to Mexican-owned Albavisión. Chilevisión was sold to Turner Broadcasting System (United States). In the case of Colombia, the Santo Domingo family, owners of Caracol, sold 60 percent of its shares of Caracol Radio to Prisa in 2002; however, the family retained full ownership of Caracol TV (Arango-Forero et al., 2010). In Mexico, 43 percent of Televisa is owned by the Mexican Azcárraga family. Present in both the Mexican SEM and the NYSE, Bill Gates holds 8 percent of Televisa's stock, protected as neutral investments. Dog & Cox, First Eagle Global, Bank Morgan, and Cascada Investment also have a presence in Televisa with minor participation (Institut für Medien- und Kommunikationspolitik, n.d.). In the case of the United States, the law allows partial foreign ownership up to 25 percent. Mexican Televisa owns 5 percent of Univision Corporation, with options to grow to 30 percent (Fontevecchia, 2010). The public-oriented Vme has 42 percent of shares owned by the Spanish Group Prisa ("V-Me," n.d.). Azteca America, a US corporation, is 100 percent owned by Mexican TV Azteca, but does not break US law because TV Azteca has no ownership of its television stations, since they are the corporation's independent affiliates ("Azteca America," n.d.).

 In spite of provisions that allow partial foreign ownership in countries such as Colombia and Brazil, in both countries there is a lack of foreign ownership in national television networks, and the main media corporations in Latin America have been held by powerful families. For instance, Televisa and TV Azteca are controlled by Emilio Azcárraga Jean and Ricardo Salinas Pliego and their families, respectively. Venevision is the property of the Cisneros family. TV Globo is owned by the Marinho family. TV Caracol and RCN are owned by powerful corporate groups over which the Santo Domingo and Ardila families have ownership. These family-owned media corporations, while working in collaboration with foreign entities, have functioned as de facto barriers of entry for foreign media ownership within their companies and national industries.

While limits on foreign investment and ownership set up a barrier, production houses conceived as content providers for television networks have no limits on ownership and investment. Owning or partially investing in independent production companies is shaping up to become a decisive factor in the regional production output.

Furthermore, some independent producers have arranged decisive transnational production agreements. This has become an important strategy for transnational entities to enter Latin American television industries and markets.

Foreign presence has played a prominent regional role, since the interests of foreign entities have been deployed through production agreements with national networks for domestic market consumption. Such are the cases of Dori-Media (Argentinean-Israeli–owned), Fox Telecolombia (owned by News Corp), Plural (owned by Prisa), Promo-film-US Imagina (owned by Spanish Globomedia), RTI (owned by Telemundo/NBC), Teleset (owned by Sony), Venevision Studios in Miami (owned by the Cisneros Group), and the position of Vista Producciones as the exclusive producer for ABC/Disney formats for the Colombian market.[1] Further, RTI has been a key player in making Telemundo/NBC productions available to the Colombian market through Caracol TV. Vista Producciones with Disney, Fox Telecolombia for Fox/News Corp, and Teleset for Sony all produce for the Colombian and hemispheric markets, mainly through the RCN television network. Argentinean Underground was partially acquired by Endemol, a company based in the Netherlands but owned by Mediaset Italia. This operation cemented the various coproduction agreements of the European producer with Underground and Telefe. Dori-Media Group, owned by Yair Dori, has linked the Argentinean and Israeli television markets. Plural-Prisa through Vme also has a window of distribution. The trend of foreign corporations co-opting local independent production houses or coproducing with them is one of the most salient ways in which transnationalism has entered the market of fictional programming. This trend is also particularly evident with *telenovelas*, given the linguistic, cultural, and professional resources of the main television-producing Latin American countries.

US and European media companies are also very active in localizing formats and ideas for the region. This transnational route is exemplified in the strategies of global media corporations such as Sony Pictures Television (SPT), ABC/Disney Networks, MTV Latin American Networks/Viacom, Nickelodeon/Viacom, Fox/News Corp, and HBO/Time Warner. For instance, Sony Pictures Television has been a very active player in the localizing process due to the relevance and quantity of the company's coproduction agreements with almost all the main television networks and independent houses in the region. This strategy reflects the new preferred avenue for US corporations to reach mass hemispheric audiences in US Latino and Latin American television industries.[2]

Sony, MTV, Disney, Fox, NBC, and HBO produce telenovelas and series with local professionals, using national or well-known Latin American talents widely familiar to regional audiences. Because of this strategy, and in contrast to the original flow of English-language television and US programs that have not had the massive appeal that telenovelas have enjoyed, these transnational networks have been able to enter the local market with productions that seem more culturally proximate. The cultural proximity of these productions stems from language use, talent, locations, scripts, and their embeddedness in well-established industrial formulas in which either the local, national, or regional is televisually produced. Telenovelas such as *A corazón abierto*, a coproduction of Disney with Colombian Vista Producciones and RCN; *La reina del sur*, a coproduction of NBC-Telemundo, RTI Colombia, and Antena 3 with the collaboration of Argos; and *Amas de casa desesperadas*, a coproduction of Disney and Pol-ka, have earned high ratings in their intended domestic and regional markets. For instance, *A corazón abierto* has earned the distinction of being the most successful production in Colombian history, in the country of the super-famous *Yo soy Betty, la fea* (Henao, 2010).

Programming Flows and Transnational Circuits of Exhibition

Brazil and Mexico are the Latin American countries with the largest number of hours in fictional production. Argentina, Chile, Colombia, Venezuela, and the US Hispanic market have joined them as the group of leading producers in the region (Obitel, 2008–2012). However, production capacities do not always reflect the countries' programming distribution presence in the region. While Brazil has been the leading Latin American producer for global markets, counterflows have favored Mexican, Colombian, and US Hispanic productions as the main providers of new fictional titles in the region.[3]

Describing the flows of programming only in numbers among Latin American countries may conceal the specific industrial conditions that have produced the rise of Mexico, Colombia, and the US Hispanic market as major programming distributors. These distributors are part of a web of corporate relationships developed strategically across borders at regional levels. To understand the logics of transnational programming flows, we need to recognize that they are the result of specific corporate strategies. These corporate strategies are shaped by the television networks' production capacities, their business models, and the institutional identities they aspire to. For instance, scarcity of domestic market resources or weak production capabilities compared to those of other competitors may push a network to rely on imported programming. The programming flows that are responding to this transnational landscape, these pressures, and these market conditions are what I term circuits of exhibition.

The rise of new television networks around the region that compete for limited economic and creative resources at home has reinforced the need to look abroad for lucrative transnational exchanges. Depending on the network's capacity for making economic and technological gains, the corporation may further decide to produce its own programming to gain creative and legal control over it. The corporation may also decide to contract with local independent house productions or to rely on imports. In this competitive industrial scenario, television networks face a vital question about what business model best enables their chances for economic survival and growth: should they be television producers or distributors? The question implies positioning themselves as either producers of original content, programming distributors, or some combination thereof. When it comes to fictional production, Televisa, TV Azteca, TV Globo, Rede Record, and TVN's business model have developed mainly as producers and net exporters, while Univision, UniMás (formerly Telefutura), Azteca America, La Red, Megavisión, and SBT have clearly positioned themselves as net importers. Other television networks with robust original productions and regional visibility, such as Telemundo, Caracol TV, RCN, Venevisión, and Telefe, have embraced a mixed business model in which their lineups combine their original content with imported programming.

The relationships among network producers, network importers, and mixed importing-exporting networks are not fortuitous; in many cases they have been forged through programming agreements that mirror domestic corporate rivalries across the whole hemisphere. An important factor in production and programming distribution within the region has been the increased influence on the region of the US Hispanic market and the Spanish-language television industry. The US Hispanic market has become an economically appealing marketplace for Latin American producers willing to expand their business north of the Mexican border, and also for Spanish-language television produced by US corporations. These US corporations, producing in Miami, Los Angeles, or elsewhere, are expanding their presence with new production strategies designed to gain entry to the Latin American region.

One circuit of programming distribution and exhibition rivalry was born across the Mexico-US border, with Mexicans representing the largest segment of the US Hispanic population. Televisa and Univision signed a Programming Licensing Agreement (PLA) in 1992 for twenty-five years, resulting in Univision becoming the overwhelming Hispanic-market media leader. Telemundo, as Univision's main contender for the US Hispanic market, fought this programming agreement by partnering with TV Azteca, the rising Mexican competitor of Televisa in the 1990s ("TV Azteca and Telemundo," 1999). The agreement stopped with the launch of Azteca America in 2001 in the US market, making TV Azteca a direct competitor with Telemundo. The need for Mexican programming or a Mexican narrative and production touch was filled by Argos TV, TV Azteca's former independent house producer (Sutter, 2000). For years, this has translated into a flow of programming with TV Azteca's—and later Argos's—programming directly competing with Televisa's for Mexican audiences on both sides of the border.

This rivalry will be prolonged because of the growing relevance of Colombian production for the US Hispanic market and the alliances forged with RCN and Caracol TV, two of the main competing national networks in Colombia. The early coproduction and programming agreements between Telemundo and Caracol TV resulted in an exchange of programming for the US and Colombian markets. A key player in this alliance has been RTI-Colombia, an independent Colombian production house that sided with Telemundo since around 2000 and offered programming with Colombian flavor for Caracol TV ("Telemundo, Caracol Television and RTI," 2001). Meanwhile, programming agreements between Univision and RCN opened the screens of both

Univision and UniMás for the Colombian channel ("No. 1 U.S. Span-ish-Language Network," 2001). The battle of both RCN and Caracol TV networks in Colombia was reenacted on Univision's and Telemundo's screens in the United States. Furthermore, the transnational alliances were cemented by the aligning of Televisa and RCN with coproduction and programming agreements ("Televisa y RCN," 2010). The inclusion of the Mexican networks Cadena Tres and Argos, which reached pro-duction and programming agreements with Caracol TV, also helped to cement this alliance (E. Díaz, 2012). The rivalries among the alliances forged between Univision-Televisa-RCN against Telemundo-Argos/ Cadena Tres-Caracol TV reinforced a particular circuit of program-ming exhibition through the hemisphere, mirrored in production agreements in which Miami, Mexico City, and Bogotá became the nodes of these alliances.

TV Globo represents an interesting case. In Brazil this network is the hegemonic television power (Rego, 2011), with a decisive presence in Portugal's market through the television network SIC and regu-lar exports to African Portuguese-speaking countries (GTVI, 2010). As Televisa does for the US Hispanic market through Univision, the positioning of TV Globo in Portugal's SIC and the Portuguese-speak-ing world underlines the existence of geo-linguistic markets (Sinclair, 2004). While TV Globo is often hailed as the most successful telenovela exporter in the world television marketplace (La Pastina, n.d.), its pres-ence within the US Hispanic and Latin American television markets is not homogenously felt. TV Globo's programming is highly visible in Argentina, Uruguay, and Chile, but the number of titles exported to the rest of the hemisphere is far lower than those of its Mexican, Colom-bian, and US Hispanic competitors. In the region there is no program-ming alliance with TV Globo that strongly defines the identity of any regional network with the Brazilian telenovela style; however, one or two titles from TV Globo are always included in the lineups in almost every country in the hemisphere. In some countries the Brazilian net-work has been successful in selling programs to competing networks within the same domestic markets.

Presumably to circumvent any assumed linguistic or cultural barrier, TV Globo is pursuing an aggressive strategy of coproduction. The net-work has struck coproduction deals with the US Hispanic Telemundo

(*El clon, Marido en alquiler*), the Mexican TV Azteca (*Between Love and Desire*), and the Portuguese SIC (*Blood Ties*) ("Globo Bets," 2012). The telenovela *El clon* was distributed to more than fifty countries and made it onto the list of the most-watched telenovelas in Mexico and Venezuela (Obitel 2011).

The Venezuelan television market reveals a complex scenario, due in part to the dramatic decrease of fictional production and the resulting reliance on imports. RCTV's closing and Venevision's increasing production in Miami are two different sides of the domestic production crisis. Venevision is bound to Univision by the same PLA signed in 1992 with Televisa. The programming agreement has provided a window for Venevision to enter the US Hispanic television market; however, Venevision's telenovelas have been left out of the prime-time schedule largely occupied by Televisa's productions. As a result of the former conflict with Televisa on the PLA, Univision sought a coproduction strategy with Venevision to produce an alternative in case the relationship with the Mexican company went bad. From that strategy *Eva Luna* was coproduced by Univision Studios and Venevision Studios in Miami. As the network property, *Eva Luna* was scheduled in prime time, and entered into the top ten most watched fictional programming in 2010, and topped the list in 2011 (Obitel 2011, 2012), becoming the domestic production with the highest ratings in US television history (Gorman, 2011). The achievement of *Eva Luna* was first considered a new strategy for success that triggered a path of coproductions among Univision Studios and Venevision Studios in Miami with *El talisman* (2012) and *Rosario* (in production in 2012). This coproduction strategy has underscored the prominent position of Venevision Productions as a transnational player for the US Hispanic market, the Venezuelan market, and the regional markets. Furthermore, Venevision has also been part of the chain already formed by Univision, Televisa, and RCN, by making Televisa and RCN a center of its programming strategy. However, the network has differed partially from the others by also including in its lineup some production from Caracol TV. Mirroring hemispheric rivalries, Televen, the competing Venezuelan network, has relied primarily on Telemundo's programming. Like Venevision, however, Televen has done it partially, by including also to a lesser degree programming from Televisa, TV Azteca, Caracol TV, RCN, TV Globo, Telefe, and Rede Record.

However, while the dynamics of circuits of exhibition are established to secure TV screens across the region, with the support of more or less stable corporate transnational relationships, they show fissures in some specific contexts, or are reordered in moments of market structural changes. For instance, from 2006 to 2010, the transnational programming alliance between Televisa and Univision was imperiled because of years of legal fighting between the two corporations, due to Televisa's failed attempt to acquire Univision in 2006 at an auction that was ultimately won by Broadcasting Media Partners (BMP) (Sorkin, 2006). As a result of this selling process, Televisa withdrew its investment in Univision and fought to stop the PLA signed between both companies in 1992. This bitter battle led Televisa to seek ways to weaken Univision's position in the United States, using two programming and production strategies. The first strategy was to open the door to Telemundo when it inked a programming distribution agreement allowing Telemundo to show its programming through Televisa's broadcasting network Channel 9-Galavisión (James, 2008).[4] The consequences of this programming strategy still persist, with Telemundo making strong inroads in Mexican audiences with telenovelas such as *El clon, ¿Dónde está Elisa?* and *La reina del sur*. These productions have surpassed TV Azteca's audience ratings points in Mexico. However, Univision and Televisa's partnership was saved in October 2010, when the corporations signed an extension of the PLA—from 2017 to 2025—giving Internet distribution rights to Televisa and programming rights to Univision. The Mexican company also returned as owner of the Hispanic corporation, with an initial participation of 5 percent and the opportunity to increase this participation up to 40 percent (de Cordoba and Schechner, 2010).

Today the launch of MundoFox by RCN and News Corp/Fox in the summer 2012 is already changing the face of this hemispheric balance ("MundoFox Goes Live," 2012). By siding with Fox, the Colombian RCN has become a new competitor to its former partners Univision and Televisa. As a consequence, Univision's Telefutura network has been rebranded as UniMás. In UniMás, Univision will schedule RTI and Caracol TV productions. Televisa has signed an agreement with the Colombian RTI (N. Díaz, 2012) with plans to include Caracol TV programming on its Mexican broadcasting networks (Guthrie, 2012). The rivalry of RCN and Caracol TV will be moved and reproduced through MundoFox's RCN and UniMás's Caracol TV programming. Telemundo will seek to reinforce its relationship with the Mexican Argos and Cadena Tres from Mexico because the programming agreement it signed with RTI was to expire by the end of 2012. Actually, Telemundo has again sought TV Azteca as a possible source of programming, despite a frosty corporate relationship resulting from legal battles in the past. While Fox Telecolombia has aligned with MundoFox, and the network has scheduled only original production from RCN, there is still room to see where the production of the independents such as Teleset and Vista Producciones are going to be scheduled. The consequences of these corporate changes at hemispheric levels are still to be seen, but they seem to change the balance of power that had been in place for two decades.

Conclusions

The Latin American broadcasting landscape is an increasingly complex and multilayered transnational industrial space, characterized by regional counterflows from competing national, regional, and global media corporations deploying a variety of strategies to produce and distribute appealing programming to audiences in several domestic markets. The incorporation of Latin American national television industries into regional and global competitive scenarios has been a by-product of the processes of deregulation deployed by neoliberal policies, while the surge of new competitors has also resulted in a process of media concentration that has ended up securing the hegemonic position of regional and global media powerhouses. Furthermore, while broadcasting regulation has historically set up barriers that prevented the entry of foreign citizens and entities as owners of national television corporations, the need for financial flows to be competitive at regional levels is undermining that barrier, with an increase in different modalities of foreign participation.

While Latin American families such as the Azcárragas, Cisneros, Marinhos, Ardilas, and Santo Domingos are still the main holders of their broadcasting media corporations, the expansion of these industries into different media sectors as conglomerates through processes of concentration has resulted in the transitioning of family-structured

firms into corporate groups (Mastrini and Becerra, 2011). The positioning of these media corporations within national holdings or corporate
groups has opened the door for the participation of transnational capital or entities in different sectors, with diverse legal modalities, forcing
changes in corporate governance and participation. Broadcast television has become only one media sector within corporations that have
interests in sectors such as the telecommunications industry, which has
different regulations on foreign participation, defying long-standing
legal media frameworks. The key role of foreign media participation
in Latin America has become evident with the participation of Spanish
and Venezuelan media groups in the failed Colombian bidding process
of a third network (Ferreras, 2012), the lift on limits on foreign ownership in cable television in Brazil (Rabello and Harrison, 2011), and the
recently signed telecom law in Mexico that frees foreign ownership in
telecom and lifts foreign participation in the broadcasting industry up
to 49 percent (Tarbuck, 2013).

Limited foreign ownership has not stopped foreign presence in the
broadcasting industry, and the concentration process has strengthened media groups, offering more windows of distribution and reinforcing the concentration of programming flows and distribution to a
few powerful regional players. The programming agreements reached
by these corporations at transnational levels are signed to grant their
presences through the circuits of exhibition that structure the programming in the region and reinforce the hegemonic position of the few in
a landscape of many windows. However, today the manufacture of the
national for broadcasting television is no longer solely the prerogative
of national producers. The slow entry of global corporations, such as
Sony, Disney, News Corp, Viacom, and Endemol into Latin American
industries, through ownership in local production houses or through a
variety of coproduction agreements, has allowed Hollywood to reach
massive audiences through telenovela production in broadcast television, a space once reserved for Latin American corporations.

The participation of national, regional, and global corporations in the
Latin American broadcasting space leads to the convergence of a series
of competing economic, legal, cultural, and linguistic forces with differentiated televisual impact in the different national markets. While audience preferences are still largely driven by the cultural proximity of the

local and the national (Straubhaar, 1991), regional programming still holds relevance in audience preferences, underscoring the relevance of Latin America as a geo-linguistic market (Sinclair, 2004). However, the national and the regional are far from being natural, homogeneous categories, but rather are televisually manufactured and market-tailored products. The "national" as an assumed factor for audiences' preferences is clearly a constructed industrial category in which some corporations have enjoyed hegemonic positions in contrast to others. Not only is the national in televisual terms manufactured, the idea of a natural geo-cultural linguistic market (Sinclair, 2004) is also a space of structured economic and material conditions that cause certain cultural cues to be more valuable in industrial terms than others. The notion of a geo-cultural-linguistic market, while useful in understanding cultural commonalities, may simultaneously conceal the cultural heterogeneousness of the different regional markets and the different competing forces trying to succeed with culturally appealing products. There is no such thing as a Latin American culture; rather, there are cultures, integrated by a variety of cultural expressions, different languages, and dialects within the region, many enclosed in the notion of a "nation," but many largely ignored by the hegemonic and official discourses of the national culture. By the same token, the geo-linguistic region as a television market is an industrial construction, manufactured through the long-standing visibility of certain commodified televisual narratives produced by hegemonic media corporations within national markets and at regional levels.

A unique and interesting outcome has been the increasing transnationalization of the US Hispanic industry. On the one hand, Latin American and Iberian corporations have taken advantage of the legal provision that allows no limits on network ownership, boosting the presence of foreign groups as owners in the last decade with the incursion of the Mexican TV Azteca, the Spanish Prisa, and the Colombian RCN, which have joined the ranks of longtime players like the Mexican Televisa and the Venezuelan Venevision. On the other hand, the distribution and exhibition patterns in Latin America have raised the visibility of US Hispanic productions. While Telemundo lags far behind Univision in the domestic market share, its position as a producer and distributor of programming at regional and global levels sets the network apart from others that also lag in market shares in their respective countries. Telemundo's fictional programming, produced in Miami, Bogotá, or Mexico City, is being distributed in many countries around the region, with increasing acceptance from Latin American audiences. The support of its parent company, NBC/Comcast, a global media corporation, and NBC's commitment to conquer the Spanish-language network in both the United States and Latin America have been key driving forces behind Telemundo's growth as a producer and distributor. NBC's incursion through Telemundo's Spanish-language programming has been reinforced by the distribution infrastructure of the American corporation, transformed into Telemundo Internacional, making the US Hispanic player visible in regional and global levels.

The transnational within the category of the regional in inter–Latin American programming flows is largely represented by a small group of television corporations that have achieved their exporting status by exerting a disproportionate influence within their own domestic markets. The power and long-standing presence of some regional players, such as the Mexican Televisa, have produced programming flows of industrially manufactured regional proximity in which the network has become the second most popular source for programming in the region after nationally produced programming, a place that Hollywood has traditionally enjoyed at global levels. The competition for the US Hispanic and Latin American market plays out at different levels through different industrial layers. Transnational corporations are trying to co-opt audiences using an array of strategies, and the increasingly interwoven relationship of global corporations and national corporations has become the new regional, which forces us to leave behind past perspectives in which both were distinctive categories.

NOTES

1. While Vista Producciones is Colombian-owned, its close relationship with Disney has positioned the independent producer as the de facto adapter of ABC's programming for the Colombian market.

2. Over the last five years SPT has coproduced many successful telenovelas and series with Telemundo, Televisa, TV Azteca, Cadena Tres, Caracol TV, RCN, Bandeirantes, Telefe, Venevision, and Televen, among many others (Vinaja, 2012). While European media houses such as Endemol and FremantleMedia have traditionally been active in the region with the production of reality TV for local markets, they have also recently worked in coproduction agreements

for telenovela and series production. Some of the productions representing the entrance of US corporations through localization are *Amas de casa desesperadas* (2008, Disney, Pol-ka, Univision), *A corazón abierto* (ABC/Disney, RCN, Vista Producciones), *¿Dónde está Elisa?* (2012, Disney Network, Telemundo, RCN), *Violetta* (2012, Disney, Pol-ka), *Patito feo* (Disney, Televisa, Ideas del Sur), *Una maid in Manhattan* (2011, Sony Pictures Television, Telemundo), *Doña Barbara* (2008, Sony, Telemundo, RTI-Colombia), *Zorro* (2007, Sony, Telemundo, RTI-Colombia), *Los caballeros las prefieren brutas* (2011, Sony, TV Caracol), *Amar y temer* (2011, Sony, Caracol TV), *El sexo débil* (2011, Sony, Cadena Tres, Argos), *El octavo mandamiento* (2011, Sony, Cadena Tres, Argos), *Niñas mal* (2010, MTV Latin America, Teleset-Sony Colombia), *Si me miras bien* (2010, Sony, Laura Visconti Productions), *Isa TKM* (Nickelodeon Latino America, Sony), *Los simuladores* (2008, Sony, Televisa), *Grachi* (2011, MTV Networks, Nickelodeon), *Sueña conmigo* (2010, MTV Networks, Nickelodeon, Televisa), *La maga* (2008, MTV Networks/Nickelodeon, Dori Media Group, Illusion Studios Argentina), *Capadocia* (2007, HBO Latino, Argos Mexico), *Mandrake* (2005/2007, HBO Latin America, Conspiração Films Brazil), among the most important.

3. In terms of programming flows, the overwhelming force has been Mexico, with more than 300 titles released in the other six major markets, followed by Colombia, with 144 titles (solely from the three years 2007, 2010, and 2011), and 101 titles from the US Hispanic companies. There were only eighty-one Brazilian titles released in these markets, distantly followed by Argentina with twenty-three, and Chile with six (Obitel, 2008–2012).

4. Galavisión is a Mexican broadcasting network, a totally different entity from the US Galavisión, a Hispanic cable network owned by Univision, even though it is also filled with Televisa's programming.

REFERENCES

Arango-Forero, G., M. Arango, L. Llaña, and C. Serrrano. (2010). "Colombian Media in the XXI Century: The Re-Conquest by Foreign Investment." *Palabra Clave* 13 (1), January–June. Accessed October 23, 2012, http://www.scielo.unal.edu.co/scielo. php?script=sci_arttext&pid=S0122-82852010000100005&lng=pt&nrm=.

"Azteca American Television Stations." (n.d.). Stations Index.com. Accessed October 20, 2012, http://www.stationindex.com/tv/by-net/azteca.

Carter, B. (2000). *Mass Communication Law in a Nutshell*. Eagan, MN: West Group.

de Cordoba, J., and Schechner, S. (2010). "TV's Hottest Couple: Univision and Televisa Strengthen Ties." *Wall Street Journal*, October 5.

Díaz, E. (2012). "La ruta blanca apasionante como la realidad: Hoy se estrenó la primera coproducción internacional de Cadena tres y Caracol Televisión." Excelsior. com.mx (Mexico), August 13.

Díaz, N. (2012). "RTI firma alianza con Televisa." *El Tiempo* (Bogotá), August 16. Pro-Quest Database.

Ferreras, I. (2012). "Colombia Sees Necessity of Third Network." *Rapidtvnews*, February 21, http://www.rapidtvnews.com/index.php/2012022119909/colombia-sees-necessity-of-third-network.html.

Fontevecchia, A. (2010). "Televisa Revamps U.S. Strategy." *Forbes*, October 15. Accessed October 18, 2012, http://www.forbes.com/2010/10/05/televisa-univision-deal-markets-equities-television.html.

Fox, E. (1997). *Latin American Broadcasting: From Tango to Telenovela*. Bedfordshire, UK: John Libbey Media, University of Luton Press.

Fox, E., and S. Waisbord, eds. (2002). *Latin Politics, Global Media*. Austin: University of Texas Press.

Georgiou, M. (2006). *Diasporas, Identity and the Media: Diasporic Transnationalism and Mediated Spaces*. Cresskill, NJ: Hampton.

"Globo Bets on Co-Productions to Grow Internationally." (2012). *NexTV Latam*, June 6. Accessed December 4, 2012, http://nextvlatam.com/index.php/6-content/globo-bets-on-co-productions-to-grow-internationally/.

Gorman, B. (2011). "*Eva Luna* Finale Reaches 9.7 Million Viewers." *TV by the Numbers*, April 12. Accessed December 4, 2012, http://tvbythenumbers.zap2it.com/2011/04/12/%E2%80%9Ceva-luna%E2%80%9D-finale-reaches-9-7-million-viewers-ranks-as-one-of-top-10-novela-finales-of-all-time-and-the-highest-rated-domestically-produced-novela-in-history/89225/.

GTVI. (2010). "100% of Portuguese Africa Uses TV Globo Products." Press release, August 31. Accessed October 15, 2012, http://www.globotvinternational.com/news-Det.asp?newsId=133.

Guthrie, M. (2012). "Univision Rebrands Telefutura as UniMás." *Hollywood Reporter*, December 3. Accessed December 4, 2012, http://www.hollywoodreporter.com/news/univision-telefutura-rebrand-unimas-396702.

Henao, M. (2010). "*A corazón abierto* es la producción más exitosa de la historia según Fernando Gaitán." Colombia TV Blog, July 12. Accessed August 10, 2012, http://colombiatv.wordpress.com/2010/07/12/a-corazon-abierto-es-la-produccion-mas-exitosa-de-la-historia-segun-fernando-gaitan/.

Institut für Medien- und Kommunikationspolitik. (n.d.). "Grupo Televisa: Revenues 2011." Accessed October 18, 2011, http://www.mediadb.eu/en/data-base/international-media-corporations/grupo-televisa.html?cHash=2e1dc49af2d8e87a75cc4846cfb41516&type=98&PHPSESSID=7c113ba295f9ebd85dca6e76ab38c76b.

Investment Development Agency, Republic of Argentina. (n.d.). "Inversión extranjera: Comparación del marco jurídico en América Latina." Accessed August 10, 2012, http://www.argentinatradenet.gov.ar/sitio/datos/material/adi4.pdf.

James, M. (2008). "NBC Unit Crosses Border." *Los Angeles Times*, March 18, C3. ProQuest Database.

Keane, M. (2006). "Once Were Peripheral: Creating Media Capacity in East Asia." *Media, Culture & Communication* 28 (6): 835–55.

LAMAC. (2011). "Reporte: Penetración de TV paga en América latina seguirá creciendo en 2011 (TV Latina)." Latin American Multichannel Advertising Council.

Accessed September 18, 2012, http://www.lamac.org/america-latina/prensa/reporte-penetracion-de-tv-paga-en-america-latina-seguira-creciendo-en-2011-tv-latina.

La Pastina, A. (n.d.). "Telenovelas." Museum of Broadcast Communication. Accessed October 23, 2012, http://www.museum.tv/eotvsection.php?entrycode=telenovela.

Lotz, A. (2007). *The Television Will Be Revolutionized*. New York: New York University Press.

Mastrini, G., and M. Becerra. (2011). "Media Ownership, Oligarchies, and Globalization: Media Concentration in South America." In *The Political Economies of Media: The Transformation of the Global Media Industries*, edited by D. Winseck and D. Yong Jin, 63–86. London: Bloomsbury Academic.

Miller, T., N. Covil, J. McMurria, R. Maxwell, and T. Wang. (2005). *Global Hollywood 2*. London: British Film Institute.

Monroe, P. (2000). *Television, the Public Sphere, and National Identity*. Oxford, UK: Oxford University Press.

"MundoFox Goes Live: New Network Launches for Latino Audiences across the U.S." (2012). *Marketing Weekly News*, September 1, 379.

"No. 1 U.S. Spanish-Language Network, Univision, and No. 1 Colombian Network, RCN, Form 5-Year Exclusive Programming Alliance for the U.S. and Puerto Rico." (2001). *Business Wire*, June 18, 1. ProQuest Database.

Obitel. (2008). *Global Markets, Local Stories*. Edited by M. Vasallo and L. Vilches. Ibero-American Observatory on Television Fiction. Sau Paulo: Globo Universidade.

———. (2009). *Television Fiction in Iberoamerica: Narratives, Formats and Advertising*. Edited by G. Orozco and M. Vasallo. Ibero-American Observatory on Television Fiction. Sau Paulo: Globo Universidade.

———. (2010). *Convergencias y transmediación de la ficción televisiva*. Edited by G. Orozco and M. Vasallo. Ibero-American Observatory on Television Fiction. Sau Paulo: Globo Universidade.

———. (2011). *Quality in Television Fiction in Iberoamerica and Audiences' Transmedia Interactions*. Edited by G. Orozco and M. Vasallo. Ibero-American Observatory on Television Fiction. Sau Paulo: Globo Universidade.

———. (2012). *Transnationalization of Television Fiction in Ibero-American Countries*. Edited by G. Orozco and M. Vasallo. Porto Alegre, Brazil: Universidade Globo and Editora Sulina.

Rabello, M. L., and C. Harrison. (2011). "Brazil's Senate Approves Opening Cable TV to Phone Carriers, Foreigners." Bloomberg.com, August 17, http://www.bloomberg.com/news/2011-08-17/brazil-s-senate-approves-opening-cable-tv-to-phone-carriers-foreigners.html.

Rego, C. (2011). "From Humble Beginnings to International Prominence: The History and Development of Brazilian Telenovelas." In *Soap Operas and Telenovelas in the Digital Age: Global Industries and New Audiences*, edited by D. Rios and M. Castañeda, 75–92. New York: Peter Lang.

Robles, D. (1999). *El régimen jurídico de los extranjeros que participan en sociedades mexicanas*. Guadalajara, Mexico: Editorial Themis.

Schiller, H. (1991). "Not Yet the Post-Imperialism Era." *Critical Studies in Mass Communication* 8: 13–28.

Sinclair, J. (1999). *Latin American Television*. Oxford, UK: Oxford University Press.

———. (2004). "Geo-Linguistic Region as Global Space: The Case of Latin America." In *The Television Studies Reader*, edited by R. Allen and A. Hill, 130–38. London: Routledge.

Sorkin, A. (2006). "Univision Is Sold for $11 Billion to Saban Group." *International Herald Tribune*, June 28, 18. ProQuest Database.

Straubhaar, J. (1991). "Beyond Media Imperialism: Asymmetrical Interdependence and Cultural Proximity." *Critical Studies in Mass Communication* 8: 39–59.

———. (2007). *World Television: From Global to Local*. Los Angeles: Sage.

Sutter, M. (2000). "U.S. Net Telemundo Pacts with Argos." *Variety*, October 16, 124. Accessed June 25, 2007, http://find.galegroup.com.ezproxy.lib.utexas.edu/itx/start.do?prodId=AONE&userGroupName=txshracd2598.

Tarbuck, E. (2013). "Mexico: New Telecommunications Law Introduced." *Argentina Independent*, June 11, http://www.argentinaindependent.com/currentaffairs/newsfromlatinamerica/mexico-new-telecommunications-law-introduced/.

"Telemundo, Caracol Television and RTI Join Together in Unprecedented Co-Production Force." (2001). *PR Newswire* (New York), March 22, 1.

"Televisa y RCN amplían su alianza para coproducir y adaptar telenovelas: México-Televisión." (2010). *EFE News Service* (Madrid), October 19. ProQuest Database.

Thussu, D. K. (2007). "Mapping Media Flow and Counter-Flow." In *Media on the Move: Global Flow and Contra-Flow*, edited by D. K. Thussu, 10–20. New York: Routledge.

"TV Azteca and Telemundo Sign Strategic Alliance." (1999). *Financial News*, June 17, in *PR Newswire*. Accessed October 22, 2012, http://www.thefreelibrary.com/TV+Azteca+And+Telemundo+Sign+Strategic+Alliance.-a054923049.

Vinaja, V. (2012). "Large Scale Co-Production." *TTV MediaNews*. Accessed October 22, 2012, http://www.ttvmedianews.com/scripts/templates/estilo_nota.asp?nota=eng%2FEjecutivos%2FEntrevistas%2F2012%2F04_Abril%2F19_Donna_Donna+Cunningham_SPT.

"V-Me." (n.d.). TV commercial in Portugal and the United States. Prisa TV.Com. Accessed October 19, 2012, http://www.prisatv.com/es/pagina/v-me/.

2

Converging from the South

Mexican Television in the United States

RODRIGO GÓMEZ, TOBY MILLER, AND ANDRÉ DORCÉ

The history of audiovisual exchange between the United States and most of the world has been structured in dominance: one side's content and technology have reigned supreme. Latin America is no exception. But there are important counterexamples, and they animate this chapter. Latin America, particularly Colombia, Brazil, Venezuela, and Mexico, has a global niche in the export of *telenovelas*, including massive sales to the United States. The mobilization of dominant stereotypes, working with local imaginaries embedded in "universal" love stories, makes telenovelas symbolically and economically popular with differentiated domestic audiences and "normalized exotic" imports in regional and foreign markets. They are "glocalized" products (Paxman, 2003; Mato, 2003). Successful format sales[1] derive from the transformation of culturally specific origins into geographically "neutral" formulae (Colombia's *Yo soy Betty, la fea*, whose format was exported to dozens of countries, is a paradigmatic reference). By developing locally adapted formats, the industry re-territorializes audiovisual texts, increasing the use-exchange and sign-value of investments and diminishing risk. Apart from the venerable telenovela, a second TV genre has distinguished itself in the last decade: sports, especially football (which we'll call "soccer," deferring to

Yanqui readers). The pay-TV channels ESPN Deportes, Fox Sports, and Univision Deportes are notable successes. Each draws extensively on Mexican and other suppliers (Gómez, 2012).

The 2010 US census estimates the overall Latin@ population at 50.5 million, or about 16 percent of the national total (Pew Hispanic Center, 2012). The large number of Spanish speakers and people of Latin American origin in the United States has produced significant ratings for the dominant *hispano-hablante* broadcast TV networks, Univision and Telemundo (Arnoldy, 2007; Bauder, 2008). These stations seek to bridge intergenerational divisions between Spanish- and English-dominant Latin@ audiences to expand, deepen—and exploit—family togetherness (Loechner, 2009; Livingston, 2010). Over the last few years, additional players have emerged. Since 2000, six new TV networks directed at US Latin@s have appeared: Azteca America, LATV, TeleFutura, Vme, Estrella TV, and MundoFox. Televisa USA plans to develop hybrid English-language prime-time programming that unites the telenovela model with top US talent (Young, 2012). In 2012, CNN announced it would launch a broadcast channel, CNN Latino, and the following year saw Jennifer Lopez and Robert Rodriguez announce rival *anglo-parlante* networks aimed at Latin@s. And on cable, Fox Sports, Fox Deportes, ESPN Deportes, CNN en Español, and HBOLA have succeeded (James, 2012).[2] The major players import large amounts of programming from Mexican networks: Univision and Telemundo have long-term arrangements with Televisa and TV Azteca, as well as Argos, an independent production house (Coffey, 2007; Beck, 2010; Piñón, 2011b; Umstead, 2013). Univision is frequently considered the second network in the United States after Fox for audiences ages eighteen to thirty-four, and it controls the biggest Spanish-language radio network as well as being the largest Spanish-language music distributor (Gómez, 2007). Such counterflows signal new political-economic and diasporic intercultural norms.

This chapter focuses on the converging alliances, pacts, and interactions between Mexican media and Latino media and audiences in the United States. We take as our starting point the fact that economic and symbolic dynamics flow from transnational migration and media exchange, producing new conditions for both US and Latin American stakeholders that are best understood through a blend of cultural studies and political economy of communication. Mexican companies dominate at the level of the corporate political economy, but the hegemony of Mexican programming among *hispano hablantes* does not necessarily induce identical audience responses across platforms. Exchanges and power relations between companies, contents, and consumers all have parts to play in reconfiguring media convergence.

In 1940s sociology and 1960s economics, convergence referred to capitalist societies becoming more centrally planned, even as state-socialist ones grew more capitalist (Galbraith, 1967). In 1980s communications, convergence explained the processes whereby people and institutions share expressions and issues (Bormann, 1985). Both these political-economic and ethnographic realities are at play in this case: a formerly protectionist economy, Mexico, enters vigorously into a counterflow of goods with a similarly protectionist but avowedly open economy, the United States, which favors truly open markets only in audiovisual trade. A supposedly dependent economy (Mexico) sells symbolic goods to a traditional exporter of such texts (the United States). The target for this content is a diverse people bound together through language and/or racialization by state, capital, and self. In addition, convergence is occurring across media platforms, as TV and tablets produce what the Television Advertising Bureau calls a "Great Circle of modern consumerism"—while audiences watch programs, they buy products that are advertised ("What Topped," 2012).

The cultural hybridization produced by transnational flows of media and people structures new relationships and possibilities for media conglomerates in the United States to invest in Latin America and vice versa—for example, Time Warner's interests in Chilean, Brazilian, and Colombian media, Carlos Slim's stake in the *New York Times* (Edgecliffe-Johnson, 2012; "Carlos Slim," 2011), or Televisa's stake in Univision; hence our desire to look at the political economy. At the same time, ownership and control do not guarantee how texts are made, distributed, or interpreted (Miller, 2009); hence the need to consider new senses of belonging within Latin@ viewing communities.

Ownership and Control

The North American Free Trade Agreement (NAFTA)/Tratado de Libre Comercio de América del Norte (TLCAN) has restructured the Mexican economy. Commodities, capital, and companies have comparatively free access to each country. But even though the United States relies so much on Mexican labor, its government permits neither free exchange of labor nor free transit for Mexican citizens. Meanwhile, Mexico's rural employment base has been undermined by prohibitions on subsidies, at a time when crime-related violence displaces vast groups of people. These twin forces have stimulated a massive movement of people northwards in the last three decades, when the number of Mexican migrants, with or without papers, has been at least seven million (the Mexican government says that twelve million of its citizens reside in the United States).[3] In contrast with immigrants in general, Mexican-born citizens are young and male, have less formal education, lack familiarity with English, and are poor. Perhaps a quarter are US citizens, compared to half of other migrants ("Mexico: Special Report," 2012; Nielsen, 2012).

In the audiovisual industries, NAFTA/TLCAN has favored Grupo Televisa and TV Azteca, which import licenses, shows, and Hollywood films from the United States and export licenses and content (Gómez, 2007). Although the relationship between Televisa and Univision is the most intense in Latin@ and Mexican media history, other strategic alliances have emerged in the last two decades. Before Azteca America was launched, TV Azteca, Argos, and the Colombian network RTI had important ties with Telemundo (Piñón, 2011a). There are strategic alliances such as the one between Sony and Colombia's Caracol, which signed a three-year coproduction agreement in 2011 to create television series, in the same way that Univision is in partnership with Venezuela's Venevision. Other examples include the participation of Spain's Grupo Prisa in Vme[4] and News Corp and Colombia's RCN launching MundoFox in 2012. MundoFox targets young people and a notion of "living on the hyphen" between social and national identities—hence its tagline, "Americano como tú."[5] It embodies new media-business relations between the United States and Colombia, suggesting a cultural turn that will leaven the Mexican character of much Spanish-language US television. Meanwhile, Telmex, a dominant economic actor across Latin America in telecommunications and pay-TV, is also expected to take a role in the United States.[6] In Mexico, it operates the Internet TV channel UNOTV Noticias.

Nevertheless, for all this apparent pluralism, Univision Communications dominates Spanish-language media in the United States.[7]

Univision has several convergent distribution windows: Univision, Telefutura/UniMás, Galavisión, Univision on Demand, Univision Móvil, Univision Music, and Univision Deportes. In 2009, the firm generated $1.973 billion, making it the forty-eighth largest audiovisual company in the world (European Audiovisual Observatory, 2011).

In 2000, Univision and Televisa consolidated their alliance, agreeing to reciprocal use of content until 2017 and forming a new network called Telefutura. Univision Music Group bought rights from the Mexican record company Fonovisa (Sutter, 2001). This accord responded to market changes that also saw NBC buy Telemundo for $2 billion and TV Azteca incorporated into the market through Azteca America.

In 2005 and 2006, Univision and Televisa disagreed over digital signal distribution rights and the terms of their broadcast agreement. The group that controlled the US firm expressed interest in selling it for more than $13 billion. In 2009, the companies settled: Univision agreed to pay Televisa $25 million and advertising time worth $65 million a year for content until 2017. Grupo Televisa productions have been key elements, mainly through telenovelas, Mexican movies, and the Mexican soccer league and national team.[8]

In 2010, Univision announced that Televisa was investing $1.2 billion in it (Univision, 2011). In 2011, Televisa paid $49.1 million for common stock in BMP, Univision's parent company, increasing its stake from 5 percent to 7.1 percent. Univision has exclusive Spanish-language digital rights to Televisa programming until 2020. Under their program license agreement (PLA), Televisa will provide Univision with at least 8,531 hours of programming yearly. Royalty payments to Televisa increased from 9.36 percent of television revenue to 11.91 percent in 2011, excluding certain sporting events. In 2017, royalties will be 16.22 percent and Televisa will receive 2 percent of Univision's revenues above $1.65 billion (Televisa, 2012).

Univision gained access to Televisa's online content, broadcast, and pay-television programming (TuTV) for use across its own networks and interactive platforms, such as Univision.com, Univision Móvil, and Video on Demand. Univision also signed a "Mexico License Agreement," "under which Televisa . . . received the right to broadcast Univision's content in Mexico, . . . in exchange for . . . royalty fees to the Company of $17.3 million each year through 2025" (Univision, 2012: 14).

Finally, Televisa has broadcast rights to various Mexican soccer matches and grants Univision the right to screen them in the United States. Univision achieved historic ratings for the CONCACAF Gold Cup Final in 2011, when 10.9 million viewers watched all or part of the match between Mexico and the United States. Televisa owns the TV rights to ten teams in the Mexican League (Univision, 2011). Grupo Televisa's US income since 2000 averages $100 million, 80 percent of its foreign sales. After the new agreement in 2009, royalties and profits to Televisa increased, to $225 million in 2011 (Televisa, 2009–2012). The companies signed another agreement in 2011, launching Univision Deportes in competition with ESPN Deportes and Fox Sports, the most important sports channels in the Americas. In 2009, Grupo Televisa granted Telemundo broadcasting rights to key Mexican soccer matches for 2010 and 2011.

Telemundo, owned by Comcast/NBCUniversal, is the second-largest Spanish-language television network in the United States. It has had various alliances and contracts with Mexican firms. Telemundo has branded itself through Argos-Azteca telenovelas, which boast higher production values than Televisa's and incorporate complex stories that refer to sociopolitical events and use sophisticated visual and narrative strategies (Dorcé, 2005; Gómez, 2004). Several segments of Telemundo programs are in both English and Spanish.

Telemundo's ratings record is a 2010 World Cup match between Mexico and Argentina, which garnered 9.3 million viewers (Gorman, 2010). The network has the rights to broadcast the 2018 and 2022 World Cups in Spanish, at a cost of approximately $600 million—more expensive than the Anglo equivalent. The agreement also gives Telemundo rights to the 2015 and 2019 Women's World Cups and various international tournaments (Longman, 2011).

Prior to the new century, Telemundo had an agreement covering distribution and exchange with TV Azteca, for both soccer matches and telenovelas. Back then, many of Azteca's telenovelas came from Argos. During the 1990s in Mexico, Argos and TV Azteca produced six telenovelas, three of which matched and sometimes bettered Televisa production ratings in prime time. This positioned Argos as a key actor in Mexico and the United States.[9]

After conflict between Argos and TV Azteca in 2000, Telemundo and Argos signed coproduction and rights deals from 2001 to 2008. They produced nine telenovelas and two series, many of which were first broadcast in the United States, deploying the new international division of cultural labor via a "multi-Latin" crew of actors, with the idea of attracting wider Latin@ audiences. In 2011, 85 percent of Telemundo's telenovelas were filmed in Miami, generally with Mexican or Mexican American stars.

Argos signed a coproduction deal with HBO Latin America in 2007 to produce *Capadocia*. In 2012, Argos and Telemundo contracted with the Mexican company Cadena Tres to produce series and telenovelas in Mexico, and agreed to a global distribution deal with Cadena Tres and Televen in Venezuela. The relationship between Argos and Cadena Tres began in 2010 with an initial investment of around $21 million. They have produced eight telenovelas, giving Cadena Tres its best ratings since launching in 2007.[10] *Las Aparicio*, its first telenovela, got a 2.5 rating in 2010, a significant figure for a local station.

In 2000, TV Azteca,[11] the second-largest Mexican TV company, launched Azteca America in the United States.[12] It broadcast in-house productions, including a library of over 200,000 hours of telenovelas, Mexican soccer league, live shows, news, and variety. The network complements Mexican programming with shows produced in its Los Angeles headquarters.

TV Azteca was initially a joint venture with Pappas Telecasting, but became independent a year later. The agreement between TV Azteca and its affiliates divides advertising revenue equally. This is possible because TV Azteca has a programming license under NAFTA/TLCAN rules (Gómez, 2007). The Pappas-Azteca relationship broke down in 2003, and TV Azteca pays $9.6 million yearly to lease its Los Angeles station. Azteca America now reaches 91 percent of Latin@ households across forty markets (TV Azteca, 2012). In 2006, Azteca America claimed a 5 percent share of Latin@ audiences, and 12 percent on weekend evenings (de la Fuente, 2006). In 2012, it became the fifth Spanish-language network with a 0.6 household rating (*Advertising Age*, 2012: 24). In the pay market, TV Azteca has Azteca Mexico, which closely mirrors the network's Mexican channel Azteca 13.

TV Azteca has become Mexico's second-biggest audiovisual exporter, to the value of $7.5 million in 2009, $8.1 million in 2010, and $8.6 million in 2011 (TV Azteca, 2012). Like Televisa, TV Azteca has broadcast rights to ten Mexican soccer teams, giving it many advantages over competitors in attracting Mexican American and Mexican audiences. TV Azteca sells those rights to pay-TV channels such as Fox Sports and ESPN Deportes.

Texts and Subjects

To gain a clearer picture of what this infrastructure means culturally, we have to look beyond owners and address contents and audiences. The Observatorio Iberoamericano de la Ficción Televisiva (OBITEL) provides some insight. If we review fictional genres on TV by country of origin across the five major US *hispano-hablante* networks, Mexican productions lead by far (table 2.1). If we compare those figures with the most-viewed Latin@ programs of 2010 (table 2.2), a pattern of minimal diversity emerges.

To understand the economic viability of Latin@ television, we need to look at the US advertising industry and the commodification of Latin@ tastes and practices. In 2010, the nation's advertising expenditure rose to $131.1 billion, and $144 billion the following year. TV advertising amounted to $59 billion and $60.7 billion, respectively. Television retains the greatest share of US advertising, at around 39 percent. Spanish-language TV saw significant advertising investment growth of 10.7 percent from 2010 to 2011 (see table 2.3). By contrast, English-language TV ad expenditure declined by 2 percent (*Advertising Age*, 2012: 6).

According to Nielsen, Latin@ purchasing power is around a trillion dollars (Nielsen, 2012). Spanish-language advertising has increased by an annual average of 6 percent over the last decade (*Advertising Age*, 2012: 6). These figures make Latin@ TV a bigger market than Spain and Mexico (see table 2.4).[13]

Univision is routinely the fifth-most-watched network in the country, just after CBS, ABC, NBC, and Fox. The top six Latin@ television markets are Los Angeles, New York, Miami–Fort Lauderdale, Houston, Chicago, and Dallas–Fort Worth (*Advertising Age*, 2012: 18). Univision beat ABC, NBC, and CW in the 2010–2011 season's opening ratings week, and was number three among adults aged eighteen to thirty-four. These successes were due to a Televisa telenovela, *Hasta que el dinero nos separe* (Sanjenís, 2010). Univision was also the second broadcast network in prime time among children two to eleven, and fifth among all viewers older than two years, adults eighteen to forty-nine, and teens twelve to seventeen ("Week 15," 2011). In May 2012, Univision won the ten leading prime-time broadcasting network TV programs among Latin@s with three Televisa *novelas: La que no podía amar, Una familia con suerte 2,* and *Abismo de poder,* with eighteen- to twenty-point ratings in Latin@ households (*Advertising Age*, 2012: 20).

Historically, Mexican immigrants and second- and third-generation arrivals have maintained strong bonds with Mexican audiovisual products. Before there were TV networks in Spanish, Mexican cinema was a cultural link, forming part of what Carlos Monsiváis (2001) understood as cultural migration. We should also remember that the same markets with many Latin@s once boasted movie theaters that projected only Mexican cinema (Miller, 2005). No wonder that Nielsen says the Latin@ population "is visible in every aspect of the US landscape, including popular culture, the workforce, consumerism, politics and US American national identity" (2012: 2).

Telenovelas are reconstituted through practices of consumption, which may vary by social identity. For instance, Mexican women living in the United States interviewed by Ana Uribe expressed their pleasure in watching Mexican telenovelas, because they actualized affective and symbolic ties with their homeland. Interestingly, many men in the same study felt embarrassed and estranged by telenovelas, because they found the depiction of Mexican everyday life unrealistic (Uribe, 2009).

Jade Miller suggests that "South-to-North flows of people via migration can be considered an engine of South-to-North flows of culture along with the converse: North-to-South flows of capital in payment for content" (2010: 210). In that sense, according to Catherine Benamou,

Table 2.1. Fiction Premieres by Country of Origin in Latin@ Networks, 2010

Country	# Titles	%	Episodes	%	Hours	%
Brazil	3	4.8	140	3.3	136	3.2
Colombia	10	16.1	557	13.3	579	13.5
United States	17	27.4	935	22.3	911	21.1
Mexico	26	41.9	2,107	50.2	2,242	52.2
Venezuela	5	8.1	458	10.9	427	9.9
Total	61	100	4,197	100	4,295	100

Source: Piñón, 2011a: 366–67.

Table 2.2. Top Ten Broadcast TV Programs among Latin@s, 2010

Rank	Title	Network	Produced	Format	Rating	Share
1	Soy tu dueña	Univision	Televisa	Telenovela	22.5	34
2	Sortilegio	Univision	Televisa	Telenovela	22	33
3	Hasta que el dinero nos separe	Univision	Televisa	Telenovela	19.1	30
4	En nombre del amor	Univision	Televisa	Telenovela	18.3	29
5	Eva Luna	Univision	Univision Venevision	Telenovela	16.1	25
6	Mi pecado	Univision	Televisa	Telenovela	13.6	25
7	Mujeres asesinas 2	Univision	Mediamantes/ Televisa	Series	14.6	23
8	Llena de amor	Univision	Televisa	Telenovela	12.1	21
9	La rosa de Guadalupe	Univision	Televisa	Telenovela	11.4	21
10	Un gancho al corazón	Univision	Televisa	Telenovela	9.6	25

Source: Adapted from OBITEL, 2011: 372.

Table 2.3. Latin@ TV Advertising Expenditure, 2009–2011, in Millions of Dollars

	2009	2010	2011
Network TV	3,047	3,307	3,491
Spot TV	1,131	1,316	1,224
Cable TV networks	184	189	227
Total	4,362	4,812	4,942

Source: *Advertising Age*, 2011 and 2012.

Table 2.4. Most Important Markets in TV Ad Spending in Spanish, 2009–2011, in Millions of Dollars

	2009	2010	2011
US Latin@	4,361	4,813	4,941
Spain	3,327	3,411	3,200
Mexico	2,480	2,945	3,030
Total	10,168	11,169	11,171

Sources: *Advertising Age*, 2011 and 2012; European Audiovisual Observatory, 2011; and Marketingdirecto, http://www.marketingdirecto.com/actualidad/publicidad/el-mercado-publicitario-espanol-cayo-un-65-en-2011-segun-el-estudio-infoadex/ (accessed 20 July 2012).

televisual melodrama is not only a site where the tensions among the national, the local, and the global are articulated and made manifest, it is also a communicative bridge that links viewers across national, expanded regional, and global realms of transmission and reception, working to shape new cultural and intercultural communities. (Benamou, 2009: 152)

Thus telenovela consumption is as much a modernizing national ritual as a practice that structures belonging for emergent transnational traditions.

In May 2011, the nation's top prime-time network programs included *Triunfo del amor* and *Teresa*, another Televisa telenovela. That same year, *Eva Luna*, a Venevision production in association with Univision, was the fourth-top-rated program in the United States: about ten million people watched its finale. Much telenovela success is also attributable to promotional strategies that mobilize its star system: "[Maria] Morales [executive editor of *People en Español*] said stories about telenovela stars comprise up to 50% of *People en Español*, which has a circulation of 6.5 million, compared to the roughly 3.5 million circulation of the English-language version of *People*" (Gutman, 2012).

Again, advertising and the commodification of the audience's attention are crucial factors. Univision announced product placement (the industry's euphemism is "brand integration") into *Eva Luna*: "we were able to work upstream in the process with the *Eva Luna* creators, we could understand the characters, what motivates them, and make integration decisions based upon that information so our presence feels authentic to the overall storyline," said General Motors' director of branded entertainment and marketing alliances (quoted in Gorman, 2010). Univision did not only formulate sponsoring strategies suitable for its content, it also adapted plot structures to advertising opportunities within the dramatic scheme, thus expanding the intertextual reach of its programs:

The plot allowed for multiple vehicle storylines to be woven thru *Eva Luna*. In the *telenovela*, the female lead (Eva, played by Soto) wins the Buick Regal account for the advertising agency she works for. The ad created by her team will become the first real Spanish-language commercial for the Buick Regal and will run on a regular media schedule on Univision, TeleFutura, and Galavisión. *Eva Luna* will also feature the Chevy Cruze as the embodiment of Danny and Eva's love story, playing a major part in the pivotal scenes throughout their relationship; as well as the Chevy Traverse, playing the role of a trusted companion, helping Danny and those closest to him during important moments. (Gorman, 2010)

Finally, we point out that Argos telenovelas represent two landmarks of Latin@ cultural consumption. On the one hand, the telenovelas attracted new segments of audiences that hadn't shown interest in the genre or Mexican TV more generally—mainly the urban middle classes; on the other hand, their success demonstrated that telenovelas could relate their stories, in an intelligent and explicit way, to social, economic, and political issues.

Final Remarks

Convergence is a complex, multisited, and far from uniform process. Clearly, Mexican content remains dominant in Latin@ media, though new players may change that situation. It is also clear that telenovelas and sports are the main genres in Latin@ TV. Do Azteca America, Telemundo, and Univision currently enrich the Spanish audiovisual landscape? Will future Latin@ audiences in the United States enjoy more diverse televisual content, beyond the traditional Mexican base? And if so, what kind of cultural, political, economic, and environmental citizenship will be shaped by new cross-border TV alliances? What are the cultural profiles and practices of Latin@ audiences? Given the poverty experienced by many Latin@s in the United States, how will the newer media affect their television viewing? And what are the prospects for alternative, open-access TV in an era when cable companies are seeking repeal of their social obligations? How will new networks, aimed at young Latin@s rather than families, change the landscape and challenge the hegemony of Mexican exports? Will convergent economic and interpretative tendencies continue or dissipate? These seem fruitful lines of inquiry for future research.

NOTES

1. Mato points out that "these formats consist of the sale of the basic structure of the telenovela: the concept, the plot and the main characters. Subsequently, subplots and other characters are added to such a format using both local actors and modes of speech to 'localize' the product and thus adapt to specific internal markets" (2005: 427).

2. In 2012, Univision announced it would rename Telefutura UniMás (Guthrie, 2012).

3. There are signs that incompetent management of the US economy and renewed growth in the Mexican economy may change things.

4. Vme is available free to air and on basic cable and satellite packages and via IPTV Verizon FiOS and AT&T U-verse. It has an association with PBS stations and is the fourth-largest Spanish-language network in the United States. The Spanish Grupo Prisa owns 42.6 percent of shares.

5. See http://www.youtube.com/watch?v=aWAxbq3qbJc&feature=player_embedded.

6. América Móvil (the Telmex mobile branch in Latin America, better known as Claro) operates in eighteen countries and has about 38.6 percent of wireless subscribers in Latin America and the Caribbean. In addition to its Mexican dominance, the company has 70 percent of the market in Ecuador, 61 percent in Colombia, 25 percent in Brazil, and about a third in Argentina (Harrison, 2012).

7. Univision operates nineteen full-power stations and seven low-power stations, mainly in Los Angeles, New York, Miami, Houston, Dallas, and Chicago. In Puerto Rico, it has three full-power stations. The company reports 64 broadcast affiliates and 1,357 cable and Direct Broadcast Satellite affiliates. Univision began in 1986. Before that it was called the Spanish International Network (SIN) and was owned by Televisa. That arrangement changed following a Federal Communications Commission and Justice Department resolution in the 1980s that foreign investment in broadcast TV not exceed 25 percent.

8. Grupo Televisa is the twenty-fourth-largest audiovisual company worldwide, with 2010 turnover of $4.67 billion (European Audiovisual Observatory, 2011: 14).

9. *Nada personal* (1996–1997), *Demasiado corazón* (1998), and *Mirada de mujer* (1997–1998).

10. *Las Aparicio* (2010), *El sexo débil* (2011), *El octavo mandamiento* (2011), *Bienvenida realidad* (2011), *Infames* (2012), *Rosa Diamante* (2012), and *La patrona* (2012).

11. TV Azteca operates two national television networks in Mexico, Azteca 13 and Azteca 7, and Channel 40. Through more than three hundred owned and affiliated stations across the country, it has a 26 percent to 30 percent audience. In 2011, the company's net income was $982 million (TV Azteca, 2012).

12. When it began, Azteca America covered 28 percent of Latin@ audiences in the United States.

13. We converted Euros and pesos to dollars, which does not necessarily reflect national performances in those markets. In the case of Spain, the decrease in 2011 could be explained by the success of the digital media and the country's economic crisis.

REFERENCES

Advertising Age. (2009). *Hispanic Fact Pack 2009.* Ad Age Data Center.

———. (2011). *Hispanic Fact Pack 2011.* Ad Age Data Center.

———. (2012). *Hispanic Fact Pack.* Ad Age Data Center.

Arnoldy, Ben. (2007). "Among Networks, Spanish-Language Univision Is Now a Top Contender." *Christian Science Monitor,* September 17.

Barrera, Vivian, and Denise D. Bielby. (2001). "Places, Faces, and Other Familiar Things: The Cultural Experience of Telenovela Viewing among Latinos in the United States." *Journal of Popular Culture* 34, no. 1: 1–18.

Bauder, David. (2008). "Univision Takes 18–49 Demo Crown." *TVNewsday,* December 31, http://www.tvnewscheck.com/article/28301/Univision-takes-1849-demo-crown (accessed December 8, 2012).

Beck, Chad Thomas. (2010). "Azteca America's Performance of Mexicanness in the Pan-Hispanic Television Market." *International Journal of Cultural Studies* 13, no. 3: 271–89.

Benamou, Catherine L. (2009). "Televisual Melodrama in an Era of Transnational Migration: Exporting the Folkloric Nation, Harvesting the Melancholic-Sublime." In *Passion, Pathos and Entertainment: Latin American Melodrama,* ed. Darlene J. Sadlier, 139–71. Chicago: University of Illinois Press.

Bormann, Ernest G. (1985). "Symbolic Convergence Theory: A Communication Formulation." *Journal of Communication* 35, no. 4: 128–38.

"Carlos Slim Increases Stake in NY Times." (2011). Reuters, October 6, http://www.reuters.com/article/2011/10/06/newyorktimes-idUSN1E7951NY20111006 (accessed December 2, 2012).

Coffey, Amy Jo. (2007). "Trends in U.S. Spanish Language Television, 1986-2005: Networks, Advertising, and Growth." *Journal of Spanish Language Media* 1: 4–31.

de la Fuente, Anna Marie. (2006). "Azteca's Aboard Nielsen: Web Will Be Reported within NTI, NHTI." *Variety,* August 29, http://www.variety.com/article/VR1117949228 (accessed August 1, 2012).

Dorcé, André. (2005). "The Politics of Melodrama: The Historical Development of the Mexican Telenovela, and the Representation of Politics in the Telenovela *Nada personal,* in the Context of Transition to Democracy in Mexico." PhD diss., Goldsmiths College, University of London.

Dorfman, Ariel, and Armand Mattelart. (2000). *Para leer al pato Donald: Comunicación de masa y colonialismo.* Mexico City: Siglo Veintiuno Editores.

Edgecliffe-Johnson, Andrew. (2012). "Time Warner Eyes LatAm and Europe Opportunities." *Financial Times,* August 6.

European Audiovisual Observatory. (2011). *Yearbook 2011: Film, Television and Video in Europe*. Vol. 2, *Television and On-Demand Audiovisual Services in Europe*. Strasbourg: European Audiovisual Observatory.

Galbraith, John Kenneth. (1967). *The New Industrial State*. Boston: Houghton Mifflin.

Gómez, Rodrigo. (2004). "TV Azteca y la industria audiovisual mexicana en tiempos de integración regional y desregulación económica." *Comunicación y Sociedad* 14: 51–90.

———. (2007). "El impacto del Tratado de Libre Comercio de América del Norte (TLCAN) en la industria audiovisual mexicana (1994–2002)." PhD diss., Universidad Autónoma de Barcelona.

———. (2012). "News Corp in Latin America: The Prominence of Fox Entertainment." In "A Round-Table on the International Dimensions of News Corp in the Light of the UK Phone Hacking Scandal." *Global Media and Communication* 8 (April 2012): 3–25, doi:10.1177/1742766511434730.

Gorman, Bill. (2010). "Univision Announces Branded Entertainment Partners for *Eva Luna*, Univision Studios' First Primetime Dramatic Production." *TV by the Numbers*, October 29, http://tvbythenumbers.zap2it.com/2010/10/29/Univision-announces-branded-entertainment-partners-for-"eva-luna"-Univision-studios'-first-primetime-dramatic-production/70139/ (accessed December 3, 2012).

———. (2011). "Network TV Ad Spending Grows 5.3%; Cable TV Ad Spending Up 9.8% in 2010." *TV by the Numbers*, March 17, http://tvbythenumbers.zap2it.com/2011/03/17/networktv-ad-pending-grows-5-3-cable-tv-ad-spending-up-9-8-in-2010/86088/ (accessed July 2, 2012).

Guthrie, Marisa. (2012). "Univision Rebrands Telefutura as UniMás." *Hollywood Reporter*, December 3.

Gutman, Matt. (2012). "As American Soap Operas Bust, Telenovelas Boom in US." *ABC News*, August 16, http://abcnews.go.com/Entertainment/american-soap-operas-bust-telenovelas-boom-us/story?id=16553245 - .ULwrYaXmeX1 (accessed December 2, 2012).

Harrison, Crayton. (2012). "World's Richest Man Faces Clampdown in Latin America." *Bloomberg*, December 4, http://www.bloomberg.com/news/2012-12-04/worlds-richest-man-faces-clampdown-in-latin-america.html (accessed December 4, 2012).

James, Meg. (2012). "CNN Set to Launch Spanish-Language Service for Broadcast TV Stations." *Los Angeles Times*, December 3.

"*Las Aparicio* calientan a Cadenatres." (2010). *CNN Expansión*, November 1, http://www.cnnexpansion.com/monstruos-de-la-mercadotecnia-2010/2010/10/20/cadenatres-aparece-en-la-pantalla (accessed August 20, 2012).

Livingston, Gretchen. (2010). "The Latino Digital Divide: The Native Born versus the Foreign Born." Pew Hispanic Center, July 28, http://www.pewhispanic.

org/2010/07/28/the-latino-digital-divide-the-native-born-versus-the-foreign-born/ (accessed December 8, 2012).

Loechner, Jack. (2009). "Bi-Lingual Hispanics Live with Ease in Both Worlds." Center for Media Research, February 16, http://www.mediapost.com/publications/ article/100359/#axzz2WMRv3krq (accessed June 16, 2013).

Longman, Jere. (2011). "Fox and Telemundo Win U.S. Rights to World Cups." *New York Times*, October 22.

Mato, Daniel. (2003). "The Telenovela Industry: Markets and Representations of Transnational Identities." *Media International Australia Incorporating Culture and Policy* 106: 46–56.

———. (2005). "The Transnationalization of the Telenovela Industry, Territorial References, and the Production of Markets and Representations of Transnational Identities. *Television & New Media* 6 (4): 423–44.

"Mexico: Special Report." (2012). *Economist*, November 24, http://www.economist. com/news/special-report/21566773-after-years-underachievement-and-rising-violence-mexico-last-beginning (accessed December 8, 2012).

Miller, Jade L. (2010). "*Ugly Betty* Goes Global: Global Networks of Localized Content in the *Telenovela* Industry." *Global Media and Communication* 6, no. 2: 198–217.

Miller, Toby. (2005). "El cine mexicano en los Estados Unidos." In *Situación actual y perspectivas de la industria cinematográfica en México y en el extranjero*, ed. Néstor García Canclini, Ana Rosas Mantecón, and Enrique Sánchez Ruiz, 87–134. Guadalajara: Universidad de Guadalajara-IMCINE.

———. (2009). "Media Effects and Cultural Studies: A Contentious Relationship." In *The Sage Handbook of Media Processes and Effects*, ed. Robin L. Nabi and Mary Beth Oliver, 131–43. Thousand Oaks: Sage.

Monsiváis, Carlos. (2001). *Aires de familia*. Barcelona: Ariel.

Nielsen. (2012). *State of the Hispanic Consumer: The Hispanic Market Imperative*. Report, Quarter 2, 2012. Nielsen Company.

Passel, Jeffrey, D'Vera Cohn, and Ana Gonzalez-Barrera. (2012). "Net Migration from Mexico Falls to Zero—And Perhaps Less." Pew Hispanic Center, April 23, http:// pewresearch.org/pubs/2250/mexican-immigration-immigrants-illegal-border-enforcement-deportations-migration-flows (accessed December 8, 2012).

Paxman, Andrew. (2003). "Hybridized, Glocalized and Hecho en México: Foreign Influences on Mexican TV Programming since the 1950s." *Global Media Journal* 2, no. 2, http://lass.purduecal.edu/cca/gmj/sp03/gmj-sp03-paxman.htm (accessed December 8, 2012).

Perrilliat, Jessica A. (2012). "Spanish Language Television." In *The State of Spanish Language Media: 2011 Annual Report*, 9–22. Denton, TX: Center for Spanish Language Media.

Piñón, Juan. (2011a). "Estados Unidos: Crecimiento, reestructura y diversificación de la televisión hispana." In *OBITEL 2011: Calidad de la ficción televisiva y participación transmediática de las audiencias*, ed. Guillermo Orozco and I. Vasallo, 354–73. Rio de Janeiro: Globo Universidade.

———. (2011b). "The Unexplored Challenges of Television Distribution: The Case of Azteca America." *Television & New Media* 12, no. 1: 66–90.

Sanjenís, Elizabeth. (2010). "Univision: The Real Winner during the 2010/2011 Season's Opening Week." Univision, September 29, http://u.Univision.com/contentroot/uol/10portada/sp/pdf/corp_releases/2010/NOMETA_09-29-2010-1-en.pdf (accessed June 30, 2012).

Sutter, Mary. (2001). "Televisa Ready to Cross the Border: Company Pacts with Univision on Programming, Pay TV, Music." *Variety*, December 20, http://www.variety.com/article/VR1117857619 (accessed August 15, 2012).

Televisa. (2009). *Annual Report 2008, 20-Form.* http://www.televisa.com/inversionistas-espanol/forma-20-f/ (accessed June 9, 2012).

———. (2010). *Annual Report 2009, 20-Form.* http://www.televisa.com/inversionistas-espanol/forma-20-f/ (accessed June 9, 2012).

———. (2011). *Annual Report 2010, 20-Form.* http://www.televisa.com/inversionistas-espanol/forma-20-f/ (accessed June 15, 2012).

———. (2012). *Annual Report 2011, 20-Form.* http://www.televisa.com/inversionistas-espanol/forma-20-f/ (accessed June 10, 2012).

Trejo, Raúl. (2008). "Intolerancia en el Grupo Imagen." *Revista Zócalo* 102: 14–17.

TV Azteca. (2010). *Informe Anual TV Azteca 2010.* https://www.irtvazteca.com/downloads/anuales.aspx (accessed June 26, 2012).

———. (2011). *Informe Anual TV Azteca 2011.* https://www.irtvazteca.com/downloads/anuales.aspx (accessed June 26, 2012).

———. (2012). *Informe Anual TV Azteca 2012.* https://www.irtvazteca.com/downloads/anuales.aspx (accessed June 24, 2012).

Umstead, R. Thomas. (2013). "Cable Show 2013: Lopez, Rodriguez Tout Network Plans to Industry." *Multichannel News*, June 12, http://www.multichannel.com/index.php?q=distribution/cable-show-2013-lopez-rodriguez-tout-network-plans-industry/143868 (accessed June 17, 2013).

Univision. (2011). *2010 Year End Reporting Package.* http://corporate.Univision.com/investor-relations/financial-information/quarterly-filings/#axzz24n7shI6B (accessed June 22, 2012).

———. (2012). *2011 Year End Reporting Package.* http://corporate.Univision.com/investor-relations/financial-information/quarterly-filings/#axzz24n7shI6B (accessed June 22, 2012).

Uribe, Ana Berta. (2009). *Mi México imaginado: Televisión, telenovelas y migrantes.* Colima: Editorial Porrúa, El Colegio de la Frontera Norte, and Universidad de Colima.

"Week 15: Univision Begins 2011 as #3 Ranked Broadcast Network." (2011). *Radio and Television Business Report*, January 4, http://rbr.com/week-15-univision-begins-2011-as-3-ranked-broadcast-network/ (accessed June 16, 2013).

"What Topped TV's Holiday List? Tablets!" (2012). Television Advertising Bureau, December 21, http://www.tvb.org/4685/about_tvb/commentary/commentary_article/1339337 (accessed January 28, 2013).

Young, James. (2012). "Televisa Sets Sights on U.S. Market: Mexico Firm's Anglo Arm Remakes Telenovelas for the States." *Variety*, August 4, http://www.variety.com/article/VR1118057436 (accessed August 10, 2012).

3

NuvoTV

Will It Withstand the Competition?

HENRY PUENTE

The Pew Hispanic Center reported in 2013 that 85 percent of Latinos between the ages of five and seventeen, and nearly 60 percent over the age of eighteen, either speak English only at home or speak English very well (Motel and Patten 2013). This language shift has left traditional Spanish-language networks like Univision ill-prepared to target the growing market segment of English-speaking Latinos. The shift from Spanish to English, however, was precisely what NuvoTV (formerly Sí TV) anticipated. NuvoTV was the first cable network to exploit this growing niche market and produce entertainment programming specifically for English-speaking US Latinos. This chapter examines whether or not NuvoTV will be able to withstand increasing competition from current rivals and a pair of emerging, well-funded rivals set to debut in 2013. The essay begins by chronicling NuvoTV's emergence and notable successes, and then identifies NuvoTV's competitors in pursuit of this increasingly valuable audience. The chapter concludes by pinpointing several of NuvoTV's future challenges and explores why its future is uncertain at best.

When Jeff Valdez's and Bruce Barshop's Sí TV (renamed NuvoTV in 2011) evolved from a production company to a cable network, it had the opportunity to transform the television landscape for US Latinos.

Historically, this market has been dominated in terms of viewership by two Spanish-language television networks, Univision and Telemundo, and a cable network, Galavisión, owned by Univision. One of the primary reasons that these networks have survived this highly competitive marketplace is their ability to construct and tap into a valuable US Latino market. These networks paid $20 million to Nielsen, a market research company, in 1992 to change its measurement methodology by adding bilingual enumerators. This development led to more participation from Spanish-speaking viewers, which increased the market's value. Nielsen also essentially packaged all Latinos, including monolingual English speakers, into one homogeneous category for these two networks and Spanish-language advertising agencies (Rodriguez 1999, 51, 132). Through its efforts, Nielsen developed an audience profile that crystallizes the typical Latina/o as a foreigner, regardless of individual acculturation level and English-language ability. Valdez's Sí TV had the opportunity to significantly alter Nielsen's carefully constructed audience profile of US Latinos, which has remained in place for over twenty years, through the production of new English-language content featuring US Latino talent and stories.

Perhaps more importantly, Sí TV's founder and CEO, Jeff Valdez, represented one of the first US-born Latino entrepreneurs to champion and acknowledge English-speaking and bilingual US Latinos in the cable television industry. Historically, Spanish-language and English-language network executives alike ignored this segment of Latinos. Both assumed that bilingual and English-speaking Latinos did not watch their content, which essentially placed nearly 31 million viewers in a "no man's land" in the television landscape (Motel and Patten 2013). Valdez's Sí TV set out to fill this void by creating English-language content targeting Latina/os between the ages of eighteen and thirty-four (Piñón and Rojas 2011). Ignored by the television industry, ironically, these English-speaking Latina/os are considered more valuable to advertisers because this group tends to be better educated and have more disposable income. However, this niche audience has either not built a large enough middle class or has been considered too elusive to target effectively (Rodriguez 1999, 134). Or perhaps English-speaking and bilingual Latinos lacked someone like Valdez, who had the vision to start a cable network that resonated with this potentially valuable audience.

If Valdez's Sí TV (and later NuvoTV) produced content that success-fully targeted this audience and generated significant ratings for adver-tisers, it would challenge Univision's and Telemundo's dominance. It would also reduce the two networks' importance and value in the US television landscape, since these networks would no longer attract "all of the Latino viewers." NuvoTV represents a direct threat because it is better positioned to reach the over 60 percent of US Latinos who are either monolingual English-speaking or bilingual (Taylor et al. 2012). NuvoTV's long-term success could force a change to the old business model of importing inexpensive Mexican or Venezuelan programming instead of more culturally relevant and costly content produced in the United States. Valdez's successful cultivation of English-speaking and bilingual Latino viewers could represent a dramatic shift in both the US Latino market and the overall US television landscape.

Without a significant competitor, NuvoTV slowly increased its sub-scription base over the past decade. English-speaking and bilingual Latinos suddenly have become an audience worthy of pursuit for cable networks because they are a lot younger than the mainstream popula-tion (twenty-seven versus forty-one), perceived to be more brand-loyal than other niche audiences, and watch more television than non-Latino whites (Morello 2011; Piñón and Rojas 2011). Spanish-language cable networks like Mun2 have begun to develop, produce, and televise more programming like *RPM Miami* that targets bicultural Latinos. New cable networks like El Rey are set to launch and produce programming for bicultural Latinos specifically. NuvoTV now finds itself in a race to see which network emerges as the leading cable outlet for bicultural US Latino viewers, who represent over 50 percent of a $1.2 trillion market ("Behind the Rebrand" 2012).

NuvoTV's Emergence

Jeff Valdez was raised in a bilingual housing project in Pueblo, Colo-rado. He arrived in Los Angeles in 1993 with hopes of making it big as a stand-up comedian. When Valdez began to produce English-language programming for Latinos, he stated that "Latinos want to see them-selves on screen. They want to hear their stories" (Navarro 2006). He initially produced *Comedy Compadres*, which aired on KTLA-TV, a local Los Angeles TV network (de la Fuente 2006). He secured a venue and vital funds from Bruce Barshop, a San Antonio investor, in 1996 to produce the Latino Laugh Festival in San Antonio, which was eventually acquired by Showtime (Saldana 2013). He also started to produce cable television programming like *Funny Is Funny!* for Galavisión in 1997. After producing several Latino-oriented programs, Valdez raised capital for a new cable network and attempted to secure fast food and beer advertisers (Fitzgerald 1999). Shortly afterwards, Sí TV produced its most successful program, *The Brothers Garcia*, which aired on Nickelodeon from 2000 to 2004 and Nick on CBS in 2004.

During the television run of *The Brothers Garcia*, Valdez managed to develop Sí TV into the first cable network dedicated to targeting bicultural and assimilated Latinos. Sí TV's original slogan, "Speak English, Live Latino," illustrated how the company differentiated itself from traditional Spanish-language television networks like Telemundo and Univision. Valdez's goal for Sí TV was to produce entertainment programming for Latinos who rarely watched Spanish-language television, those "who were raised on *Brady Bunch*, not *Sábado Gigante*" (Esparza 1998). Valdez's argument for creating Sí TV clearly resembles Robert Johnson's motivation for establishing Black Entertainment Television (BET) in the 1980s. Johnson claimed that African American audiences needed a space to view their content and a channel that could provide a platform for African American artists (Smith-Shomade 2007, 179; Mullen 2003, 123). Valdez accomplished his goal of securing a space for a US Latino cable network on a multiple system operator's (MSO) or satellite carrier's lineup when Sí TV completed its initial carriage deal on Dish Network (Calvo 2003). Sí TV was supposed to launch on Dish Network in the summer of 2003; however, it did not officially debut until February 2004 (Hofmeister 2004).

NuvoTV's Successes

Despite operating in a difficult marketplace for an independent cable network, NuvoTV successfully secured carriage on several of the largest MSOs and satellite carriers. The network, however, expanded quite slowly. Without being affiliated to a media conglomerate, NuvoTV was unable to secure a quick overall deal from various MSOs. Instead, it managed to secure only a "hunting license," which enabled NuvoTV to approach a cable system's individual affiliates. The hunting license, however, does not ensure affiliate carriage. The duration of the carriage agreement is also left to the discretion of the cable system's affiliate. Valdez describes how he managed to expand Sí TV's carriage: "I was on the road a lot—going to each individual affiliate and trying to convince them. It was like *Groundhog Day*. Well, corporate says it is a good idea, but we (the affiliates) don't know if it is good for us" (personal communication). Valdez and the current management have overcome this challenge, and as a result NuvoTV has grown steadily over the past decade to over 30 million subscribers (Moore 2013).

NuvoTV was the first cable network to successfully create a distinction for advertisers between first-generation, Spanish-speaking Latino parents and their bicultural children who grew up with the popular culture of the United States and generally preferred English-language programming. As a result, NuvoTV built stronger relationships with advertisers and justified the advertisers' extra expense in order to produce culturally relevant Latino advertisements. This strategy appears to be gaining traction slowly. For example, a recent Nielsen survey indicated that NuvoTV viewers felt that the advertisements on this cable network were more culturally relevant to them than advertisements on other networks (45 percent versus 32 percent) ("New Nielsen Data" 2012). For NuvoTV to generate more advertising revenue, the network will need to work closely with advertisers, providing them with information about US Latino trends in order to help these companies build brand awareness.

To a certain extent, NuvoTV has successfully altered the language of the advertisements that air on the network. Valdez described how difficult it was to get advertising agencies to produce English-language advertisements for US Latinos:

> We initially approached general market agencies. They told us that Sí TV was either not big enough or that they could not help us because "You are Hispanic. You have to go to the Hispanic agencies." Hispanic agencies would say that "This is great. But your programming is in English. We could only put commercials in Spanish on your channel. That's all we do! We are not allowed to do English-language commercials." We eventually bypassed the advertising agencies and went to the brands directly. (Personal communication)

Despite NuvoTV's best efforts, some advertisers continued to deliver Spanish-language advertisements that were not culturally relevant for bicultural viewers (James 2005). Valdez, however, contends that advertising agencies are slowly producing more culturally relevant English advertisements (personal communication).

Although the network debuted in 2004, Sí TV's management did not feel that it had strong enough brand awareness with advertisers. The network subsequently launched a rebranding campaign on July 4, 2011, that changed its name to NuvoTV, which combines the initial letters of the words "nuevo" and "voice"; they also changed the tagline to "America's 'nu' voice" in order to better reflect the dual cultures of the target audience ("Behind the Rebrand" 2012; Morabito 2011). Despite the fact that Sí TV had already successfully attracted some large advertisers, like General Motors and Wal-Mart, that rarely advertised to US Latino viewers, the name change resulted in an instant increase in advertising revenues for the network (Wentz 2004). NuvoTV doubled the number of advertisers airing spots to about forty or forty-five at its 2011 upfront (Whitney 2011). These industries included consumer-packaged goods (CPGs), retail, wireless, and movie studios looking to attract more highly educated and bicultural US Latino consumers. NuvoTV's rebranding campaign appears to have attracted more advertisers and generated more advertising revenue.

NuvoTV's name change and new programming also have attracted more US Latino viewers. The CEO, Michael Schwimmer, argued that potential audiences confused the Spanish word *sí* with the English words *sea* or *see* (B. Steinberg 2011). Along with the network name change, NuvoTV generated new programming like *Operation Osmin* and *Mission Menu* in 2011 that have boosted prime-time viewership by 53 percent. The network also has increased its early fringe viewership by 200 percent (Seidman 2012). The network recently announced at the New York upfront for 2012–2013 that it was going to debut five new programs, including *Fight Factory* and *Mario Lopez 1-on-1* ("NuvoTV Unveils" 2012). NuvoTV also has developed a partnership with Jennifer Lopez's Nuyorican Productions (B. Steinberg 2012). She announced at the NuvoTV 2013 upfront that she will be the subject of a biographical documentary entitled *Jennifer Lopez: Her Life, Her Journey* and another documentary entitled *Gotta Dance*, which will air on the network

(Moore 2013). NuvoTV's name change and new programming appear to resonate with a growing number of bicultural Latino viewers.

NuvoTV successfully secured funding for a slate of new shows—$40 million in 2012 from its early investors Columbia Capital and Rho Capital Partners and two new investors, Veronis Suhler Stevenson and Tennenbaum Capital Partners (James 2012). According to Schwimmer, "this is the largest injection of capital into NuvoTV since it was founded in 2004" (Gates 2012). NuvoTV will utilize these funds to produce original English-language entertainment programming for US Latinos. Schwimmer said, "We're looking for that unique show and that's what this investment is all about" (de la Fuente 2012). This investment could be an enormous boost to NuvoTV's goal of producing programs with Latino talent that reflect Latino culture.

Lastly, NuvoTV has made good use of Nielsen's research data that indicated that the network was attracting high-income viewers and that its advertisements were making a positive impact with the US Latino public. According to Nielsen, NuvoTV's audience median income is $61,000, which ranks in the top ten among cable networks ("New Nielsen Data" 2012). Its viewers earn nearly twice the average income of Spanish-language network viewers. These Nielsen data support Mayer's assertion that "Sí TV needed to reach the wealthiest segments of the national, pan-ethnic Mexican American market" in order to survive (2003, 14). Nielsen data also indicated that Latino viewers are more likely to trust brands advertised on NuvoTV as compared with viewers of other networks (40 percent versus 21 percent) and are more interested in the brands seen on this cable network than are viewers of other networks (42 percent versus 20 percent) ("New Nielsen Data" 2012). This information is consistent with Dávila's argument that Latino viewers are often packaged and sold as more brand-loyal than non-Latinos (2001, 70). NuvoTV needs to continue to utilize these Nielsen data to prove to advertisers that it is attracting high-income, brand-loyal, and underserved viewers.

NuvoTV's Current Challenges

Despite being a trendsetter in this market, NuvoTV is encountering several current challenges from current and emerging competitors. The network needs to find a new and influential face to replace its cofounder Jeff Valdez. When Michael Schwimmer became the chief executive officer, Valdez began to disagree about what the network should be (personal communication). Valdez left shortly afterwards to become the cochairman of Maya Entertainment, a Latino-oriented film distributor (Kilday 2006). In founding the network, Valdez played a vital role in securing the initial financing of $60 million from major pay-television distributors like Time Warner and EchoStar Communications and several private equity investors in 2004 (J. Steinberg 2004). Valdez also successfully pitched NuvoTV's initial concept to MSOs and secured its early carriage on Cox and Dish Network. Perhaps more importantly, he helped create NuvoTV's most successful television program, *The Brothers Garcia*. Although NuvoTV's new management has subsequently raised $24 million in 2010 and $40 million in 2012, the management team has been unable to replace the face of Sí TV ("Sí TV Raises $24 Million" 2010; Gates 2012).

The lack of a recognizable leader to attract more investment dollars in NuvoTV may have been resolved with its recent partnership with Jennifer Lopez. Named the network's chief creative officer, Lopez will have a minority stake in NuvoTV (Vega and Elliott 2013). Lopez's Nuyorican Productions will work closely with Bill Hilary, the new head of programming, to produce content (Ng 2013). Lopez's production company could bolster NuvoTV's current content, having produced motion pictures like *Bordertown* (2006) and *El Cantante* (2007). Lopez also has coproduced or produced television programs like *South Beach* (2006) and *The Fosters* (2013). NuvoTV hopes that Lopez's name will enable the network to attract other talent to strengthen its programming. Lastly, Lopez will be involved in the network's marketing initiatives (B. Steinberg 2012). NuvoTV has already leveraged the Lopez partnership by featuring her at a recent upfront ("Hispanic Upfront" 2013). This collaboration could further enhance the network's brand and may generate more interest from potential investors, advertisers, and cable/satellite distributors.

A significant challenge for NuvoTV will be to strike a balance between appealing to the broadest audience possible while providing a channel where Latinos truly see themselves on screen. For example, Mayer (2003) asserts that Sí TV changed some elements of *Brothers*

Garcia in order to appeal to a broader audience, like relocating the family from San Antonio to Los Angeles and changing the program's original name from *Barbacoa* to *Brothers Garcia* (91). Mayer also argues that media producers striving to cross over to a broader audience may ignore common images of working-class Mexican American families (92). Although NuvoTV has not produced a new scripted drama or sitcom, the network needs to be careful that it does not exclusively center its stories on the middle-class family experience, which already is the dominant image on US television (Mayer 2003, 172). The network also needs to avoid focusing its stories strictly on the two largest segments of the US Latino market—Mexican Americans and Puerto Ricans. The struggle will be whether or not NuvoTV can truly depict the US Latino experience and still cross over to a non-Latino audience, attracting mainstream advertisers.

NuvoTV also faces a challenge in producing programs that avoid old Latina/o stereotypes like the bandito or half-breed harlot. When this cable network was founded, it operated with a clean slate because the marketplace lacked an archive of English-language Latino-oriented programming. Instead of producing dramas or situation comedies that realistically featured this diverse population, it has developed reality television programming like *Curvy Girls*, *Miami Ink*, and *Model Latina*. Some of these reality TV programs perpetuate the old Latina stereotypes like the half-breed harlot (sexual Latina) and Latina spitfire (emotional Latina), which have plagued the community since the beginning of motion pictures. Charles Ramirez-Berg (2002) notes that the repetition of stereotypes can become so normalized that audiences are surprised when they are not presented (19). Though it can be quite challenging to avoid stereotypes, NuvoTV has a unique opportunity to produce more television shows that truly capture US Latino culture and depict US Latina/os in a nonstereotypical manner.

One of the greatest difficulties of running any network is filling the channel with enough content. During hard economic times, when advertising revenues are down, mainstream channels can license inexpensive archived television shows from decades of classic television production. In contrast, NuvoTV encounters a unique programming difficulty because there are very few Latino-oriented, syndicated television programs in network archives to supplement its schedule.

Mainstream and Spanish-language television networks historically have not produced many English-speaking or bilingual Latino-oriented programs. In fact, Latina/o characters have been continually invisible on English-language network television programs because producers avoided casting Latina/os. While recent Latino-oriented hit programs like *The George Lopez Show* and *Ugly Betty* and programs with prominent Latino/a characters such as *Modern Family* have had significant television runs, the number of high-quality, older Latino-oriented programs or programs featuring prominent Latina/o characters remains quite low. NuvoTV consequently needs to overcome the lack of inexpensive older programming that fits its brand.

In addition to programming challenges, NuvoTV needs to convince MSOs to place the network in a more appropriate basic tier instead of relegation to expensive or specialized Spanish-only channel bundles. Valdez described the difficulty in securing placement in basic tiers: "Cable owners often wanted to place Sí TV in a Spanish-language bundle. I always had to remind cable system owners that Sí TV was an English-language cable network and it should be on an English-language tier" (personal communication). By securing basic tier placement, NuvoTV can expand its subscriber base significantly. A basic tier position would also enhance its per-subscription fee revenue from various MSOs and satellite carriers. These fees range from five dollars per subscriber for powerful basic cable networks like ESPN to about sixty cents for some well-known cable networks like USA (Flint 2012). NuvoTV will find it difficult to demand this type of per-subscriber fee. However, basic tier placement would improve the chances of crossing over to non-Latino audiences (Trevino 1999). Simultaneously, NuvoTV needs to avoid being placed in too many Spanish-language channel bundles, which would be a poor fit for the network's English-language content. This type of bundle placement stifles NuvoTV's reach and limits its ability to attract new advertisers. NuvoTV needs to work closely with various MSOs and satellite carriers to secure placement in basic tiers and appropriate bundles in the future.

Despite having success in convincing some sponsors to run more English-language advertising, NuvoTV is still struggling to create a distinction for advertisers between itself and traditional Spanish-language networks like Univision. While sponsors acknowledge that the US

Latino market is evolving rapidly, the top five hundred US advertisers have not significantly altered their advertising strategy for this market. They still spend the vast majority of $4.3 billion on Spanish-language advertising by securing spots on traditional Spanish-language networks like Univision (Koyen 2012). They simultaneously appear to be holding onto the image of Latinos being a monolithic Spanish-speaking ethnic group by placing their Spanish-language advertisements on a network that targets English-speaking Latinos. Valdez points out how slowly advertising agencies are adapting to the changing demographics of the US Latino market:

> To this day, if you watch NuvoTV, you will see Spanish-language advertisements on English-language content. I do not believe running Spanish-language advertisements are the current management's choice. It certainly was not our choice. Our choice was English-language advertisements. But agencies did not have advertisements for English-speaking Latinos. It was kind of shocking if you think about it. (Personal communication)

As a result, advertising agencies place NuvoTV in a no-win situation. These Spanish-language advertisements obviously provide the network with vital advertising revenue. However, if NuvoTV continues to accept these Spanish-language advertisements, it fails to create a distinction between itself and Spanish-language networks for advertisers, which is imperative for its long-term success.

Although NuvoTV has made good use of Nielsen data, it will need to continue to illustrate to media buyers that it has strong Nielsen rating numbers. Since the cable network's origin, media buyers who reserved space and time assumed that NuvoTV was the best vehicle for reaching the elusive bicultural Latino viewers, because it did not have any direct competitors. Media buyers, however, did not have Nielsen ratings to support their purchases. Nielsen did not rate NuvoTV because it did not have 30 million subscribers (B. Steinberg 2011). NuvoTV recently reached that figure. However, NuvoTV could have a tougher time convincing media buyers and advertisers to secure space and time on its network if it has low ratings, if its ratings drop significantly, or if a new direct competitor can illustrate that it has better ratings. NuvoTV cannot afford to provide media buyers with "make goods." A "make good" normally is a free advertisement that is provided by the media outlet to an advertiser if the media outlet makes an error. A make good, however, also could occur if the advertisement is placed in an under-performing program. NuvoTV will need to sustain respectable Nielsen ratings in order to avoid future make goods, continue to justify more media buys from current advertisers, and attract new advertisers. Thus far, the cable network's Nielsen ratings in 2011 and 2012 were good (Seidman 2012). The network, however, will now be more scrutinized by media buyers and advertisers in the future, especially with the growing number of direct competitors.

New Competitors

More recently, NuvoTV has expanded rapidly into new markets by taking advantage of cable system operators' new technology and their heightened focus on Latino subscribers. MSOs expanded their bandwidth in order to accommodate more high-definition content. But the expanded bandwidth it also enabled them to effectively target a growing number of Latino households in their local affiliate markets by adding Latino-oriented channels to their lineups. For example, Time Warner, Comcast, Cox, and Dish Network recently either developed special Latino-oriented bundles or added more Latino cable networks to their current lineups (Gibbons 2009). The number of Latino-oriented cable networks consequently has grown to eighty-eight, up from seventy-eight the previous year (Winslow 2008). Thus, NuvoTV has benefited from this new technology, but the increase in bandwidth and better equipment has allowed an increasing number of significant competitors to enter the marketplace.

Mun2, owned by NBCUniversal, became NuvoTV's direct competitor when it changed some of its programming. In 2011, Mun2 debuted new shows like *I Love Jenni* and *RPM Miami*, which target bicultural Latinos. NuvoTV can no longer claim that its focus on English-speaking Latinos sets it apart from competitors (Ben-Yehuda 2008). *I Love Jenni* centers on the personal and professional life of the Mexican American singer Jenni Rivera and became one of Mun2's biggest hits (Villarreal 2013). The cable network, however, suffered a huge setback after Rivera was killed in a tragic airplane crash. The family has decided to continue the program, and part of the new season will focus on how the family is dealing with Rivera's untimely death. *RPM Miami* is a bilingual drama that centers on Alejandro Hernandez, an Iraq War veteran. These two shows have diversified Mun2's programming and have begun to blur the difference between the two networks. An advertiser or viewer can no longer make a clear distinction between NuvoTV and Mun2. If Mun2 continues to produce this type of programming, it could become a formidable competitor, especially if NBCUniversal agrees to finance more Latino-oriented content.

Another potential competitor on the horizon is El Rey, which is set to launch in the near future. El Rey is part of an agreement that Comcast is fulfilling with the Federal Communications Commission (FCC) when it purchased NBCUniversal (Vega 2012), whereby Comcast agreed to create minority-owned cable networks like El Rey. The network is a partnership between the director Robert Rodriguez and FactoryMade Ventures. The cable network recently secured additional investment funds from Univision ("Hispanic Upfronts" 2013). Rodriguez will lead the network and its creative focus (Allen 2012). He will also attract top Latino talent. El Rey's diverse lineup could feature reality TV, originally scripted TV series, animated TV series, feature films, documentaries, music, and sports. With Comcast's financial support and Rodriguez's name recognition with Latino audiences, this network appears to be a formidable challenger in the future. Valdez asserts that this network is going to break out and set a new paradigm for programming because Rodriguez has real rock star talent and money (personal communication). If Valdez's prediction is correct and El Rey produces high-quality Latino-oriented programming, it will have an excellent opportunity to attract NuvoTV's core audience away from the network.

The last big NuvoTV challenger could be Fusion, a new cable channel that has resulted from a partnership between Disney and Univision. This English-language cable network will be a twenty-four-hour news channel and is set to launch in the summer of 2013. Univision will be responsible for the programming and hiring of employees. Disney will handle the channel's distribution by leveraging its other cable network assets like ESPN in order to secure a place in MSO or satellite carrier lineups. Fusion has already secured placement on cable systems like Cablevision, Charter, and Cox, which will enable the cable network to reach 20 million homes (Chozick 2013). A significant hurdle that Fusion must overcome is that its parent companies, Disney and Univision, have not produced much programming for English-speaking Latinos (James and Chmielewski 2012). Fusion represents a new opportunity for both Disney and Univision to reach bicultural Latinos. If this joint venture works, these media companies possess the financial capability to expand out of the news-only format and diversify the network's content. Both companies could also leverage their current cable network assets and create a new cable channel that targets bicultural Latinos. Either scenario would pose a serious threat to NuvoTV.

NuvoTV's new competitors like Fusion, which are financed by media conglomerates, possess huge advantages in terms of securing carriage on MSO and satellite carrier lineups simply by being able to negotiate more favorable terms with their distributors. They can easily avoid NuvoTV's lengthy process of approaching a cable system's individual affiliates. As a matter of fact, NuvoTV has still failed to secure carriage on every single US cable system, and its subscription base of a little over 30 million still lags far behind some other more established basic cable networks like Discovery or Nickelodeon, which often have about 100 million subscribers. Valdez describes the current marketplace for independent channels like NuvoTV:

A single channel in a multi-channel world is tough. It is very hard to have leverage when you have one channel and another company has twenty channels. Those channels are well established. They have an audience and they can leverage those assets. The first channels that get beat up in negotiations are the little guys. It is the nature of the beast. (Personal communication)

With an increasing number of powerful and well-funded competitors and its current single-channel status, NuvoTV may have to accept lower per-subscription fees from MSOs in order to remain on lineups. NuvoTV will also have to work harder to differentiate itself from the growing number of similar competitors if it plans to remain on MSOs' current lineups.

NuvoTV's Future Challenges

In order to hold off current and emerging competitors, Jennifer Lopez and Bill Hilary will need to bolster NuvoTV's current programming, which primarily consists of reality TV programs like *Modelo Latina* and second-run television programs like *Prison Break*, with a new hit program. NuvoTV's present, longest-running series is the Latino version of *America's Next Top Model*, entitled *Modelo Latina*, which features models competing for a Q Management contract and a $25,000 prize. NuvoTV recently strengthened its current Latino-oriented reality TV programming with *Low-Ballers* and *Curvy Girls*, and it plans to televise multiple docu-series like *Oribe* and *Rodney's Joy* (Nededog 2013). Lopez's Nuyorican Productions may help improve NuvoTV's lineup with two upcoming documentaries, but it does not have a successful track record of producing hit television programs. Lopez's and Hilary's primary challenge will be acquiring or producing a successful scripted program that can catapult the network's popularity (Block 2013). NuvoTV's lack of a notable scripted program continues to provide an opportunity for another cable network with more financial resources, like Comcast's El Rey, to produce its own Latino-oriented hit program, which would put a significant dent in NuvoTV's ratings.

Despite having raised more than $100 million in its brief history, NuvoTV has failed to secure an investor willing to pay for new programming on a consistent basis (James 2012). Most recently, NuvoTV secured about $40 million in 2012 from a mix of new and old investors, which will enable it to produce scripted Latino-oriented shows (Gates 2012). While the investment is a step in the right direction, $40 million does not generate a lot of new scripted programming. For example, a typical cable drama's production costs is about $2 million per episode (Carter 2010). If a program has thirteen one-hour episodes per season, the production company will spend about $26 million in production costs. Hence, this most recent investment is not nearly enough money to significantly alter NuvoTV's current lineup. With the high expense of producing scripted television content, NuvoTV needs to secure investors willing to provide enough funding on an annual basis to enable the network to alter its programming significantly.

Next, NuvoTV encounters an enormous challenge in trying to target a diverse Latino audience with hit programming. The US Latino market is not as cohesive as the mainstream market, but rather consists of several submarkets, like the Mexican American, Puerto Rican, and Cuban American markets. Within these various submarkets, viewers have different immigration experiences and are at different stages of acculturation. This viewership consequently is attracted to different content. For example, Latino-oriented film distributors like Arenas Entertainment or Maya Entertainment have historically struggled to draw a significant number of moviegoers. Mainstream television networks currently have had little success in attracting US Latino viewers to their existing scripted programming (Vega and Carter 2012). NuvoTV will need to produce a hit Latino-oriented program that will attract English-speaking Latinos and cross over to other viewers, all of which have proven to be difficult for producers and distributors of Latino-oriented films and television programs.

Finally, NuvoTV, analogous to BET in the early 1980s, needs to make a tough decision between producing programming that will cross over to a broader non-Latino audience and meeting its original goal of providing bicultural Latinos with entertainment programming. For BET, which had a similarly unproven target audience, the biggest obstacle in securing MSO carriage and attracting new advertisers was that African American viewers were not perceived as a lucrative audience by advertisers (Mullen 2003, 159). BET consequently needed to convince cable operators and advertisers that its programming would cross over and attract other lucrative audiences like teenagers and white adults. As a matter of fact, BET's ability to attract a white audience may even have been more of a priority than sustaining an African American audience (Smith-Shomade 2007, 187). BET's ability to cross over to other audiences was vital to maintaining a spot on cable systems' lineups. NuvoTV will need to make a similar decision, which will likely determine its future success or failure. An incorrect decision may result in NuvoTV suffering the identical fate of AZN Network, a cable channel that targeted Asian American viewers. AZN went out of business because it could no longer attract advertisers and secure cable system carriage (Haugsted 2008).

Will NuvoTV Survive?

Without a doubt, Valdez's Sí TV was a trendsetting cable network that overcame significant obstacles and achieved notable accomplishments in its short history. A large part of NuvoTV's growth stems from its promise to target bicultural Latino viewers with unique television shows. NuvoTV's content, however, remains reliant on inexpensive reality television programs because it has not been able to attract a significant amount of consistent financing in order to produce original, scripted content. NuvoTV simultaneously cannot purchase a considerable amount of inexpensive syndicated programming because many of these programs do not feature notable Latino characters. With a dearth of available financing and limited programming options, NuvoTV's existing programming strategy is effective in the short term because it is easy for a cable network to offset the inexpensive production and/ or acquisition costs of reality television with advertising revenue and per-subscriber fees. Relying on reality TV, however, does not generate strong branding among bicultural Latina/o viewers because several cable networks already air a significant amount of reality television programming. This strategy also fails to fulfill Valdez's original goal for Sí TV, which was having a channel where Latinos can see unique stories about themselves.

In order to increase brand awareness, Sí TV changed its name to NuvoTV. While the name change has been positive, NuvoTV now finds itself in a race with other cable networks like El Rey or Mun2 to brand itself with bicultural Latino viewers. NuvoTV certainly has improved its chances of becoming the leading US Latino cable network by developing a new partnership with the powerful Jennifer Lopez. Unfortunately, as bicultural US Latinos continue to become an increasingly important target audience, NuvoTV will encounter competition from a growing number of cable networks. Armed with more capital to produce original US Latino-oriented content and with the ability to leverage current cable assets in order to secure broad distribution, NuvoTV's competitors like Fusion or El Rey currently appear to be better positioned to brand themselves with this audience and overtake NuvoTV in this marketplace.

REFERENCES

Allen, Greg. 2012. "Media Outlets Adapt to Growing Hispanic Audience." National Public Radio, *Morning Edition*, Apr. 3.

"Behind the Rebrand, One Year Later: Network for Bicultural Latinos Finds Its New Brand Is Paying Off." 2012. *Multichannel News*, June 25.

Ben-Yehuda, Ayala. 2008. "The Expanding Channel." *Billboard*, Apr. 5, 24.

Block, Alex Ben. 2013 ."Jennifer Lopez at the Cable Show: I Want to Change the Face of Television." *Hollywood Reporter*, June 12, http://www.hollywoodreporter.com/news/jennifer-lopez-at-cable-show-567517 (accessed June 12, 2013).

Calvo, Dana. 2003. "Dish TV Service to Carry Si Network." *Los Angles Times*, Jan. 28, C3.

Carter, Bill. 2010. "Weighty Dramas Flourish on Cable." *New York Times*, Apr. 4.

Chozick, Amy. 2013. "Disney Give Details of Fusion, a Channel for Latinos." NYTimes. com, Feb. 11, http://mediadecoder.blogs.nytimes.com/2013/02/11/univision-and-abc-news-give-details-of-cable-channel-aimed-at-latinos/ (accessed June 11, 2013).

Dávila, Arlene. 2001. *Latinos, Inc.: The Marketing and Making of a People*. Berkeley: University of California Press.

de la Fuente, Anna Marie. 2006. "Jeff Valdez." *Daily Variety*, Mar. 9, A12.

———. 2012. "NuvoTV Raises $40 Mil from Investors." Variety.com, Aug. 28, http://variety.com/2012/tv/news/nuvotv-raises-40-mil-from-investors-1118058334/ (accessed June 29, 2013).

Esparza, Elia. 1998. "Must SíTV." *Hispanic*, May, 20–30.

Fitzgerald, Kate. 1999. "Latino Lifestyle Missing from English-Language Fare." *Advertising Age*, Aug. 30, S18–S19.

Flint, Joe. 2012. "Is Fox Pondering a National Cable Sports Network?" *Los Angeles Times*, Mar. 29.

Gates, Sara. 2012. "Latino TV Shows: NuvoTV Raised $40 Million to Create English Programming for Hispanic Audience." *Huffington Post*, Aug. 28, http://www.huffingtonpost.com/2012/08/28/latino-tv-shows-nuvotv-40-million-investors_n_1836645.html?utm_hp_ref=email_share (accessed Sept. 1, 2012).

Gibbons, Kent. 2009. "Cox Adds SíTV in Arizona." *Multichannel News*, Jan. 12.

Haugsted, Linda. 2008. "Comcast Shutting Down AZN Network." *Multichannel News*, Jan. 25.

"Hispanic Upfronts: The Good, the Bad and the Pretty." 2013. *Multichannel News*, May 20, 20.

Hofmeister, Sallie. 2004. "In Brief/Entertainment: SíTV Cable Channel Secures $60 Million." *Los Angeles Times*, Apr. 6, C3.

James, Meg. 2005. "Networks Have an Ear for Spanish." *Los Angeles Times*, Sept. 11, A1.

———. 2012. "NuvoTV Secures Additional $40 Million in Financing." *Los Angeles Times*, Aug. 28.

James, Meg, and Dawn C. Chmielewski. 2012. "ABC News, Univision to Launch English-Language News Network." *Los Angeles Times*, May 8.

Kilday, Gregg. 2006. "Valdez Joins Maya Ent. as Co-Chairman." *Hollywood Reporter*, Oct. 11, http://business.highbeam.com/2012/article-1G1-154005659/valdez-joins-maya-ent-cochairman (accessed Aug. 20, 2013).

Koyen, Jeff. 2012. "The Truth about Hispanic Consumers: Myth vs. Reality." *Adweek*, Mar. 11, http://www.adweek.com/sa-article/truth-about-hispanic-consumers-138828 (accessed Aug. 12, 2012).

Littleton, Cynthia. 2011. "Latino Leverage." *Daily Variety*, Apr. 5, 1, 13.

Mayer, Vicki. 2003. *Producing Dreams, Consuming Youth: Mexican Americans and Mass Media*. New Brunswick: Rutgers University Press.

Moore, Frazier. 2013. "Jennifer Lopez Named NuvoTV's Chief Creative Officer." *Huffington Post*, May 15, http://www.huffingtonpost.com/2013/05/16/jennifer-lopez-named-nuvo_n_3285150.html (accessed June 10, 2013).

Morabito, Andrea. 2011. "SíTV Branding to NuvoTV: Network Relaunches July 4; Becomes Nielsen Rated in October." *Broadcasting and Cable*, Mar. 14, http://www.broadcastingcable.com/article/465252-Si_TV_Rebranding_To_nuvoTV.php (accessed Sept. 30, 2012).

Morello, Carol. 2011. "Demographics among Children Shifting Quickly." *Washington Post*, Apr. 5, A18.

Motel, Seth, and Eileen Patten. 2013. "Statistical Portrait of Hispanics in the United States, 2011," Table 20: Language Spoken at Home and English-Speaking Ability by Age, Race and Ethnicity. Pew Hispanic Center, Feb. 15, http://www.pewhispanic.org/2013/02/15/statistical-portrait-of-hispanics-in-the-united-states-2011/#20 (accessed July 12, 2013).

Mullen, Megan. 2003. *The Rise of Cable Programming in the United States: Revolution or Evolution?* Austin: University of Texas Press.

Navarro, Mireya. 2006. "Changing U.S. Audience Poses Test for a Giant of Spanish TV." *New York Times*, Mar. 10, A1.

Nededog, Jethro. 2013. "Jennifer Lopez Named Chief Creative Officer of NuvoTV." thewrap.com, May 16, http://www.thewrap.com/tv/article/jennifer-lopez-named-chief-creative-officer-nuvotv-92006 (accessed June 10, 2013).

"New Nielsen Data Reveals NuvoTV Delivers an Audience with One of Television's Highest Median Incomes." 2012. *PR Newswire*, Apr. 23.

Ng, Philiana. 2013. "NuvoTV Names Former Comedy Central Exec as Head of Programming." *Hollywood Reporter*, May 3.

"NuvoTV Unveils 2012–2013 Programming Slate." 2012. *PR Newswire*, Apr. 24.

Piñón, J., and V. Rojas. 2011. "Language and Cultural Identity in the New Configuration of the US Latino TV Industry." *Global Media and Communication* 7 (2): 129–47.

Ramirez-Berg, Charles. 2002. *Latino Images in Film: Stereotypes, Subversion, Resistance*. Austin: University of Texas Press.

Rodriguez, America. 1999. *Making Latino News: Race, Language, Class*. Thousand Oaks: Sage.

Saldana, Hector. 2013. "S.A. Comedy Club Celebrates 20 Years of Laughs." MySA.com, May 29, www.mysanantonio.com/entertainment/stage/article/20-years-of-laughs-4554633.php (accessed June 23, 2013).

Seidman, Robert. 2012. "NuvoTV: Ratings Growth Strong Right from the Start." *TV by the Numbers*, Jan. 27, http://tvbythenumbers.zap2it.com/2012/01/27/nuvotv-ratings-growth-strong-right-from-the-start/117802/ (accessed Aug. 4, 2012).

"SíTV Raises $24 Million in Equity and Debt Financing." 2010. *Business Wire*, June 7.

Smith-Shomade, Beretta E. 2007. "Target Market Black: BET and the Branding of African America." In *Cable Visions: Television beyond Broadcasting*, edited by Sarah Banet-Weiser, Cynthia Chris, and Anthony Freitas, 177–93. New York: New York University Press.

Steinberg, Brian. 2011. "SíTV to Change Name as It Aims for Bicultural Latinos." *Advertising Age*, Mar. 14.

———. 2012. "Jennifer Lopez to Take Minority Stake in Cable's NuvoTV." Adage.com, Sept. 12, http://adage.com/article/media/jennifer-lopez-minority-stake-cable-s-nuvo-tv/237139/ (accessed Sept. 14, 2012).

Steinberg, Jacques. 2004. "Network Hopes to Attract Hispanics by Speaking English." *New York Times*, Apr. 5, C5.

Taylor, Paul, Mark Hugo Lopez, Jessica Hamar Martínez, and Gabriel Velasco. 2012. "When Labels Don't Fit: Hispanics and Their Views of Identity." Pew Hispanic Center, Apr. 4, http://www.pewhispanic.org/2012/04/04/when-labels-dont-fit-hispanics-and-their-views-of-identity/ (accessed Dec. 20, 2012).

Trevino, Joseph. 1999. "Bilingual Television Grows an Audience." *Hispanic*, Oct., 14–16.

Valdez, Jeff. 2013. Telephone interview by Henry Puente, April 4.

Vega, Tanzina. 2012. "Ad Executive Makes Leap to Comcast's El Rey Network." NYTimes.com, Aug. 10, http://mediadecoder.blogs.nytimes.com/2012/08/06/ad-executive-makes-leap-to-comcasts-el-rey-network/ (accessed Aug. 10, 2012).

Vega, Tanzina, and Bill Carter. 2012. "Networks Struggle to Appeal to Hispanics." *New York Times*, Aug. 5.

Vega, Tanzina, and Bill Elliott. 2013. "Media Companies Aim to Woo Advertisers and Latinos." *New York Times*, May 16.

Villarreal, Yvonne. 2013. "*I Love Jenni*'s Harsh Reality." *Los Angeles Times*, Apr. 13, D1.

Wentz, Laurel. 2004. "The Biz: SíTV Reaches Out to Young Hispanics." *Advertising Age*, Feb. 23, 37.

Whitney, Daisy. 2011. "Upfront 2011: Spanish Language Market 50 Million Reasons to Be Optimistic." Reelgrok.com, http://www.reelgrok.com/news-article.cfm?id=263&t=n (accessed Sept. 28, 2012).

Winslow, George. 2008. "More Choices for Hispanic Viewers." *Broadcasting and Cable*, Oct. 20, 1A–4A.

4

One Language, One Nation, and One Vision

NBC Latino, Fusion, and Fox News Latino

CHRISTOPHER JOSEPH WESTGATE

Throughout the last two decades, scholars have analyzed the production of English-language news that focuses on Latin@s. One recent study revealed that ABC, CBS, NBC, and CNN have underrepresented and misrepresented 17 percent of the US population. Less than 1 percent of those networks' evening news stories have centered on Latin@s, and of that percentage, most of the content has been negative. The study's author concluded that the television networks "still do not consider Latinos to be an integral part of the American social fabric. . . . The nation's portrait of US Latinos is distorted."[1] The four English-language networks' low quantity and poor quality of Latin@ news coverage interfere significantly with the potential for an informed culture.

Although it is but one aspect of culture, language is nonetheless an important consideration in Latin@ journalism studies. Several scholars, for example, have found that the language of news reports influences how audiences understand political and economic issues.[2] Just as transnational news channels attempt to gain export advantages by carving out geo-linguistic markets that reflect an "emerging English linguistic hegemony,"[3] select transcontinental media firms continue to uphold the dominance of the Spanish language. To be sure, the predominant language of media conglomerates affects, to different degrees, the production of journalism in digital spaces.

It may thus seem surprising that scholars have not paid much attention to the languages of Latin@ digital news. According to a 2012 Pew Hispanic Center survey of 1,765 Latin@ adults, 82 percent of Latin@s received some news in English, an increase of 4 percent from 2006 to 2012; importantly, there was a decline—from 78 to 68 percent—over the same ten-year period among those who consumed a portion of their news diet in Spanish. Additionally, 32 percent of Latin@s read, watched, or listened to news stories exclusively in English, a 10 percent increase from 2006 to 2012; meanwhile, the share of Latin@s who obtained stories solely in Spanish declined from 22 to 18 percent over that ten-year period. While those figures account for Internet, print, radio, and television news, 61 percent of Latin@s who use only the Internet for news receive content exclusively in English.[4] A larger context surrounds these consumption patterns: 40 percent of second-generation and 69 percent of third-generation Latin@s are more proficient in English than in Spanish. Of the over 52 million Latin@s older than age five, 65 percent either speak only English at home or speak English well.[5] The overall message could not be clearer for news producers: more English, less Spanish.

Major news organizations have begun to recognize that not all Latin@s watch Spanish-language news, and that it may be profitable to sell English-dominant Latin@ audiences to advertisers through websites and news applications. The strategic launch years of NBC Latino (2012), Fusion (2013)—formerly ABC-Univision (2012)—and Fox News Latino (2010) preceded and coincided with the US presidential election and debates over immigration reform. Univision in particular has a history of political programming: the network runs "an imperialist script that . . . assumes linguistic assimilation for political participation."[6] There may very well be a political agenda behind the launch of each news site, but the sites' creators also have an economic agenda driven by US census numbers, purchasing power statistics, and the twin motivations of cutting costs and maximizing returns. It would be far too naïve to think that NBC Latino, Fusion, and Fox News Latino were created either because the number of US-born Latin@s has surpassed the amount of Latin Americans who migrate to the United States or because news organizations supply products to meet audience demands; those statements may be true to various degrees, but media companies also set their own political and economic agendas.[7]

While all three news sites attempt to bring Latin@s together into national conversations that celebrate intragroup and intergroup differences, this chapter argues that the sites instead create an illusion of integration—one language, one nation, and one vision—for political and economic reasons. Just as the political reality behind that illusion is suggestive of segregation, precisely because each media company confines non–English-language news to "other" channels and sites outside mainstream mediated culture, the economic reality behind it is one of segmentation for second-generation-plus Latin@s, as well as for non-Latin@ users. NBC Latino, Fusion, and Fox News Latino are symptoms of the problematic ways that monolingual media threaten the principles and practices of linguistic pluralism. The use of one language, then, means assimilationist politics and economics.

Naysayers will certainly point out that Internet users have a choice; there are, after all, more than three English- or Spanish-language news sites in cyberspace, though not very many that focus on multiple Latin@ communities in a transnational context. Audiences may choose what to consume, but they do so from a finite number of reputable news corporations with significant clout. Independent news organizations have yet to leave a comparable number of impressions on mass audiences, due in no small part to the omnipresence of mainstream media corporations and their branding on the popular imagination. Their forms may be different, but the NBC Latino, Fusion, and Fox News Latino sites have the same function as most news sites: to deliver similar, if not identical, content in a common language.

This chapter's argument is demonstrated with a textual analysis of the three news sites, their parent or sister television news sites, related social media pages, and articles from the trade and popular presses. The positions of officials, descriptions of reporters, and reactions of users were read for references to English, Spanish, or "other" languages. The following three sections of the analysis address one English-language news site at a time. Each section begins by discussing a specific site's linguistic orientation; shortly thereafter, select social media posts are shared for what they illuminate about monolingual media. The analysis then proceeds to comment on the politics of segregation and the economics of segmentation, illustrating how "language is an economic resource with symbolic political value."[8] Each section concludes with an examination of relevant television news offerings, as well as an evaluation of the similarities and differences between a particular company's English-language news site and its related Spanish-language television news site.

NBC Latino

After its debut as a Tumblr page in 2011, NBC Latino morphed into a full-scale news site one year later with the goal of becoming "the new voice of Hispanic Americans"—the company's media workers "talk to them in English because it's the language they already speak."[9] It is important to notice the "us versus them" object pronoun positioning in this statement and how it implies an elite mentality of producers who speak to, rather than with, Latin@ audiences. Critical observers would do well to ask why the writer(s) of that statement failed to acknowledge that not all Latin@s prefer English, that some of the site's users may speak more than English or Spanish, and that culture cannot be reduced to language. The notion that a single corporation could project the voice of multiple communities is anything but democratic; one goal of a news organization, at least in an information society, should be to facilitate the auditions of multiple voices rather than aggregate their sounds into a predetermined mass for marketing convenience.

Echoing that criticism, perhaps unwittingly, one of NBC Latino's freelancers, Julio Ricardo Varela, published an opinion piece that contained the following observation about the language of media: "English media is perceived as superior in terms of reach and quality, because it has always been the mainstream and the larger market." Readers neither challenged Varela's assertion nor questioned the idea of monolingual content; instead, they confirmed that large companies have the power to "create their own version of reality." As one NBC Latino user, Bella Vida by Leddy, commented at the end of Varela's piece, "this country IS made up of people from ALL over the world and it is this diversity that makes us a strong nation."[10] Bella Vida by Leddy astutely acknowledged that NBC Latino's monolingual content does not reflect the country's linguistic pluralism. The site's English-only news stories suggest that NBC's private interest in the exchange value of one language trumps the public's interest in the use value of multiple languages. Bella Vida by Leddy's response shows how corporate executives prefer content in one language, especially when those with the largest market shares have a perceived feeling—rather than any real evidence—that different languages, merely by virtue of their existence, threaten to drown out the voices of those in power.

NBC Latino's public page on Facebook, with its 80,000-plus "likes" at the time of this writing, exemplifies how the news organization's monolingual identity is reproduced in the social communication of its users. Most of the page's posts are in English. The minority of users who post in Spanish display wide variations in their writing: several fans show careful regard for accent marks and proper punctuation, while others write as they speak, using "k" instead of "que" to mean "that," thereby illustrating the orality of new media writing.[11] NBC Latino's media workers, known as contributors, encourage questions or comments, but their responses, even to Spanish-language posts, are always in English. Users rarely post questions or comments that do not, at least in some way, react to a preexisting news agenda set by Executive Editor Chris Peña and his supervisors.

The language of the Facebook page's users is, not coincidentally, the language of corporate leaders. Comcast, NBC Latino's parent conglomerate, endorses English for a potentially global, yet primarily national, audience by publishing content only in that language on most of its news sites. By excluding any and all Spanish-language stories—in the form of original or aggregated content—from its site, NBC Latino's corporate leaders and media workers are perpetuating a reality of segregation under the guise of integration. Latin@s may report the news, but Comcast executives, the vast majority of whom do not identify as Latin@s on their public profile pages, still control the reporting.[12]

NBC Latino's decision to exclude Spanish-language news may reflect the desire of crony capitalists to maintain similar ideologies. Comcast executives, for instance, worked with government leaders on the NBCUniversal Political Action Committee (PAC). Between 2011 and 2012, the PAC received more than $3 million in individual contributions.[13] Although PACs have implications for the concentration of ownership and market competition, they can also influence national legislation on issues like immigration. Peña remarked that immigration reform has and will continue to be "widely discussed" among NBC Latino web producers who are assigned to politics.[14]

Economics are not far removed from politics. NBC Latino's segmented audience includes second-plus–generation Latin@s and non-Latin@s, particularly millennial users. The company's media kit indicates that the news site addresses acculturated "American born Latinos—bilingual, bicultural, and influential in a multi-generational household . . . a population that enjoys enormous purchasing power: $1 trillion."[15] In the process of selling some audience segments to advertisers and not "others" (e.g., Spanish-dominant Internet users), NBC Latino ironically draws on Telemundo's resources. For example, bilingual Telemundo journalists regularly translate news stories for NBC Latino's audiences.[16]

Considering that both entities share resources, it would seem logical for NBC to incorporate Telemundo's Spanish-language television news headlines into its Latino site. And yet, as the National Institute for Latino Policy confirmed, "Telemundo has been a very marginal part of the whole NBC operation."[17] Spanish must play a role in Telemundo's marginalization, especially if language is interpreted as a lever of political-economic gain or loss. While one answer to the question of why NBC Latino excludes Telemundo's stories is that the former site does not target Spanish-dominant Latin@s and first-generation immigrants—perhaps because most of the $1 trillion of Latin@ spending power is, in all probability, derived from second-plus–generation consumers[18]—the issue of English-only news remains problematic for those who support the creation, circulation, and consumption of multilingual media content on pluralistic grounds.

Although there is some content duplication between the Noticias Telemundo and NBC Latino sites—evinced in the cost-saving measure of aggregating news from cooperatives—the former publishes more stories from Latin America than the latter.[19] NBC's site is organized by nine different beats—people, parenting, food, education, politics, news, video, celebrity, and technology—with accompanying US-centric stories. In contrast, most of Noticias Telemundo's headlines and leads appear underneath a general articles header, making it difficult for users to quickly search for country-specific information.[20] The Noticias Telemundo site represents the commodification of news content for Spanish-dominant Latin@s and first-generation immigrants, many of whom watch the news more often on traditional screens than on computers, cell phones, or other digital devices.

Noticias Telemundo is clearly in the business of entertainment, one explanation for why the site's content builders and designers reserve more space for sports and *telenovelas* than for hard news. The "Noticias" (news) tab is one of ten entertainment-related tabs on the Telemundo site. This privileging of entertainment over information points to Telemundo's historical competition with Univision for television viewers—and now for Internet users—across geo-linguistic markets. It will be interesting to see whether NBC Latino eventually transitions to television, taking its cue from the Fusion website and television network.

Fusion

ABC and Univision established a joint venture in 2012—ABC-Univision, rebranded as Fusion in 2013—to target a growing audience of English-dominant Latin@s as well as non-Latin@s. Journalist Jorge Ramos, however unintentionally, suggested otherwise: "those voices that *we* hear on a daily basis in Spanish are not being heard in English. . . . It's time that that starts to happen" (emphasis added).[21] The "we" subject pronoun that Ramos uses is inclusive of Spanish-dominant Latin@s and first-generation immigrants. When interpreted in the context of Fusion, Ramos's statement may mean that Univision is developing a bilingual identity. Cesar Conde, the former president of Univision Networks, added that the joint venture was designed to reach "all Hispanics, regardless of language,"[22] though Fusion clearly holds English in the highest regard. Due to the media ecology in which audiences find themselves, and because of the language(s) that they use on a daily basis, Latin@ web users' "lives are in English."[23]

ABC News journalists Jim Avila and Serena Marshall reported on a Pew Hispanic Center study that found English to be the primary language of Latin@s. More than a dozen Fusion users critically responded to that report. From reader Charles Edward Brown's post that blamed Avila and Marshall for telling "liberal lies" to the poster James Jones's question of whether "this lie is supposed to make me feel better about the takeover of my country," respondents expressed overt skepticism if not cynicism about the story's main idea, citing their own experiences of having to "press one for English" and observing McDonald's employees who do not speak English.[24] These posts, however, did not show evidence of engagement with the Pew study itself. Responses were posted at the bottom of the Fusion—formerly ABC-Univision—news site rather than on a social media page.

Fusion takes advantage of audience labor, or, put euphemistically, the network builds "relationships with brand ambassadors who can spread messages via Facebook and Twitter";[25] indeed, Fusion has a presence on Twitter, Facebook, Instagram, Google+, and Tumblr.[26] One tweet linked to a story about an immigration reform bill proposed by US senators who argue that immigrants should learn English prior to becoming permanent residents. PastorofPLUR, one of Fusion's users, disagreed with reporter Jordan Fabian's observation that immigrants "don't need to be told to learn English; they're already doing it." The user responded in the imperative mood: "Go to a welfare office, a low-income or free clinic, or any ethnic church. . . . You will find an overwhelming number of people [who] cannot understand the simplest English sentences and need help filling out the most basic forms."[27] PastorofPLUR neither identifies as a literacy specialist nor concedes that those who are fluent in English also ask for help with federal forms.

The politics of users are closely related to the partisanship of executives. Peter Walker, Univision's former local media president, referenced the company's partisan nature when he remarked that "candidates and groups representing certain points of view have an interest in reaching our audience, and we have an interest in helping them do that."[28] Fusion contributes to the segregation of Spanish-language from English-language stories by relegating the former to the Noticias Univision news site; as was the case with NBC Latino, the Fusion news site does not contain any Spanish-language stories. Disney, its ABC subsidiary, and Univision subjugate any potential public interest in multilingual news to their private interests in monolingual content.

Like many media organizations, Univision does not take a conservative position on all issues—the network has committed itself to progressive political action on immigration. For Ramos, the political was always personal: his own immigration story propelled him to "demand changes by chronicling the stories of broken dreams and broken families" on television and in print. The journalist has openly accused President Obama of delaying immigration reform. Univision's position on immigration is "clearly pro-Latino. . . . We are simply being the voice of those who do not have a voice."[29] Perhaps that position is one reason why Fusion recently added a noticeable immigration reform section to its main page.[30]

Politics and economics are inseparable. Like NBC Latino, Fusion targets second-plus–generation Latin@s and non-Latin@ millennial users. As Univision News president and Fusion chief executive officer, Isaac Lee, admitted, "I care about influencing the people who are going to be the future of this country. Their main language is English, not Spanish."[31] Apart from segmentation, Fusion's site reveals the network's dependence on ABC and Univision for news content.[32] It is precisely this kind of dependency that allows Fusion to minimize the expense of newsgathering.

While the Fusion and Univision news sites clearly differ in language,[33] one strategy may be to lure Spanish-dominant Latin@s and first-generation immigrants—especially those who have been told by corporate owners and government leaders that they need greater exposure to English and its associated cultural capital for the purposes of assimilation and citizenship—to the Fusion site. Critical observers may wonder what will ultimately happen to the status of Spanish in the broader media ecology if English gradually encroaches on Spanish-language media under the guise of inclusivity; perhaps such "encroachment" is already under way with the addition of closed captioning to Univision's prime-time telenovelas[34] and with the creation of the Fusion site. A political-economic endorsement of English, however, probably has more to do with citizenship requirements on the one hand, and the potential for a profitable exchange between producers, advertisers, and audiences, on the other, than with the linguistic needs and preferences of media users.

Along with its website, Fusion's television channel debuted in 2013. One reporter wrote that the multimillion-dollar joint venture was created to "target a wealthier audience of 'acculturated' Hispanics who are comfortable with the English language while remaining deeply rooted in their own culture."[35] Apart from one critical response to this statement—Latin@s are members of more than one community—it is difficult to understand how a major news network could encourage its viewers to remain "deeply rooted in their own culture" when not all groups are equally represented, if they appear at all. Latin@ news coverage is, in its very nature, selective.[36]

Fusion represents an opportunity for Latin@s to talk back in an "empowered" way, however "irreverently," to mainstream media institutions and government officials about immigration and other important issues. Lee went as far as to say that Fusion "gives Latinos a voice in the American conversation,"[37] a statement that raises several questions. Why do audiences need a television network to participate in democracy? How can the idea of giving voice not perpetuate an unhealthy power imbalance between those who hold the proverbial microphone and those who ask or are asked to speak into it? Why is there only one American conversation, and who defines its parameters? What do the answers to these questions mean for Latin@s who speak "other" languages? Both the Fusion website and its television network exemplify the "production of Latinos as easily digestible and marketable within the larger structures of corporate America." Fusion's monolingual content "generalizes the totality of Latin@s from one English-speaking segment" in an attempt to "consolidate the country" with a standardized language.[38] The impact of monolingual media on linguistic pluralism matters to those who are concerned about the consolidation of corporate power and its effects on freedom of expression.[39]

Fox News Latino

Although the Fox News Latino site inches toward bilingual news, it does not quite get there, mostly because the quantity of English-language news far outweighs the number of Spanish-language stories; the site is divided into ten English-language sections and one Spanish-language section.[40] This ten-to-one ratio seems to discourage rather than encourage a truly embedded bilingual presentation of news, one that could incorporate a relatively equal distribution of English- and Spanish-language content. Considering that linguistic imbalance, it is not surprising that Fox News Latino's Facebook posts are mostly written in English, a choice that reveals how users are cultivated to select one language over another.

Fox News Latino's Facebook page, with its 81,000 "likes" at the time of this writing, includes an "about" section that describes the news site's relationship to "the Latino community living in the U.S.," incorrectly implying that Latin@s constitute a monolith of users. This kind of unitary construction is not unique to Fox News Latino, nor to NBC Latino and Fusion, for that matter; such constructions frequently appear in headlines when commentators or reporters singularize segments of society. Similar to the missions of the NBC Latino and Fusion sites, Fox News Latino attempts to bridge two worlds, "reflect[ing] a sensibility of Latino traditions but also deep engagement and commitment to American society. We will showcase videos and content in both English and Spanish."[41] It is difficult to discern what the writer(s) meant by Latino traditions, or why the "but" conjunction was used; that conjunction dichotomizes Latin@s and Americans, implying that Latin@ traditions, whatever they are, do not constitute a part of the American way of life. The writer(s) may not have anticipated this interpretation, but it is nonetheless one possible reading of the text.

In response to a story that recounted the removal of Spanish-language signs from a Delaware playground, one Fox News Latino Facebook user, Pedro Dabalsa, asserted the following: "I think the lesson is clear—learn English, do not rely on others people translations, drop the Spanish television, the Spanish language soap opera, and switch to English channels."[42] This statement is more powerful for what it does not say than for what it does, insofar as it implies that media companies like Fox have some degree of influence on how audiences think about their own language acquisition and retention. This is not to suggest that media organizations are omnipotent and determine how audiences behave, nor that audiences are completely autonomous, but that messages have cumulative effects insofar as audiences are cultivated— not only by their peers, parents, or teachers, but also by and through media—to use particular languages.[43] The mediated cultivation of language does not display signs of either technological determinism or social constructivism, but rather works subtly and unceasingly between both extremes.

Johnny Kasitz, another Fox News Latino Facebook user, reacted to English-language news for Latin@s by asking NBC, ABC, and Fox why they do not "offer a trial run of all programming and advertisements with Spanish captioning, and vice-versa with the Spanish-speaking networks." Theresa Jarvis, another Fox News Latino Facebook user, responded to Kasitz's post: "Anyone living here should learn our language. Sounds like you want to continue to enable them to not learn. . . . Johnny, learning a language won't happen by reading captions. Again, it just enables them to avoid learning."[44] In her response, Jarvis incorrectly asserts, without credible evidence, that subtitles do nothing to contribute to learning or reinforcing a language. Her position illustrates how Fox News users influence—and are influenced by—the political orientations of corporate executives and government leaders, particularly those with right-wing ideologies.

The executive chair of News Corporation and 21st Century Fox, Rupert Murdoch, has been critiqued for his excessive influence on US politics. In addition to "pressuring the FCC and Congress to alter the laws of the land and regulatory standards" so that his conglomerate can gain unfair advantages over competitors, Murdoch regularly displays what one media critic called "far too much control" over the media landscape.[45] The CEO has been shown to use his business operations to "penetrate new markets, expand audience shares . . . and leverage public opinion."[46] Murdoch's high degree of control over his media assets has undeniably affected Fox News Latino's segregation of Spanish from English, exemplified by a separate Español token tab.

And yet not all media assets of News Corporation and 21st Century Fox project equal amounts of conservatism on all issues. When President Obama's administration announced that it would streamline the process by which undocumented immigrants apply for permanent residency, Fox Nation (the Fox News Channel site) and Fox News Latino could not have been more different from each other in tone. The latter site reported the story with the headline "U.S. Eases Path to Legalization for Some Immigrants, Keeps Families Together" and a photograph of an immigration reform rally, while the former site released the same story with the title "Obama Begins Amnesty Push" and an image that Fox had previously used to criticize President Obama's administration for its decision to cease deportations of undocumented children.[47]

Based on the way Fox Nation framed that story, it is easy to see why the National Hispanic Media Coalition concluded that Fox's viewers hold a more negative view of Latin@s than viewers of other networks do. Moreover, some conservatives have denounced Fox News Latino for its apparent lack of credibility.[48] Fox News Latino may be willing to assume the risk of a less regressive position on immigration in order to build a larger base of Latin@s who could take conservative stands on other issues.

Like NBC Latino and Fusion, Fox News Latino attempts to reach English-dominant Latin@s and non-Latin@ millennial users. According to its director, Francisco Cortes, the site's "target audience is second- and third-generation U.S. Hispanics."[49] Additionally, much of Fox News Latino's stories are collected from the Associated Press, Nuestra Tele Noticias (NTN 24), Radio Cadena Nacional de Televisión (RCN), and Agencia EFE. These newsgathering cooperatives illustrate how Fox News Latino relies on prepackaged programming in order to conserve funds.

Critics may question why Fox invested in a Spanish-language television network in light of the historical relationship between US conservatives and that language, Fox Nation's overt conservatism, and Fusion's strategic choice to program in English. One possible answer seems to lie in the potential for MundoFox—a 2012 joint venture between Fox International and RCN Televisión—to lure Telemundo's and Univision's Spanish-dominant viewers away from those networks by disseminating content that is modeled on mainstream English-language news and entertainment. The television network is clearly transnational in its approach: most shows are produced by RCN in Colombia as well as by RCN's NTN 24, Fox's Spanish-language sports network (Fox Deportes), and 21st Century Fox's Shine America.[50]

The apparent irony that Fox News Latino has included Spanish-language news on its site while NBC, generally regarded by some observers as more liberal, has not, should not be surprising. Fox may have decided to publish news stories in two languages to differentiate its brand, but the arguably quasi-bilingual decision also creates a synergy between Fox News Latino and the Spanish-language television network's news site, Noticias MundoFox—the latter's headlines appear at the bottom of select pages across the former's site.[51] Noticias Mundo-Fox provides fewer stories and beats than Fox News Latino, a fact that may well reflect the television news program's early stage of development. Only time will tell whether Noticias MundoFox will thrive in the already competitive television news economy.

Conclusion

NBC Latino, Fusion, and Fox News Latino have endorsed one language as an official medium for the transmission of information. All three news sites produce an illusion of integration for the political and economic purposes of segregation and segmentation. The sites certainly do not prevent bilingual or multilingual users from accessing content in more than one language across various forms of media; not all Latin@s visit the news sites, just as not all of the sites' visitors are Latin@s. Nevertheless, all three sites, due to the long-term influence of conglomerates on media life in the United States,[52] marginalize non-English languages through the absence of multilingual stories. Most national media are monolingual, one primary reason for monolingual audiences' lack of fluency in "other" languages.[53] NBC Latino, Fusion, and Fox News Latino are not simply responding to the reality of English-dominance among Latin@ millennial users; they are also shaping and sustaining that very reality as they inform and entertain audiences in one language on a daily basis. Telemundo, Univision, and MundoFox are, of course, doing the very same thing for Spanish-dominant Latin@s and first-generation immigrants.

The English-language news sites do not offer the alternatives that critics predicted; instead, NBC Latino, Fusion, and Fox News Latino reproduce the predictable effects of deregulation on localism. ABC and Univision selected Doral, a suburb of the transnational city of Miami, for Fusion's home base. MundoFox opted for Los Angeles as the site for its headquarters, a city that was chosen because of its geographic proximity to Mexico and because two-thirds of Latin@s identify as Mexican or Mexican American. And yet even with Los Angeles's regional-Mexican character, MundoFox relies on prepackaged content from Colombia and Spain for its Noticias program.[54]

NBC Latino, Fusion, and Fox News Latino could build multilingual editions of their sites by fully integrating content produced by their sister/parent companies Telemundo, Univision, and MundoFox,

respectively, or by hiring media workers to offer dialectal translations—of Cuban Spanish, Brazilian Portuguese, and so on—for different audiences. CNN created two foreign-language editions of its news
site, one in Spanish and another in Arabic, as well as CNN Latino, a
bilingual television network. Television viewers can already select subtitles in multiple languages, so it seems that web users should be able
to choose multilingual editions with content that is carefully selected
by web editors who are trained to pay attention to medium, context,
purpose, audience, dialect, and register. This solution could contribute to a "multicultural liberal perspective that encourages Latinas/os
to express their cultural and political lives in the language(s) of their
choice . . . to politicize Spanish (subject it to political debate, reevaluate
it as a citizenship right) and to denaturalize the English-centric way of
defining political rights."[55] That solution is especially important in light
of audience studies that reveal a lack of Spanish-language content on
the web.[56]

It may be useful to theorize why English-language news conglomerates do not provide multilingual translations of their content. Apart
from conserving funds, one reason may be that the market demand for
translations remains unarticulated or, more likely, unheard. Another
reason may relate to the movement toward English as a global language
of business. As one critic remarked, "in the same way that American
power creates asymmetrical geopolitical and economic relationships
with certain parts of the world, so too does the reliance on English
as an international lingua franca engender cultural asymmetries with
non-Anglophone cultures."[57] A final reason may be that English-only
corporate executives tacitly subscribe to or, at the very least, unknow-
ingly exhibit the ideology of the English-only movement, an organized
effort that has resurfaced in recent calls by Oklahoma senator James
Inhofe and Iowa representative Steve King to make English the official
language of the United States. Acting in clear opposition to difference,
the English-only movement has intervened in elections to remind voters that their loyalty to the country would be questioned if they did not
use that language. Despite the movement's inability to make English the
country's official language, thirty-one states have designated it the official language of all public documents; in the process, these states have
not only hindered multilingualism, but also cultivated a culture of fear

to prevent separatism and sedition. At the national level, the question framers of the US census have "used language as an index of race,"[58] perpetuating a long practice of "linguistic apartheid"[59] that dates back to the colonial period of US history. Crony capitalists implicitly support English-only rhetoric by not valuing multilingualism in all of their products and services.

It will be interesting to see whether all three sites begin to recognize the unique characteristics of Latin@ communities, or whether Latin@ media workers' impact on production adds authenticity to each company's news agenda. The question of who not only writes, but also manages and owns, content is fundamental when one considers that the very concept of Latin@ news is, in its current form, a misguided by-product of a mentality that replaces particularity with universality.[60] If news organizations are "educational communicators," and if most Latin@s have "stopped watching or listening to Spanish-language media by the third generation,"[61] then this shift in usage poses a problem for the currency of that language in US society. From the perspectives of English-only corporate executives, media cultivation may prove to be less combative than government legislation; it may also be more effective at inducing bilingual or multilingual audiences—and ultimately, Spanish- or Portuguese-dominant audiences—to choose English.

NOTES

1. Otto Santa Ana, *Juan in a Hundred: The Representation of Latinos on Network News* (Austin: University of Texas Press, 2013). See also America Rodriguez, *Making Latino News: Race, Language, Class* (Thousand Oaks: Sage, 1999); and Allan Bell, *The Language of News Media* (Oxford: Blackwell, 1991).

2. Erika Franklin Fowler, Matthew Hale, and Tricia D. Olsen, "Spanish and English Language Local Television Coverage of Politics and the Tendency to Cater to Latino Audiences," *International Journal of Press/Politics* 14 (2009): 232–56; Regina Branton and Johanna Dunaway, "English- and Spanish-Language Media Coverage of Immigration: A Comparative Analysis," *Social Science Quarterly* 89, no. 4 (2008); Kristin C. Moran, "Is Changing the Language Enough? The Spanish-Language 'Alternative' in the U.S.A.," *Journalism* 7 (2006).

3. Joseph Straubhaar, *World Television: From Global to Local* (Thousand Oaks: Sage, 2007); Juan Piñón, "New Hierarchies of TV Broadcasting Distribution: The Case of Hispanic Networks," *FLOW* (2013).

4. Mark Hugo Lopez and Ana Gonzalez-Barrera, "A Growing Share of Latinos Get Their News in English," Pew

Research Hispanic Center, 2013, http://www.pewhispanic. org/2013/07/23/a-growing-share-of-latinos-get-their-news-in-english/.

5. Paul Taylor et al., "When Labels Don't Fit: Hispanics and Their Views of Identity," Pew Hispanic Center, 2012, http://www.pewhispanic. org/2012/04/04/when-labels-dont-fit-hispanics-and-their-views-of-identity/; Seth Motel and Eileen Patten, "The 10 Largest Hispanic Origin Groups: Characteristics, Rankings, Top Counties," Pew Hispanic Center, 2012, http://www.pewhispanic.org/2012/06/27/ the-10-largest-hispanic-origin-groups-characteristics-rankings-top-counties/.

6. Hector Amaya, *Citizenship Excess: Latino/as, Media, and the Nation* (New York: New York University Press, 2013).

7. See Andrew Calabrese and Colin Sparks, eds., *Toward a Political Economy of Culture: Capitalism and Communication in the Twenty-First Century* (Lanham, MD: Rowman and Littlefield, 2003).

8. S. Gal, "Language and Political Economy," *Annual Review of Anthropology* 18 (1989). See also Judith T. Irvine, "When Talk Isn't Cheap: Language and Political Economy," *American Ethnologist* 16, no. 2 (1989); and Paul Manning, "Words and Things, Goods and Services: Problems of Translation between Language and Political Economy," *Language & Communication* 26, nos. 3–4 (2006).

9. NBC Latino Facebook page, http://www.facebook.com/NBCLatino; also see its website: http://nbclatino.com/.

10. Julio Ricardo Varela, "Opinion: Three Reasons Why There Are Almost No Latinos in English-Language Newsrooms," NBC Latino, December 3, 2012, http:// nbclatino.com/.

11. NBC Latino Facebook page; Walter Ong, *Orality and Literacy: The Technologizing of the Word* (New York: Routledge, 2012).

12. Comcast, "Executive Biographies," http://corporate.comcast.com/ news-information/leadership-overview.

13. Federal Election Commission, "Financial Summary—Comcast Corporation & NBCUniversal Political Action Committee- Federal," http://www.fec.gov/ fecviewer/CandidateCommitteeDetail.do.

14. George Winslow, "Exclusive: NBC News Plans Latino-Targeted Site," *Broadcasting & Cable*, December 14, 2011, http://www.broadcastingcable.com/news/ technology/exclusive-nbc-news-plans-latino-targeted-site/48885.

15. "2012 Media Kit: NBC Latino," 2012, http://nbclatino.files.wordpress. com/2012/04/nbc-latino-mediakit.pdf.

16. Winslow, "Exclusive: NBC News Plans Latino-Targeted Site."

17. David Folkenflik, "Eyeing Latinos, NBC News Snuggles Up to Telemundo," *NPR's Morning Edition*, August 14, 2012, http://www.npr. org/2012/08/14/158690903/eyeing-latinos-nbc-news-snuggles-up-to-telemundo.

18. "2012 Media Kit: NBC Latino."

19. Noticiero Telemundo, http://msnlatino.telemundo.com/ informacion_y_noticias/Noticiero_Telemundo/.
20. Arlene Dávila, "Mapping Latinidad: Language and Culture in the Spanish TV Battlefront," in *Globalization on the Line: Culture, Capital, and Citizenship at U.S. Borders*, ed. Claudia Sadowski-Smith (New York: Palgrave, 2002); Amy Jo Coffey, "Growth and Trends in Spanish Language TV in the U.S.," in *The Handbook of Spanish Language Media*, ed. Alan B. Albarran (New York: Routledge, 2009).
21. David Folkenflik, "The Next Frontier in TV: English News for Latinos," *NPR's Morning Edition*, August 15, 2012, http://www.npr.org/2012/08/15/158763308/ the-next-frontier-in-tv-english-news-for-latinos.
22. "ABC News y Univision Anuncian Nuevo Canal en Inglés Dirigido a His-panos," *EFE News Service*, May 7, 2012, http://feeds.univision.com/feeds/ article/2012-05-07/abc-news-y-univision-anuncian.
23. Arian Campo-Flores and Sam Schechner, "Disney's ABC, Univision Mull News Channel Launch," *Wall Street Journal*, February 7, 2012, http://online.wsj.com/ news/articles/SB10001424052970203315804577207501238640514.
24. Jim Avila and Serena Marshall, "English Main Language for Hispanic Americans," ABC Univision, July 23, 2013, http://abcnews.go.com/blogs/ politics/2013/07/english-main-language-for-hispanic-americans/.
25. Cesar Conde, "Nielsen Consumer 360—Cesar Conde," YouTube, http://www. youtube.com/watch?v=FhmyGTbTfqU.
26. Fusion "Social Media," http://fusion.net.
27. Jordan Fabian, "No It's Not Necessary to Make English the Official Lan-guage," ABC Univision, June 14, 2013, http://fusion.net/leadership/story/ congress-immigrants-learn-english-12121.
28. Michael Malone, "Univision's Local Vision," *Broadcasting & Cable*, May 2, 2011, http://www.broadcastingcable.com/news/local-tv/ univision's-local-vision/42864.
29. Meg James, "Univision's Jorge Ramos a Powerful Voice on Immigra-tion," *Los Angeles Times*, June 3, 2013, http://www.latimes.com/enter-tainment/la-et-jorge-ramos-immigration-20130604-dto,0,6344424. htmlstory#axzz20sbNIhwh.
30. Fusion, "Politics: Immigration Reform," http://fusion.net/Topic/ Immigration_Reform/.
31. Andrew Edgecliffe-Johnson, "Univision of the Future," *Financial Times*, April 12, 2013, http://www.ft.com/cms/s/2/d803c9e6-a2bf-11e2-bd45-00144feabdco. html#axzz20tHTtHn2.
32. *Al Punto con Jorge Ramos*, http://noticias.univision.com/al-punto/; *America with Jorge Ramos*, http://fusion.net/America_with_Jorge_Ramos/.
33. Fusion; Univision Noticias, http://noticias.univision.com/.
34. Nancy Cook, "Univision Charts Course for America's Ethnic Future," *National Journal*, June 2, 2011, http://www.nationaljournal.com/next-economy/

univision-charts-course-for-america-s-ethnic-future-20110602; Ruth Samu-elson, "No Habla Español," *Columbia Journalism Review*, September 13, 2012, http://www.cjr.org/feature/no_habla_espanol.php?page=all.

35. Zachary Fagenson, "New Hispanic Media Network to Launch in 2013," *Reuters*, October 10, 2012, http://mobile.reuters.com/article/creditMarkets/idUSBRE8991OP20121010.

36. Santa Ana, *Juan in a Hundred*.

37. Univision PR, "ABC and Univision Introduce Fusion," February 12, 2013, http://corporate.univision.com/2013/press/abc-and-univision-introduce-fusion/#.UsBo--Aq538.

38. Arlene Dávila, *Latinos, Inc.: The Marketing and Making of a People* (Berkeley: University of California Press, 2001).

39. G. Cristina Mora, "Regulating Immigrant Media and Instituting Ethnic Bound-aries—The FCC and Spanish-Language Television: 1960–1990," *Latino Studies* 9, nos. 2–3 (2011); Amy Jo Coffey and Amy Kristin Sanders, "Defining a Product Market for Spanish-Language Broadcast Media: Lessons from United States v. Univision Communications, Inc. and Hispanic Broadcasting," *Communication Law & Policy* 15, no. 1 (2009).

40. Fox News Latino, http://latino.foxnews.com/index.html.

41. Fox News Latino Facebook page, http://latino.foxnews.com/index.html.

42. Ibid.

43. For a good overview of media effects, see Jennings Bryant and Mary Beth Oli-ver, eds., *Media Effects: Advances in Theory and Research* (New York: Routledge, 2008).

44. Fox News Latino Facebook page.

45. John Nichols, "Rupert Murdoch Has Gamed Ameri-can Politics Every Bit as Thoroughly as Britain's," *Nation*, July 16, 2011, http://www.thenation.com/blog/162083/rupert-murdoch-has-gamed-american-politics-every-bit-thoroughly-britains.

46. Amelia Arsenault and Manuel Castells, "Switching Power: Rupert Murdoch and the Global Business of Media Politics," *International Sociology* 23, no. 4 (2008).

47. Hilary Tone, "Fox Nation v. Fox News Latino on Obama's New Immigration Rule," Media Matters for America, January 3, 2013, http://mediamatters.org/blog/2013/01/03/fox-nation-v-fox-news-latino-on-obamas-new-immi/192000.

48. National Hispanic Media Coalition, "The Impact of Media Stereotypes on Opinions and Attitudes towards Latinos," 2012, http://www.nhmc.org/sites/default/files/LD%20NHMC%20Poll%20Results%20Sept.2012.pdf.

49. David Folkenflik, "How Fox Pioneered a Formula for Latino News," *NPR's All Things Considered*, August 8, 2012, http://www.npr.org/2012/08/09/158416047/fox-pioneers-formula-for-latino-news.

50. Tanzina Vega, "MundoFox to Enter the Latino TV Market," *New York Times*, August 12, 2012, http://www.nytimes.com/2012/08/13/business/media/mundofox-new-spanish-language-network-to-make-debut.

html?_r=0; Natalia Trzenko, "Hollywood también compite en cas-
tellano," *La Nación*, August 14, 2012, http://www.lanacion.com.
ar/1498961-hollywood-tambien-compite-en-castellano.

51. Fox News Latino, http://latino.foxnews.com/index.html.

52. Mark Deuze, *Media Life* (Cambridge: Polity, 2012).

53. Tsedal Neeley, "Global Business Speaks English," *Harvard Business Review*, May
    2012, http://hbr.org/2012/05/global-business-speaks-english/ar/1.

54. Andrea Morabito, "ABC News/Univision Network to Be Based in Miami,"
    Broadcasting and Cable, October 10, 2012, http://www.broadcastingcable.com/
    news/programming/abc-newsunivision-network-be-based-miami/64676;
    Meg James, "Fox Launching Spanish Language Network," *Los Angeles Times*,
    August 12, 2012, http://articles.latimes.com/2012/aug/12/entertainment/
    la-et-ct-0813-mundofox-network-20120813.

55. Amaya, *Citizenship Excess*.

56. Nielsen, "In Any Language, Content Is Still King: New Survey Finds Spanish-
    Speaking U.S. Hispanics Interested in More Spanish-Language Digital Content,"
    2012, http://www.nielsen.com/us/en/newswire/2012/in-any-language-content-
    is-still-king-new-survey-finds-spanish-speaking-us-hispanics-interested-in-
    more-spanish-language-digital-content.html.

57. Paul Cohen, "The Rise and Fall of the American Linguistic Empire," *Dissent: A
    Quarterly of Politics and Culture*, Fall 2012, http://dissentmagazine.org/article/
    the-rise-and-fall-of-the-american-linguistic-empire. See also U.S. English Foun-
    dation, "Making English the Official Language," http://www.us-english.org/
    view/9; Lisa García Bedolla, "The Identity Paradox: Latino Language, Politics
    and Selective Dissociation," *Latino Studies* 1 (2003); and Deborah Schildkraut,
    Press One for English: Language Policy, Public Opinion and American Identity
    (Princeton: Princeton University Press, 2005).

58. Jennifer Leeman, "Racializing Language: A History of Linguistic Ideologies in
    the US Census," *Journal of Language and Politics* 3, no. 3 (2004). See also Sarah
    Allen Gershon and Adrian D. Pantoja, "Patriotism and Language Loyalties:
    Comparing Latino and Anglo Attitudes toward English-Only Legislation," *Eth-
    nic and Racial Studies* 34, no. 9 (2011); and Ana Celia Zentella, "The Hispano-
    phobia of the Official English Movement in the U.S.," *International Journal of
    the Sociology of Language* 127 (1997).

59. Pierre W. Orelus, "Linguistic Apartheid and the English-Only Movement,"
    ENCOUNTER: Education for Meaning and Social Justice 24, no. 3 (2011);
    Donaldo Macedo, "The Colonialism of the English Only Movement," *Educa-
    tional Researcher* 29, no. 3 (2000); Dennis Baron, *The English-Only Question:
    An Official Language for Americans?* (New Haven: Yale University Press,
    1990).

60. Arlene Dávila, "Talking Back: Spanish Media and U.S. Latinidad," in *Latino/a
    Popular Culture*, ed. Michelle Habell-Pallán and Mary Romero (New York:
    New York University Press, 2002); Angharad Valdivia, *Latina/os and the Media*

(Cambridge: Polity, 2010); Federico A. Subervi-Vélez, ed., *The Mass Media and Latino Politics* (New York: Routledge, 2008).

61. Christopher Joseph Westgate, "Fellow Travelers at the Conjunction: Williams and Educational Communicators," in *About Raymond Williams*, ed. Monika Seidl, Roman Horak, and Lawrence Grossberg (London: Routledge, 2009); Peter Schrag, *Not Fit for Our Society: Nativism and Immigration* (Berkeley: University of California Press, 2010).

5

The Gang's Not All Here

The State of Latinos in Contemporary US Media

FRANCES NEGRÓN-MUNTANER

This chapter highlights findings from "The Latino Media Gap," a comprehensive report released in collaboration with the National Association of Latino Independent Producers and the Center for the Study of Ethnicity and Race at Columbia University.[1] Using a wide range of methodologies, including statistical analysis, historical research, case studies, and interviews, this chapter provides a state-of-the-art picture of the status of US Latinos in movies, television, radio, and the Internet. It also explores obstacles to and strategies for a more diverse media landscape.

The first three sections focus on the relative stagnation of Latino participation in media over the last decades as well as the significant lack of Latino decision makers in studios and networks. The final three emphasize the limits and potential of policies, advocacy campaigns, and storytelling innovations, and how these are transforming the industries and expanding opportunity for Latinos in media.

The Incredibly Shrinking Latino Presence, 1940–2013

According to the 2010 US census, Latinos constitute 16.7 percent of the population of the United States. In all of the most densely populated cities such as New York, Los Angeles, and Miami, Latinos constitute an even greater share: from 27.4 percent to 68.2 percent of residents.[2] In addition, Latinos have $1.2 trillion spending power—more than any other minoritized group, including Asian Americans, African Americans, and women. They also currently constitute 20 percent of eighteen- to thirty-year-olds, the advertising industry's most coveted demographic. The rate of Latino population growth is no less noteworthy: over the last thirty years, Latinos have grown seven times faster than the rest of the population.[3]

Yet these numbers do not align with mass media participation. Although Latinos have been part of the mainstream media industries from their inception and a range of Spanish-speaking networks currently aim to serve this audience, the level of inclusion in mainstream English-speaking media remains stunningly low. This is the case across all traditional media—film, television, radio—and genres, including entertainment and news.

If one considers standard reference measures such as the participation of Latinos in the professional media guilds—Directors Guild of America (DGA), Writers Guild of America (WGA), or the Screen Actors Guild (SAG)— Latino participation in 2010–2013 ranges from 2 percent in DGA and 3 percent in WGA to 6 percent in SAG. Available figures for on-camera representation in movies and television at the most visible levels are even lower in some categories. In the ten top-rated shows of 2010–2013, Latinos made up 0 percent of the total leads, 2.8 percent of directors, and 1.7 percent of producers. In the top ten movies, Latinos accounted for 1.9 percent of leads, 2 percent of directors, and 6 percent of writers. Significantly, the movie sample included only one US-born and -raised Latino.[4]

While the news media claim to represent the "real America," reality is often worse than fiction. In newsrooms, all minorities are under 13 percent of the workforce, and their numbers have declined steadily in recent years.[5] Our survey of nineteen prime-time shows revealed that of twenty-two anchors featured in news shows through 2013, twenty (90.9 percent) were white and two (9 percent) were black. No anchor was Latino. Equally dramatic, all available studies suggest that over the last decade, less than 1 percent of all news featured Latinos.[6] Latinos are also generally excluded from talk shows, accounting for less than 3 percent of all guests.[7]

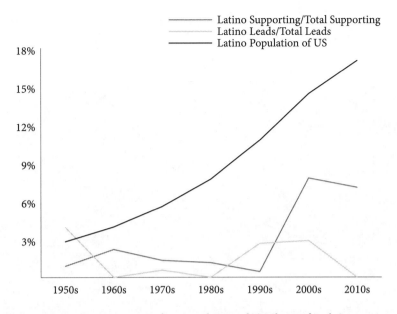

Figure 5.1. Latino Actors in Ten Highest-Rated Scripted TV Shows of Each Season, Averaged by Decade

Importantly, the assumption that Latino participation will simply follow growing demographics is not borne out by our research. A comparison between Latino inclusion today and in earlier periods shows that Latinos actually enjoyed higher per capita rates of participation in three prior moments: during the 1940s (film), 1950s (television), and 1970s (television). Whereas in the 1950s, on average, Latinos were 3.9 percent of the leading TV actors and 2.8 percent of the population, in 2010–2012 they were over 16.7 percent of the population and 0 percent of leading actors (see figure 5.1). Even when we expand the scope, the pattern holds: In the top twenty-five scripted TV shows, there is not a single year since 1950 in which more than two shows with Latino leads aired.[8]

Likewise, although among the top ten films with the highest domestic gross, the percentage of lead roles filled by Latinos is slightly increasing, proportionally it has not caught up with the 1940s. During that period, when the percentage of Latinos in the United States was 2 percent, the percentage of Latino leading actors in the ten top-grossing films was also 2 percent. By the early twenty-first century, when the

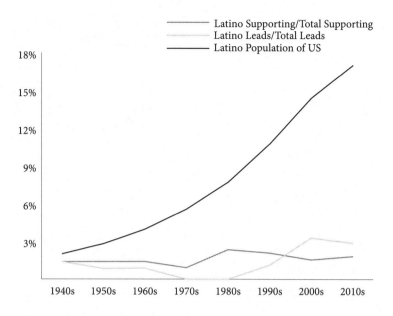

Figure 5.2. Latino Actors in Ten Highest-Grossing Yearly Films, Averaged by Decade

Latino population had skyrocketed to nearly 17 percent of the US population, the average percentage of Latino lead actors declined to less than 2 percent (see figure 5.2).

In other words, whereas in earlier decades there were relatively few Latinos in the media industry, per capita, there was at times a more proportional level of participation. For Latinos to enjoy population-appropriate representation in the current decade, the film and television industries would have to hire Latinos for 23.5 percent of leading roles for all media released between 2013 and 2019, and a greater share for writers and directors. Otherwise, the gap between representations and population will persist as a structural feature of US mass media.

Stereotyped, Still

Numbers, of course, do not tell the whole story. In fact, if the number of Latinos in front of the camera suddenly increased, the media landscape would, in some ways, worsen. This is not only because Latinos are underrepresented in media, but also because in the relatively rare

instances when Latinos appear, they tend to embody the same stereotypes first visualized in cinema in the 1900s: criminals, domestic servants, sexual objects, and comic relief.

The persistence of stereotypes has been noted by all major studies of
the past decade: A comprehensive 2002 study, for instance, observed
that the "vast majority of Latino male characters appeared in prime
time television as police employees or criminals" and that "the vast
majority of Latina characters appeared in prime time television as
nurses, clerical workers, or domestic workers."[9] More recently, a 2012
brief by Latino Decisions similarly concluded that "non-Latinos report
seeing Latinos in stereotypically negative or subordinate roles (gar-
deners, maids, dropouts, and criminals) most often in television and
film."[10]

Focusing on the last few years, we found that not only do stereotypical storylines and characters continue to dominate both fictional and
nonfictional shows and movies, but Latinos remain confined to a few
genres, mostly television crime dramas and action movies. Among the
top ten shows from 2010 to 2013, for instance, only one of the main
adult characters played by a Latino/a actor was not a member of law
enforcement. This was Sofia Vergara, who plays the sexy spitfire role of
Gloria Delgado-Pritchett in *Modern Family*.

Similarly, in the ten highest-grossing movies from 2010 to 2012, Latinos primarily played law enforcement, criminal, and/or working-class
roles. In fact, Latinos were more than three times as likely to play blue-
collar workers, such as construction workers and waitresses, than were
actors as a whole. They were also more likely to play blue-collar criminals, involving theft of goods and cash, kidnapping, the manufacture
and sale of illegal drugs, and physical violence over white-collar/corpo-
rate criminals, involved in embezzlement, bribery, cybercrime, and/or
identity theft. Not surprisingly, of the Latino criminals who appeared
in the highest-grossing films from 2010 to 2012, all were gang-affiliated.
Taken together, criminal and law enforcement roles made up 38.64 percent of all roles played by Latinos.

Latinas remain similarly restricted to stereotypical parts. A good
case in point is the role of the maid. Once dominated by African American actresses playing "Mammy" characters, the role has shifted deci-
sively toward Latina actresses in the last thirty years. Beginning in 1996,

Latina actresses played eleven of sixteen featured maid characters in film and television. In 2013, this trend was the subject of much controversy when the actress and political activist Eva Longoria became executive producer of *Devious Maids*, an ABC show featuring five Latina actresses as maids working for affluent households.

Although most studies emphasize fiction film and television, nonfiction characterizations are equally, if not more, stereotypical. In news, 66 percent of stories focusing on Latinos are about crime, terrorism, or illegal immigration. In some ways, the news category is more alarming, as the majority of people still primarily rely on television news for basic information[11] In the end, the quantity and quality of Latino representation—as well as the debate around it—remain relatively unchanged.

The Deciders: Who Is Running the Show?

The direness of the media landscape begs the question of who is responsible, ultimately a matter of how media are produced. As it has been widely studied, major media corporations are based on a top-down model with tightly controlled decision-making structures. This means that only executives high on the corporate ladder approve the movies and television shows available to the public. In television, a producer or showrunner can also have a significant influence on all talent decisions. When considering the profiles of who has greenlight and hiring power, the underrepresentation of Latinos as writers, directors, and actors pales in comparison with their underrepresentation in such positions as company CEOs and television showrunners.

Beginning at the top of the ladder, in the leading twenty-two English-language television, film, cable news, and radio broadcast companies, all CEOs are white men except Kevin Tsujihara, the Asian American CEO of Warner Brothers Entertainment, and Paula Kerger, CEO of PBS.[12] If one considers the chairmen and CEOs of these studios' parent companies, all but Kazuo Hirai of the Japan-based Sony Corporation are white men.

When we examine the roster of company entertainment presidents, the picture is not very different. Of twenty-two top English-language television, film, cable news, and radio broadcast companies, twenty-one studio presidents are white and nineteen are men. Only one studio president, Nina Tassler, who is head of CBS, is Latina. Moreover, there is no Latino who acts as a greenlight executive on any major English-language news show or is the head of a major, English-language radio broadcast company.

The picture on showrunners is no less alarming (see table 5.1). In the period from 2010 to 2012, Latinos accounted for less than 1 percent of producers of new pilot shows. In 2011, 4.9 percent of all actors were Latino. Yet only 2 out of 352 producers were Latinos, resulting in the stunningly low figure of 0.57 percent. In 2011 and 2012, there were no Latino writers for network TV pilots at all.

From 2010 to 2013, the number of writer and producer positions filled by Latinos actually increased. But the numbers remain small in relation to population: in 2013, only 10 out of 447 writer, producer, and director positions for network TV pilots were Latino, representing 2.24 percent. It is also unclear whether increases will be sustained. Between 2010 and 2011, for example, the proportion of Latino writers, producers, and directors fell. Additionally, in the past four years there has been only one Latina or Latino working in any of these categories for a network pilot: Sofia Vergara, who is executive producing the upcoming ABC drama *Killer Women*.

In TV news, the view is strikingly similar: our survey of nineteen prime-time shows revealed that of twenty-one executive producers, all were white, including three women. Of the eight shows that posted information on their websites about their producing staff, only 2 of 114 producers, or 1.75 percent, were Latino. Media decisions are also driven

Table 5.1. Latinos behind the Camera in Network TV Pilots, 2010–2013

	2010 (%)	2011 (%)	2012 (%)	2013 (%)
Latino Writer/Producer/Director	1.5	0.7	1.0	2.2
Latino Writer	1.6	0.0	0.0	5.2
Latino Producer	1.8	0.57	0.93	2.07
Latino Director	1.47	1.30	3.70	2.70
Pilots with a Latino Writer, Producer, or Director	4.82	3.49	4.65	9.00

Note: I thank Jeff Valdez, co-chairman of Maya Entertainment, for pointing out this trend to me.

by those who own the airwaves. According to a study by the Minority Media and Telecommunications Council, in 2009 Latinos did not own any studios and owned only 2.5 percent of television stations and 2.9 percent of radio stations. The Federal Communications Commission (FCC) released similar figures in late 2012. According to the FCC, between 2009 and 2011, the increase of Latino ownership of television stations was negligible, from 2.5 percent to 2.7 percent.[13] Latinos hold majority voting interests in just 2.9 percent of radio stations, demonstrating stagnation in this category.[14]

The lack of Latino decision makers is evident in other bodies, such as the Academy of Motion Picture Arts and Sciences, which routinely recognizes talent in the film industry. As of 2012, 94 percent of the Academy members were white, and fewer than 2 percent were Latino.[15] This composition is arguably evident in the selections made and in the public awarding of the Oscars. From 2002 to 2012, only 4 percent of Oscar nominees in the major categories were Latino, and none of them won an award.[16] No Latino has received an Oscar for acting since Benicio del Toro won best supporting actor for the 2000 film *Traffic*. In the years since, there have been 240 nominations in acting categories, including only one nomination of a US Latino—again del Toro, in 2003.

Diversity Trouble

These low levels of participation clash not only with changing demographics but also with the corporate discourse on diversity. During the 1990s, studios and networks coped with the pressure brought on by social movements and advocacy groups by creating diversity departments and appointing people of color, mostly African Americans, as diversity executives. The term "diversity" emerged as a less confrontational term than race, gender, or sexual orientation.

While it would be an exaggeration to conclude that diversity departments have been completely ineffectual, it would not be unfair to say that they have not significantly changed the face of the industry. This is partly related to the fact that in most instances, diversity executives gather data and can exert influence but generally have little or no power to enforce compliance. This may account for the striking result that although all twenty-seven diversity and other executives interviewed in our study favored diversity as a policy, four out of five agreed that diversity departments had largely failed to achieve their main objective.

Interviewees identified a broad range of reasons at multiple levels, including interpersonal, institutional, and social, to account for why diversity departments had not been highly effective. Here, I will highlight five that capture some of the key dynamics.

First, an overwhelming majority of diversity officers expressed that while marketing to Latinos has become a strategic imperative in the face of changing demographics, diversity itself had not become an institutional value, but rather "a Christmas ornament that you bring out and after it's over, you put it away."[17] Or as a diversity officer bluntly stated, "Diversity officers are managers of discontent and get paid well to do it."[18] Even further, some felt that diversity initiatives were in fact a conservative mechanism to maintain the status quo. In the words of one guild advocate, "Diversity is the product of white backlash. Taking some of our language and using it on us."[19]

In addition, there was a strong consensus that the "comfort zone" of decision makers played a significant role in hiring decisions.[20] All interviewees agreed that producers and executives tend to hire people whom they know, people who are recommended by acquaintances, and/or people with whom they feel comfortable. "The industry is hostile, dog eat dog and very stressful," one guild advocate commented. "In that world, you want people who have your back."[21] Due to the class and racial hierarchies that organize US society and the fact that the vast majority of top media industry management is currently white and male, hires tend to be made along the same racial and gender lines. The assumption is that people outside the network will not be loyal or supportive to those already inside.

Most interviewees also believed that Latinos, in contrast to African Americans, are perceived as recent immigrants and foreigners; hence, their inclusion is not understood as a public good. In the words of a guild advocate, "Whites do not feel responsible. Their sense is 'I didn't do it.'"[22] Consistently, executives feel no urgency about increasing opportunity. As one press relations executive observed, "At our company, people tend not to leave. So we can't keep up with outside demographics. We don't have many opportunities for promoting minorities."[23]

In a broader sense, despite extensive documentation that racial exclusion persists in the workplace and in the media, beginning in the 1990s and culminating in the immediate aftermath of President Obama's 2008 election, there is a growing sense, particularly among whites, that the United States is now a postracial society. According to one guild advocate, "There is no discrimination. People just look for where the money is."[24] The fact that racial discrimination does not look or feel as it did in the first two-thirds of the twentieth century produces a context for "racial fatigue," or the exhaustion of racial discourse as a compelling means to address persistent exclusion. There is also a general rejection of the argument that collective rights take precedence over individual talent and preparation. As one studio executive put it, "The days of affirmative action are over."[25]

Moreover, for major studios and networks, diversity is understood globally. This means that employment and programs involving Latin America and Latin Americans are understood as contributing to Latino diversity. An example of this is that when pressed for evidence of Latino participation, most diversity and human resources officials cited their overseas divisions and Latin American–born and –bred talent. "We have produced shows with Argentina, Venezuela," a cable executive pointed out.[26] On the ground, this conflation also means that when opportunities open, it is often Latin Americans rather than US Latinos who benefit, as the former tend to come from middle-class backgrounds, are light-skinned, and/or are better educated than many Latinos and are therefore perceived as more competent.

Lastly, the description of the media industry as a family business or a business based on relationships tends to conceal a greater anxiety experienced by people already working in the industry: fear of displacement and change. As one guild advocate observed, "They say that the business is based on relationships. But the fact is that people just don't want to change. We do a lot of network mixers and it goes nowhere. The business is so competitive, no one wants to open it up to new people for fear of displacement."[27] Or in more direct terms, there is the sense that, as a diversity executive put it, "When someone is up, someone is down."[28]

Significantly, the fear factor is not only a white and Latino issue. Some interviewees pointed out that African Americans were also reluctant to work on behalf of Latinos. In the words of one producer, "There

is a fear of black displacement because blacks had been standing in for
all diversity until now."[29] The fact that inclusion is largely understood in
racial terms reinforces racial solidarity and perpetuates fear of others.

Despite the enormous reluctance by decision makers to diversify talent, however, our research shows that greater diversity produces tangible
economic benefits for media entities. The classic case may well be ABC. In
2004, ABC was at the very bottom of the pile in ratings. In response, the
CEO, Steve McPherson, designed a strategy based on the idea that given
US demographics, diverse shows could help revive network ratings and
increase revenue. To this end, McPherson greenlighted three shows with
key Latino talent in quick succession: *Desperate Housewives* (2004), *Lost*
(2004), and *Ugly Betty* (2006). The results were remarkable: By 2005, ABC's
ratings had climbed from 3.2 in the 2003–2004 season to 4 in the 2005–
2006 one. The network's advertising revenue also jumped to an unprecedented $50 million in the *Ugly Betty/Grey's Anatomy* Thursday slot.[30]

Equally important, the ABC experience is not unique. Similar outcomes have ensued in a broad range of contexts, from hit shows like
American Idol, which stopped its rating drop when it hired Jennifer Lopez as a jury member in 2011, to KPCC, a public radio station
in Southern California. In 2012, the station decided to hire a Latino
cohost, A Martinez, for its morning news program, *The Madeleine
Brand Show*. Even after the show's star host, Madeleine Brand, quit in
protest,[31] the station's ratings and revenue increased substantially: the
percentage of Latino adults listening to the station more than doubled,
while the show's AQH (a measure of listenership) increased by 15 percent and the audience share by 20 percent. Donations to the station hit
record highs.[32]

Uploading Stories: Latino Producers Online

The fact that most decision makers resist diversification even when it
makes business sense suggests that they may be acting against their
own economic interests to preserve other forms of power. This partly
accounts for an important new development: the increasing Latino
flight from some traditional English-language media, particularly television, to new media. While the vast majority of research and advocacy
efforts continue to be aimed at incorporating Latinos into television and

studio filmmaking, this focus overlooks various important converging trends of Latino creativity in the Internet and the industry at large.

First, not only are studios increasingly searching for talent online, but Internet and media companies may be the future of high-quality content production—or at least a growing part. An indication of this shift is the recent decision by DreamWorks Animation to stream three hundred hours of episodic television content via Netflix, bypassing the obvious choice of cable television.[33]

Second, Latino media engagement is increasingly taking place online and in multiple platforms. A wide range of studies suggests that the rate of Latino participation online exceeds or over-indexes in relation to other groups. For instance, a 2011 Nielsen study showed that, on average, Latinos have considerably higher rates of Internet consumption and watch 15 percent less television than other groups.[34] Moreover, Latinos spend 68 percent more time watching Internet videos than non-Hispanic whites, and 20 percent more time watching these videos on their phones.[35] Latinos also engage more frequently with social media than non-Hispanic whites: 54.2 percent of Latinos were found to be regular Facebook users, compared to 43 percent of whites.

Third, and even more important in this context, much of Latino media creativity is taking place online. A recent study of college students found that Latinos are more likely than white students to be online content creators.[36] Furthermore, the Latino online presence is substantial not just when it comes to downloading, but uploading as well. According to the Forrester Social Technographic Ladder, 47 percent of online Latinos are "content creators." This represents an over-index of 263 when the activity of non-Hispanics is indexed at 100.[37]

Consistently, our study also found that in some genres, Latinos are far more visible on YouTube than they are on network television. Of the two hundred YouTube channels with the most subscribers, thirty-four feature content created by Latinos in the United States and Latin America (17.5 percent). Among the top two hundred channels, there are twenty-five VEVO channels dedicated to specific musical artists; five of these are Latino artists (16 percent).[38] In the popular genre of young women's fashion advice, two of the top three independent YouTube creators are Latinas.[39] Comparable trends are evident in music-related videos as well: The highest-rated YouTube channel featuring a rock band is Boyce Avenue, made up of three Puerto Rican brothers. Latinos, including Boyce Avenue and Megan Nicole, make up two of the top three serious, independent musicians on YouTube.[40] *diversitication*

These consumption and production trends will only amplify over *dc-* time, due to larger demographic factors. Users of social media tend *central* to be young people, and Latinos represent one of the youngest ethnic groups in the United States: over 60 percent of Latinos are younger than thirty-five, and 75 percent are younger than forty-five. Yet the importance of Latinos in media is not only about consumer online production or consumption, as important as these practices are. Even when Latinos have limited access to educational training and/or to the mainstream media industries, they are producing major media innovations. A case in point is the Latino transmedia pioneer Jeff Gomez.

Born in the Lower East Side in 1963 to a US Jewish mother and a Puerto Rican father, Gomez has become a pivotal figure in the consolidation and recognition of transmedia, an interactive form of storytelling in which people collectively create new worlds in various media, including books, comic books, ads, computer games, films, television, computers, and phones. His contributions to the field include a paradigm shift regarding the nature of studio film storytelling, as evidenced by the transmedia universes that he created for Disney's *Pirates of the Caribbean*, *Prince of Persia*, and *Tron*, Microsoft's *Halo*, and James Cameron's *Avatar*. To a large extent due to his work's impact, in 2010 the Producers Guild of America (PGA) ratified a credit called "Transmedia Producer" to recognize those who create worlds across multiple media platforms.

Whereas most of Gomez's work since the 2000 founding of his company, Starlight Runner Entertainment, has focused on creating "blockbuster universes," he is increasingly focused on original storytelling and introducing transmedia education in schools:

> What disappoints me from my peers is that they say that transmedia is hypercomplicated, that it requires a mathematical mind. That's not the case. Transmedia is like a *novela*, you expand the characters. The true path that I am on is to show people, young people, that there are alternative ways of thinking, so that you are not locked into a way of being that is self destructive.

agency

Ultimately, Gomez views transmedia as a symptom of a much larger social shift in which consumer power extends beyond just purchasing commodities: "Large companies are underestimating the potency from which the consumer owns the dialogue. The paradigm shift is among the most dramatic ever seen."[41]

Power to the Mouse: Unleashing Latino Consumer Power in the New Century

As Gomez suggests, the current juncture is a historically new one. In this last section, we will shift the accent from consumer to power in considering the ubiquitous phrase "Latino consumer power." When invoked by the media and even media advocates, the term tends to refer to the amount of money Latinos spend in purchasing consumer goods: over $1.2 trillion, or close to 10 percent of the US total. It also comes from future projections: According to the market analysis company IBISWorld, by 2015, Latino buying power will hit $1.6 trillion, "growing at a 48 percent clip, compared to about 27 percent for the entire nation."[42] To put this figure in perspective: If Latinos constituted a nation, their economy would rank among the largest in the world.

In the media world these numbers are particularly relevant, as Latinos are among the most avid of consumers. As previously noted, in the key advertising demographic of eighteen to thirty-four years, Latinos have the highest rates of media consumption of any racial or ethnic group in the United States.[43] Overall, Latinos purchased 26 percent of movie tickets in the United States in 2012. While the average moviegoer went to the movies 4.1 times in 2010, Latino moviegoers went 6.4 times.[44] Latinos were also the only ethnic group to purchase more tickets in 2012 than in 2011.[45] The high rate of Latino attendance is one of the main reasons why the US and Canada box office hit a record total of $18.8 billion in 2012.[46]

The allusions to Latino consumer power, however, tend to be accompanied by the assumption of passivity. Even when studies show that Latinos actually switch brands at higher rates than non-Hispanics, the news media tend to portray Latino consumers as brand-loyal.[47] Furthermore, some corporate executive interviewees represented activist consumers as detrimental to achieving media change. In the words of one executive, "Protests are outdated. They ruffle feathers."[48]

Yet the mobilization of Latino media advocates and consumers has been key in the acceleration of change. Since the introduction of cinema in the late nineteenth century, Latinos have been aware of the power of media to shape perceptions and have organized accordingly. Starting in 1918 there have been at least twenty-five protests of national impact led by Latinos against media products and/or companies.

The rate of these protests increased substantially in the late 1960s and through the 1970s as Latino civil rights movements identified media access as a civil right; the rate declined during the 1980s. Triggered in part by demographic changes, protest picked up once more in the mid-1990s, and the last three years have seen an increase in activity reminiscent of the late 1960s (see figures 5.3 and 5.4). Significantly, in addition to their frequency, recent Latino media advocacy campaigns are becoming increasingly effective in comparison with prior decades. Of seven protests since 1998, all but one (86 percent) achieved all or part of their objectives in considerably less time than in earlier decades.

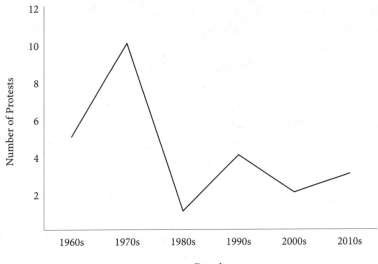

Figure 5.3. Number of Media-Rated Campaigns Led by Latinos

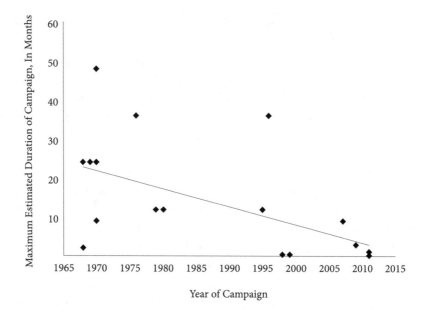

Figure 5.4. Length of Media-Rated Campaigns Led by Latinos

Furthermore, whereas activists did not generally utilize consumer discourse as a way to argue for greater Latino access to media until the 1990s (protests before were more often based on claims of racial discrimination), Latino campaigns since the 1960s have been the most effective when targeting advertising in radio and television. In fact, all Latino protests against products using stereotypical advertisements after 1968 have achieved the advocates' goals. These include mobilizations against Bell Telephone, Granny Goose, Liggett and Myers, Frito-Lay, American Motors, and Coors Light.

Not surprisingly, given the media's reliance on advertising for revenue, boycotts or campaigns aimed at television and radio programs have also often met with considerable success. They have been responsible for banning a *Seinfeld* episode that featured the burning of a Puerto Rican flag (1998) and accelerating the canceling of television shows like *Work It* in 2012. Only one ongoing campaign, started in 2012 by the National Hispanic Media Coalition against the *John and Ken* radio show, has yet been unable to take the program off the air, although it has triggered an exodus of advertisers.

Overall, the least successful campaigns have been against movie studios, which have been historically less dependent on advertisement dollars. Beginning in the late 1990s, however, some campaigns like "No nos quieren," launched again by the National Hispanic Media Coalition against ABC and Disney, became the seed of successful writing programs that provide access for Latinos to entry-level creative opportunities. Still, the vulnerability of studios is likely to increase with the rise of transmedia, as film revenue will also stem from merchandise and other products that rely heavily on advertisement.

A compelling example that showcases new forms of media advocacy in the Internet age is the 2009 campaign demanding an end to the CNN TV news show *Lou Dobbs Tonight*. As is well known, since its establishment in 2003, the show had become a site for anti-immigrant and racist rhetoric, often presenting exaggeration as fact. In 2005, for instance, Dobbs made the claim that immigrants were importing leprosy across the Mexican border at a very high rate, a total of seven thousand cases in three years, when in fact this was the total number in the past thirty years.[49] Regardless, CNN did not act to hold Dobbs accountable to journalistic standards. Instead, CNN supported the show, which experienced a significant ratings bounce of 72 percent between 2003 and 2007.[50]

Dubbed "Basta Dobbs," the campaign was led by the media strategist Roberto Lovato and called on CNN to fire Lou Dobbs. Organized through the website Presente.org, the effort was composed of over forty grassroots organizations spanning twelve states and twenty-five major media markets. In pressing its case, the campaign made two main arguments: first, that CNN could not retain Dobbs and hope to be considered a politically neutral news site in relation to MSNBC and Fox; and second, that CNN could not simultaneously hope to court Latino viewers with its *Latino in America* series to be aired in November and retain Dobbs as a host.

In addition to mobilizing traditional media by recruiting writers to contribute op-eds in the *New York Times*, *Chicago Tribune*, *El Diario*, and *La Opinión* and gathering 125,000 signatures, the campaign made use of new media to amplify its claims. Even further, the effort included the creation of a text-message shortcode publicized via radio and on-the-ground events in eighteen of the largest Latino media markets, which enabled ten thousand people to join the campaign via cell phone by texting the word "enough" to number 30644. Moreover, "Basta Dobbs" organized a digital sit-in on CNN's website, which allowed thousands of Presente.org members and supporters to deliver their comments and pictures directly to CNN.

The "Basta Dobbs" campaign's innovation, however, was not only about technology. It was fundamentally about *how* to conceptualize a campaign for the global digital age. The campaign, for instance, used the media to critique the media: it was launched at the same time that Dobbs chose to participate in an anti-immigrant conference organized by the Federation for American Immigration Reform (FAIR) in September, and relaunched a month later when CNN's *Latinos in America* was to be broadcast. As Lovato sums it up, "On their big day in the limelight with *Latinos in America*, all coverage was about how Latinos wanted CNN to cut its ties to Lou Dobbs."[51] The negative attention both hurt the brand and jeopardized the resources and hopes invested in *Latinos in America* to bring Latinos back to the network.

Fully grasping both the fact that CNN is a global brand and that Latinos are a transnational group, Presente.org subtitled some of its media materials so that Spanish-speaking Latinos could learn what was being broadcast about them, and threatened to take the campaign throughout Latin America and beyond if CNN did not budge. In this way, Presente.org turned a potential disadvantage—the amorphousness of studio and television diversity standards that favor Latin Americans over US Latinos—into an advantage. They approached CNN's "diversity" challenge not as a national civil rights issue but as one with the potential to mobilize news consumers transnationally.

After nearly six months of the campaign, on November 11, 2009, Lou Dobbs announced he was leaving the network. CNN's president, Jonathan Klein, denied that the protests played a role in this outcome. Activist pressure was likely not the only variable in terminating the show. By July, Dobbs's strategy of building an audience by mobilizing anti-immigrant feelings and fueling the President Obama "birther" controversy was no longer working: he had lost 15 percent of his overall viewership.[52] One month before his exit, the show was "dead last" in the critical age demographic of twenty-five to fifty-four.[53] But the show's decline and ouster were greatly accelerated by media and immigrant activist pressure. At the end, CNN actually paid Dobbs an $8 million severance package so he would leave before his contract expired.[54]

Conclusion: Changing Media in the Digital Age

As "Basta Dobbs" suggests, an effective campaign requires the circulation of new stories that link broad networks and leverage their strength via online technology and on-the-ground connections. In contrast to the film and television eras, the success of media today increasingly depends on a network of consumers who deliberate and communicate on quality content at a fast rate. Or, as the writer Michael Walsh put it, "early visibility is a crucial factor that determines ultimate popularity in a networked environment."[55]

This new environment also affects political action. In the words of Lovato, "The compression of time that is characteristic of digital reality and acceleration of communication systems also accelerates political time."[56] The power of a Latino consumer boycott of a studio or network is on the rise. On the one hand, while protest has been the realm of media activists in the past, today more people can participate. On the other hand, due to the demographic shift, a consumer protest involving only a small percentage of the population over a month or less can seriously cut into a media company's profit margin and stain a brand's prestige.

At the same time, the current juncture is not without major challenges. The slight rise in employment for acting positions over decision-making ones indicates that change will more likely take place in front of the camera than behind, not altering fundamental power dynamics. In addition, the accelerated shift to Internet media production will likely continue to depress wages in creative employment and can result in double exploitation: as producer and consumer. Yet, if Latino consumer power is organized and mobilized at a higher rate than at present, it could become a major force in reshaping the media landscape. A "consumer population" with $1.2 trillion in buying power should be capable of that—and more.

NOTES

1. For more information, please see full report, Frances Negrón-Muntaner with Chelsea Abbas, Samuel Robson, and Luis Figueroa, "The Latino Media Gap:

A Report on the State of Latinos in U.S. Media," 2014, http://www.columbia. edu/cu/cser/. The report was funded in part by the Social Science Research Council.

2. Jason Koebler, "11 Cities with the Most Hispanics," *U.S. News and World Report*, n.d., http://www.usnews.com/news/slideshows/11-cities-with-the-most-hispanics (accessed March 27, 2013).

3. "Hispanic Demographic Information," Tucson Hispanic Chamber of Commerce, http://www.tucsonhispanicchamber.org/hispanic-demographics (accessed April 18, 2013).

4. Of the twenty-five writers, one, Guillermo del Toro, was a Mexican national.

5. "Journalists of Color Decline for Third Year," Maynard Institute, April 7, 2011, http://mije.org/richardprince/journalists-color-decline-3rd-year#ASNE (accessed March 17, 2013).

6. Serafín Méndez-Méndez and Diane Alverio, "Network Brownout 2003: The Portrayal of Latinos in Network Television News," National Association of Hispanic Journalists, 2003.

7. Fairness and Accuracy in Reporting (FAIR), "Taking the Public Out of Public TV: PBS Fare Differs Little from Commercial TV," 2010; and Media That Matters, "Gender and Ethnic Diversity in Prime-Time News," 2007.

8. Multiple sources were consulted to obtain lists of the top-ranking films and television shows in this report. These include the website Deadline, ABC Medianet, IMDB, and Box Office Mojo, as well as the book by Tim Brooks and Earle Marsh, *The Complete Directory to Prime Time Network and Cable TV Shows, 1946–Present* (New York: Ballantine, 2007). Television rankings were based on Nielsen prime-time network ratings, and followed the fall-to-spring television schedule.

9. National Hispanic Foundation for the Arts, "Latinos on Primetime," 2002, 7.

10. Latino Decisions, "How Media Stereotypes about Latinos Fuel Negative Attitudes towards Latinos," 2012, http://www.latinodecisions.com/blog/2012/09/18/how-media-stereotypes-about-latinos-fuel-negative-attitudes-towards-latinos/.

11. Ibid.

12. This report defines studio heads as the presidents of individual film and television studios and radio companies. Paula Kerger, president and CEO of PBS, is double-counted as a studio head and CEO. So are David Field of Entercom, Lewis Dickey of Cumulus Media, and Gary Knell of NPR.

13. Joe Flint, "FCC Media Ownership Survey Reveals Lack of Diversity," *Los Angeles Times*, November 14, 2012.

14. Alton Drew, "Dearth in Minority Media Ownership Persists, MMTC Offers Capital Solution," Politic365.com, November 19, 2012, http://politic365. com/2012/11/19/dearth-in-minority-media-ownership-persists-mmtc-offers-capital-solution/ (accessed March 12, 2013).

15. John Horn, Nicole Sperling, and Doug Smith, "Oscar Voters Overwhelmingly White, Male," *Los Angeles Times*, February 19, 2012.

16. Russell K. Robinson, Su Li, Angela Makabali, and Kaitlyn Murphy, "Not Quite a Breakthrough: The Oscars and Actors of Color, 2002–2012," UCLA Chicano Studies Research Center, Latino Policy & Issues Brief, no. 27 (March 2012): 2; "Nominees and Winners for the 84th Academy Awards," http://www.oscars.org/awards/academyawards/84/nominees.html (accessed March 19, 2013).

17. Interview with television executive, Washington, DC, 2010.

18. Interview with guild advocate, Los Angeles, December 2009.

19. Ibid.

20. For further discussion, see John Downing and Charles Husband, *Representing Race: Racisms, Ethnicity and the Media* (London: Sage, 2005).

21. Interview with guild advocate, Los Angeles, December 2009.

22. Ibid.

23. Interview with press relations executive, New York, May 2010.

24. Interview with guild advocate, New York, December 2, 2009.

25. Interview with studio executive, Los Angeles, 2010.

26. Interview with VP of human resources for television network, New York, 2010.

27. Interview with guild advocate, Los Angeles, December 2009.

28. Interview with studio diversity executive, Los Angeles, 2009.

29. Interview with Latino producer, Los Angeles, 2009.

30. Claire Atkinson, "*Ugly Betty* Looks Pretty Good to ABC," *Advertising Age*, September 29, 2006, http://adage.com/article/media/ugly-betty-pretty-good-abc/112151/.

31. Dru Sefton, "Co-Host Pairing Prompts Brand to Exit KPCC," Current.org, October 9, 2012, http://www.current.org/2012/10/co-host-pairing-prompts-brand-to-exit-kpcc/ (accessed April 17, 2013).

32. Arbitron, "Survey Schedules," January 2013, http://www.arbitron.com/home/surveysched.asp.

33. Brook Barnes, "DreamWorks and Netflix in Deal for New TV Shows," *New York Times*, June 18, 2013, B14.

34. Nielsen Company, "National Television Audience Report," 2011, http://www.nielsen.com/us/en.html.

35. Nielsen Company, "State of the Hispanic Consumer: The Hispanic Market Imperative," 2012, 8.

36. Teresa Correa and Sun Ho Jeong, "Race and Online Content Creation," *Information, Communication & Society* 14, no. 5 (2011): 638–59.

37. David Chitel, "Latinos Have the Power to Change Media and Entertainment and Create a New Image," *Huffington Post*, October 11, 2011, http://www.huffingtonpost.com/david-chitel/latinos-have-the-power_b_1004145.html (accessed March 23, 2013).

38. These artists include Pitbull, Selena Gomez, Demi Lovato, and Shakira.

39. These include lady16makeup creator Yuya and Macbarbie07 creator Bethany Mota.

40. All statistics as of May 15, 2013. See http://vidstatsx.com/youtube-top-200-most-subscribed-channels.

41. Telephone interview with Jeff Gomez, June 22, 2013.

42. Jeff Koyen, "The Truth about Hispanic Consumers," *AdWeek*, March 11, 2012, http://www.adweek.com/sa-article/truth-about-hispanic-consumers-138828.

43. "Si TV Launches Groundbreaking Collective of Community-Driven Lifestyle and Culture Websites," *PR Newswire*, http://www.prnewswire.com/news-releases/si-tv-launches-groundbreaking-collective-of-community-driven-lifestyle-and-culture-websites-connecting-young-latino-artists-and-consumers-while-creating-authentic-integrated-opportunities-for-advertisers-and-strategic-partners-58784207.html (accessed March 22, 2013).

44. Motion Picture Association of America, "Theatrical Market Statistics 2012," http://www.mpaa.org//Resources/3037b7a4-58a2-4109-8012-58fca3abdf1b.pdf (accessed March 23, 2013), 13, 16.

45. Nielsen Company, "Popcorn People: Profiles of the U.S. Moviegoer Audience," http://www.nielsen.com/us/en/newswire/2013/popcorn-people-profiles-of-the-u-s-moviegoer-audience.html (accessed March 22, 2013).

46. Motion Picture Association, "Theatrical Market Statistics 2012," 9.

47. Koyen, "The Truth about Hispanic Consumers."

48. Interview with studio executive, Los Angeles, 2009.

49. David Leonhardt, "Truth, Fiction and Lou Dobbs," *New York Times*, May 30, 2007.

50. Jorge I. Domínguez and Rafael Fernández de Castro, *United States and Mexico: Between Partnership and Conflict* (New York: Routledge, 2009), 190.

51. Interview with Roberto Lovato, New York City, June 17, 2013.

52. Felix Gillette, "Controversy Surrounding Lou Dobbs Has Failed to Increase His Ratings," *New York Observer*, August 30, 2009, http://observer.com/2009/07/controversy-surrounding-lou-dobbs-has-failed-to-increase-his-ratings/.

53. Julia Hollar, "Dropping Dobbs: A Victory for Media Activism, and the Challenge Ahead," NACLA, January 4, 2010, https://nacla.org/news/dropping-dobbs-victory-media-activism-and-challenge-ahead.

54. Ibid.

55. Mike Walsh, *Futuretainment: Yesterday the World Changed, Now It's Your Turn* (New York: Phaidon, 2009), 136.

56. Lovato, interview.

6

Latinos at the Margins of Celebrity Culture

Image Sales and the Politics of Paparazzi

VANESSA DÍAZ

The paparazzi are a notorious fixture in Los Angeles, and their inescapable presence has become emblematic of celebrity and Los Angeles culture.[1] In contrast to other types of celebrity photographers—such as red-carpet photographers or celebrity portrait photographers—paparazzi work on the street in an effort to capture candid, photojournalistic shots of celebrities. Despite the ubiquity of their photographs, paparazzi continue to operate largely outside the formal economic channels of celebrity media. Paparazzi are not on staff at any media outlet. Many work on a freelance basis and provide their photos to one or more photo agencies in exchange for a percentage of any revenue from the sale of their photos. Others participate in under the table sales of photographs to other paparazzi who act as "image brokers" to the agencies on their behalf (Gürsel 2012). The informal, unregulated nature of the paparazzi reduces barriers of entry into the profession and helps fuel the celebrity media system, but at the same time it also positions paparazzi as public scapegoats for what is wrong with celebrity media today.

Despite playing a critical role in the system of celebrity media production, Los Angeles paparazzi are routinely the objects of scorn both within the media industry and among the public at large. In Los

Angeles, the center of celebrity media production, the current paparazzi are predominantly Latino men, including US-born Latinos and both documented and undocumented Latin American immigrants who generally have no previous training in photography. The shift to this demographic over the past decade aligns with heightened social and physical hostility toward paparazzi, a hostility that has been normalized in Los Angeles and encouraged by celebrities and the very media that purchase and publish paparazzi photos.

This research is part of a larger ethnographic project on the production of the celebrity weekly magazines—*People*, *Us Weekly*, *In Touch*, *Life & Style*, *OK!*, and *Star*—that builds on my experience as an intern and freelance reporter for *People* magazine since 2004. My experience working as a celebrity reporter provided me with invaluable access to these cultural producers and background knowledge of the entertainment and media industries. My particular interest in paparazzi stems largely from my frustration at the disparaging ways I have heard them discussed by the media producers who need them most; the Latino dominance among Los Angeles paparazzi has been accompanied by shifts in daily discourse on paparazzi, and their overall racialization.

Based on ethnographic fieldwork and interviews conducted with paparazzi and photo agency workers in Los Angeles, and with reporters and editors of celebrity weekly magazines in New York and Los Angeles from 2010 to 2012, this chapter explores the current state of the paparazzi industry in Los Angeles, the formal and informal economy of paparazzi images, and how the racialization of this new and predominantly Latino workforce has affected the discourse and stereotypes around paparazzi. Ultimately I argue that the low barriers of entry into paparazzi work coupled with the racial/ethnic makeup of the new Los Angeles paparazzi have heightened hostility toward the photographers, as they are made scapegoats for all that is wrong with the celebrity media industry by both the media producers (who need paparazzi photos to make their product) and consumers (who voraciously consume that product). I also argue that the Latino dominance of the paparazzi—or the "browning" of the profession—has created a crisis for a profession that requires invisibility for productivity (e.g., to get candid shots, the photographer should be invisible to the subject); within a predominantly white industry, these media laborers of color are often rendered highly visible and, thus, easily targeted and ridiculed. Still, despite accusations by white media producers that this new workforce lacks professionalism and skill, an issue explored in the sections that follow, the new paparazzi have developed a new economic system and strategy for image sales that is transforming the business. Overall, not only are the new paparazzi workforce responsible for the production of so many of the iconic celebrity images circulated today, but they are also responsible for the creation of a new informal economy that is fueling an important part of the entertainment industry.

The Paparazzi Boom and the New Workforce

Although there were paparazzi working in Los Angeles since before the term "paparazzo" was coined in Federico Fellini's 1960 film *La Dolce Vita* (Loker 2009: 164), the number of paparazzi working in the city increased exponentially in the first decade of the twenty-first century (Tiegel 2008: 97). A former photo editor of a celebrity weekly magazine, whom I will call Phoebe,[2] described the period of expansion from 2002 to 2008 as the "paparazzi boom," while a photo agency owner termed those years "the gold rush." The "boom" was triggered by an explosion in demand for photographs by the celebrity weekly magazines, which remain the key customers for paparazzi photos. Prior to 2000, the weekly magazine *People*, which launched in 1974, had no direct competition in the magazine market. In 2000, *Us Magazine*, which had existed as a more trade-focused bimonthly and then monthly publication since 1977, relaunched as a weekly to compete with *People* (Kuczynski 1999). Two years later, the magazine *In Touch* began publication. Then in 2004, *Life & Style* entered the market and the tabloid newspaper *Star* was relaunched as a magazine to compete with the other celebrity weeklies. The US version of the British weekly celebrity magazine *OK!* was launched the next year. These new magazines brought about a competition for content that had not previously existed in the industry.

The expansion from one celebrity weekly magazine to six in the span of only five years created a market in which the magazines struggled to make their product distinctive. In contrast to posed red-carpet photos, which are obtained by multiple photographers at any premiere or special event and typically sell for about $150, candid shots are unique, and thus have the potential to be much more valuable. In this newly competitive environment, procurement of "exclusive" paparazzi shots became a crucial selling point for the magazines. Phoebe believes that the paparazzi boom started after the first major bidding war over photos among the celebrity weekly magazines, which was over a set of photos of Ben Affleck and Jennifer Lopez kissing that was purchased for around $75,000 by *People* magazine (Carr 2002). The highly publicized nature of the bidding wars worked as an advertisement for the new demand for paparazzi photographs. Phoebe recalls that this period of increased competition coincided with the expansion of digital photography, which reduced costs for aspiring paparazzi and for the magazines as well, allowing them easier access to photographs:

> One of the big reasons we started to see more was: (a) photographers flooded the market because it was all of a sudden really profitable and (b) they could get us pictures by just pushing a button and putting them into our FTP [File Transfer Protocol—a standard for the exchange of program and data files across a network]. When it became easier for us to get pictures, more people were game to buy them.

The boom ended in 2008, not coincidentally at the beginning of the financial crisis. According to editors, paps, and agency heads, the magazines reduced their budgets for photo acquisition and scaled back to pre-boom pricing standards for photos.[3]

When the number of the paparazzi in Los Angeles drastically increased during the "boom," Latino immigrants made up the majority of these new paps, joining the workforce in such large numbers that by 2008 a shift in the demographics of the profession from "all white guys" to mostly Latinos was noticeable and routinely commented upon (Pearson 2008). As media producers who are not included in the formal decision-making processes of the media outlets that publish their photos, paparazzi are seen as informal contributors to the celebrity media industry and thus are at the bottom of the celebrity media food chain. That the paparazzi are predominantly Latino is significant, not only because it exemplifies how people of color are left out of formal production processes, but because there is no other area within the celebrity media industry that shares this demographic makeup.

In an interview in 2011, a former paparazzo who now co-owns an agency told me that he was the only person of color papping in the 1990s. "We started out as photographers, and [the demographic] was the exact opposite ten years ago. I was considered a minority; everyone else was Anglo," the former pap, whom I will call Gregory, said. Based on the accounts of many paparazzi, however, before the Latino influx that started in 2002, most of the Los Angeles paps were European immigrants. Frank Griffin, a British pap-turned-agency owner, was quoted in 2005 saying, "An interesting question is: Why aren't there more American paparazzi in Los Angeles? What I don't understand is why they're all French, British, and German. Most of the photographers out there are European, not from the United States. . . . there's only one American" (qtd. in Howe 2005: 41). Thus, the paps were previously an immigrant-heavy group, but the immigrants were predominantly European. As Arlene Dávila has pointed out, the educational and cultural experiences, coupled with the continued racialization of Latino immigrants, set their experiences apart from the experiences of European immigrants (2008: 12).

The precise demographics of paparazzi are difficult to tabulate. It is certain, however, that the first noticeable group of Latino immigrant paparazzi were Brazilian. One of the photo agencies that specializes in paparazzi photos, started by a French journalist and photographer, is X17. During the boom, Regis Navarre, the owner of X17, started hiring parking attendants and other restaurant workers who happened to be predominantly Brazilian (Samuels 2008). In 2008, his team alone reached sixty to seventy paps; unlike the other agencies, many of X17's paps are on staff, creating security for the workers, but preventing them from being able to keep the full profit from their shots. During this time, his paps were paid a "stipend of $800 to $3,000 a week plus the occasional four- or low-five-figure bonus in exchange for global rights to their images, which Regis owns" (Samuels 2008). For the Brazilians he hired, it came down to the money. Luiz Pimentel immigrated to the United States from Brazil in 1999; he had friends who started working as paps as early as 2002. "They started talking about the excitement of getting the pictures and making good money," Luiz told me during a 2011 interview. "At the same time, they were trying to keep the business more closed off. Not many people knew about it. I said you cannot make that kind of money at any job here [in the United States]. But it was real."

As Brazilians started to expand the business through their networks of fellow Brazilians, a technique prominent in immigrant labor (Gomberg-Muñoz 2011), they began to "change the way photographers worked," Luiz said.

> One of the things that really differentiated the Brazilians working [as paps] was that Regis was kind of fascinated with Britney [Spears]. We started working 24/7. [In the past] paps worked regular business hours. Then we came and we started staying late, and the later we stayed, the more stuff we would get. And that turned into 24/7, groups working in shifts.

Though the agency owner preferred to pay in checks, he made special arrangements with undocumented paps.

In 2011, the agency owner Gregory said, "We would hear about [the Brazilians] from our photographers. We would tell them to go cover Britney Spears and they would say, 'We felt like we were in Rio [de Janeiro]. There were 20 photographers there and they were all from Brazil.' And then eventually it became more of a standard fact." The agency owner recognizes Navarre as responsible for the Brazilian influx in the industry. "He imported them, in a sense. It was like a boat stopped over at X17." His phrasing of the "importation" of these Latin American laborers insinuates illegality and likens them to imported products or chattel. The reputation of these Brazilian paps represents the worst of Black and brown male racial stereotypes and circulated not only among the paps, but also in popular media. In a *Vice* magazine article, people are warned to "be careful" of the "territorial" Brazilian paps, also referred to as "crazy capoeira motherfuckers." The article suggests that, should you run into these Brazilians, you should "be ready to fight" (Randolph 2012).

Still, the Brazilians were only the beginning of the shift in paparazzi demographics and the new set of stereotypes that surround Los Angeles paparazzi today. Other Latino immigrants, US-born Latinos, Filipinos, and African-Americans began joining the workforce as word spread about the money that could be made in the industry; agencies needed to compete with the new X17 model, and so agency owners took chances

Figure 6.1. Paparazzi shoot contestants from *Dancing with the Stars* from the parking lot next door to the studio on Mateo Street in downtown Los Angeles. Photograph by Ulises Rios.

on young men ready and willing to work "24/7." This new immigrant and minority workforce transformed the nature of the paparazzi work and has brought with it a shift in the economics of paparazzi image sales.

The Economics of Image Sales

The field of paparazzi photography is not regulated. There are no formal barriers to entering the business because the work does not take place in regulated elite spaces, like red carpets, private events, or press junkets. The work is done in public spaces to which anyone has access. "There are no requirements to be a paparazzi. Tomorrow you could decide you wanna be one. There's no, 'Where's your resume?'" according to the paparazzo Ulises Rios, a first-generation Mexican-American.

Paparazzi generally work on a freelance basis and give their photos to one or more photo agencies in exchange for a percentage of any profits made on the photos. There are a small number of paparazzi who are on staff at agencies, though this is less common. The benefit of being on staff is steady pay; the downside is that the agencies maintain copyright ownership of the images and the paps do not reap much of the reward, if any, when their photos sell for large amounts. In some cases, a pap might see his photos sell for an amount many times his annual salary. Today staff paps make around $30,000, which is down from up to $100,000 during the boom.

Today, the main photo agencies selling paparazzi photos in the United States include X17, Splash News, AKM/GSI, Fame Pictures, Bauer-Griffin, and INF (Insight News and Features). These agencies sell paparazzi photos to all media outlets; still, despite the changes in media production and the increase in online media, the bulk of these images are purchased by the celebrity weekly magazines. According to one pap who runs his own agency, "The weekly magazines are still my bread and butter and that's about 75 percent of my sales. Then about 20 percent of sales are the blogs now for me. The final 5 percent are interesting new customers and TV."

In general, freelance paparazzi make between 60 and 70 percent of the sale price for their photographs. Since the freelance paparazzi do not deal with the sales at all, however, it is difficult for them to know whether they get paid based on what their photos actually make. But paparazzi stay freelance for a few reasons. One pap who briefly tried to start his own agency to sell directly to the magazines quickly realized that "they are two full-time jobs and you can't do both." Not just anyone can sell to the magazines. In order to be seen as a legitimate company in the magazines' eyes, "You have to have about 500,000 images for magazines to see what you have and then they might agree to do business with you. You have to get permissions to upload images to the magazines' FTP sites," Luiz told me.

Early on as a staff pap for Fame, the Salvadoran-born pap Galo Ramirez took a photo that sold for $300,000; he received a $500 bonus for that shot. These types of sales, in which paparazzi receive less than 1 percent of the amount paid for their photos as a bonus, provide a large incentive for paps to work freelance in hopes of earning a higher percentage from their sales. When Galo first went freelance, he staked out the home of the actors Katie Holmes and Tom Cruise while Holmes was pregnant, waiting for her to go into labor so he could follow her to the hospital. He made only $700 in those three months.

Figure 6.2. The paparazzo Galo Ramirez shoots the singer Fergie's baby shower in Beverly Hills. He shoots from a precarious position in a tree, since his goal is to not be seen in order to get a truly candid shot and to not disrupt the celebrity. Photograph by Lalo Pimentel.

In recent years, paps and agency heads alike say that bids for their photos generally do not approach the high prices seen during the boom. For example, X17 made over $3 million from photos of Britney Spears in 2007 (Lambert 2012); in 2011, a sought-after set of photos of Spears sold for $50,000, which was considered high in today's market. When I spoke with him in 2011, Luiz's last major sale was of Kristen Stewart and Robert Pattinson filming a movie in Brazil, for which a set of photos grossed between $100,000 and $150,000, of which he received a percentage. Sales like these, however, are "not often anymore," he said. "But you can still get big numbers, it just depends on the story." A set of shots Galo took of Justin Bieber immediately after Bieber assaulted a pap in 2012 has made about $25,000 to date, of which Galo will receive 70 percent; but since he works with a partner pap, they will split that percentage. In general today, the average paparazzi photo sells for anywhere between $50 and $4,000, though one agency owner calls the $500 to $4,000 range the "meat and potatoes" of their business and says that this price range reflects 90 percent of their image sales. Without any bidding wars on a photo, the standard magazine photo rates have been cut at least in half since the boom. For example, one pap said, "It used to be standard to get $1,500 for a quarter-page photo in *People*; now it's $750. Exclusive images that would have earned $3,000 will only get me about $500."

Galo, like many paparazzi, believes that prices have declined because the market is "oversaturated." To understand this oversaturation, we need to note how many photos are sent to the weekly magazine offices—which all maintain similar programming for receiving photos. A photo transmission manager who has worked for multiple celebrity weekly magazines explained to me that, in ten years, the number of digital photos being uploaded to the magazines' FTP sites multiplied exponentially. In 2001, the magazines received approximately 50,000 photos. By 2011, that number had jumped to over 8 million. Today, the magazines receive about 800,000 photographs per month, the majority of which are paparazzi shots. This increase not only is based on technological advancements, but also correlates to the huge increase in the number of paparazzi working on the street every single day. As a result of this oversaturation of the paparazzi photo market, some paparazzi have sought out new ways of securing income through their work.

Informal Economy of Paparazzi Images: Paps as Image Brokers

While the agencies serve as the "image brokers" to the magazines (Gür-sel 2012), an informal economy of paparazzi images has also developed in which some paparazzi serve as intermediary image brokers between other paps and the agencies. This informal system revolves around certain freelance paps—whom I will call the informal paps—who evade dealing with photo agencies by selling their photos to other freelance paps for a small, flat fee (generally about $50 a set). The brokering freelance pap then owns the photos and gives them to whatever agency (or agencies) he might work with and will then earn the same percentage from the brokered photos that he would from his own images. This new form of pap image sales facilitates increasing openness within the industry in a way that allows for more undocumented workers to compete in the market on their own, without having to engage in any formal business channels and without having to provide any personal information.

From my interviews and observation in the field, I have found that undocumented paps are more likely than others to sell in this fashion, as they attempt to avoid formal business transactions. However, undocumented paps are not the only ones informally selling their photos—some paps sell this way to avoid negotiations with the agencies or to avoid taxes. Regardless of any potential correlation between Latinidad and the undocumented status of some paps, every pap my closest collaborators in this research have witnessed selling their images informally has been Latino. The informal sales are often negotiated in Spanish. Though a significant number of paps are Brazilians, they generally do not participate in this new informal realm. The informal image-broker market has become an established part of the pap business, and adds another layer to the complex labor hierarchy already in place in this industry.

On the particular occasion I will examine, the sale of a video of Halle Berry becoming enraged with a paparazzo outside her daughter's school became an example of the complicated intertwining of the informal economy of paparazzi images and the ethical codes observed by the paparazzi. On May 9, 2012, I sat in Galo's grey Prius around the corner from the homes of the actresses Vanessa Hudgens and Dakota Fanning in Studio City. As a group of paps gathered around another pap's car, Galo and I went to say hello. The paps we approached were part of a group nicknamed "the Home Depots." As with all pap nicknames, they embrace the often playful, if insulting, names assigned to them by their fellow paps. As Galo said, "If you don't have a nickname, you're not 'in.' And if you're not 'in,' you're probably not going to make it."

The Home Depots are a group of paparazzi who generally sell and circulate their photos informally through other paps (or multiple agencies). Through their name, the Home Depots, their role in the pap economy and their racialized bodies/physical appearance are bundled together. One Latino pap explained, "We call them the Home Depots because they look like a group of guys standing outside of Home Depot looking for work." Another pap says they were given the name because "They're like the guys at Home Depot. They're there every day to get pictures to sell for $50, which is what they do at Home Depot. Pick me up and, for $50, I'll paint your house."

The Home Depots were watching a video of Halle Berry. She had become irate at a pap, Andy Deetz ("Halle Berry" 2012), because he went inside her daughter's school to take photos, instead of remaining outside the entrance, as other paps do. This act violated the self-regulated ethical code, mainly revolving around legal restrictions, that paparazzi understand they are supposed to adhere to. In this case, Galo instantly made an ethical judgment upon seeing the video. "She was right," he said, explaining that he felt Berry had reacted appropriately. Galo did not approve of Deetz's behavior; thus, he wanted to ensure circulation of the video to expose this pap's lack of adherence to ethical codes—and, of course, because he saw the potential for monetary gain. "What are you going to do with the video?" Galo asked the Home Depots. "I'll sell it to you," one of them offered.

As the paps talked about the video, they discussed ethics, right, wrong, and whiteness, as the pap who crossed the ethical line was Anglo-American. The Home Depots described what led up to them shooting the video. "I was following Halle [Berry], and he was following Vanessa [Hudgens]. While I was waiting for Halle, he [Deetz] went inside of the school." "I guarantee the video will sell," Galo told them. "He is a fucking idiot," they agreed, referring to Deetz.[4]

Galo, who normally does not play a part in the informal pap economy, offered $200 for the video, which the Home Depots would normally have sold for $50. They agreed, and sold the video to Galo for $200, which he hoped to turn around and sell for at least ten times that amount. Galo began calling different agencies and organizations attempting to sell the film. His main agency didn't want it. Initially, TMZ did not want it, because it thought that the video made paparazzi look bad, which it wants to avoid in order to maintain its brand. X17 had purchased another version of the video (there were about three versions of the video circulating). Galo hadn't really gotten any shots that day, and so this was another way to potentially make money. Ultimately, Galo was unable to sell the video as quickly as he had hoped, so he returned the video and, since he normally does not buy from the Home Depots and is well respected by the other paps, they returned his money. Eventually, the Home Depots sold the video through other paps and agencies.

This informal economy of images contributes to the inundation of photos available to the magazines, the corresponding lower cost for images, and the relative unimportance of an "exclusive" photo today compared to during the boom. The informal paps generally do not sell their photos as exclusives, since it would prohibit them from selling their photos multiple times. Sometimes the informal paps sell the same photo set to multiple image brokering paps, and, more often, the image brokering paps attempt to sell the informally acquired set through multiple photo agencies; thus, both parties involved in the informal sale contribute to the flooding of the pap photo market. Yet paps like Galo place more blame on the brokering paps, since they feel that the informal paps are taken advantage of because they are not paid anywhere near the potential value of their photos.

Galo believes that this cooperative informal economy is generally disruptive to the overall pap business. "They flood the market with pictures," he said. "Before, if there were three paps, there were only three agencies buying pictures. Now, if there are three guys, there could be ten agencies buying because one guy could give his [photos] to six agencies and another guy gives it to another four and it's like everyone has it now." Though less common, some informal paps sell their photos under the table to agencies for the same flat fees they receive from the image brokering paps. This, again, disrupts the regular pap image sale system because it drives down the overall prices of the images. As Galo elaborates,

> Because the [informal paps] sell the pictures so cheap, those agencies can sell the pictures for cheap to get placement and it doesn't matter to them because they are already making profit because they paid 50 bucks. They turn around and sell it for $500. That's 90 percent profit and it doesn't matter to them because they are making 450 bucks. Whereas with my boss, he wants to sell pictures expensive, so everyone wins. He'll get a placement in *People* magazine, a full page. They're going to pay around $6,000, depending on what story it is. That is non-negotiable, whoever has it, because those are the prices he gets. The other places who get the pictures off of these guys, they sell them cheap—*People* magazine full page, $500.

This informal economy of images adds another node to the chain of working relationships, creating an even more substantial labor hierarchy. It further distances the actual image producer from the final media products in which the images appear and ensures that there is no dialogue or acknowledgement of the informal paps, as they are rendered professionally invisible in this process. Their position as informal workers—as the "Home Depots"—again reinforces notions of the invisible (Latino) immigrant workers and fully interconnects their racialization with their professional, legal, and (presumed) immigrant status (McDonald and Sampson 2012: 63).

Through this informal economy, the originating producer of the image that leads to the final media product does not have a relationship with either the agencies that place his/her images or the media outlets that ultimately publish them. Still, even without the informal economy of pap images, the paparazzi who sell their images formally are not given any acknowledgement by the media outlets who rely on their images. The paparazzi perform the labor, but seldom have any relationships with the actual media outlets that use their work; they are intentionally left out of the formal media production process and rendered invisible by the media outlets and organizations that demand their labor.

Skill, Visibility, and Perceptions of the New Paps

This is your camera, this is your weapon. Me and my partner, we don't have room for mistakes. This isn't a game. We're out here because we have to feed our children.
—Sergio Huapaya, pap[5]

The idea that unskilled immigrants, particularly Latinos, dominate low-skill work and bid down the wage scale in local markets (Espenshade 2000: 128) is widespread, and reflects an assumption "that all immigration is unskilled" (Dustmann and Glitz 2005: 17). As the paparazzi demographic of Los Angeles shifted, immigration and lack of skill were directly correlated in descriptions of this new wave of paps.

For example, a *Los Angeles Times* article reported, "Agencies use foreigners working on what some say are questionable visas. Photographers are hired less for their camera skills than their ability to navigate the rough-and-tumble of the celebrity chase" (Winton and Alanez 2005). A *New York Times* article called the new paps "hordes of untrained or corner-cutting paparazzi . . . willing to make their presence known, even to jump out at celebrities on the street, if it means a chance for quick cash" (Halbfinger and Weiner 2005). In a 2011 interview, Stanley—an Anglo-American paparazzo—brought up the demographic shift of the paparazzi: "Certainly you have the unprofessionalism brought into the paparazzi field by all these guys who aren't professional. All these guys were gang members or valet parkers. Now they're carrying around cameras, so they're not really trained." Interestingly, Stanley himself had no formal training as a photographer. He had worked odd jobs on film sets before transitioning to paparazzi work by specializing in sneaking shots on set, exploiting his access to these hard-to-reach settings. Another pap/agency owner, who had no previous training before entering the pap business as a teenager, said,

In the past, all the photographers were trained. There was a certain level of pride associated with it because they were photographers who were trained as photographers, and they knew each others' work and talent. Now it's like no one takes pride. It's more about the hunt. There are

some good pictures being done, but a lot of the better pictures are generally done by the trained photographers. There's a lot of shit coming out
because [the newer paps] are not photographers.

These ideas, coming from self-taught photographers with no formal
education or training in photography, demonstrate the ways appearance—racial, ethnic, presumed immigrant status—dictate assumptions
about skill level and "professionalism," even in the eyes of other photographers who entered the business with no professional training in
photography.

Ironically, perhaps, given the lack of formal space provided to them
within the celebrity media industry, one particular area of skill that the
new paparazzi are often accused of lacking is an ability to "be invisible." This is precisely because of their seeming displacement as people
of color occupying rich white spaces to photograph the predominantly
white celebrities. Still, the idea of Black and brown bodies, especially
immigrant bodies, being socially invisible but fulfilling necessary social
roles, is a familiar one (McDonald and Sampson 2012: 63). Thus, there
is a tension between the notion of their inability to be invisible as Black
and brown laborers, and their need to be invisible for the job. The
new paparazzi have been critiqued for failing to "adhere to an unwrit-
ten code of Los Angeles paparazzi—that the ideal picture is one that a
celebrity does not even suspect has been taken, shot by a photographer
who is neither seen nor heard" (Halbfinger and Weiner 2005). But this
criticism of the new paparazzi workforce is inaccurate. For example, in
October 2012, Galo—a Latin American immigrant photographer with
no formal training in photography—captured a highly sought-after
shot of Gwyneth Paltrow, Chris Martin, and their children by using a
long lens without their knowledge. Celebrity media fawned over the
photograph, calling it "the celebrity sighting equivalent of a unicorn,"
and it made his photo agency around $20,000 in the first week of sales
(Serpe 2012). Likewise, the recent iconic images of Kristen Stewart
sharing an intimate moment with her paramour, Rupert Sanders, could
not have been taken if the celebrities weren't completely oblivious to the
presence of the paparazzi. The extent to which the paps remain invisible, allowing them to capture such elusive shots, factors heavily into
the respect they get from peers, as well as the amount of money they

can make. "This is how we separate the men from the boys," Galo said when he shot the Paltrow/Martin family. A Salvadoran-born pap who goes by the nickname "el Diablo," who also joined the workforce after the paparazzi boom with no formal photography training, had the same understanding of what it meant to be a good pap: "Do the job the right way. Never leave your car, or shoot from a bush on a long lens."

The notion of the paparazzi's invisibility, namelessness, and facelessness is problematized by their status, particularly in Los Angeles, as predominantly immigrants and even undocumented immigrants. Essentially, these are people who are marginalized by their race, ethnicity, and "legal" status in this country, and yet they are performing a task that is in demand by major corporate organizations who further marginalize them by keeping them on the outskirts of the actual production process. At the same time, this position as "outsiders" in terms of the media production process and the nature of paparazzi work as an unregulated field are also what allow undocumented people, individuals without formal training or education, and individuals without access to elite spaces (like the red carpet) to do this kind of work at all.

The fact that some paparazzi are immigrants, and some undocumented, is an issue that has been casually mentioned, but not critically evaluated, in the media and among consumers ("Crashes and Deception" 2008; Pearson 2008). In the comment section of the video of an incident involving a wedding for the show *The Bachelor*, in which paparazzi attempting to take photos were beaten, one person posted, "Literally [paparazzi are] the scum of the Earth. Why are they always Latinos? Are they even citizens? Maybe they should show their green card so they can be deported . . . la migra!" ("Photographers Sue" 2010).[6] This comment exemplifies how all "Latinos"—US-born or immigrant— are presumed undocumented. In the comment section of a YouTube video reporting on Justin Bieber's assault of a paparazzo, one viewer said, "Poor Justin. That Mexican (yeah I said it) paparazzi was trying to antagonize Justin. Well things didn't go the Mexican's (the aggressor's) way. . . . I don't blame Justin. Enough is enough."[7] This example begins to link the Latino—in this case, the presumed Mexican—with aggression. A *New York Times* article also referred to Los Angeles paparazzi as "hyper aggressive" (Halbfinger and Weiner 2005), a trait stereotypically associated with "hot-blooded" Latino men (Carroll 2003: 263).

An Associated Press article from April 2008 refers to paparazzi as "pack animals," without regard for how that term might be interpreted, considering the demographic shift in paparazzi (Pearson 2008). Perhaps not coincidentally, the central focus of the article is on this demographic shift:

> This L.A. story merges with another one: immigration. "There's a lot of illegals out there, and X17 has a lot of them," said [Gary] Morgan of Splash [News, another photo agency]. Veteran paparazzi like Frank Griffin, who runs the Bauer-Griffin agency, complain that the new LA shooters know nothing about their cameras or subjects. "I call them knuckle-scraping mouth breathers," Griffin said. "They can either make $1,500 a month running around with cameras, or they can go rob a 7-Eleven." (Pearson 2008)

This article reifies stereotypes of immigrants and men of color as uneducated, animalistic, uncivilized, and violent (Jeffries 2011; Way 2011: 225). The harshest critiques and racialized comments come from the paps' white counterparts, who stand to lose from these new paparazzi's success. Griffin's status as a British immigrant in the United States and his complaints about these new immigrants demonstrate the ways white Western European immigrants are treated and understood versus the way that Latino immigrants are treated and publicly observed, hated, and seen automatically as unskilled labor. As opposed to the European immigrants who once dominated the field, these racialized Latinos are seen as "illegal alien" invaders. H. Roy Kaplan's book *The Myth of Post-Racial America* explains *why* these types of characterizations persist: "If people of color did not aspire to be upwardly mobile and seek the resources heretofore controlled by whites, they would not be perceived as threats to the existing social order—an order dominated not only in numbers but in power and privilege by whites since the formation of this nation" (Kaplan 2011: 76). It is important to note that there are divisions even among the Latino paps. Some US-born Latino paps talk openly about the undocumented-ness of the Latino immigrants in a negative way, suggesting that it is disrupting their business (Ruy 2008).

Nonetheless, for many, the informal economic system of paparazzi has provided an avenue into the entertainment industry and its lucrative economy, particularly in comparison to other jobs available to immigrants and men of color without college educations. With it, however, has come a discourse of everyday racism (Hill 2008) that is encouraged by the entertainment industry. The magazines, in particular, need the paps to be "the bad guys" so that the magazines can continue to build cooperative relationships with the celebrities and Hollywood insiders they need to guarantee interviews. Though paparazzi in Los Angeles had previously been European immigrant-dominated, there was never a discourse about them working illegally (Winton and Alanez 2005). However, when the color of the "foreign" paparazzi operating within the informal economy changed, so too did the discourse surrounding them.

Conclusion

This chapter has examined the causes and effects of the "paparazzi boom," which took place between 2002 and 2008. The new predominantly Latino workforce that resulted from the boom led to a shift in the paparazzi culture of Los Angeles. The work is around-the-clock, and the image sales informal. Perhaps most significantly, there is a workforce within the entertainment industry, as peripheral as this workforce may be, that is dominated by Latino people. While negative stereotypes continue to be thrust upon this group of laborers, their work is an indispensible part of celebrity media production and of the entertainment industry more broadly.

NOTES

1. This article is dedicated to the late Chris Guerra, who lost his life while on the job as a paparazzo in Los Angeles on January 1, 2013. He was twenty-nine years old.
2. I use pseudonyms throughout my ethnography in order to protect my collaborators. Exceptions are Galo Ramirez, Ulises Rios, and Luiz Pimentel, who requested that their real names be used.
3. In this chapter, the terms "pap" and "paparazzi" will be used interchangeably. "Pap" is the informal term used by paparazzi, and others in the entertainment industry, to refer to paparazzi photographers.
4. This dialogue was translated from Spanish to English.
5. Quoted in Ruy 2008.
6. "La migra" is an abbreviated Spanish slang term for the former Immigration and Naturalization Services (INS) and the Border Patrol.

7. This quote was originally posted on the video: http://www.youtube.com/
watch?v=VRZ3iM4oWeM. The video was posted on May 26, 2012, and the comment was left by the viewer dardaf9049. This video has since been removed for
copyright issues.

REFERENCES

Carr, David. 2002. "Paparazzi Cash In on a Magazine Dogfight." *New York Times*,
November 4.

Carroll, Bret E. 2003. *American Masculinities: A Historical Encyclopedia*. Thousand
Oaks, CA: Sage.

"Crashes and Deception: Paparazzi on Getting Too Close." 2008. Associated Press,
April 4.

Dávila, Arlene M. 2008. *Latino Spin: Public Image and the Whitewashing of Race*. New
York: New York University Press.

Dustmann, Christian, and Albrecht Glitz. 2005. *Immigration, Jobs and Wages: Evidence
and Opinion*. London: CEPR, CReAM.

Espenshade, Thomas. 2000. "Immigrants, Puerto Ricans, and the Earnings of Native
Black Males." In *Immigration and Race: New Challenges for American Democracy*,
ed. Gerald D Jaynes. New Haven: Yale University Press.

Gomberg-Muñoz, Ruth. 2011. *Labor and Legality: An Ethnography of a Mexican Immigrant Network*. New York: Oxford University Press.

Gürsel, Zeynep Devrim. 2012. "The Politics of Wire Service Photography: Infrastruc-
tures of Representation in a Digital Newsroom." *American Ethnologist* 39 (1): 71–89.

Halbfinger, David M., and Allison H. Weiner. 2005. "As Paparazzi Push Harder, Stars
Try to Push Back." *New York Times*, June 9.

"Halle Berry Puts Paparazzi on Trial." 2012. TMZ.com, August 16.

Hill, Jane H. 2008. *The Everyday Language of White Racism*. Malden, MA:
Wiley-Blackwell.

Howe, Peter. 2005. *Paparazzi*. New York: Artisan.

Jeffries, Michael P. 2011. *Thug Life: Race, Gender, and the Meaning of Hip-Hop*. Chicago:
University of Chicago Press.

Jordan, Mary. 2008. "Paparazzi and Driver Found Negligent in Princess Diana's Death."
Washington Post, April 8, C1.

Kaplan, H. Roy. 2011. *The Myth of Post-Racial America: Searching for Equality in the Age
of Materialism*. Lanham, MD: Rowman and Littlefield Education.

Kuczynski, Alex. 1999. "Striking Back at the Empire; Wenner Media Takes on the
Mighty Time Inc. in Transforming US to a Monthly Magazine." *New York Times*,
September 27.

Lambert, Molly. 2012. "The Kristen Stewart Mess: Forget It, Jake, It's Twilight Town."
Grantland.com, August 6.

Loker, Bradford E. 2009. *History with the Beatles*. Indianapolis: Dog Ear Publishing.

McDonald, John, and Robert J. Sampson. 2012. *Immigration and the Changing Social Fabric of American Cities*. Philadelphia: Sage.

Pearson, Ryan. 2008. "'Britney Beat': Paparazzi Are No Longer Faceless Pack Animals." Associated Press, April 3. http://www.foxnews.com/story/0,2933,346212,00.html.

"Photographers Sue! *Bachelor* Wedding Airs, ABC Exploits Security's Attack on Photographers." 2010. X17.com, March 8, http://www.x17online.com/celebrities/the_bachelor/photographers_sue_bachelor_wedding_airs_abc.php#mjp52AAI935IRhkH.99.

Randolph, Steven. 2012. "Pap Smear: Giving the Paparazzi a Taste of Their Own Disgusting Medicine." *Vice Magazine*, April 30.

Ruy, Frank. 2008. *Giving It Up*. New York: New Amsterdam Entertainment.

Samuels, David. 2008. "Shooting Britney." *Atlantic Monthly* 301 (3): 36–51.

Serpe, Gina. 2012. "Gwyneth Paltrow, Chris Martin and Kids Out Together (Really) on Toy Run." *E! Online*, October 26, http://www.eonline.com/news/357591/gwyneth-paltrow-chris-martin-and-kids-out-together-really-on-toy-run.

Tiegel, Eliot. 2008. *Overexposed: The Price of Fame: The Troubles of Britney, Lindsay, Paris, and Nicole*. Beverly Hills: Phoenix.

Way, Niobe. 2011. *Deep Secrets: Boys' Friendships and the Crisis of Connection*. Cambridge: Harvard University Press.

Winton, Richard, and Tonya Alanez. 2005. "Paparazzi Flash New Audacity." *Los Angeles Times*, October 16.

PART II

Circulation, Distribution, Policy

7

Anatomy of a Protest

Grey's Anatomy, Colombia's A corazón abierto,
and the Politicization of a Format

YEIDY M. RIVERO

In July 2009, Radio Cadena Nacional (RCN), a private Colombian television network, announced the cast of *A corazón abierto,* the Colombian adaptation of the US series *Grey's Anatomy.* Coproduced by Disney
Media Networks Latin America, Vista Productions, and RCN, *A corazón
abierto* was advertised as following the "spirit," characters, and creative
universe of *Grey's Anatomy* while presenting the realities of Colombia's
health and medical systems. Soon after RCN announced *A corazón abierto*'s cast, an unexpected controversy emerged and eventually led to a
protest. Several Afro-Colombian organizations accused RCN of racism
due to the network's exclusion of the black characters who were present
in the original *Grey's Anatomy.* As the leader of one of the Afro-Colombian organizations involved in the protest declared, "There are no solid
reasons for the producers of the series to change the [black] characters
when, in the original version, those characters add interesting elements
to the drama and that would not have to be different in the Colombian
version" ("Afrocolombianos protestan" 2009). The RCN producers' adaptation collided with the audiences' expectations, as at least one segment of
the Colombian audience anticipated that *A corazón abierto* would maintain its fidelity to the original series and reproduce its multiethnic cast.

Considering the circulation of Colombian formats across the region and the Colombian television industry's integration into the US Spanish-language and English-language television markets (see the chapters by Juan Piñón and Omar Rincón and María Paula Martínez in this anthology), the conflict between Afro-Colombian organizations and RCN not only sheds light on the complexities of format adaptations and transnational business arrangements, but also reveals the plurality of identities of those generically (and exclusively) described as Colombian, Latin American, and US Latinos/as. My goal in this essay, then, is to use *A corazón abierto*'s casting controversy as a case study to explore audiences' expectations of Hollywood formats as well as to problematize the monolithic conceptualization of ethnic identities. Hence, relying on press coverage, Internet postings, a radio show, and a television show about the *A corazón abierto* controversy, and personal interviews with Colombian media professionals, I ask the following three questions.[1] First, what do the Afro-Colombian organizations' casting expectations tell us about the process of format adaptation? Second, how do ethnic groups or the notion of ethnic groups translate across national and cultural borders? Third, to what extent does the *A corazón abierto* incident challenge the construction of a pan–Latin American and pan–US Spanish-language Latino/a media space? To answer these questions, I engage with Hans Robert Jauss's concepts of "horizon of expectation," "horizon of experience," and "horizon change."

In "Literary History as a Challenge to Literary Theory" (1982), Jauss addresses the reception of literary work, focusing especially on how readers, who are situated in a specific historical moment and who are also familiar with literary trends, understand a text. He conceptualizes the reading process and the relationship among author, text, reader, and the historical moment as the "horizon of expectation." The horizon of expectation influences both the author of a text, who tends to reproduce literary conventions to successfully communicate with the audience, and the readers' responses to a text, which are informed by a knowledge of literary elements such as genre and form. Another factor that permeates the understanding of a text is the readers' "horizon of experience," which encompasses not only the readers' literary horizon but also their experience in life. Whereas these two horizons play an important role in the creation and interpretation of literature, some instances in literary work present new experiences and thus produce a "horizon change." According to Jauss, this literature "negates familiar experience or articulates an experience for the first time" (14). By paying attention to these "horizons" in historical moments when literature confronts moral taboos or "offer[s] the reader new solutions for the moral casuistry of his life," scholars can begin to understand literature's impact on society (37).

Drawing on Jauss's theory of reception, in this essay I argue that the Afro-Colombians' familiarity with *Grey's Anatomy*, their own position as a marginalized television public, and the history of Afro-Colombian political mobilizations created expectations that transcended Colombian television's programming. These expectations were inspired by African American representations on US television, African Americans' fight for civil rights, and the Afro-Colombians' efforts to fight discrimination. Collectively, globalization, the exportation of US programming, and Afro-Colombians' awareness of the US civil rights movement were part of the Afro-Colombian organization members' "horizon of expectation." In other words, the Afro-Colombian organizations' protest against the *A corazón abierto* casting related not only to Colombia as a multiethnic/racial nation, but also to the ways Afro-Colombians saw themselves and others who are part of the African Diaspora. This Afro-diasporic space, as we shall see, also included television. In short, the *Grey's Anatomy* format came with a history that went way beyond the confines of ABC, Disney Latin America, and RCN. Hence, to understand the anatomy of the *A corazón abierto* protest, we need to begin with *Grey's Anatomy* and its creator, Shonda Rhimes.

Grey's Anatomy: The Inadvertent Formation of
an Afro-Diasporic Television Format

Grey's Anatomy is a highly successful ABC network medical drama that focuses on the personal and professional lives of the doctors and residents of Grace Mercy West Hospital in Seattle, Washington. Since its premiere in 2005, one of the series' key features was the use of a multiethnic cast. Industrially promoted as presenting a "color-blind cast" (a generic way to describe the casting of ethnically diverse actors for roles that were not necessarily envisioned with a particular ethnic background in mind), the doctors and nurses who populate *Grey's Anatomy's* fictional world are African American, Asian American, Latino/Hispanic, and white. As a *New York Times* article noted one month after *Grey's Anatomy's* premiere, the series has a "diverse world of doctors," who, although rarely discussing racism or prejudice, nonetheless represent an accurate demographic depiction of US society (Fogel 2005). Shonda Rhimes, *Grey's Anatomy's* creator and showrunner, reaffirmed the "color blindness" of her characters. As the *New York Times* article explains, when Rhimes conceptualized the series, the characters were not imagined as members of any specific ethnic group. Rhimes subsequently selected the actors based on their auditions, not their ethnicity.

The industry's (and to a certain extent, Rhimes's) initial promotion of *Grey's Anatomy's* color blindness is an example of what Dale Hudson refers to as Hollywood's "multicultural whiteness" (2007). By including racially diverse characters in minor roles, multicultural whiteness "negotiates contradictions between an overstated racially blind inclusiveness of multiculturalism and an understated racial exclusiveness of whiteness" (Hudson 2007, 130). Even though *Grey's Anatomy's* African American, Latina, and Asian American characters are important players in the series, their color blindness (which in the narrative translates into a lack of dialogues about race and racial oppression), like multicultural whiteness, also "universalize[s] experience by divorcing history and power from representation" (Hudson 2007, 132).

Certainly, as we know today, Rhimes's approach to color blindness has more shades than her 2005 interview led us to believe. In a 2012 story about media diversity, Rhimes revealed her political intentions behind her casting choices for *Grey's Anatomy*. As she observed, "*Grey's* was about me making a statement. I was making a television show that I wanted to watch and part of that was putting people of all colors in it so that you saw people like you on television" (Springer 2012). Rhimes's casting choices for her other two series—*Private Practice* and *Scandal*, whose lead is an African American woman—in addition to her strong criticism of showrunners who exclusively cast white performers, demonstrate her efforts to transform Hollywood's racial (white) homogeneity (Ekin 2012; Haulsey 2012). As the first African American woman to create and be the executive producer of top-ten–rated dramas ("She

Made It," 2008), Rhimes has used her power to alter Hollywood's casting practices.

Yet, despite Rhimes's clear push for ethnic diversity, her conceptualization of color-blind characters was ingrained in *Grey's Anatomy*. This color blindness, plus industrial parameters that detach formats from any ethnic and culturally specific attributes (Keane and Moran 2008; Moran 2009), eliminated all possible traces of a US conceptualization of ethnicity and race from the *Grey's Anatomy* format. The exported *Grey's Anatomy* program visually represented ethnic diversity nonetheless, and in theory, the exported *Grey's Anatomy* format was a blank slate. As I will soon explain, this ethnic/racial ambiguity, along with Shonda Rhimes's ethnicity, became important factors in the anatomy of the *A corazón abierto* protest. Still, before the casting selection was made, the main worry for those behind the adaptation of *Grey's Anatomy* was having the freedom to indigenize the format.

One year before the announcement of *A corazón abierto*'s cast, I had the opportunity to interview Fernando Gaitán, the creator of *Yo soy Betty, la fea* and the person selected by Buena Vista International Television Latin America and RCN to adapt *Grey's Anatomy* for Colombia and Latin America, excluding Brazil. My conversation with Gaitán revolved around the impact of the *Yo soy Betty, la fea* global phenomenon in Colombia's television industry, the theme of another research project I was conducting at the time. In May 2008, when I talked to Gaitán, I was unaware of RCN's plans to adapt *Grey's Anatomy*; however, the topic surfaced in the conversation. Gaitán was working on the preproduction phase of *Grey's Anatomy*, and his main concern then was having the freedom to indigenize the series' concept. As he observed,

> I told RCN, if they are going to send me a script just to translate it, I am not interested. The theme [of *Grey's Anatomy*] is very interesting but the health system in the US is different from the one in Colombia. The fast response to crises, the service, and the science . . . well, we do not have that here. It does not work. In fact, we would be seen as clowns if we just reproduced *Grey's Anatomy*'s story lines. (Personal communication)

Gaitán's specificity regarding translating *and* adapting *Grey's Anatomy* instead of merely performing a translation was related to *Amas de casa desesperadas*, the Latin American version of *Desperate House-wives*. When Buena Vista International Television Latin America and the Argentinean company Pol-ka Productions produced the *Desperate Housewives* format for the Latin American market, the format stipulation agreement did not allow for an actual adaptation, only a translation. *Amas de casa desesperadas* became a major financial flop, leading Disney's executives to realize that successful formats must be adapted. Therefore, the *Desperate Housewives* "disaster" (as it was described to me by some Colombian media professionals) opened the doors to a "purely Colombian" *Grey's Anatomy*. And it was precisely this Colombianness that legitimized the selection of an all-white cast. In other words, Colombia's "hegemonic values of whiteness" (Wade 2000) and its impact on television, wherein black performers and/or actors with strong indigenous features are consigned to minor roles, influenced the casting selection for *A corazón abierto*. Given RCN executives' "horizon of expectation," those behind the *A corazón abierto* team were surprised when Afro-Colombian organizations publicly accused RCN of racial discrimination. At the core of the Afro-Colombian organizations' allegations was a vision of Colombianness that embraced multiculturalism and that, as a result, coincided with the visual—multicultural—narrative of *Grey's Anatomy*.

The principal document that articulates the activists' position is a July 21, 2009, press release by Cimarrón Nacional, one of the country's most important Afro-Colombian groups (Perea Garcés 2009; Williams Castro 2011). The document, "Racism and Exclusion on RCN Television," grounds the protest in the network's violation of three legal procedures: Colombia's Constitution (1991), Law 22 of 1981, and Law 70 of 1993. Although drafted in different years, these measures reassessed the nation and its citizenry as multicultural and addressed racial and ethnic discrimination. For instance, the Constitutional Reform of 1991 acknowledges the country's ethnic, cultural, and linguistic diversity and reconceptualizes Colombia as a pluri-ethnic nation. Law 22 of 1981, on the other hand, denounces all types of racial discrimination, paying particular attention to discriminatory practices in the labor market. Law 70 of 1993, a revolutionary measure for Colombia's black populations, recognizes Afro-Colombians as an ethnic group, prohibits discrimination, promotes the incorporation of Afro-Colombian themes in educational curricula, and encourages Afro-Colombian political participation in the government (Wade 1997, 2000; Williams Castro 2011). Hence, by citing the aforementioned legal documents, the Afro-Colombian organizations criminalized RCN, implying that by casting white actors only, the company was racially discriminating against Afro-Colombians and thus defying the Constitution, Law 22, and Law 70.

In addition to positioning *A corazón abierto*'s casting selection as an example of racial/ethnic discrimination, the Cimarrón Nacional press release indicates that RCN and other local production companies "do not recognize that Afro-Colombians can be portrayed as professionally successful people." To demonstrate RCN's "racism and exclusion," Cimarrón Nacional used *Grey's Anatomy*'s authorship, casting, and what the organization understood as Shonda Rhimes's sociopolitical intentions with the series, as its justification for the protest. As stated in the press release,

> The successful US series *Grey's Anatomy* was created by the Afro-American Shonda Rhimes to promote intercultural relations and the elimination of racial prejudice and to exalt cultural diversity. In the original script, the leading roles are enacted by two African-American actors and an Afro-American actress, who, together with white and Asian-American actors, portray the role of talented doctors.

Clearly, the Afro-Colombian leaders were familiar with *Grey's Anatomy*. Nonetheless, what is interesting about the press release's description is that the showrunner's ethnicity and the inclusion of an ethnically diverse cast triggered a new reading of the original show and its format.

First, Shonda Rhimes's ethnicity repositioned her as a creator whose main intention with the series was to promote multiculturalism and to fight discrimination. Even though Rhimes advertised her characters as color-blind and even though racial discrimination was not at the center of the series' narrative, the Afro-Colombian organizations added racial politics to the show. To be sure, and as I mentioned earlier, Rhimes's casting selections were clearly politicized. Nonetheless, what is interesting about the Afro-Colombian organization members' reading of Rhimes and her cast is how their ethnicities transformed the content of the show. As the leader of Cimarrón Nacional (Juan de Dios Mosquera) stated in the newspaper interview cited earlier, "There are no solid reasons for the producers of the [Colombian] series to change the [black] characters when, in the original version, those characters add interesting elements to the drama" ("Afrocolombianos protestan" 2009). Considering that the characters' ethnic and cultural backgrounds are rarely discussed in *Grey's Anatomy*, one can say that the visual cues were the main source for the Afro-Colombian leader's claim. In some ways, the Afro-Colombian organizations both imposed and lifted the burden of representation from Rhimes. On the one hand, her blackness situated her in a position in which she needed to embrace and represent her ethnic community. On the other hand, her blackness—together with the ethnic diversity of *Grey's Anatomy*—already incorporated politics into her creations. The episodes' dialogues and themes were irrelevant because, in the Afro-Colombian organization members' "horizon of expectation," the body of the creator and the series' visual narrative seemed powerful enough to transform the narrative.

Another intriguing factor in the Afro-Colombians' interpretation of *Grey's Anatomy* is the characterization of the African American characters as leads in the show. Certainly, as I previously mentioned, the African American characters, together with the Asian American and Latina characters, are important components of the series. However, white performers play the leading couple in *Grey's Anatomy* (Meredith Grey and Derek Shepherd). Thus, the Afro-Colombian leaders reposition the lead characters (played by white performers) as secondary characters and some of the secondary characters (played by African Americans) as leads. Somewhat interconnected to the transformation of the series' white and African American characters' casting is the invisibility of Callie Torres, the only Latina character in *Grey's Anatomy*. No discussions of the US show mention Callie or her ethnicity. There are two possibilities for this absence. One explanation is that perhaps the Afro-Colombian leaders were unaware of Callie, given that the character was incorporated in the second season of *Grey's Anatomy* and obtained her prime status only in season three. Another reason for Callie's invisibility might have been associated with the actress's skin color, coded in Latin America as white. In other words, Callie's body merged her with the white characters, rendering her ethnicity nonexistent. Given that the Afro-Colombian organization members' reading of *Grey's Anatomy*'s racial politics was framed by visual cues, the invisibility of *Latino-ness* is quite likely. But regardless of the alteration of roles, the invisibility of a particular character, and the imposition or lifting of the burden of representation, the important aspect of *Grey's Anatomy* relates to the utilization of the series and format as a tool for political mobilization at the local level.

Cimarrón Nacional's press release listed six demands targeting Colombian television networks and society in general. The group sought (1) the creation of a national campaign to tackle the racism against Afro-Colombians on TV and in other areas of Colombian society; (2) the production of *Grey's Anatomy's* original concept; (3) collective efforts by all media outlets to protect Colombia's cultural identity and its Constitution; (4) an investigation by the minister of communication into RCN's casting practices for the Colombian *Grey's Anatomy*; (5) an invitation to all people who believed in the ideals of Martin Luther King, Jr., and Nelson Mandela to stop watching RCN; and (6) a request to all Colombians to join the Afro-Colombian organizations' efforts to fight discrimination. Together with the press release, the organizations Cimarrón Nacional, Palenque Vivo, and Colombia Negra organized a protest outside the RCN building (Perea Garcés 2009).

Inadvertently, *Grey's Anatomy* created a "horizon change," a cultural artifact that promised new types of representations on Colombian television. The fact that the promise of change was not fulfilled unlocked the frustration of those involved in Afro-Colombian organizations, many of whom, like Cimarrón Nacional's leader, have been fighting for years to improve the rights of their communities (Wade 2009; Williams Castro 2011). This long-lasting frustration was palpable in the demands listed in the press release. Through these statements, the organizations linked their struggles to those endured by others in the African Diaspora. More importantly and interrelated, by including the names of Martin Luther King, Jr., and Nelson Mandela, the press release brought to light the history of Afro-Colombians' cultural, political, and social activism, which, as scholars have documented, was influenced by the US civil rights and South African anti-apartheid movements (Wade 1997, 2009; Williams Castro 2011). From the names of cultural centers and groups (for example, the Frantz Fanon Research Center and Soweto) to stories about members of the Black Panther Party allegedly visiting Colombia in the 1970s, Afro-Colombians have created affinities with black people in the United States and other parts of the world (Williams Castro 2011, chap. 2). Shonda Rhimes, *Grey's Anatomy*, and television became part of this connectedness, symbolically serving as circuits that wired the Afro-Colombian organizations' past to their present and their national politics to their ideological bond with members of the African Diaspora.

As expected, Cimarrón Nacional's press release attracted the immediate attention of RCN as well as other media outlets. Initially, the main participants in the controversy were Fernando Gaitán, who, in his role as vice president of production at RCN, served as the company's spokesperson, and Juan de Dios Mosquera, founder of Cimarrón Nacional and the lead person behind the protest. However, when the debate between these two individuals moved to newspapers, radio, and television, other Colombian citizens joined the discussion. And, even as *Grey's Anatomy* was the center of the dialogue, the topic of racial exclusion expanded to address the limited opportunities for black performers on Colombian television.

In every interview, Gaitán followed a similar script, which included a description of all RCN shows that had cast Afro-Colombians, the reasons for not casting Afro-Colombians for *A corazón abierto*, and a sketch of two future RCN projects that would need black actors. On the other hand, Juan de Dios Mosquera repeated the information included in the press release, emphasizing the need for television networks and production companies to expand the pool of black actors through national casting calls.

During interviews for Caracol Radio and *El Universal* newspaper, Gaitán began the conversation by noting that Cimarrón Nacional's accusation of racism was "unfair." As he explained, "We believe it is absolutely unfair, particularly since RCN has produced . . . important series with ethnic themes such as *Azúcar* [Sugar], *Los colores de la fama* [The colors of fame], and *Guajira*" ("Corporación afrocolombiana" 2009; "Fernando Gaitán responde" 2009). In addition to citing the aforementioned series, he listed a number of Afro-Colombian actors who had worked for RCN (in the radio interview, RCN sent a list to the show's host of all the Afro-Colombians who were working for the channel at the time). After providing this information, Gaitán proceeded to explain the three reasons for the network not casting Afro-Colombians as doctors in *A corazón abierto*.

Gaitán's first justification was the fact that *Grey's Anatomy* was a format. "First of all, I need to clarify something and that is that this [*Grey's Anatomy*] is a franchise of Vista and Disney. This last company is the owner of *Grey's Anatomy* in the world" ("Fernando Gaitán responde" 2009). Whereas Gaitán did not indicate that Disney was behind the casting selection, he seemed to imply that RCN was not in total control of the series. Then, he entered the terrain of adaptation by mentioning the failure of *Amas de casa desesperadas*. By recounting the *Amas de casa desesperadas* ratings flop, he conveyed that producing an exact US version of *Grey's Anatomy* would not work in Colombia.

The topic of translation and adaptation gave Gaitán the opportunity to provide the second reason for the absence of black actors in the Colombian version of *Grey's Anatomy*: the lack of black doctors in Colombia. "The US medical world has a strong presence of black doctors and it is not our fault that here it is not the same. It is an economic problem, a social problem, and it is related to the lack of opportunities" ("Fernando Gaitán responde" 2009). Even though Gaitán might have touched upon some aspects related to the interconnection of race and class in Colombia, his generalized statement drew angry reactions from readers and listeners, as I explain below. Yet the second justification gave him the chance to present the third reason for not casting black actors: the dearth of black actors. "We looked for actors to play the character of Burke. . . . We invited four actors but we did not find what we needed, something that is not related to racial discrimination" ("Corporación afrocolombiana" 2009; "Fernando Gaitán responde" 2009). Whereas sources documenting the number of black performers in Colombia do not exist, one might assume that, if there is a scarcity of black actors, it might be a product of the limited job opportunities in theater and television.

Cimarrón Nacional's Juan de Dios Mosquera was also interviewed on the Caracol Radio show *Hoy por hoy*, where, echoing the words of the press release, he deplored Colombia's racial discrimination. Furthermore, he insisted that the Colombian version of *Grey's Anatomy* needed to follow the casting of the original series. As he stated at the beginning of the interview, "We totally reject racial exclusion. It is inconceivable that in Colombia there is an ongoing aggression against us, the 18 million inhabitants who are Afro-Colombians. Our *Grey's Anatomy* needs to respect the original format that includes black actors as protagonists in addition to convey[ing] a message that favors diversity and inclusion" ("Corporación afrocolombiana" 2009). To emphasize the topic of racial marginalization, Mosquera used the opportunity to mention two letters allegedly sent by Televisa and TV Azteca to Colombian television networks asking these corporations not to include black actors in products sold to Mexico. By bringing Mexican television networks into the discussion, Mosquera expanded the topic of racial exclusion beyond the confines of the nation, indirectly hinting at the problem of anti-black racism in Latin America. This move also expanded the geolinguistic region (i.e., the Latin American and the US Spanish-language television markets) to one that was not exclusively formed by the commonality of language; it was also constructed through whiteness and racial exclusion.

The most significant Gaitán/Mosquera interview took place on the RCN television program *El defensor del televidente.* The entire August 12, 2009, show was devoted to the *Grey's Anatomy* adaptation controversy. The main protagonists behind the debate were interviewed, and the program also featured interviews with Afro-Colombian actors and actresses, who discussed not only the adaption of the US series in Colombia but also the exclusion of black performers in leading roles.

Without exception, all actors and actresses interviewed on *El defensor* insisted that *A corazón abierto* needed to be faithful to the casting of the original series. Furthermore, as in Cimarrón Nacional's press release, Shonda Rhimes's ethnicity played a key role in the performers' arguments to include Afro-Colombians. As one actress observed, "An African American woman created the series and she clearly developed the protagonists as Afro. In the US it is a law [to include black performers]. If the format is going to be produced in Colombia the company behind the production" needs to respect it [the format] 100%" (*El defensor del televidente* 2009). For this actress, Rhimes's ethnicity and *Grey's Anatomy*'s multicultural cast erased the color blindness behind Rhimes's casting selection. Also, in what seems to be a misunderstanding of the Civil Rights Act of 1964, the actress implied that in the United States a racial quota system influenced commercial television's casting selections. Given that neither of the show's hosts, Mosquera or Gaitán, corrected the information, the implication passed as truth.

Besides discussing *Grey's Anatomy*, Afro-Colombian performers used the opportunity to address racial discrimination on Colombian television. Comments such as "all Colombian productions should have at least one Afro"; "Television series should represent the diversity of Colombia's society"; "We need to be judged as actors regardless of race"; and "why is it that in Colombia, Afro-Colombians are not cast . . . as leads?" were common among the actors and actresses. To emphasize the Afro-Colombian performers' comments and the importance of television, Juan de Dios Mosquera observed,

> Television is an impressive medium. It educates or miseducates. It includes or excludes. It acknowledges or negates a presence. We consider it intolerable that we are excluded from the representation of *Grey's Anatomy*. An Afro-American woman created the series to promote inclusion. . . . To be clear, I do not demand inclusion based only on the color of the skin. I demand inclusion based on talent. (*El defensor del televidente* 2009)

In some ways, similar to Shonda Rhimes in the context of the United States, what Mosquera and the Afro-Colombian actors seemed to want was openness in casting selections and the promotion of Colombia's ethnic diversity. They were not the only ones who shared these goals.

Newspaper readers, radio listeners, and television audiences were also part of the *Grey's Anatomy* adaptation discussion. While these engaged citizens responded to both Gaitán's and Mosquera's views, most of the reactions targeted the RCN creator and executive. For instance, Gaitán's generalized statement regarding the lack of black doctors in Colombia drew angry reactions from some readers and listeners who posted comments on the newspaper and radio station's online forums as well as other online sites. One *El Universal* reader wrote, "Mr. Gaitán, what a deception. Have you visited the Pacific? Come and see how many Afro-Colombians work in that area of employment." Afro-Colombian citizens residing outside Colombia also joined the debate. In the online magazine *Barûle Gazette*, a Florida resident took the opportunity to criticize Gaitán's explanation for the absence of Afro-Colombians in the adaptation of *Grey's Anatomy* (Arango Valencia 2009).

Listeners of the radio program *Hoy por hoy* also commented on Gaitán's and Mosquera's words, providing different perspectives on the topics of racial discrimination, racial/ethnic inclusion, and television. For example, in reference to Mosquera's views regarding the need to cast Afro-Colombians in lead roles, a listener expressed that selecting black people for particular jobs, regardless of the candidates' capabilities, was racist. This listener also noted that, instead of forcing diversity, the Afro-Colombian organizations should "invest their energies in training their members to be competitive" in the job market ("Corporación afrocolombiana" 2009). In addition to utilizing the argument of reverse discrimination, this listener blamed the lack of Afro-Colombians in various professional positions on the leaders of Afro-Colombian communities. Left out of this listener's comments were the problem of systematic institutional racism and the role of the state in fighting discrimination beyond the confines of the law.

Responding to the previous comments as well as to Gaitán's justifications for not casting Afro-Colombians in *A corazón abierto*, another listener used herself as an example of one of many Afro-Colombians who are highly educated and professionally successful. "I am Afro-Colombian . . . a civil engineer from the Javeriana University. There are 'hundred[s]' of cases, of professionals, of capable, highly prepared, and intelligent Afro-Colombians. . . . The justification for not showing Afro-Colombians in the Colombian version is ridiculous" ("Corporación afrocolombiana" 2009). An interesting aspect of this listener's posting relates to the ways she conceptualized local television and Afro-Colombian politics. Making a direct connection to Cimarrón Nacional's press release, she wrote,

> Juan de Dios [Mosquera], I invite you to leave aside Martin L. King and follow Malcolm X. . . . I consume neither Caracol TV [the other commercial network in Colombia] nor RCN TV. . . . Let's watch FOX and BET, any [television] except Colombia's. ("Corporación afrocolombiana" 2009).

Embracing the radicalism characteristic of Malcolm X and the Black Power movement, and supporting US networks that, in particular moments in time (in the case of Fox), have targeted African Americans, this Afro-Colombian put aside the Colombianness of her identity, favoring the "Afro" that connected her with African Americans.

The aforementioned readers,' listeners,' and audiences' views, similar to those expressed by Afro-Colombian organization leaders, represented the broader objectives of the Afro-Colombian movement. As Joseph Jordan argues,

> Afro-Colombians have articulated a new black cultural identity as a strategy for mobilization within the current historical process of Colombia's nation definition. Reimagining "blackness," African consciousness, Afro-Colombian ethnicity, and maroon identity provides a means for an extra-national citizenship, and it connects Afro-Colombians to struggles waged by other communities of African-descent throughout the Americas. (Jordan 2008, 90)

This political understanding of blackness framed Afro-Colombian organization members' and some of the online participants' "horizon of experience." It was difficult for these audiences to conceptualize a different casting strategy for Colombia's Grey's Anatomy not only because the Constitution, Law 22 of 1981, and Law 70 of 1993 promised them equal participation in society, but also because Shonda Rhimes had created the series. For many Afro-Colombians, Grey's Anatomy was their cultural product; it was a television show created by an African American woman—someone who, like them, shared an African/Afro ethnic identity. Shonda Rhimes and her creation, Grey's Anatomy, cohabited in the symbolic yet also palpable and transcontinental space that forms the African Diaspora. For them, Grey's Anatomy was an Afro-Diasporic television format.

Lessons in Formats: The Grey's Anatomy Controversy and Beyond

On April 26, 2010, RCN network began to broadcast A corazón abierto (2010–2011). Following the telenovela genre, A corazón abierto broke ratings records in its premiere, beating Colombia's original Yo soy Betty, la fea (Seidman 2010). Whereas A corazón abierto did much better in Colombia than it did in the United States when it began to air on Telemundo in 2010, the format adaptation was so successful in the South American country that TV Azteca bought the rights. The Mexican version, mostly described in the Spanish-language press as Colombia's *A corazón abierto* (instead of Shonda Rhimes's *Grey's Anatomy*), began to air in September 2011, and it gave TV Azteca a rating hit ("DMNLA and TV Azteca" n.d.). Broadcast on TV Azteca and by its sister US company, Azteca America, Mexico's *A corazón abierto* ended in May 2012.

The casting controversy did not translate/move with the adapted format to Mexico. That information remained local yet available for those who, like me, were interested in researching the background of Colombia's *A corazón abierto*. It was through these explorations that I discovered that, according to a 2010 online article entitled "Protesta anti-racismo dio fruto," RCN had hired an Afro-Colombian actor for several episodes of *A corazón abierto*. Indeed, as the title of the article suggests, this was a positive outcome of the earlier antiracism protest. Nonetheless, the *Grey's Anatomy*/*A corazón abierto* casting controversy did not change the actors selected for the principal roles. Nor did it create a massive mobilization against prejudice in Colombia. Instead, the debates provided a new arena for addressing the specificity of anti-black racism on Colombian television. In addition, the controversy crystallized many Afro-Colombians' affinities and interconnections with members of the African Diaspora. Shonda Rhimes's *Grey's Anatomy* and the "in-betweenness" of format adaptation wherein, as Vinicius Navarro writes, "one culture looks at and interprets another," provided a space for the articulation of black struggles, political activism, and Afro-Diasporic affinities (Navarro 2012, 36).

The *A corazón abierto* controversy and the "in-betweenness" of formats also demonstrate that the process of adaptation does not only involve the indigenization of a script, concepts, casting, and sets (to mention just a few elements); sometimes it also engages in the reinterpretation of the particular historical, social, political, and cultural conditions that directly and indirectly influenced the original concept. Thus, one can say that formats—particularly from a major exporter such as Hollywood—carry with them a variety of expectations hidden in industrially unconstrained, invisible, and malleable appendixes of information. These expectations surface with the adaptation and are triggered by the audiences' familiarity with and interpretation of the original text, as well as local sociocultural and political conditions. As a product of globalization, the Grey's Anatomy format carried with it the original show's textual and visual narratives as well as its metanarrative: from magazine interviews and news stories to the fight for civil rights and the end of racial discrimination to issues regarding ethnic minorities on US television, and so forth. Furthermore, the format also came with some assumed narratives about US history. For example, the Afro-Colombian actress's statement that in the United States, by law, networks have to cast African Americans stemmed from a false assumption about the Civil Rights Act of 1964.

Considering the varying aspects and influences that inform format adaptations, I would like to expand Vinicius Navarro's conceptualization of formats in which he states that "to adapt is to make sense of a format created elsewhere" (34) and add that to adapt a format is to make sense of a television concept, culture, and history formed elsewhere. During the process of adaptation, new interpretations of format, culture, and history can emerge that may or may not be accurate for those who created the original concept, but that might make perfect sense for those at the local level who are producing the interpretation and adaptation. Equally important and interrelated, we can say that in some cases formats can provide new parameters of representation and thematic discussions that are absent or marginalized at the local level. Through the unpredictable and industrially unexpected rereadings of formats, culture, and history, or simply by importing a format that tackles themes not discussed locally, industrial products can produce a "horizon change."

The topic of "horizon change" brings me back to questions regarding ethnic and cultural affinities across Latin America and in US Latino/a communities. As evidenced in the Afro-Colombian organizations' demands and some of the audiences' online postings, some members of the Colombian nation seemed to be more attuned with African Americans' civil rights struggles, history, and televised representations than with those of other Latin Americans and US Latinos. In fact, their voices reminded me of the challenges against anti-black racism on Puerto Rican television that took place in the 1970s and that were influenced by the US civil rights and Black Power movements as well as changes on US commercial television (Rivero 2005). In both the

Grey's Anatomy/*A corazón abierto* example and the Puerto Rican case, the empathies of actors and audiences with those in the African Diaspora erased or diminished a potential pan–Latin American and pan-Latino/a construct.

Stuart Hall reminds us that "[i]dentity is not as transparent or unproblematic as we think. . . . [Identity is] a production which is never complete, always in process, and always constituted within, not outside, representation" (Hall 2000, 704). Let me state the obvious. People are more than their ethnicities. Our job as media scholars is to go beyond the "horizon of expectation" regarding identities and affinities within an ethnic group (for example, Latinos/as) and analyze the moments in which productions, texts, or audiences (to mention some aspects of the encoding-decoding process) challenge ethnic-political solidarities or expand creative or social relations among people from different ethnic groups or within the confines of a single (pan-)ethnicity. We need to expand our scholarship and examine the multiple identities that form those who are lumped together as Latinos/as and who consume (or desire to consume) media artifacts that are not targeted to "Latinos." Closely interrelated, we also need to recognize that many people who are singularly labeled Latino/a or Hispanic, like the Afro-Colombian organization members presented in this chapter, empathize with the struggles of other groups beyond the "Latino/a" community.

NOTE

1. These interviews were conducted in May 2008 and were designed for a research project on the impact of *Yo soy Betty, la fea* as a global phenomenon in Colombia's television industry. While none of my questions covered *A corazón abierto* (at the time of the interviews *A corazón abierto* was in the initial pre-production stages), issues regarding the adaptation of US formats, including *A corazón abierto*, came up in the conversations.

REFERENCES

"Afrocolombianos protestan por ausencia de actors negros en serie de RCN." 2009. *Semana*, August 1. Accessed July 4, 2011. http://www.semana.com/problemas-sociales/afrocolombianos-protestan-ausencia-actores-negros-serie-rcn/126885-3.aspx.

Arango Valencia, Edubar. 2009. "TeleRacismo en la Colombia?" *Barûle Gazette*, August 30–September 5. Accessed December 10, 2012. http://www.barulegazette.com/bar%C3%BBle_gazette_-_zona_de_archivo_-_00059.htm.

"Corporación afrocolombiana acusa al Canal RCN de segregación en versión de la serie *Grey's Anatomy*." 2009. Caracol Radio, *Hoy por hoy*, July 24. Accessed December 1, 2012. http://www.caracol1260.com/noticia/corporacion-afrocolombiana-acusa-al-canal-rcn-de-segregacion-en-version-de-la-serie-greys-anatomy-fernando-Gaitán-explica-motivaciones-del-canal/20090724/nota/850458.aspx.

El Defensor del Televidente. 2009. RCN, August 12. Accessed May 20, 2011, on Movimiento Cimarrón Nacional, Youtube channel. http://www.youtube.com/user/movimientocimarron/featured.

"DMNLA and TV Azteca Confirm Production of *A corazón abierto* for Mexico." n.d. *Todo TV News*. Accessed December 4, 2012. http://www.todotvnews.com/scripts/templates/estilo_nota.asp?nota=35173.

Ekin, Jaimie. 2012. "Shonda Rhimes Tweets about Lack of Diversity on 'Bunheads' on ABC Family." *Huffington Post*, June 13. Accessed December 10, 2012. http://www.huffingtonpost.com/2012/06/13/shonda-rhimes-bunheads_n_1594251.html.

"Fernando Gaitán responde a líderes afrocolombianos." 2009. *El Universal*, July 26. Accessed March 5, 2011. http://www.eluniversal.com.co/cartagena/actualidad/fernando-gaitan-responde-lideres-afrocolombianos.

Fogel, Matthew. 2005. "*Grey's Anatomy* Goes Colorblind." *New York Times*, May 8. Accessed March 5, 2011. http://www.nytimes.com/2005/05/08/arts/television/08foge.html?pagewanted=print&_r=0.

Hall, Stuart. 2000. "Cultural Identity and Cinematic Representation." In *Film and Theory: An Anthology*, edited by Robert Stam and Toby Miller, 704–14. Malden, MA: Blackwell.

Haulsey, Kuwana. 2012. "With *Scandal*, Shonda Rhimes Is Upending Racist Hollywood Formulas and Changing TV." *Atlanta Black Star*, May 17. Accessed December 10, 2012. http://atlantablackstar.com/2012/05/17/with-scandal-shonda-rhimes-is-upending-racist-hollywood-formulas-and-changing-the-tv-landscape/.

Hudson, Dale. 2007. "Vampires of Color and the Performance of Multicultural Whiteness." In *The Persistence of Whiteness: Race and Contemporary Hollywood Cinema*, edited by Daniel Bernardi, 127–56. New York: Routledge.

Jauss, Hans Robert. 1982. "Literary History as a Challenge to Literary Theory." In *Toward an Aesthetic of Reception*, translated by Timothy Bahti, 3–45. Minneapolis: University of Minnesota Press.

Jordan, Joseph. 2008. "Afro-Colombia: A Case for Pan-African Analysis." In *Transnational Blackness: Navigating the Global Color Line*, edited by Manning Marable and Vanessa Agard-Jones, 37–98. New York: Palgrave Macmillan.

Keane, Michael, and Albert Moran. 2008. "Television's New Engine." *Television and New Media* 9, no. 2: 155–69.

Moran, Albert. 2009. "Introduction: Descent and Modification." In *TV Formats World Wide: Localizing Global Programs*, edited by Albert Moral, 9–24. Bristol, UK: Intellect.

Navarro, Vinicius. 2012. "More than Copycat Television: Format Adaptation as Performance." In *Global Television Formats: Understanding Television across Borders*, edited by Tasha Oren and Sharon Shahaf, 23–38. London: Routledge.

Perea Garcés, Ademir. 2009. "Racismo y exclusión en RCN Television." July 21. Accessed April 12, 2011. http://216.121.116.75/atlantico-negro/afrolatinos-caribenhos/colombia/1760-racismo-y-exclusion-en-rcn-television.

"Protesta anti-racismo dio fruto." 2010. Chocosabor.com, April 19. Accessed May 5, 2011.

Rivero, Yeidy M. 2005. *Tuning Out Blackness: Race and Nation in the History of Puerto Rican Television*. Durham: Duke University Press, 2005.

Seidman, Robert. 2010. "*Grey's Anatomy* Adaptation *A Corazón Abierto* Premieres to Huge Ratings in Colombia." *TV by the Numbers*, April 27. Accessed May 5, 2011. http://tvbythenumbers.zap2it.com/2010/04/27/greys-anatomy-adaptation-a-corazon-abierto-premieres-to-huge-ratings-in-colombia/49914/.

"She Made It: Women Creating Television and Radio." 2008. Paley Center for Media. Accessed December 4, 2012. http://www.shemadeit.org/meet/biography.aspx?m=165.

Springer, Sarah. 2012. "*Grey's Anatomy* Creator, Actress Discuss Media Diversity." CNN, May 22. Accessed December 10, 2012. http://inamerica.blogs.cnn.com/2012/05/22/greys-anatomy-creator-and-actress-discuss-media-diversity/.

Wade, Peter. 1997. *Race and Ethnicity in Latin America*. Chicago: Pluto Press.

———. 2000. *Music, Race, and Nation: Música Tropical in Colombia*. Chicago: University of Chicago Press.

———. 2009. "Defining Blackness in Colombia." *Journal de la Société des Américanistes* 95: 165–84.

Williams Castro, Fatimah. 2011. "The Politics and Everyday Experience of Race in Post-Constitutional Reform Colombia." PhD diss., Rutgers University.

8

Colombianidades Export Market

OMAR RINCÓN AND MARÍA PAULA MARTÍNEZ

In the past few years many TV series have been filmed in studios that resemble Hollywood, but that are actually located in Bogota. A new phenomenon of coproductions between local companies and enterprises such as Telemundo, Sony, Disney, Fox, and Univision is reshaping the Latin@ TV market that Colombia had dominated with *telenovelas* back in the 1990s.[1] This essay explores how Colombian TV production is adapting to American and Latin@ audiences, and how Bogota is being reimagined and reinventing itself as a reference for Latin@ TV production.

According to Jesús Martín-Barbero, the most important researcher on *telenovelas* and popular culture in Latin America, "There's much more of the Colombian nation that passes through the telenovelas than the news programs." The best way to know the country's recent history is to look at television fictions, consisting of comedy and melodrama. "In the midst of the complexity of the country's armed conflict," notes Martín-Barbero, "the soccer games and the telenovelas had become some of the few ways we were held together as a nation."[2] We do not know how to do real or documentary portrayals of our violence, our narco-culture, and our modern dreams. In order to do that, we do telenovelas. That's how we recognize ourselves, how we define our identity:

through stories of love, vengeance, justice, and humor. Telenovelas are the best cultural product we have invented and developed into a successful industry because the format is not limited to melodrama, but also includes a neo-realistic comedy/tragedy. Telenovelas and their reach into other countries are a matter of national pride that has earned Colombia a prominent share of the US Latin@ industry and market.

Currently, Colombia is the top producer of TV fictions for Latin@ media in the United States. Some people even talk about "Bogolly-wood," as many series are being filmed in studios that look like Hollywood but are actually in Bogota. Why is this happening? Although the Mexican producer Televisa is (and has been) the leader of TV production in Latin@ America, it appears Colombia is emerging as a strong competitor. American enterprises like Sony, Disney, Telemundo, Fox, and Univision have coproduced many TV series and documentaries in Colombia since 2001, such as *Mental, Kdabra, Tiempo final, Lynch, Isa TK+, Mujeres asesinas, Tabu, Migrópolis, El capo,* and *El rescate perfecto.*

Regarding TV production, what is it that Colombia does better than other countries? Why has the American market preferred Colombia instead of other Latin@ American countries? This essay will try to answer these questions.

The Colombian TV Phenomenon

Colombia is the top producer of TV fictions for the Latin@ market in the United States due to its highly regarded talent, the deregulated TV labor market, and creative approaches to the new media industry dynamics.

According to Invest in Bogota, the investment promotion agency of Bogota, the audiovisual production industry increased from US$628 million in 2005 to US$1,200 million in 2011, with 90 percent of it stemming from television revenues.[3] This major leap is mainly a result of the merger of American enterprises and local companies: Fox with Telecolombia,[4] Sony with Teleset,[5] Vista Producciones with Disney,[6] Telemundo with RTI,[7] Be-TV with Caracol,[8] and MundoFox with RCN.[9]

Also, the audiovisual industry has grown because of the country's economic stability and the government effort to create an optimal environment for foreign investment. Since the beginning of 2000, Proexport, the government entity that promotes international tourism, foreign investment, and nontraditional exports in Colombia, included the audiovisual industry in its investment promotion catalogue. According to its report, Colombia offers the following "opportunities for recording studios and content development for the film, television and media industries":

- Colombia is one of the five countries in the world considered as megadiverse.
- Locations: there are ecosystems covering all the way from snow peaks, tropical rainforests, moorlands, large valleys, two oceans, deserts, countless rivers, lakes, lagoons, and thousands of plant and animal species.
- Colombian television is currently exporting its products successfully to the United States, Mexico and Costa Rica, among others.
- Over 45 thousand graduates per year from technical and professional careers related to the creative industries (Ministry of Education, Colombia).
- Academic training programs in high-level audiovisual animation and production, according to the National Learning Service (SENA).
- Competitive wages in the region for engineers and technicians. US$9,714 per year for an electronic engineer and US$10,548 per year for an audiovisual technician (Salary Expert).[10]

Colombia is the fourth-largest economy in Latin America, and in 2012 the country became a member of the Organization for Economic Cooperation and Development (OECD). According to Ángel Gurría, the OECD general secretary,

Colombia has accomplished much in the past few years. Good economic policies have provided a higher level of macroeconomic stability and living standards have gradually risen. Improved security has also contributed to a better economic environment. Now that the global economy is recovering, Colombia is enjoying high inflows of foreign investment, growing demand for its exports and more favorable terms of trade.[11]

In Colombia there are more than 135 national audiovisual companies, which sell more than US$1,000 million a year. According to Dinero. com, a monthly economics magazine, Vista Productions, through its alliance with Disney, increased its operating profit from US$14 million in 2009 to US$20.6 million in 2010. RTI has produced over forty telenovelas for Telemundo and recorded incomes of over US$36.5 million. According to Samuel Duque, chief executive officer of Fox Telecolombia, his company increased its revenues three times, from $10 million to $30 million in four years, and the staff increased from 150 employees to about 600.[12]

These alliances work in three different ways: offering original and high-quality productions, such as *Escobar, El patrón del mal* (Caracol, 2012); making remakes of proven successes, such as *Pasión de gavilanes* (Telemundo RTI, 2003); or making adaptations of American TV hits such as *A corazón abierto* (adaptation of ABC's *Grey's Anatomy*).[13]

In 2013 new agreements took place between Televisa, Univision, and Caracol in order to deliver Colombian content in the United States and Mexico. The UniMás-Univision sister network will be able to broadcast, in prime time, a specified minimum of hours of TV series, telenovelas, and entertainment shows made by Caracol. Meanwhile, from January 1, 2013, Televisa will broadcast original TV shows of Caracol on public television channels and pay-TV chains in Mexico and Latin@ America.[14] On the other hand, the RCN television channel (a direct competitor of Caracol) has made an alliance with Fox TV to broadcast (on the MundoFox channel) several series, telenovelas, and news shows produced by RCN.

There has yet to be much of a reaction to these new alliances and distribution strategies. Neither the media nor academics have engaged in public debate about these changes. The lack of critical response could stem from the duopoly enjoyed by the two major Colombian channels, RCN and Caracol. Mexican media and other Latin American media announced these alliances before RCN or Caracol did.

To challenge the dominance of these private channels, small TV producers are developing their own strategy. Small producers in Colombia aren't limiting themselves to telenovelas or drama series, but are also creating children's TV shows and documentaries. Señal Colombia, a public Colombian channel, has produced children's TV shows that have been very popular among Colombians and elsewhere.[15] For example, the TV series *La lleva*, which is a mix between a reality show and a documentary, tells stories from the children's cultural points of view.

One kid visits another kid in a different country to discuss their different habits, food, weather, clothes, and other cultural aspects. *La lleva* already has four additional versions, in Argentina, Mexico, the Dominican Republic, and Ecuador. The first season was made in Colombia and limited to Colombia, where children traveled within different regions, but due to its success, the producers started a Latin American model where children try to define their own culture by telling stories about their way of life.[16]

On the other hand, regarding private TV production, other companies like Televideo,[17] Mauricio Vélez Producciones, Telecolombia,[18] LuloFilms,[19] and Laberinto Producciones[20] are working in the panregional documentary market producing popular TV series such as *Tabu* (Nat Geo Latin America) and several series about Colombian armed conflict that are broadcast on the Discovery Channel Latin America and Discovery Channel US Hispanic. That is the case for the documentary *Narcosubmarinos* (2011), produced by LuloFilms and aired on the Discovery Channel, which won the silver world medal as best news documentary and the Golden Aurora Awards.

Recently it has become clear that American TV companies seek Latin American local content. To improve the diversity of TV grids, channels are including more and more telenovelas, TV series, dramas, and documentaries that appeal to universal emotions at the same time that they offer popular cultural narratives. According to the Teleset producer Camila Misas, American TV companies that are interested in conquering the US Latino market must compete against Univision to bid on original content.[21] This desired content is one that is global, emotional, and different. And that's precisely where Colombia has begun to play an important role. Colombia offers a unique capacity for production of high-quality content that is wide-reaching and broad in its universal appeals to familiar sentiments and narratives.

In the American and Latin American market, Colombia is a new competitor growing quickly. Why is this happening? Why has Colombian content become attractive to the American market? Is it because Colombia is the best value in the TV industry or just because it offers lower costs in comparison to other countries? Could it be the Sofía Vergara effect? To answer these, we will build an argument based on three key factors: (1) the particular history of TV fiction production in

Colombia; (2) the creation of the telenovela model of narrative; and (3) the existence of an industry that produces high-quality content, great locations/people, and cheap prices.[22]

The Creation of Fictional TV in Colombia

Colombia celebrates a unique TV production style influenced by a fusion of classic literature, Latin American narratives and tropes (love stories where justice wins, family and religious values are reinforced, poor people are always good, rich people are always bad), Cuban and Mexican melodrama (love triangles, music, women heroines), and the national sense of humor. For instance, in the fiction of telenovelas, becoming successful doesn't have anything to do with money, employment, or education, but with love, morality, and popular values.

Colombia television broadcasting began on June 13, 1954, at 9 p.m. That day marked the first year of the government of General Gustavo Rojas Pinilla.[23] Contrary to what happened in other Latin American countries like Venezuela, Mexico, or Argentina, where television was developed primarily as a private, commercial industry, in Colombia cultural concerns dominated. The first transmissions sought to make television that was guided by "principles of good taste," which included music, theater, comedy, popular folklore, and education. Until 1995, Colombian TV was considered exclusively a cultural and educational vehicle. The state offered eight public channels construed solely as educational, and other channels that were called "cultural varieties," which included public opinion, film and cinema, religion, entertainment, and religious music. According to Professor Germán Rey, television broadcasting was seen as a vehicle to bring culture to the people, to save "lost souls."[24] Nonetheless, while television tried to accomplish this, regional habits and tastes, as well as people's desires and sense of humor, became evident.

In the first decade of television broadcasting (1953–1963), the state determined that in fiction, television needed to present drama of global significance (Albert Camus, Molière, Franz Kafka). Then, from the 1960s to the 1980s , the state decided to change the focus of TV content and established that national television needed to be inspired by Latin American literature and Colombian literature.[25] By the end of the 1980s, the Colombian industry had shaped a national model that combined classical heritage and its own regional and local stories. That's how Colombian telenovelas were born: as a combination of foreign and local tastes, pretensions to high culture, music, melodrama, and humor.

In 1995, private TV channels were created, and Caracol and RCN stopped being producers and became twenty-four-hour channels with total autonomy.[26] Many producers disappeared in that moment, while a new industry was born: a Colombian TV brand with a strong heritage of Cuban and Mexican melodrama, international literature, and its own reality (a mix of social neo-realism and Caribbean taste and humor).

The Colombian Telenovela Model of Narrative

In 2009, telenovelas were included in a temporary exhibition at the National Museum of Colombia. Telenovelas are popular, provocative, magical, and full of music. According to Jesús Martín-Barbero, *telenovelas* recognized the diversity and complexity of Colombian emotions and desires before politics or laws did.[27] For instance, the values of diversity and cultural and ethnic pluralism, which were recognized by the National Constitution of 1991, were already being explored by the telenovelas back in the 1980s. Telenovelas became a medium to express plurality and the the different ways of being Colombian, including the Colombian Caribbean ways of life (*Pero sigo siendo el rey* [1984] and *Escalona* [1991]); the Colombian coffee and mountain ways (*Quieta Margarita* [1988], *La casa de las dos palmas* [1990], and *Café, con aroma de mujer* [1994]); the culture of the Colombian tropical and Pacific region (*San tropel* [1986] and *Azúcar* [1989]); and the jungle and Amazonian culture (*La potra zaina* [1993]).

The telenovela forever changed the representation of Colombia in national television. According to Germán Rey, professor and former television critic, the key to its success lies in

> the selection of stories very close to the everyday. . . . The emergence of a regional experience of cultural expression, a manifestation of a heterogeneous country crossed by numerous cultures. . . . In addition, the melodrama retrieves the humor and irony, satire and self-confidence. . . . The soap opera of the '80s transformed the craft of storytelling, the use of

technical resources, and more than anything, it took the melodrama away from love stories and into culture-specific and regionally located stories.[28]

Telenovelas are conceived as a cultural vehicle in which the nation faces its diversity and enjoys self-recognition. For instance, we can learn about Colombian journeys from the countryside to the modern cities on *Café, con aroma de mujer*; city life and new beauty trends on *Yo soy Betty, la fea*; the representation of Colombian men's roles on *Pedro el escamoso, Juan joyita, Pobre Pablo, Martín el inútil, Muñoz vale por dos, Oscar el vecino,* and *El encantador*; and more recently, about the narco-style (narColombia) on *Sin tetas no hay paraíso, El cártel, El capo, Rosario Tijeras, Escobar, El patrón del mal, Los tres caínes,* and *La prepago*.[29]

Patricio Wills, CEO at RTI Production Company, based in Miami, the epicenter of the television industry in Latin@ America, explains that the Colombian strategy is "grounded in an important creativity, a different way of doing drama, the neutral accent[30] of the actors and relevant political stability in the country." Nonetheless, how is it that the Colombian brand works? What is it that makes it original, popular, and more and more valued in the market? The Colombian telenovela is a blend between local and popular culture and a local style of narrative. It remains true to the Mexican formula of melodrama (whose stories have the same pattern, a love triangle structure and fairy tale characters: the pure but valiant warrior princess, the witch/villain, the stepmother/family against the princess, the buffoon or best friend, and the Prince Charming/macho). While the Brazilian narrative dares to think about national values and its great dilemmas, and the Argentinian narrative tends to explore psychological matters or issues, Colombian telenovelas talk about urban/rural stories and center the stories on the woman warrior. Also, they introduce comedy as a narrative tool. Finally, the Colombian model of telenovela plays with contradictions and ambiguities: archaic and postmodern values, rural and globalized societies, Christian morality and new commercial values, good taste and narco-style, understood not only as a business related to drug traffic but as an aesthetic sense and morality linked to the Colombian culture and represented in music, television, language, architecture, and consumer goods. Narco, as a style, is flashy, flamboyant, and kitschy: a recognition of popular taste and morality. While intellectuals and high culture defined this style as bad taste, telenovelas are recognized as a medium through which popular classes can get a glimpse of modernist values. To summarize, Colombian telenovelas can be defined by these ten criteria:

1. The woman is not Cinderella: In Colombia's telenovela, women are warriors. The woman is not going to be saved by a man, so in order to succeed she'll need to struggle at work. In the end, she is the one who saves the man.
2. Men have no power: Men matter little; they are often the comedians or just auxiliaries of female power.
3. Classic genres are mixed: Telenovelas are melodramatic as well as funny, tragic, and suspenseful. Besides all that, they are fun and daring.
4. Multiple stories are told: The real story develops around the secondary characters, their narrative universes, and their ways of speaking and being in the world.
5. It has a musical component: Colombian telenovelas are always very musical, mainly using Caribbean and popular rhythms; the music marks the timing and rhythm of the stories.
6. It captures popular aesthetics: It shows urban innovations and rural culture; it talks about sexuality while maintaining traditional and religious values.
7. It dares to explore controversial issues: All topics are examined: sex, drugs, easy money, beauty, corruption.
8. It has an ambiguous ethics: Anything is acceptable in order to climb the social ladder. The idea is "do whatever it takes to earn money," no matter how.
9. Fernando Gaitán is known worldwide as the creator of *Yo soy Betty, la fea* and *Café, con aroma de mujer*, extremely successful telenovelas.
10. It is a growing industry: Due to talent, creativity, innovation, and low production costs, telenovelas have become Colombia's most popular cultural product.

In recent years, the Colombian TV market has found a new and successful way to conquer Latin@ TV media: with narco-series that feature easy money, women who look like Pamela Anderson, and the endorsement of killing as a valid means of social advancement.[31] These narratives take narco-values as a guide: money as the goal of life, fun as the mood of life, and the cocaine business as the only way to achieve power and social visibility. Narco-fictions are usually well produced, are very entertaining, and achieve very high ratings. It seems like the industry has left behind the traditional love stories (drama) to talk about the actual Colombian way of life (tragedy); and, right now, they are focused on new matters such as desires for economic and social advancement (epic), and the existence of illegal activities like drug dealing ("tragimedy").[32]

However, the production/distribution of narco-series has drawn criticism and sparked many public debates about the impact of selling these fictions worldwide and the possible damage they are inflicting on the country's image. "Tragimedy" has become the best-selling product of Colombian television. The question is whether this new genre is authentic to Colombian culture and identity, or exploits, sensationalizes, and debases the everyday lives of Colombians.

Colombian TV Industry: High Quality and Low Prices

According to Amelia Andrade, a former producer at Fox Telecolombia, Bogota is nowadays the best value for TV production.[33] It is cheaper to bring an entire team of directors and actors to Colombia than to film a TV series in the United States or any other country in Latin@ America. A studio based in Hollywood costs at least US$500,000 per episode, in Brazil US$200,000, in Mexico US$150,000 and in Colombia US$50,000. That is the case for the Fox drama series *Mental*, each episode of which cost between US$50,000 and $70,000 including the special effects needed in the series.[34]

At the same time, the international market has laid eyes on Colombia for the quality and low costs of television production and postproduction. Colombian people are nice to work with, and the country offers an immense diversity of locations. For all these reasons, people in the industry talk about the BoBoom, Collywood, or Bogollywood, as Bogota has become a very attractive location to film TV series for the Latin@ market and the American market.

At the beginning of 2007, Fox Telecolombia started filming series for the Latin@ version of the Fox Channel. *Tiempo final*, which was the first series filmed entirely in Bogota, experienced great success and earned as high a rating as other TV series like *24* or *Nip/Tuck* that were produced entirely in Hollywood. A total of fifty-four one-hour episodes were filmed and aired in three seasons between 2007 and 2009.

In 2008, Fox Telecolombia decided to film the TV drama *Mental* entirely in Bogota. It became the first original TV production, in English, filmed in Latin America and aired worldwide. For the first time, the production team as well as the actors moved from the United States to Colombia to film thirteen one-hour episodes, which were aired on Fox International Channels in the United States, Latin America, Europe, and Asia. For this project, a new 1,500-square-meter studio (a US$9 million investment) was built near Fox Telecolombia offices to re-create the facilities of a psychiatric hospital, where much of the action took place.[35]

In 2010, Sony Pictures Television, in alliance with the Colombian producer Teleset, announced that the second season of the acclaimed teen television series *Isa TK+* would be filmed in Bogota, rather than in Venezuela, where the first season was filmed. A total of 120 episodes were filmed at indoor studios in Bogota and broadcast by the Nickelodeon channel in Latin America. It enjoyed resounding success, and in 2010 earned Meus Nick Awards in Brazil and Kids' Choice Awards in Mexico.[36]

In 2011, a new comedy series called *Lynch* was produced in Bogota in an alliance between Fox Telecolombia and Moviecity.[37] It was filmed between Buenos Aires and Bogota and performed by actors from different countries, including Chile, Peru, Mexico, Colombia, and Argentina. It was aired in Moviecity and Cinecanal channels.

The following factors have helped Bogota transform into Bogollywood:

1. Low prices: Filming a TV episode in Hollywood costs US$500,000; filming it in Bogota costs US$50,000. Colombia has become the best value for Latin@ TV production as it maintains the quality of the series produced in California, at a much lower price.

2. Locations: According to Samuel Duque, CEO at Fox Telecolombia, the country offers a great deal regarding locations, not only because you can find varied and beautiful landscapes (mountains, beaches, jungles, and urban settings), but also because Colombian production companies

have over twenty years of experience shooting in real/outdoor locations (which is not the case in Venezuela and Mexico, where only 10 percent of the shooting is done outdoors; the other 90 percent is in studios).[38]

3. Enterprise alliances: The merger and alliances between international TV chains and local production companies have strengthened the TV industry in a very important way. Colombian TV series, documentaries, and telenovelas are now distributed worldwide in high-audience channels such as Fox, Discovery, Moviecity, and Nickelodeon. Those alliances have also made possible the creation of indoor studios with the most up-to-date audiovisual technology.

4. Worldwide fame: Colombia is the world's third-largest exporter of telenovelas in the world. Since the 1990s it has found great success with telenovelas like *Café, con aroma de mujer* and *Yo soy Betty, la fea* that were sold to dozens of TV channels worldwide. *Yo soy Betty, la fea* (1999–2001) had 338 episodes, which were sold to over a hundred countries at prices between US$1,200 and US$8,000. It was translated into fifteen languages, and more than twenty-two script adaptations were made worldwide. The premiere of the American version, *Ugly Betty*, was seen by over 18 million Americans, and the Chinese adaptation, *De Wudi*, was seen by 73 million people.[39]

5. Talented and kindly people: The Colombian TV industry is highly regarded for its quality. It's recognized for its creativity and talent (good actors, scripts, and directors). Also, Colombians have developed a reputation as "friendly and easygoing people" to work with in the audiovisual area, perhaps because of their greater willingness to accommodate in order to compete and join in all types of new productions. However, we should also bear in mind that perhaps "cheaper labor" is construed as "friendly" and "kind," and that perhaps they are more accommodating because they're more eager to join in this new industry.

6. A unique style: As mentioned before, Colombia has built a particular model of telenovelas that has proven to be successful even though it departs from the traditional models that have proven to be commercially successful in Mexican and Brazilian soap operas.

This is why Colombia has become very attractive for the Latin American and US TV market. Regarding production and postproduction, Colombia is the continent's cheapest country. In addition, it has a very long tradition of making high-quality TV series, which gives it an advantage in the competition with Brazil and Mexico.

Colombian television fictions are very well made and well told, with neo-realism in the language, characters, and actions, and with humor, strong performances, and a great deal of music. The stories are authentic, and the locations and landscapes are always outstanding. Regarding quality, there are well-trained personnel, and there are no TV unions, as there are in Argentina, that can delay or complicate the TV production process. In addition, Colombia is only a three-hour flight from Miami, and it is near other countries in Central and South America. Also, Colombians seem to have an accent that can be easily understood in other countries.

For these reasons the Colombian TV industry is at its peak. It is an exciting new market, with a great deal of money being invested in studios, postproduction, and so forth. The various alliances between TV companies are able to take advantage of the country's landscape, technical strengths, cheap prices, and people who are willing to work long hours. However, experts agree that if the industry is to keep growing, new regulation regarding TV content production must be established. It is a paradox that Colombian film production has to rely on a law and a special budget to promote local productions, even though Colombian films have very poor audiences and recognition, and the industry's impact on the economy remains undocumented and unrecognized. In contrast, while TV production is very important for the international market in terms of the country's economy and cultural image, the industry hasn't been regulated yet, and doesn't get any promotion by the government. Also, in order to protect national production, the industry needs a new "must-carry" regulation that obliges pay-TV cable channels to broadcast a minimum of local content (as they have done in Brazil) and to promote unions to protect TV workers.

NOTES

1. We prefer to use the Spanish term *telenovelas* instead of the English translation, "soap opera," because we consider that they are different industrial television products. Telenovelas are stories with a definite end (to be reached within 80 to 120 episodes); they mix genres such as melodrama, comedy, tragedy, suspense,

and even reality; they are usually love stories with happy endings and told from the women's perspective. They also dignify premodern values such as love, justice, and family; they normally take into account the context of each country: for instance, in Colombia, the telenovelas tell stories about the violence, the cultural diversity, and the local music, while in Brazil the stories are about what it means to be Brazilian.

2. Martín-Barbero 1998.

3. Invest in Bogota is a nonprofit entity created in 2006 by Bogota's Capital District and its Chamber of Commerce to promote and strengthen sustainable economic development and the promotion of investment and commercial trade. See http:www.investinBogota.org.

4. Telecolombia was a national TV production company that was bought in 2007 by Fox International Channels. Since then it has made several TV series, such as *Mental, Kdabra, Lynch, El capo, The Walking Dead, Tiempo final,* and *La mariposa.* Additional information can be found at its website: http://www.foxtelecolombiainternational.com.

5. In 2005 Sony Pictures Television acquired a 50 percent stake in Teleset, a Colombian TV company, in order to expand its own production activities across the Latin@ market. It has made the following TV series: *Popland, Niñas mal, Isa TK+, Rosario Tijeras,* and *La prepago.*

6. Vista Producciones remains a Colombian company that has a distribution alliance with Disney Media Network Latin America. It has produced international TV remakes and adaptations such as *A corazón abierto (Grey's Anatomy), Amas de casa desesperadas (Desperate Housewives), Mujeres asesinas* (an original Argentinian production), and *¿Dónde está Elisa?*; at this moment it's doing the Latino version of *Brothers and Sisters.* See http://www.vista.com.co/producciones.

7. Telemundo, owned by NBC, established a coproduction agreement with the Colombian TV Company RTI from 2003 to 2009, and the two companies have done some projects together since 2009 as well. In 2012 RTI established an alliance with Televisa. They have produced the following TV series: *Pasión de gavilanes, El zorro, El clon,* and *La reina del sur.*

8. Be-TV is a Colombian TV production company well known for the TV series *El cártel de los sapos, Los Escobar, Look at Me,* and *Welcome y adiós.*

9. "El Hollywood criollo," *Dinero,* http://m.dinero.com/negocios/articulo/el-hollywood-criollo/135166 (accessed 5 February 2013).

10. Proexport, "Invierta en Colombia," 2012, http://bit.ly/YdXsM5.

11. OECD, "Colombia: Economic Assessment," September 2010, 5, http://bit.ly/WZemk2.

12. "El Hollywood criollo."

13. *A corazón abierto* (Vista-Disney, 2011) earned the highest TV rating in 2011. It was sold to other countries in Latin America, including Mexico, which bought the scripts to do a local adaptation.

14. "Televisa, Univision y Caracol se alían," *CNN Expansion*, 4 December 2012, http://www.cnnexpansion.com/negocios/2012/12/04/televisa-univision-y-caracol-se-alian (accessed 5 February 2013).

15. Señal Colombia's children's TV series, such as *El show de Perico, Migrópolis, Ooommm mmmooo, La lleva,* and *Guillermina y Candelario,* have been nominated for and won several times best children's TV show in the India Catalina National TV Awards.

16. Other examples are *Migrópolis,* which talks about migration from the children's point of view; *Ooommm mmmooo,* which is a yoga program aimed specifically at young ones; and *El profesor super O,* which features a superhero who protects and defends the Spanish language.

17. Since 2000, Televideo has produced fifty-six documentaries for TV channels such as Discovery Channel, Nat Geo, Infinito, Sun Channel, and Canal Caracol. See http://www.televideo.com.co.

18. Fox Telecolombia has produced two seasons of the TV series *Tabu: Latino America* (Nat Geo).

19. LuloFilms has made several documentaries about recent national events related to the armed conflict, such as *Tirofijo está muerto* (Nat Geo, 2010), *El rescate perfecto* (Discovery Channel, 2009), *Los hermanos Castaño* (Discovery Channel, 2011), *Operación sodoma: La caída del Mono Jojoy* (Discovery Channel, 2011), and *Narcosubmarinos* (Discovery Channel, 2010).

20. In 2011, Laberinto produced the TV series *Los caballeros las prefieren brutas* (Sony Entertainment Television Channel) and two documentaries about Pablo Escobar.

21. Camila Misas, interview, 10 February 2013.

22. To write this article, the authors conducted interviews with people from Laberinto Producciones, Fox Telecolombia, and Teleset-Sony. They also did extensive media research about TV production in Colombia and developments in the TV market in recent years. They have also participated in researching television projects for the last twenty years; Rincón, as a television critic, has been following the television scene for the last seventeen years.

23. General Gustavo Rojas Pinilla was the only military dictator of Colombia in the twentieth century. His rise to power was promoted by the upper class, politicians, and the media (who later overthrew him). He ruled between 1953 and 1957, a period recognized as a soft dictatorship.

24. Rey 1994.

25. Many Colombian works of literature have been adapted for the screen: *El buen salvaje* (1973), by Eduardo Caballero Calderón; *La María* (1972), by Jorge Isaacs; *La mala hora* (1975) and *Tiempo de morir* (1984), by the Nobel winner Gabriel García Márquez. Other Latin American literature has been produced as well: *La tregua* (1980) and *Gracias por el fuego* (1982), by Mario Benedetti; *La tía Julia y el escribidor,* by the Nobel winner Mario Vargas Llosa; and *Los premios,* by Julio Cortázar.

26. Caracol and RCN are television networks belonging to one of Colombia's three richest families (Santodomingo and Ardila-Lulle); the other family in 2012 bought *El Tiempo* newspaper and a local private network called City TV.

27. Martín-Barbero 1998.

28. Rey 1994, 436–37.

29. See also a previous article about narco-TV: Omar Rincón, "NarcoTv o lo narco como marca actual de la telenovela colombiana," *Quimera* 315 (February 2010): 40–45.

30. In comparison with accents from other countries like Mexico or Argentina, the Colombian Spanish accent is believed to be easily understood everywhere, a soft way of speaking that could be adapted easily to a global public. However, it is important to mention that a typical feature of Colombian telenovelas is colloquial language and regional slang, a trait that speaks to the extent to which the so-called generic nature of "Colombian Spanish" is ultimately an ideological construction rather than a fact.

31. The most popular narco-series made in Colombia in the past few years are *Pasión de gavilanes* (Julio Jiménez, 2003), *La viuda de la mafia* (Nubia Barreto and Paula Peña, 2004), *Sin tetas no hay paraíso* (Gustavo Bolívar, 2006), *Soñar no cuesta nada* (Jorg Hiller, 2007), *Los protegidos* (Juana Uribe, 2008), *El cártel* (Andrés López, 2008), *El capo* (Gustavo Bolívar, 2009), *Las muñecas de la mafia* (Be-TV, 2009), *Pandillas, guerra y paz 2* (Gustavo Bolívar, 2009), *Rosario Tijeras* (Carlos Duplat, 2010), *El cártel 2* (Jorg Hiller, 2010), *El capo I* and *II* (Gustavo Bolívar, 2009 and 2012), *La bruja* (Alberto Quiroga, 2011), *La mariposa* (Alberto González and Augusto Ramírez, 2012), *La ruta blanca* (Cristina Palacios, 2012), *Escobar, El patrón del mal* (Uribe y Cano, 2012), *La prepago* (Carlos Duplat and Luz Mariela Santofimio, 2012), *Los tres caínes* (Gustavo Bolívar, 2013).

32. Narco-TV series present a multiplicity of styles and perspectives: melodrama (*Pasión de gavilanes* and *Pandillas, guerra y paz 2*), women's perspectives (*Sin tetas no hay paraíso, Las muñecas de la mafia*, and *Rosario Tijeras*), men's perspectives (*Soñar no cuesta nada, El cártel*, and *El capo*), and social criticism (*La viuda de la mafia* and *Los protegidos*).

33. Amelia Andrade, interview, Bogota, 15 January 2013.

34. "*Mental*: Television hecha en Colombia," *El Espectador*, 3 June 2012, http://m. elespectador.com/entretenimiento/arteygente/medios/articulo143814-mental-television-hecha-colombia (accessed 20 January 2013).

35. "Llega a Colombia la serie *Mental*," *Cromos*, 1 June 2009, http://www.cromos. com.co/entretenimiento/farandula/articulo-llega-a-colombia-la-serie-mental (accessed 5 February 2013).

36. "*Isa TKM* grabará su segunda temporada en Colombia," Estereofonica.com, 10 June 2009, http://www.estereofonica.com/isa-tkm-grabara-su-segunda-temporada-en-colombia/ (accessed 5 February 2013).

37. The script, the production, and postproduction were done in Colombia; the showrunner was an Argentinian, Fernando Altschul; and it was aired on Moviecity and Cinecanal channels in Latin@ America.

38. "Colombia es el epicentro de la TV en América Latina," *El Colombiano*, http://www.elcolombiano.com/BancoConocimiento/O/olac_colombiaepicentrodela TVenamericaLatin@a_13082007/olac_colombiaepicentrodelaTVenamericaLati n@a_13082007.asp (accessed 5 February 2013).

39. Posada 2011, 119–34.

REFERENCES

Martín-Barbero, Jesús (1998). "Un nuevo mapa: Debate al periodismo cultural en Colombia." *Número* (Bogota), no. 19, December.

Martín-Barbero, Jesús, and Sonia Muñoz, coordinators (1992). *Televisión y melodrama.* Bogota: Tercer Mundo.

Ministerio de Cultura (2000). "Dossier Telenovela." *Revista Gaceta #47*, Bogota.

Monsiváis, Carlos (1999). *Del rancho al internet.* México: Biblioteca del Issste.

"Pensar la ficción televisiva." (2005). Conference, Universidad Javeriana, Bogota, 24 February. http://www.javeriana.edu.co/Facultades/comunicacion_lenguaje/ficcion_tv/memorias.htm.

Posada, Simon (2011). "Betty la fea." In *Dios es Colombiano*. Bogota: Editorial Planeta.

Rey, Germán (1994). "Ese inmenso salón de espejos: La telenovela colombiana en los 80 y 90." In *Historia de una travesía*. Bogota: Inravisión.

Vasallo de Lopes, Immacolata, and Guillermo Orozco (2012). *Transnationalization of Television Fiction in Iberoamerican Countries* (Obitel Yearbook, 2012). Río de Janeiro: Globo Universidade.

9

The Role of Media Policy in Shaping
the US Latino Radio Industry

MARI CASTAÑEDA

The history and development of the Latino corporate radio industry in the United States have been profoundly impacted by US media policies that have supported commercialism and consolidation under the guise of diversity, localism, and competition. Since its establishment as the federal regulatory agency in charge of overseeing the structural management of communications in the United States, the Federal Communications Commission (FCC) has had the responsibility of producing media policies that promote the "public interest, convenience and necessity" of the communications infrastructure (US FCC 2012). The promotion of the public interest has been especially important since it has largely been interpreted as facilitating "diversity, localism and competition" (US FCC 2012), meaning that the public (and democracy overall) is best served when the communications infrastructure fosters and reflects, for instance, diverse content, local outlets, and competitive markets. These bedrock ideals of media policy have shaped the development, expansion, and composition of Latino commercial radio in the United States, but in today's deregulated media environment dominated by corporate giants, the sector has been used to achieve these goals within the general radio market and not within the Latino radio industry itself. This is very problematic, given that Latino radio has a higher listenership than the general radio market, and more Latinos rely on radio for news, information, and entertainment (Castañeda 2008).

The current neoliberal growth of the corporate US Latino media industry, which emphasizes market rather than community interests, provides an excellent context in which to reexamine the historical record in order to better understand the complicated role of the state in the diversification of broadcasting as well as Latino radio's development as a commercial, for-profit system. Although Latino public radio also exists in the United States, the emphasis in this chapter will be the commercial sector, since it reaches the majority of Latino audiences and is a premier site for examining the tensions between Latino media inclusion and neoliberalism. Consequently, revisiting the history of Latino commercial radio is important for both mapping out a media landscape that is often taken for granted and for demonstrating the creation of media property within communication industries, which does not occur by chance but through policy decisions, economic imperatives, and cultural practices. In this regard, media policy has been an important factor in the contemporary reorganization of Latino radio within the broader US commercial, advertiser-supported media system (Castañeda 2008).

One can explain this reorganization by applying a transcultural political economy framework to the analysis of how media policy shapes US Latino radio. The application of such a framework is appropriate because it "places communication within broader political economic and cultural processes and treats communication research as an inherently integrative exercise that cuts across disciplinary, [global, and historical] lines" (Chakravartty and Zhao 2008, 10). By intersecting the processes of transculturation with political economy, we may demonstrate how encounters between different cultural spheres do not always occur on level playing fields (for instance, federal media policy and local Latino media), and thus it is important to recognize how racial, ethnic, gender, sexuality, citizenship, and linguistic differences "shape political struggles over globalized information and cultural flows" (Chakravartty and Zhao 2008). The historical record of US media and its related public policies demonstrates that the development and expansion of communication institutions and practices are not only the result of political (state) and economic (capital) actions, but also transnational and transcultural imperatives that have deeply influenced those transactions. Radio has thus embodied not only a new era of modernity, but also a national vision in which whiteness as well as the social, political, and economic marginalization of minorities has been reinforced.

Additionally, the specificity of Latino commercial radio requires that the present study take into account Latino and Chicana media studies scholarship in order to specify the transcultural aspects of the political economic analysis, such as the ethno-linguistic racialization of Latino cultural consumers as well as the industry (Rodríguez 1999; Dávila 2001; Rivero 2005). Ultimately this chapter argues that despite attempts by Latino media makers to take seriously the communications bedrock principle of serving the public interest, and despite social justice efforts to hold media more accountable to communities of color, the corporate, liberal, racialized, and gendered orientation of the US media (policy) system has made it very difficult for Latinos (and people of color overall) to make significant headway in the areas of media ownership, media employment, and media programming. Although Latino commercial radio and Spanish-language media more broadly have historically represented potential spaces for community engagement, the pressure imposed by media policy makers' adherence to digital capitalism, including corporate consolidations and commercialized diversity, has created a tense media landscape that is fraught with opportunities, contradictions, and difficulties (see also the chapter by Dolores Inés Casillas in this volume). In an effort to explain the development, expansion, and composition of Latino commercial radio and the role that media policy has played in bolstering the sector, the chapter will first review the historical foundations of Latino radio. It will then examine the state of the industry in light of changing media policies and regulation through the inclusion of radio producer interviews, and will conclude with a discussion of Latino media policy activism as examples of important efforts to broaden and democratize communication resources in the digital era.

Early Foundations of Ethnic Radio Programming

The United States has a long history of ethnic radio programming that dates back before the passage of the 1934 Communications Act. As early as the 1920s, local radio stations in urban metropolitan areas hosted an array of Polish, German, and Italian programs that were often aired as hour-long programming blocks and directed at non–English-speaking immigrant communities (Matsaganis, Katz, and Ball-Rokeach 2011). Radio was still under development, and thus radio owners welcomed white ethnic producers to fill airtime with programming that would bring listeners to their radio dial. Black radio producers also found some radio owners to be amenable to their purchase of programming blocks. In New York City, the Harlem Broadcasting Corporation brokered time with WRNY in order to feature black performers, music, and storytelling (Browne 2005), and in Los Angeles, the Tejano music performer Pedro González aired his Spanish-language radio show *Los madrugadores* on KELW during the early-morning "dead airtime" hours of 4:00 to 6:00 a.m. (Rodríguez 1999; Albarran and Hutton 2009).

Indeed, the historical presence of minority voices on the airwaves (albeit limited) was an incredible feat given that radio was "owned, operated by and programmed for the white majority, and the few mainstream shows that featured ethnic performers and lifestyles confined portrayals to servants, entertainers, or comic figures" (Browne 2005, 20). Consequently, the practice of brokered programming created a space for alternative programming in which racial and linguistic minority representation, music, and public affairs were not confined to white Anglo-Saxon interpretations of content but organized by minority radio producers themselves. The for-profit orientation of broadcast radio certainly shaped station owners' openness to block programming, since it was inexpensive and convenient, although the low rate of advertising earnings consistently threatened the sustainability of non-mainstream programming, thereby affecting the accessibility of information resources by racial and linguistic minority communities. The FCC's historical record confirms that "in many cases, the time broker indirectly subsidize[d] the specialized programming by accepting economic compensation below that usually necessary to produce a comparable commercial program" (US FCC 1980). It was quite common for white Anglo-Saxon station owners to sell programming slots to Latino radio brokers who would then broadcast (largely Spanish-language) music and information in addition to advertising. Latino commercial radio programming, however, was often relegated to the late hours of the day or throughout the middle of the night, when English-speaking audiences were not tuning to the radio dial in profitable numbers. Despite the success of ethnic-brokered programming, by the mid-1930s a media policy emerged that emphasized the "ideological consolidation of the status quo" and a "favoritism toward big commercial networks . . . [that] led to the curtailing of many innovative, independent experiments in radio programming by racial minorities that had flowered during the early days of radio" (McChesney 1993, 226; González and Torres 2011, 207).

For instance, soon after the Communications Act of 1934 was approved by Congress, the newly instituted FCC began investigating the legitimacy of brokered programming practices and the level of responsibility broadcast licensees carried in the airing of questionable block programs, which negatively impacted foreign-language and ethnic radio programming (US FCC 1980). McChesney (1993) attests that labor activists and radical political radio producers were also under fire once the new legislation solidified the commercial, advertiser-supported broadcast system as best serving the public interest. Barbara Savage (1999) also notes that the "highly capitalized white-controlled national media of film and radio" left very few opportunities for African Americans and Latinos to influence the popular images of ethnic communities at a moment when the federal government was conflicted about minorities in the United States, and "radio broadcasting remained an inaccessible political medium for the expression of dissident views, especially on race" (44). Therefore, despite the perceived notion that liberal democratic principles of free speech and the marketplace of ideas always guide media regulation, the early history of ethnic programming demonstrates that US media policy aimed to protect the established political and racialized status quo by utilizing policies (such as licensing rules and seditious laws) to regulate communications content and ownership.

Ironically, full-power radio stations from Mexico City were also crossing the ether's transnational boundary, along with radio stations located on the US-Mexico border, which in some cases were established by white Anglo-Saxon broadcasters seeking to bypass overly restrictive US regulators by utilizing their Mexican-granted radio frequencies to establish stations and sell their wares (Fowler and Crawford 2002).

Since the airwaves were not restricted by geopolitical boundaries, the radio programming from Mexico-based radio stations reached Spanish-speaking listeners located in Texas, California, and Arizona, particularly in their border regions. Consequently, the creation of the Latino commercial radio infrastructure as we know it today began through this transnational and transcultural juncture. In the United States, the development of a corporate-driven radio infrastructure provided the framework through which Latino commercial radio programming could become available. In Mexico and Puerto Rico, and particularly in Cuba, the genres of Spanish-language radio programming were being developed, and as such, were later transplanted to the US context, along with each country's musical genres. These two continental processes, along with the debates about minority access to media, were thus central to the creation of the racialized broadcast infrastructure in the United States. Not only were there implications for the cultural production of mass media, but racial inequality was also experienced across the educational, political, social, and economic spectrums, an inequality that was also reinforced by media themselves. Consequently, African American and Latino social movements in the 1930s and 1940s created fissures in the oppressive system of racial discrimination and segregation in the postwar era. This was a response to the fact that as radio grew, the diversity from the early days of radio lessened and the racism in US-produced programming became more widespread. It is in this historical context that the first full-time Latino commercial radio station emerged.

A Case Study of the First Latino Commercial Radio Station

The year 1946 marked the moment in which the first US Latino commercial, full-time radio station became officially licensed and owned by a Latino/Mexican American: KCOR-AM 1350 in San Antonio, Texas, which is still on the air today. The station's emergence occurred during the decade-long battle, particularly by African Americans, to challenge mainstream radio's hold on the linguistic, cultural, and racial imagination of the American public in the 1930s and 1940s. Not only were African Americans unable to purchases radio stations (although they were US citizens, as required by federal law), but the content on mainstream radio delegitimized black culture. Additionally, the new technology of television was emerging and thus more AM (and FM) radio stations were being established in order to ensure that radio broadcasting would not die in the new era of communication technologies. US media policy was aiming for a broader structural approach, in an effort to preserve radio competition, rather than promote ownership diversity, as it would later do in the post–civil rights Blue Book era, when the FCC was forced by the judicial system to address the inequities in radio. González and Torres (2011) note that it was not until after World War II that narrow windows of opportunity materialized for African Americans, Latinos, and First Nation people to become radio station owners in the United States, despite their finding that John Rodríguez was the first Latino granted a license, in 1922, for WCAR-AM 530 in San Antonio, Texas. Unfortunately, virtually nothing is known about Rodríguez or his station's programming, but this important finding confirms that Latinos have been involved with US broadcasting from its earliest days. KCOR-AM's establishment demonstrates that its continuous broadcast of Latino commercial programming is what marks the station as distinctive in US Latino radio history.

The historical record demonstrates that Raúl Cortez filed an application with the FCC for a new 1,000-watt radio station in San Antonio, Texas, with the call letters KCOR-AM in 1944, two years before it was officially granted a license. This is significant not only because it was the first radio station offering full-time Latino commercial programming, especially during the daytime, but also because Cortez was only the second Latino to ever be granted a federal radio license, especially at a moment when segregation and discrimination against minorities were widespread. Yet there seems to be some indication that the FCC viewed KCOR's application as a test case for challenging the established radio owners and addressing the concerns of minority populations regarding the dearth of ethnic programming. Thus, it was a confluence of other factors that also created the necessary conditions for KCOR-AM to emerge. For instance, AM radio was also being expanded at the time, given the growing challenges from emerging technologies, particularly FM radio and television. Thus, a construction permit for the new radio station was granted a year later, but two weeks after the approval, Austin Broadcasting Company petitioned the FCC to either rescind the construction permit or force Cortez to move his frequency to the 1350 kilocycles location on the AM radio dial rather than staying at the 1300 location as originally requested. According to the FCC's historical records, Cortez "voluntarily" agreed to the new frequency and as a result, the commission dismissed ABC's petition. However, this move 50 kilocycles down the radio dial was significant because access to the 1350 frequency on the radio dial was sometimes shoddy.

Nevertheless, a year later, in a 1946 issue of *Radio Annual*, there was a quarter-inch advertisement for KCOR-AM with the tagline that it was "San Antonio's *only* Spanish *radio station*" (emphasis in the original). It further noted,

> National manufacturers can cash-in on the tremendous buying power of the Spanish-speaking population in San Antonio and trade territory. KCOR features programs directed at this great listening audience . . . broadcast both in English and Spanish. Rate card on request. Calcasieu Building, San Antonio, Texas. (599)

As America Rodríguez (1999) notes, "advertisers had begun to recognize the potential profitability of this audience," and by the mid-1940s in certain regional areas, Latinos were in fact becoming imagined as viable and valuable consumers (30). KCOR's commercial strategy—offering full-time Latino commercial programming to Latino listeners—was different from that of the other San Antonio radio stations. The other radio stations noted on the same page of the 1946 *Radio Annual* had already been on the air for two decades: KABC was established in 1926, KONO in 1927, and KMAC in 1930. Thus, the announcement became an attempt to differentiate KCOR from the other stations, both as a bilingual station and as the only one with four times the power, at 1,000 watts.

Revisiting the early historical record of KCOR-AM is important because it demonstrates how the structural contours of Latino radio were imagined and organized from the very beginning. For instance, a Latino was initially the FCC license holder and owner of KCOR, but in less than a decade, the radio station was sold to a corporation, and Raúl Cortez no longer continued as its proprietor. Second, KCOR was marketed to advertisers as one of the first commercially based Latino commercial radio stations, and its listeners were treated as a viable consumer group that advertisers would be interested in targeting, especially given the success of other brokered programs. Third, the station's Latino commercial programming was local as well as transnational, through its reliance on programming from Mexican radio networks such as Radio Gemas in Mexico City. Thus, KCOR became a Spanish-language representation of commercial radio modernity in North America as well as an embodiment of the FCC's goals toward "diversity, localism and competition" within the US media landscape (US FCC 2012). Yet despite KCOR's success and the establishment of other local stations, over the years, the growth of the Latino commercial radio industry failed to match the growing demographic percentages of Spanish-speaking populations. For instance, in 1998 there were only 533 Latino commercial radio stations, compared to 10,000 stations of mainstream radio (Arbitron 2003). This meant that fifty years after the establishment of the first full-time Latino commercial radio station in the United States, the sector constituted only .05 percent of all radio stations, although Latinos constituted 11.4 percent of the US population, or 30.8 million people (US Census 2012). Ironically, the media deregulation policies enacted by the FCC have increased the number of Latino commercial radio stations since 2000, but the growth remains undersized compared to the Latino population's growth (US Census 2012). Additionally, the expansion of Latino commercial radio has not significantly expanded the programming content available to Latino listeners, nor has it met their information needs, despite claims by the two largest owners of Spanish-language radio stations, Univision Radio and Entravision Communications. The following section will examine this contradiction in the contemporary Latino radio context and the implications for Latino media access, especially since radio continues to operate as the dominant venue for news and information.

Latino Commercial Radio in the United States Today

Since the passage of the Telecommunications Act of 1996, the US Latino commercial radio industry has experienced expansion into new markets while simultaneously experiencing a deepening of market-led consolidation, consequently placing limitations on the prospects for a civil rights–based diversity in programming and ownership. At several FCC diversity hearings in the past two years, community members have been vociferous about the lack of diverse management in mainstream and ethnic media outlets, and the impact such control and operations have on the production of broadcast content to serve minority populations (US FCC 2010). While Latino radio may in theory continue to fulfill the FCC's bedrock goals of diversity, localism, and competition, it is doing so in relationship to the broader radio market, not within the Latino radio sector itself, which is the direct result of political and economic actions. What is at stake in this new neoliberal era of media policy making is the slow dismantling of a broadcast communications infrastructure that represents and fosters local communities. The corporate liberalism of US broadcasting has regularly placed limits on the promise of Latino radio, and turned a blind eye to treatment of the sector as a second-class and unequal participant in the US media landscape despite the profitable growth of the industry.

For instance, Clear Channel Communications, the largest owner of radio stations in the United States, is consistently criticized for broadcasting more nationally syndicated programming rather than local content (US FCC 2012). This is especially problematic for Latino radio since the sector is much smaller than the mainstream radio market, which is why the recently announced partnership between Clear Channel and Univision Radio raises serious concerns for programming diversity, since the range of information and cultural content that reaches those listeners will be dreadfully compromised. Clear Channel will thus broadcast nationally syndicated content from Univision Radio rather than make efforts to produce regional content that better serves local communities, and Univision Radio will be beholden to a media corporation that is considered one of the staunchest anti-union and right-leaning in the country. This can potentially impact (or completely disallow) on-air critical discussions of immigration policy, labor and wage conditions, and Latino political exclusion. The preservation of wide-ranging community expression and the access to information that is meaningful for listeners, such as KCOR's broadcast of content from Mexico for its largely Mexican listeners, creates the potential for a social justice approach to media resources despite the commercial environment (Castañeda 2008). The corporate partnership between Clear Channel and Univision Radio limits this possibility within a Latino commercial radio industry that boasts less than one thousand station outlets, which is minuscule compared to mainstream radio's fourteen thousand stations. Additionally, Clear Channel's practice of dismantling local programming has in some cases created dire informational consequences for local communities (Klinenberg 2007). Therefore, the struggle over democratic access to the airwaves and media policy's role in this process far from over, especially in today's communications landscape, where the implications extend beyond broadcasting and include the digital sphere as well.

In the summer of 2011, the FCC released an important report titled *The Information Needs of Communities: The Changing Media Landscape in a Broadband Age*, developed by Steven Waldman and his working group. They argued that the information needs of communities of color were not being met, and media entities (including those serving African Americans and Latinos) were not covering or addressing the day-to-day issues that are affecting those populations (252). In a societal moment where information is critical for economic development, educational attainment, public safety, and political as well as cultural representation, the report notes that communities of color, especially those with lower financial resources, risk the possibility of falling further behind in all the indicators for wider social inclusion. Ultimately, the report argues, "democracy requires and citizens deserve a healthy flow of useful information and a news and information system that holds powerful institutions accountable" (US FCC 2011, 30).

Making changes in ownership rules was one area of media policy that was viewed as vital for creating a context in which information and cultural resources could be provided to local communities. The report referred to the 1960s Kerner Commission and its recommendation that "greater minority ownership of media . . . would allow for more balanced depictions of [minorities] and create entrepreneurial and employment opportunities for minorities" (US FCC 2011, 248). Yet in today's radio landscape, only 20 percent of Latino-owned radio stations consistently reach Latino listeners, and the number of Latino radio owners has declined drastically through media policy actions such as the deregulation of ownership rules that have decimated minority access to the airwaves (US FCC 2012). For Latino commercial radio, however, the odds were stacked against Latinos from the very beginning, due to the FCC's preference for US-based companies and the inaccessibility to capital by potential minority owners.

First, the 1934 Communications Act stipulated that no foreign entity could acquire ownership of a radio license. This practice dated back to the early days of broadcast-based telegraphy, when the federal government realized that the Marconi Company owned a large majority of the wireless telegraph system in the United States. Soon after War World I, the US government seized the assets of the company, later acquired by RCA, because it was considered a threat to national security for a foreign entity to control or own parts of the communications infrastructure, which was increasingly undergirding the US economic and military system. Consequently, this early telecommunications regulation shaped what later became known as broadcast ownership rules. In terms of Latino radio, the fact many of the pioneers were from Mexico and other Latin American countries made it impossible for them to own a radio license in the United States, which is why the practice of programming blocks thrived. Latino radio producers could lease several hours of airtime although they had little or no voice in station operations. Even if a Latino radio producer was a US citizen, the acquisition of a radio license was extremely difficult and often required corporate partnerships in order to secure the large financial capital necessary to demonstrate the ability to erect a radio station and tower (Rodríguez 2001; US FCC 2001). As noted earlier, even the first Latino commercial radio station, KCOR-AM, was owned by a Latino for only a short time.

The post–civil rights era aimed to change media policies pertaining to broadcasting, since there was evidence that minority ownership positively influenced programming directed at cultural and linguistic minorities (US FCC 2010). Media activists have also historically argued that the preferential treatment of racial minority and white women owners has been necessary because they have not had the access to the airwaves that white men have had (Schement 1978). Yet even at the height of affirmative action in the post–civil rights era, in which radio rules were modified to address inequities in ownership, many minority-owned radio stations still had a significant number of non-minority partners as partial owners (US FCC 2000). And when communities of color increased their demands that local broadcast stations address their information and entertainment needs, the policies of preferential treatment came under fire by the media industry for being discriminatory against "neoliberal economic thinking [and] unrestrained market forces" (Blevins and Martinez 2010, 230–31). Additionally, the Office of General Counsel at the FCC has noted that various political-economic barriers have inhibited Latino, and minority, ownership of broadcast properties. The most important barriers are lack of access to capital, pervasive discrimination in the broadcast interpretive community, and changes to media policy in relation to station licenses (US FCC 2000). Together, these challenges have made it incredibly difficult for minorities to overcome barriers of market entry and become potential broadcast owners. Although the FCC aimed between 1970 and 1995 to ameliorate discriminatory practices within the agency and reexamine the unconscious biases that may have pervaded media policy making, the congressional (and larger political) shift toward market-based interpretations of diversity has led to the dismantling of many race-specific rules and policies that were designed to offer modest gains to potential minority owners. The report notes that media policy has been historically uneven with regard to minorities and women in the following ways:

> Uneven enforcement of EEO policy; under utilized distress sales/license renewals; repeal of the tax certificate program; permitting use by non-minority men of minority and female "fronts" during the comparative hearing process; the lifting of the ownership caps; and minimal small business advocacy. [The policy obstacles] stand high atop a persistent legacy of discrimination in the capital markets, industry, advertising, and [broadcast regulatory] community. (2012, 1)

Unfortunately, the passage of the Telecommunications Act of 1996 and the FCC's media policies that have followed have worsened the situation. At a 2004 FCC field hearing on broadcast localism in San Antonio, Texas, community and media leaders from the predominantly Latino city demanded that the commission rethink its ownership rules, because "without a fair share of minority ownership and control . . . Latinos will continue to be absent from the airwaves . . . despite Latino commercial media" (44).

Indeed, eight years after the hearing in San Antonio, Latino commercial radio in particular is a vastly consolidated industry, with global media owners taking charge of Latino commercial radio outlets. A music producer from a Latino commercial station in Massachusetts commented confidentially that very little local information is broadcast on air, and it is a struggle to work against station managers' preferences for nationally syndicated music shows, many of which are not produced by US Latinos. At a very local level, this music producer is witnessing on a daily basis how media policy has shaped, and is transforming, the reorganization of US Latino radio into a global media property, despite local broadcasters' limited success in utilizing it as a public resource. Another Massachusetts music producer shared that he was reprimanded by his station manager for making comments about immigration, and particularly touting the "Drop the I-Word" campaign by Colorlines, a nonprofit news site committed to media and race justice. He said he believed the campaign was worthy of mention, since saying "illegal immigrant" (in either English or Spanish) communicated something very different from "undocumented worker." Indeed, the former signifies a dangerous criminal, whereas the latter merely connotes a paperless laborer. The music producers I interviewed all agreed that as debates about Latinos' social conditions increase in the mainstream political and media spheres, there was increased pressure to not address these issues and broadcast depoliticized content. One producer joked that most of her radio show's content centered on the love lives of celebrities, friendly crank call pranks, and advice on settling family disputes, although she noted that news and information vital for the local community could sometimes be found on her station's websites. This is ironic, given that most of the radio producers I interviewed entered the media field because as minorities within the broader industry they saw themselves as being committed to "actively intervening and transforming the established mediascape" (Rodríguez 2001, 20). Unfortunately these days, the producers' on-air broadcasts were far from having a social justice orientation due to the commercial imperatives of station owners and advertisers.

Another issue that was mentioned were the ways media policy was also responsible for creating conditions that transformed radio from serving the public to serving the marketplace, despite the fact that the broadcast airwaves are still regarded as a public good. The Orwellian nature of (digital) capitalism, where the marketplace is equated with diversity, has fostered spectrum auctions and competition in the name of expansive consumption. In this context it becomes difficult to argue against media policy makers' interpretation of capital as providing an array of superficial choices and good outcomes. One producer I interviewed noted that one of those goods was the notion that Latino commercial radio was no longer an "ethnic other" but simply another format, like jazz, and therefore now part of the mainstream. And although the producer appreciated the move away from marginalizing Latino media audiences, she felt that this mainly benefitted companies such as Univision Radio rather than Latino listeners because of the pressure to maintain the same rotation of popular music and keep commentaries lighthearted. Thus, while station owners and managers are now better able to convince advertisers that their audience commodity is a conventional, mainstream product, the ability to meet the information needs of Latinos, especially those who depend on Spanish-language radio, remains tenuous at best.

At a moment when Latinos are contradictorily lauded as consumers but dispirited as citizens, the access to media resources is more imperative than ever. As González and Torres (2011) concur, "the white racial narrative has always been more virulent and exclusionary whenever our information system was most centralized and controlled from the top"; therefore, the hope is that if Latinos gain access to communication outlets, a social justice narrative will prevail and counter the dominant neoliberal discourse about Latino cultural citizenship (376). Nonprofit Latino media advocacy organizations have especially taken up the charge of challenging FCC media policy that negatively impacts Latino audiences. One of the most important advocacy groups that have pressed the FCC to rethink how it considers Latino commercial radio is the National Hispanic Media Coalition. The organization, along with others, has argued before the FCC that corporations need to do more to adequately serve Latino communities nationwide by providing meaningful news, information, and entertainment in both Spanish and English. Recently, the president and CEO of the NHMC made the point that "historically, non-Latino owners have done a poor job of lifting up authentic Latino voices. . . . In the worst cases, non-Latino owners have allowed [hate speech] attacks against Latinos over their airwaves" (Nogales 2012). Although it is important to acknowledge that there are no "authentic Latino voices," given the multiplicities of latinidad, the point Alex Nogales was trying to make is that Latinos do not control the airwaves, and thus are unable to represent the multiplicity of Latino voices from their own perspective. What it means to be a US Latina, for instance, is scripted by non-Latino producers, who often not only reproduce debasing stereotypes, but also either remain neutral or encourage hate speech against minority populations. The experiences of the music producers I previously mentioned confirm that such practices also occur in Latino commercial radio, not just mainstream outlets.

The lack of Latino diversity in the current commercial media landscape is not the result of something inherent in the technology or Latino ways of life. The recent report by the bipartisan working group on information needs of communities affirms, "there is no doubt that [media] policies have played a profound role in the development and growth of the modern broadcasting industry from its earliest days" (US FCC 2011, 276). Changes in technology as well as ideological interpretations of media policy have shifted the FCC's understanding of Latino commercial radio as no longer constituting a separate market but operating as a component of the general radio landscape in which Latino commercial stations merely add programming diversity to the field of "broadcast formats" (Nuñez 2006). Yet since the beginning of radio broadcasting, minority media activists, producers, and scholars have argued that transcultural political-economic practices of media policy, including ownership rules, have consistently impacted what it means to "serve" the community. The growing corporate and political interest in Latino commercial and bilingual media (exemplified by the emergence of new media properties such as MundoFox and the Republican Party's post-2012 presidential elections' "Latino crisis") demonstrates that capital and policy makers are increasingly becoming aware that Latinos will have a role in reshifting the political, cultural, and digital landscapes of the United States. Whether Latinos will be included in the process is the challenge at hand, and therefore it is imperative to continue pressing for a more equitable distribution of communication resources and the meaningful inclusion of Latinos into the interpretive community of media policy making, as media activists have done for a long time.

Although Latino commercial radio has considerable limitations, it continues to be important to critically examine this cultural industry, not only because Latinos listen to more radio than any other ethnic and/or racial group, but also transnational companies view this sector as a crucial entry point for marketing Latino audiences as commodities. The need for continued analysis and media activism is therefore critical, otherwise Latinos will be relegated to reliving the past. As González and Torres (2011) note,

> while politically connected publishers and the major radio networks consolidated their power over broadcasting during the 1930s, people of color saw their presence in the new medium [of radio] sharply diminished. . . . [And] President Hoover and the Federal Radio Commission ignored calls for greater racial diversity, and instead actively assisted the networks and publishers in strengthening their domination. (255)

Latino commercial radio is dangerously on the cusp of fully following this trajectory. Perhaps it is already on this track, but those who work on the front lines of the sector refuse to give up hope, and aim, even if it's on the website, to provide news and information that will be useful for their local listeners. And several mentioned that they also utilized social media to make statements or comments about Latino issues even if they cannot be followed up on-air or if the majority of their listeners don't link up with them through social media; they also participated, when possible, in media policy discussions in and outside the FCC.

Conclusion

Throughout the history of Latino commercial radio, Latino producers have persisted in their belief that broadcasting was a powerful tool for reaching Latino communities that were being consistently left out of the expanding US media landscape. Yet shifting ideological interpretations of localism, diversity, and commercialism in US media policy have placed pressures on the trajectory of Latino commercial radio to follow market forces rather than community service. As noted earlier, however, the political economic framework of the US radio industry, which emphasized commercialism and the white Anglo power structure that controlled it, were foundational structures that from the beginning placed limitations on Latino radio programming and the expansion of radio stations oriented toward Latino listeners. The sector has historically been challenged for broadcasting politically charged programming (dating back to 1927 with *Los madrugadores*), but there continued to be moments of opportunity that encouraged resistance to the limitations. In today's current neoliberal context, where communication policies largely prioritize capital accumulation and economic growth, it is more difficult than ever for Latino commercial radio to be anything except commercial. The implications of this shift are critical, since radio continues to be one of the most important informational outlets for Latino listeners in a media landscape that continues to be dwarfed by the sheer size of its mainstream counterpart.

Consequently, Latina/o media justice activists have petitioned the FCC as well as developed community radio spaces in order to provide information to communities that are being left out of the English-language, bilingual, and Spanish-language radio soundscapes (see, for instance, comments for US FCC 2010). Some success has occurred with the expansion of low-power FM radio stations and the emergence of Latino public radio within the low-power network. Additionally, Latino media justice advocates are utilizing digital media and alternative nonprofit-based outlets (like National Public Radio affiliates or college radio stations) to not only provide relevant information but also create forums for discussions about transcultural political economic issues that impact Latino communities. *Tertulia* on New England Public Radio is a great example of Latino-oriented, bilingual programming in a traditionally English-language radio station. The situation with US Latino commercial radio will not change unless communities, activists, and media scholars continue to expose the neoliberal approach to media policy that does not support meaningful localism and diversity, and are creative with alternatives. Our communities' future requires a more equitable distribution of communication resources, and media policy processes must continue to be challenged to do what is right.

REFERENCES

Albarran, A. B., and B. Hutton. (2009). "A History of Spanish Language Radio in the United States." Denton, TX: Center for Spanish Language Media.

Arbitron. (2003). *Hispanic Radio Today*. Baltimore: Arbitron.

Blevins, J., and K. Martinez. (2010). "A Political-Economic History of FCC Policy on Minority Broadcast Ownership." *Communication Review* 13, no. 3: 216–38.

Browne, R. (2005). *Ethnic Minorities, Electronic Media, and the Public Sphere: A Comparative Study*. Cresskill, NJ: Hampton.

Castañeda, M. (2008). "Rethinking the U.S. Spanish-Language Media Market in an Era of Deregulation." In *Global Communications: Toward a Transcultural Political Economy*, edited by Paula Chakravartty and Yuezhi Zhao. Lanham: Rowman and Littlefield.

Chakravartty, Paula, and Yuezhi Zhao. (2008). "Introduction: Toward a Transcultural Political Economy of Global Communications." In *Global Communications: Toward a Transcultural Political Economy*, edited by Paula Chakravartty and Yuezhi Zhao, 1-19. Lanham: Rowman and Littlefield.

Dávila, A. M. (2001). *Latinos, Inc.: The Marketing and Making of a People*. Berkeley: University of California Press.

Fowler, G., and B. Crawford. (2002). *Border Radio: Quacks, Yodelers, Pitchmen, Psychics, and Other Amazing Broadcasters of the American Airwaves*. Austin: University of Texas Press.

González, J., and J. Torres. (2011). *News for All the People: The Epic Story of Race and the American Media*. London: Verso.

Klinenberg, E. (2007). *Fighting for Air: The Battle to Control America's Media*. New York: Metropolitan Books.

Matsaganis, M. D., V. S. Katz, and S. Ball-Rokeach. (2011). *Understanding Ethnic Media: Producers, Consumers, and Societies*. Los Angeles: Sage.

McChesney, R. W. (1993). *Telecommunications, Mass Media, and Democracy: The Battle for the Control of U.S. Broadcasting, 1928–1935*. New York: Oxford University Press.

Nogales, Alex. (2012). "The FCC's Chance to Promote Diverse Media Owners, and How It May Blow It." Moyers & Company, December 7. http://billmoyers.com/groupthink/on-media-consolidation/the-fcc%E2%80%99s-chance-to-promote-diverse-media-owners-and-how-it-may-blow-it/.

Nuñez, L. V. (2006). *Spanish Language Media after the Univision-Hispanic Broadcasting*. New York: Novinka Books.

Rivero, Y. M. (2005). *Tuning Out Blackness: Race and Nation in the History of Puerto Rican Television*. Durham: Duke University Press.

Rodríguez, A. (1999). *Making Latino News: Race, Language, Class*. Thousand Oaks: Sage.

Rodríguez, C. (2001). *Fissures in the Mediascape: An International Study of Citizens' Media*. Cresskill, NJ: Hampton.

Savage, B. D. (1999). *Broadcasting Freedom: Radio, War, and the Politics of Race, 1938–1948*. Chapel Hill: University of North Carolina Press.

Schement, J. R. (1978). "Voice of the People: The Case of Spanish Language Radio." *Atisbos*, 62–83.

US Census. (2012). *Profile America Facts: Hispanics*. Washington, DC: US Census.

US FCC. (1980). *Notice of Inquiry on Part-Time Programming, Policy Statement: Time Brokerage*. FCC 80-621 BC Docket No. 78-355 RM-3055. Washington, DC: US FCC.
———. (2001). "FCC Consumer Information Bureau Launches 'Bienvenidos,' a Spanish-Language Homepage." Press release. Washington, DC: US FCC.
———. (2010). *Federal Communications Commission Advisory Committee on Diversity for Communications in the Digital Age*. Washington, DC: US FCC.
———. (2011). *The Information Needs of Communities: The Changing Media Landscape in a Broadband Age*. Washington, DC: US FCC.
———. (2012). *Report on Ownership of Commercial Broadcast Stations*. Washington, DC: US FCC.

10

Lost in Translation

The Politics of Race and Language in
Spanish-Language Radio Ratings

DOLORES INÉS CASILLAS

"guenos dias pipol in da jaus!"
—Don Cheto, Twitter post, June 11, 2013

"We espeekinglish tu!"
—El Piolín, billboard campaign, 2007

In the digital era, tweets, status posts, and pricey ad campaigns have transformed the ways listeners wittingly "tune" in to radio. For the popular Spanish-language and Los Angeles–based hosts Don Cheto and El Piolín, radio salutations are not only voiced over the airwaves but also written in phonetic English and posted on different channels of social media. True, the convergence of media is certainly not unique to Spanish-language radio. Yet the public and recurrent use of a Spanish-accented English to court a Spanish-dominant listenership demonstrates a savvy level of cultural fluency in both English and Spanish. The playful written speech pokes fun at monolingual English speakers and communicates the nuanced elements of language, accent, and immigrant syntax. The practice of listening to and reading these messages privileges Latinos familiar with US popular phrases, phonetics, and hostile English-only politics. Despite the technological gains made in broadcast radio, the larger dominant English-language radio industry struggles to understand the bilingual (Spanish-English) radio listenership. Because US Latinos are largely imagined as strictly English- or Spanish-speaking, gauging Latino listening practices that weave between English and Spanish challenges the more familiar and fixed monolingual modes of English-language radio.

As a case in point, this essay examines the public controversies that follow Arbitron, the premiere radio ratings company, in its evaluation of Latino radio listeners through two different methodologies: listener diaries and the Portable People Meter (PPM).[1] Both the larger radio industry and Arbitron have long grappled with how to approach, recruit, and then measure Spanish-dominant radio listeners. Arbitron's practice of assessing listening audiences is a critical component for structuring the economy of commercial radio. Profit margin increases correlate, in theory, to a radio ratings climb. In order to increase advertising revenue, radio stations must showcase Arbitron-approved audience profiles, despite the fact that Arbitron's measurement practices are peppered with linguistic and racial oversights.

Coverage of the diary's transition to the PPM and the mixed reactions by both English- and Spanish-language radio continues to populate trade magazines. I use two publications, *Billboard* and *Broadcasting & Cable* from 1985 to 2010, to argue that language, linked to immigrant listeners and listeners of color, is addressed only tenuously in both of Arbitron's chief methodologies. Specifically, this essay investigates how Arbitron measures and classifies Hispanic or Latina/o radio listeners and the public controversies waged by Spanish-language radio networks that followed suit soon after. Currently, the United States has the third-largest Spanish-speaking population in the world, and nearly fifty million Latinos reside within the geographical United States.[2] These staggering figures bolster the argument that Spanish-language radio, already commanding number one and number two ratings in top radio markets, will most likely maintain if not surpass its exponential growth. Currently, Spanish-language radio challenges the notions that radio listening takes place in either Spanish or English and, in doing so, stumps both Arbitron and its English-language peers. Spanish-language radio networks routinely make public comments on the linguistic fluency of their constituents, all the while calling out the outdated measurements of Arbitron.

Demographic shifts in radio listeners (from white, English-language listeners to Latino, bilingual, and Spanish-dominant listeners) and the growing economic clout of Spanish-language radio (from static AM to crisp FM), coupled with outdated audience measurement techniques, have fueled a contentious relationship between Arbitron and Spanish-language radio. These public quarrels hinge on the complexities of measuring non–English-language Latino listeners, yet race and the racialization of Latino consumers have become strong undercurrents. If Latino listeners are not correctly tabulated and reflected in Arbitron-endorsed ratings, radio stations have difficulties selling airtime, thereby affecting station revenue. Because different audience measurements can provide different accounts of audience behavior, modifications of audience evaluation techniques are often regarded with caution.[3] In the case of Spanish-language radio, the awkward handling of language preference distorts "objective" radio ratings and in doing so sustains existing hierarchies of race and language in political economies of radio.

Language matters compound issues of race, ethnicity, and media use among Latinos. Bilingual and English-dominant radio listeners dispute long-standing correlations between language preference and media choice. Indeed, immigrant Latinos are more proficient in Spanish than English; second-generation Latinos adopt more English skills; and third-generation Latinos are largely English-dominant. Yet, according to a Pew Research Center survey, a significant share of these later generations of English-dominant Latinos choose Spanish when, for instance, listening to music and watching television.[4] These patterns should push professionals in the radio industry to not only stop assuming that Latino audiences are exclusively immigrant or Spanish-dominant, but also to reassess their sampling methodology.

The Role of Ratings

Recognized as objective "third parties," audience evaluation companies serve as chief financial arbiters between radio stations or networks, potential advertisers, and listeners. Audience measurements and market research claim to identify "when" and "where" listeners tune in to radio. The term "audience" represents an economic product or coin of exchange, between advertisers, marketers, audience firms, and other media professionals.[5] Data on the media habits of Latinos are used to bait companies to purchase ad time and subsequently increase station revenue. Contrary to the popular notion that media companies (e.g., radio and television networks) merely sell advertising time to potential advertisers, in actuality, they also sell profiles of audiences.[6]

In the case of US radio, Arbitron Inc. boasts the definitive measurement of radio audiences. The largest radio ratings company in the United States, in business since 1965, Arbitron has operated without a chief rival since 1992.[7] Arbitron has monopolized radio research, garnering not only the service contracts of major radio stations but also benefiting from a larger discourse that positions Arbitron as the authoritative indicator of radio listenership. Arbitron's influence in the radio industry is demonstrated by its consistent press coverage. When Arbitron loses or gains a radio client, adopts a new radio market, or changes its audience measurement, trade publications consider it newsworthy. The company's name often occurs in the titles of articles: "Arbitron Buys Radio Ad Software Group"; "CBS Radio to Use Arbitron Portable People Meter"; "Broadcaster Cancels Arbitron." The attention given to Arbitron indicates its larger influence in the radio industry and also serves to reinscribe its dominance.

Trade journals routinely reference a radio station's "Arbitrends," a morphed term used to describe general listening patterns within three-month increments as reported by Arbitron. As an Arbitron-coined phrase, "Arbitrend" reifies Arbitron's credibility in reporting definitive patterns of listening. Arbitrends, coveted coins of exchange in the radio industry, are used to entice advertisers to court a station's listenership. More so, if ratings are favorable, radio stations attach themselves to Arbitron through radio identification clips. For instance, stations might remind listeners that they are "Arbitron rated #1 in the Bay Area," demonstrating that, in addition to the trade journals' affirmation of Arbitrends, even radio listeners are assumed to believe in the veracity of Arbitron findings.

Since the mid-1990s Spanish-language radio has unseated English-language radio stations from top standings across dials within *each* major radio market. Even with such high ratings, several Spanish-language radio networks insist that Arbitron's tallies of their audience numbers are dwarfed and not representative of their actual clout. Network executives complain of high subscription fees for a service that does not gauge their audience's bilingual listening practices. Complicating matters is the fact that advertising time sold on top-rated Spanish-language radio continues to cost less than it does at many English-language radio stations that are rated lower. Even with the backing of Arbitron, advertisers are reluctant to invest in a Spanish-language media market or to Latino listeners, as evidenced by the disproportionate amount of revenue earned by English-language radio stations compared to Spanish-language ones. Many Spanish-language executives call the courtship of advertising revenue a process of "educating the industry" about who in fact Latino consumers are. Although commercials from corporations such as Honda, Coca-Cola, McDonald's, Pepsi-Cola, Sears, and Wal-Mart have become staples on major Spanish-language networks, Spanish-language radio executives argue that there's more to Latino listeners than soft drinks, fast food, and two major apparel companies. Attracting more and diverse sources of radio revenue, however, begins with interrogating Arbitron ratings.

Transitions in Measurement

For the last forty years, Arbitron has relied primarily on personal and household listener diaries to track patterns of radio use. The diary, divided into seven-day increments, asks individuals of at least twelve years of age to write down that day's radio listening. While diary fatigue and delay are subject to human error, the general underestimation of audiences, specifically African American and Hispanic respondents, calls into question not only the validity of Arbitron measurements but also the ramifications for African American–targeted and Hispanic-targeted radio.

For instance, New York's WBLS-FM, an African American–oriented radio station, denounced Arbitron for the racial imbalance in listener diaries in 1992. In this case, Arbitron had used just seventeen diaries to determine the listening habits of the area's 77,500 African American men ages forty-five to forty-nine.[8] As a result, WBLS-FM's parent company, Inner-City Broadcasting, rightfully argued that the low sample of middle-aged African American men affected radio ratings and subsequently, the value of advertising time on WBLS-FM. Nearly ten years later, Denver's radio market voiced similar concerns when ratings from the summer of 2001 pointed to just 150 Hispanic (Spanish-dominant) diary responses.[9] Issues of participation and accuracy worsened a year later, when Arbitron reported a record low 32.6 percent rate of return for all diary users; for the largest twelve radio markets, response rates had dipped to 27.5 percent.[10] As the communications scholar Philip Napoli notes, "any sampling group that overrepresents or underrepresents certain demographic groups will produce data that will provide a distorted picture of the actual media audience."[11] In this case, Arbitron's 2002 tabulation of radio listeners using critically low rates of responses set off alarms throughout the radio industry, not just about the tool (the diary), but about the recruitment practices of diary participants.

The development of the Portable People Meter (PPM) promised to bring radio research up to date with twentieth-century technology and was pitched to Spanish-language radio networks as a means of repairing previous feuds over accuracy. The PPM, which resembles a pager, is a device worn by participants that functions as an electronic ear, detecting inaudible signals embedded in the audio portion of media and entertainment content delivered by broadcasters, content providers, and distributors. The use of these inaudible codes depends on the cooperation and subscription of radio stations. As a form of audience surveillance, however, not only does the PPM survey media consumption for up to fifteen hours a day for a month, but findings are available almost immediately, with detailed analysis promised monthly. In contrast, the diary asks for the cooperation of participants in one-week allotments, with findings for major markets released as quarterly reports.[12] Not only would the PPM produce more data, but findings would be calculated and made available much more frequently. Because the PPM is "all passive," it compensates by being more invasive; participants' media choices are tracked even when they are not voluntarily "choosing" media. For instance, the PPM can register ambient music in a store or elevator.[13] The assumed passivity, albeit invasive, has been largely ignored or recast as a positive attribute of its technological capabilities.

Spanish-language radio networks reluctantly followed Arbitron from its diary approach to the Portable People Meter. The president of the Spanish Broadcasting System (SBS), Raúl Alarcón Jr., made the following public remarks upon signing a multiyear contract to use Arbitron's Portable People Meter:

We are willing to make this commitment to PPM as the new currency for radio in order to provide our advertisers with the most accountable measures possible of our growing audiences. We are counting on the PPM to *enhance the credibility* of our programming and the value of these audiences in the eyes of our advertisers. (Emphasis added)[14]

Alarcón's overt reference to the PPM as Arbitron's "new currency" highlights the financial implications attributed to listening measurements. Despite already subscribing to Arbitron-approved services, Alarcón hopes to entice mainstream advertisers through the PPM to give "enhanced credibility" to SBS's Spanish-language radio listeners. His not-so-coded remarks gesture toward existing perceptions of his Spanish-language listenership based, according to him and others, on the underestimation of Spanish-language listeners. Read as a public relations tactic to improve the perception of Spanish-language listeners to potential advertisers, Alarcón's comment speaks to ongoing struggles to sell Latinos as a viable consumer base. The frustration lies in the fact that both Alarcón and his peers are forced to rely on "objective" modes of measurement to address factors of race and class in consumer (racial) profiling. The proposed solution to adjusting the perception of Spanish-language radio listeners is to rely on the PPM's more intrusive modes for gauging radio listening.

Arbitron also parades the PPM as the technological solution to problems with participation by Hispanic and African American listeners, yet there are two remaining key barriers to PPM implementation and the inclusion of station formats directed at Hispanic and African American listeners. First, the transition from diary to PPM raised already expensive subscription rates by 40 to 65 percent,[15] further limiting smaller radio stations from participating in the PPM process and being "counted" by Arbitron or recognized by pools of advertisers. In fact, throughout the PPM's development stages, radio groups complained of gradual increases in subscription fees for the diary system. Arbitron explained that the increase in diary fees was meant to offset PPM's mounting development costs. Second, despite the improved return rate of African American and Hispanic participants in, for instance, Houston's PPM trial, Arbitron has not drastically altered its mode of sample recruitment. Arbitron's initial promise that a PPM would make it easier to recruit more radio listeners did not take into account other equally important structural hurdles, such as fees and recruitment.

The recruitment practices of Arbitron have long been critiqued as an obstacle toward reaching a viable sample of listeners. For instance, Arbitron's use of mail and telephone is an unrealistic means of enrollment for most landless consumers, particularly Latinos. Arbitron recruits diary keepers by calling households using an electronic operator that places calls to a random selection of households. As early as 1980, Arbitron found that in New York nearly 50 percent of Hispanic households did not have a land line.[16] In 2005, 85 percent of all US Hispanic households had telephone service.[17] Even with household lines, newfound telephone screening mechanisms present challenges for soliciting any participant via phone. The arrival of answering machines, the caller I.D. function, the option for an unlisted telephone number, and the elective "Do Not Call" list helped bar marketing companies from calling residences. In an attempt to reach those with unlisted numbers, Arbitron employs a "random digit-dialing" technique that improves the chances of calling unlisted numbers. Yet once someone answers, the invitation to participate does not guarantee compliance. If anything, because of the growing popularity of random digit-dialing, the slight delay heard when answering the phone serves as a cue to listeners that the phone call is most likely from a marketer.

The increasing practice of screening phone calls reflects marketing companies' overuse of the telephone and subsequent consumer exhaustion. To further complicate matters, nearly 20 percent of the coveted eighteen- to thirty-four-year-old demographic have "cut the cord," relying solely on cellular phone service. With cellular numbers unlisted and largely private, the turn to wireless phones has eliminated a sizable portion of potential respondents. Significant to Spanish-language radio, research has found that US Latinos overwhelmingly opt for cellular phones over land lines. In fact, Hispanics spend 50 percent more time talking on cell phones than fellow non-Hispanic cellular users. Both AT&T and Verizon have taken notice; both are identified as top advertisers for Latino consumers in 2010.[18] Marketing ads for cellular companies aimed at US Latinos tout "pay as you go" or prepaid phone plans that often advertise low-rate international calling plans, thereby offering financial flexibility to mobile customers. With nearly 35 percent of all Hispanic cell phone customers without a land line, these potential listeners of Spanish-language radio are largely inaccessible to researchers.[19] Thus, the ability of Arbitron to accurately determine radio-listening practices—for either people of color or young people, two of the fastest-growing consumer markets—is highly questionable.

While Arbitron does not ensure or promise absolute accuracy, for either the diary or the PPM, as the industry leader it does define the standards of audience measurements. Shifts in Arbitron's measurement practices that account for factors of race and language have been done at the urging of Spanish-language radio networks. These public disputes highlight the struggle for English-dominant US radio to accommodate to its formidable Spanish-language peers.

Assimilating to Arbitron's Practices

Nestled within the transition from the archaic diary to the tech-savvy PPM are discourses of assimilation. Listeners of color are expected to assimilate to Arbitron's radio measurements rather than Arbitron adjusting its methodology to meet the bilingual and often public listening patterns of listeners of color. The refusal to translate existing methods serves as a larger reflection of how radio listeners as consumers are regarded across class, race, and linguistic lines.

Unsurprisingly, the listener diary's greatest challenge arrived when the "niche" of Spanish-language radio gained mainstream momentum. For instance, in 1986, Telemundo joined the newly rechristened Univision (formerly the Spanish International Network) as a major purveyor of Spanish-language television. That same year, a total of 168 Spanish-oriented stations occupied the radio airwaves, up from 65 a decade earlier.[20] By 1990 the figure had jumped to 390 Spanish-language radio stations.[21] Yet the changing landscape of Spanish-dominant viewers and listeners did not compel Nielsen or Arbitron to retool their audience techniques even when Spanish-language media industries publicly demanded more accurate measurements. Since then, the dissatisfied rumblings of Spanish-language media industries have appeared on the pages of trade journals, as they express skepticism about the modes of tracking Hispanic-specific listeners and viewers used by Arbitron and Nielsen, respectively.[22]

On the heels of the "Decade of the Hispanic," Univision and Telemundo, in conjunction with AC Nielsen, unveiled the "Nielsen Hispanic Ratings System" in 1989 to improve the audience tracking of Spanish-language television viewers. The collaboration required Univision and Telemundo to invest $36 million in the installment of Spanish-specific People Meters, in addition to their regular subscription fees.[23] At the time, Telemundo and Univision together garnered just 1 percent of advertising sales, despite having attracted 5 percent of the US viewership.[24] The agreement with Nielsen was undoubtedly made to entice advertising agencies toward the Hispanic market. Buoyed by high census numbers, Nielsen installed People Meters, devices that attach to television sets to monitor channel surfing, in only thirty Spanish-speaking US households, located in just two markets. By 1994, Nielsen had expanded to eleven markets, with eight hundred People Meters placed in Hispanic households.[25] For decades, Spanish-language television and radio have struggled to be recognized as comparable to mainstream English-language competitors rather than as a niche (and segregated) Spanish-language market.

At the same time that Neilsen renewed its attention toward Spanish-language television viewers, Arbitron implemented "Differential Surveys" for both Hispanic and African American radio listeners in 1982 and 1983, respectively. Differential Surveys, despite the name, were no different from earlier surveys; Arbitron simply invested more resources into recruiting higher rates of return among participants of color. The survey, available in Spanish (ironically, only if requested in English), compensated Hispanics with two to five dollars more than fellow non-Hispanic and non–African American participants. Midweek phone calls were placed to Hispanic and African American participating households to remind them to record their day's listening. And rather than asking participants to mail the diary back, Arbitron sent officials to physically pick up the diaries.[26] The adoption of an aggressive follow-through does little to address any possible discrepancies embedded in the actual diary measurement, mode of sample recruitment, or relationship with Arbitron. Instead, these innovations indicate that the identified "problem" Arbitron worked to solve was the "special" (nonwhite) listening audience and their perceived disorganization, idleness, and irresponsibility, not the measuring device. Rather than critique its own measurement techniques, Arbitron assumed that the fault lay with the participants' unwillingness to comply with Arbitron's methods. Despite its lack of success, since 2006, the Differential Survey continues to be administered today in forty-four Arbitron-designated Hispanic markets, determined by population numbers.

The use of Differential Surveys and later bilingual field researchers by Arbitron exemplifies the awkward handling of Hispanic and Spanish-language listeners. In particular, the merging of these two distinct ethnic and linguistic categories itself is deemed problematic because, as mentioned earlier, not all Hispanics speak Spanish. These listeners posed, in the words of the audience researcher Hugh Malcolm Belville, "special problems" to the audience industry, which required what Arbitron calls "special procedures," including cash and in-person cajoling to turn in surveys. Rather than alter audience measurements to account for the popular growth of both Hispanic- and African American–oriented radio stations, audience industries focused on assimilating listeners into already established measurements.

Accounting for Language

Over the years, language has held an ambiguous and subsequently contentious place in Arbitron's evaluation of radio audiences. Most of the language and measurement controversies covered in print centered on the Latino-populated radio market of Los Angeles. Both English- and Spanish-language radio industries have called into question how Arbitron considers language preference in audience evaluations. The relationship between a listener's language preference, their identity as "Hispanic," and penchants for radio has been curiously handled in trade broadcast journals. Ed Cohen, Arbitron's vice president of research, belatedly admitted in 2002 that "there is a connection between the language preference of Hispanics and their radio-listening behavior."[27] Spanish-language radio networks have repeatedly made the distinction that "Spanish is not a format, it's a language."[28] Their insistence on being recognized as distinct formats, rather than lumped under language, is indicative of their larger struggles of being identified as equal peers, rather than marginalized and ghettoized, in the landscape of radio.[29] It was as late as 1998 that Arbitron agreed to have Spanish-language radio stations self-identify according to musical genre, not language. (Even "newer" mediums group by ethnicity rather than genre—for instance, iTunes Latino.) Even then, Arbitron lists a Spanish-language station's linguistic identity after its genre, for instance, "Mexican Regional (Spanish)" while not marking English-language stations as "Country (English)." Methodologically, Arbitron has attempted to alleviate concerns about its handling of language differences by hiring bilingual interviewers, asking specifically where Spanish/English is spoken to determine language proficiency, as well as statistically weighting language in its computing of market ratings.

Faced with public pressure to address language as a serious factor in audience measurement, Arbitron conducted a survey in the summer of 1996 to determine what percentage of Hispanics living in major radio markets preferred to speak which language. Despite favorable radio ratings in many major Hispanic-identified markets, when released in 1997, the survey showed various results for different markets: Albuquerque had a 70 percent English-dominant Hispanic population, South Florida a 42 percent Spanish-dominant Hispanic population, and New York a 40 percent bilingual Hispanic population. Together these figures demonstrated that language and ethnicity are not always intricately related and that, yes, not all self-identified Latinos speak Spanish. More so, speaking and listening to Spanish have proven to be two distinct practices, especially in regard to media and popular culture. Arbitron's results were largely inconclusive since it did not consider that English-dominant Hispanics may tune into Spanish-language radio stations.

Over ten years later, the variable of language persisted for Arbitron. The script used during initial phone calls to Hispanic-identified households asked the following:

Thinking about the languages (you/he/she) use(s) in the home, would you say (you/he/she) speak(s) . . .

- ONLY SPANISH in the home,
- mostly Spanish but some English,
- mostly English but some Spanish,
- or ONLY ENGLISH in the home?
- DO NOT READ: Both Equally

Arbitron notes that "although the 'both equally' [option] will not be offered to the respondent, it will be accepted and will be reported as 'mostly English.'"[30] Despite the additional options to the language question, respondents are still categorized as either English- or Spanish-dominant, and it is assumed that their radio listening follows suit. The aversion to identifying bilingual listeners, in many ways, would complicate Arbitron's strict Spanish/English methodology. It also reifies mainstream misgivings that Spanish-language media cater to an exclusively immigrant base while English-language media court English-dominant Hispanic youth.

The four major Spanish-language broadcast companies teamed up in 2002 to publicly criticize Arbitron's handling of language preference, with claims that "the audience share of Spanish-language radio is undercounted by at least 20%."[31] Ratings for Spanish-language radio dropped in accordance with the lower number of Arbitron's Hispanic sample. In response to complaints that Arbitron surveyed too many English-dominant Hispanics, Arbitron publicly committed to statistically weighting audience samples to account for language preference, yet offered no timetable for implementation. Arbitron already gives equal weight to race, sex, and geography, but had been reluctant to incorporate language preference, citing the lack of software capabilities. Although Arbitron managed public pressure through a language preference survey, it ultimately blamed technological shortcomings as the culprit for reporting what major Spanish-language radio networks regarded as inaccurate numbers.

Lost in Translation

Spanish-language radio represents the fastest-growing "format" on *all* US radio, garners top ratings in all major radio markets, and caters to "minority audiences" that tune into radio at higher rates than the "average" (read: white, English-dominant speaking) US radio listener. Non-Hispanics reportedly listen to radio an average of sixteen hours a week; Hispanics tune to radio—Spanish-language specifically—an average of nearly twenty-two hours a week.[32] For these reasons, there is a compelling case to be made for Spanish-language radio gaining revenue equal to that of its English-language peers. Yet in 2006, even with mainstream recognition and Arbitron-approved numbers, Spanish-language executives continued to raise concerns regarding disproportionate sales, collecting an astonishing average of 40 percent less in revenue than their English-language counterparts.[33]

The disparity in revenue between English- and Spanish-language radio clearly reveals entrenched racial and linguistic bias. Philip Napoli argues that fixed perceptions of income and race may very well influence advertisers' views of minority consumers. His work finds a troubling and significant relationship between audience ethnicity and audience value.[34] Despite claims that "Spanish niche formats" have found a "gold mine," Spanish-language executives know that the riches lie in achieving mainstream status and parity, not niche.

Even with Arbitron-approved ratings, favorable standings given to Spanish-language radio are regarded with suspicion. Raúl Alarcón Jr., president of the Spanish Broadcasting System (SBS), expressed his dismay with advertising discrepancies, commenting in 1993, "I've got the No. 1 station in L.A., but I'm not getting anywhere near the revenues the No. 2 or 3 or 4 stations get."[35] SBS's station, KLAX-FM, rose momentously to number one in Los Angeles ratings. As a result, it raised its $120-a-minute ad price to $1,500 a minute, and was still underpricing lower-rated English-language radio stations. In 1997 its fellow top-ranked Spanish-language station, KLVE-FM, "charged $300 to $400 per Arbitron point for a 60-second ad," while lower-ranked English-language stations charged "between $375 and $480 per ratings point."

Upon learning of KLAX-FM's number one standing, Howard Stern asked, "What are advertisers going to sell on these [Spanish-language] stations, beans and tortillas?"[36] In assuming that Spanish-language radio would not be able to attract mainstream (non-Latino) revenue, Stern's statement reveals how Spanish evokes perceptions of a classed and raced listenership. In many ways his comments, crass yet sincere, underscored the uneven numbers and their relationship to larger dynamics of race and class. Stern's comment calls to mind Ien Ang's premise that media audiences, configured via audience measurements, do not exist "within a social and political vacuum."[37] Public disputes over audience measurements are indicative of larger historically rooted struggles over media access and a reluctance to accommodate all radio listeners. Latinos' social, racial, and economic standing in the United States has clearly facilitated larger struggles for parity within media industries.

Without an audience measurement that takes into account a more linguistically and racially diverse listenership, US radio will continue to falsely cast itself as English-dominant in language without regard to the thriving immigrant and Spanish-dominant transformation of US radio. Even through imperfect measurements, Arbitron consistently makes clear that the landscape of Spanish-language radio holds a commanding presence. Here, the opportunity arises for advertisers and media industries alike to regard Spanish-language listeners as more than a mere subset of a larger US radio listenership but rather the forefront of all radio.

NOTES

1. The diary has undergone minor revisions over the years, especially in its length and distribution. This essay concentrates on revisions made with the diary procedure to explicitly raise the participation rates of Hispanic (and to some extent African American) listeners. Asian Americans seem to be an elusive category for Arbitron, often being lumped with whites, with the exception of its first Chinese-language radio survey in 2005.

2. US Census Bureau, "Language Use in the United States: 2007," April 2010, http://www.census.gov/newsroom/releases/archives/american_community_survey_acs/cb10-cn58.html.

3. Philip Napoli, "Audience Measurement and Media Policy: Audience Economics, the Diversity Principle, and the Local People Meter," *Communication Law and Policy* 10, no. 4 (August 2005): 349–82.

4. Paul Taylor, Mark Hugo Lopez, Jessica Hamar Martinez, and Gabriel Velasco, "When Labels Don't Fit: Hispanics and Their Views of Identity," Pew Hispanic Research Center, 2012, http://www.pewhispanic.org/2012/04/04/iv-language-use-among-latinos/.

5. For the hallmark text on this process, see James S. Ettema and D. Charles Whitney, eds., *Audiencemaking: How the Media Create the Audience* (Thousand Oaks, CA: Sage, 1994).

6. Arlene Dávila's work on Hispanic marketers in the United States speaks cogently to issues of Latino commodification. See *Latinos, Inc.: The Marketing and Making of a People* (Berkeley: University of California Press, 2001).

7. Arbitron was formerly known as the American Research Bureau; see Hugh Malcolm Belville, *Audience Ratings: Radio, Television, and Cable*, rev. ed. (Hillsdale, NJ: Lawrence Erlbaum Associates, 1987), 28–61, 83–130.

8. Laura Bird, "Radio Station Airs Complaint over Arbitron," *Wall Street Journal*, 19 August 1992, B3.

9. Francisco Miraval, "Spanish-Language Radio Stations Wait for Better Rating System," *La Voz* 27, no. 44 (31 October 2001): 9.

10. Katy Bachman, "Consumers: Respond, S.V.P.," *Mediaweek*, 6 January 2003, 5.

11. Philip Napoli, *Audience Economics: Media Institutions and the Audience Marketplace* (New York: Columbia University Press, 2003), 69.

12. Philip Napoli, "Audience Valuation and Minority Media: An Analysis of the Determinant of the Value of Radio Audiences," *Journal of Broadcasting & Electronic Media* 46, no. 2 (2010): 169–84.

13. Louis Chunovic, "When Audiences Intersect," *Television Week*, 2 June 2003, 18.

14. "Spanish Broadcasting System, Inc. Enters into First Multi-Market Agreement for Portable People Meter (PPM) Ratings Services," *Hispanic PR Wire*, 27 February 2006, http://www.hispanicprwire.com/news.php?l=in&id=5681&cha=13.

15. Katy Bachman, "Ratings Lost, Reach Gained," *Mediaweek*, 26 September 2005, 5; Chris Walsh, "The Race to Measure Radio Is On," *Billboard*, 8 April 2006, 10; and Bill Gloede, "Mixed Signals," *Mediaweek*, 17 April 2006, 18.

16. David A. Lapovsky, "The Use of Seven-Day Diary Measurement in Radio and Television Audiences," Arbitron, http://www.amstat.org/sections/SRMS/Proceedings/papers/1980_137.pdf.

17. National Telecommunications and Information Administration, "Falling through the Net II: New Data on the Digital Divide," 28 July 1998, http://www.ntia.doc.gov/ntiahome/net2/falling.html.

18. Matt Richtel and Ken Belson, "Call Carriers Seek Growth by Catering to Hispanics," *New York Times*, 30 May 2006.

19. Ironically, this figure was reported by Arbitron; see Arbitron Radio, "The Power of Hispanic Consumers: A Compelling Argument for Reaching Out to Hispanic Consumers," 14 December 2004, http://www.selecta1050.com/sponsors/4/22664/file_18792.pdf.

20. "Hispanic Radio: A Medium on the Grow," *Broadcasting & Cable*, 3 April 1989, 49.

21. Andrea Gerlin, "Media: Radio Stations Gain by Going after Hispanics," *Wall Street Journal*, 14 July 1993, B1.

22. Lynn Berling-Manuel, "Marketing to Hispanics: Expanding Radio Market Battle Reaches Static," *Advertising Age*, 11 August 1986, S12; and Anne Moncreiff Arrarte, "Radio Data Don't Rate," *Advertising Age*, 27 November 1989, 88.

23. "Ratings Worth 40 Million? Networks Have No Doubt," *Advertising Age*, 24 January 1994, S2; and Paul Lenti, "Univision Snares Big Share in Nielsen Hispanic Index," *Variety*, 28 March 1994, 46.

24. "Marketing to Hispanics," *Advertising Age*, 27 November 1989, 88.

25. "Nielsen Expands Hispanic TV Ratings," *Broadcasting & Cable*, 8 August 1994, 1; and David Tobenken, "Nielsen Rethinks Hispanic Ratings," *Broadcasting & Cable*, 10 April 1995, 54.

26. Belville, *Audience Ratings*, 115–18.

27. Katy Bachman, "Waiting on Weighting," *Mediaweek*, 18 November 2002, 8.

28. Leila Cobo, "Radio Hooked on Latin," *Billboard*, 9 April 2005, 1; Steve Knopper, "The Spanish Market Grows Up," *Billboard*, 16 March 1996, 99; and Steve Knopper, "Radio en Espanol Makes Strides in U.S.," *Billboard*, 30 May 1998, 86.

29. For more on the generalization of all Latino media consumers, see Dávila, *Latinos, Inc.*

30. "Arbitron Announces Improved Methods for Tracking Race/Ethnicity and Language in Its Radio Surveys," *Radio Ink*, 8 January 2002.

31. Eduardo Porter, "Spanish-Radio Firms Blast Arbitron," *Wall Street Journal*, 21 November 2002, B10.

32. Leila Cobo, "Regional Mexican Radio Tops among U.S. Hispanics," *Billboard*, 21 June 2003, 30.

33. Cobo, "Radio Hooked on Latin."

34. Napoli, "Audience Valuation and Minority Media," 172–77.

35. Gerlin, "Media: Radio Stations Gain by Going after Hispanics."

36. Hildy Medina, "Spanish-Language Stations Rise in Respect, Ratings," *Los Angeles Business Journal*, October 13, 1997, http://los-angeles-business-journal.vlex.com/vid/spanish-language-stations-respect-ratings-53752410.

37. Ien Ang, "Wanted Audiences: On the Politics of Empirical Studies," in *Remote Control: Television, Audiences, and Cultural Power*, ed. Ellen Sieter, Hans Borchers, Gabriele Kreutzner, and Eva-Maria Warth (New York: Routledge, 1989), 104.

11

The Dark Side of Transnational Latinidad

Narcocorridos and the Branding of Authenticity

HECTOR AMAYA

On October 20, 2011, *Billboard* put together the first *Billboard* Mexican Music Awards. The event was co-organized with Telemundo, the second-largest Spanish-language television network in the United States. The awards would reward excellence in *Billboard*'s regional Mexican music category. Prior to 2011, regional Mexican music was recognized during the *Billboard* Latin Music Awards. Yet, as a testament to the sheer power of the regional Mexican category, *Billboard* and Telemundo bet that the stand-alone ceremony would be a television and marketing success. They were correct. Five million people, including almost 2.8 million adults in the coveted eighteen-to-forty-nine age demographic, saw the show. The ceremony also became one of the five highest-ranked entertainment shows of 2011 for Telemundo, and won the ratings war in Los Angeles *and* Miami among men eighteen to thirty-four (Cobo 2011). *Billboard*'s regional Mexican category refers to a radio format that includes *banda, norteño, mariachi, grupero,* and *ranchera* music. This format is the most popular among Mexican Americans in the United States, due in part to the large number of immigrants from northern Mexico who reside in the United States. Cementing the category's relevance is the fact that regional Mexican accounts for more than 60 percent of sales in *Billboard*'s broader Latin music category. By all these accounts and its success in Los Angeles, a city dominated by Mexican Americans, *and* Miami, a city dominated by Cuban Americans, Puerto Ricans, and immigrants from other Latin American nations, this ceremony was of huge significance to Latinos in the United States and to the media industries that court them (Cobo 2008).

In 2011, the big winners of the Mexican Music Awards were Gerardo Ortiz, who took the six major awards, including artist of the year award, and Jenni Rivera, who took home the female artist of the year award and a special award called El Premio de la Estrella for her positive influence beyond music. Ortiz's awards were garnered for two very successful albums named after two *narcocorrido* hits: "Ni Hoy ni mañana" (Neither today nor tomorrow) and "Morir y existir" (To die and to exist). Rivera got her awards for the imprint she made throughout her career and for a double-disc collection called *Joyas prestadas* (Fonovisa/Universal), in which she reinterpreted iconic Mexican ballads *banda*-style. Speaking to the sustained success of these two artists, Ortiz and Rivera also dominated the 2012 *Billboard* Mexican Music Award ceremony. Ortiz received seven more Billboards, including artist of the year. Rivera repeated as the female artist of the year and received two other awards.

This article examines the convergence of Ortiz and Rivera in these two important award ceremonies, a convergence that will not be repeated. Rivera died in a plane crash in Mexico in December 2012, during the writing of this article, and though sales of her music have skyrocketed, her success, from here on, will be posthumous and so will be her awards. Besides these two ceremonies, the careers of Ortiz and Rivera have two significant similarities, which are the reason for this article.

First, their careers are intimately tied to narcocorridos, a style of music and lyrics that narrates the lives, deeds, and adventures of people engaged in drug traffic. Ortiz is today one of the most important narcocorrido singers. Rivera began her career as a narcocorrido singer, and though over time she has shed some of her connections to the narcoimaginary, her original success was due to her ability to sing the narcocorrido from a female standpoint.

Second, their personal brands and their brands' circulation in the music industry convey notions of authenticity that, similar to gangsta rap, rely on mystifying claims about place and biography. Both singers are from California (Ortiz is from Pasadena; Rivera was from Long Beach), a place distant from the daily violence engendered by the cartels in Mexico, but this has not stopped them from performing their narco-corridos in the first person, a narrative trope that helps give authenticity to a brand that aims to connect fans with experiences of violence.

This article argues that just as the centenary magazine *Billboard* uses the industry term "regional Mexican" to designate music that may or may not originate in Mexico, Ortiz and Rivera constitute their commercial identities in relation to an imaginary, following Arjun Appadurai's (1996) use of the term, in which Mexican identity, place, and consumption are central to authenticity. According to Appadurai, whose work examines conditions of globalization and transnationalism such as those found in our cases, "the imagination has become an organized field of social practices, a form of work (in the sense of both labor and culturally organized practice), and a form of negotiation between sites of agency (individuals) and globally defined fields of possibility" (32). Considering the efforts by Ortiz and Rivera to highlight their connection to Mexico and the way their music circulates with their fans, who, for instance, regularly comment that Ortiz sings "la pura verdad" (the pure truth), in this field of social practice that is the imaginary, authenticity matters. Their efforts to construct the narcocorrido brand and *Billboard's* Mexican regional term call attention to the problems of validating this hugely successful music genre among Mexican American fans even though the narcocorrido is bound to Mexico and to experiences of violence.

Narcocorridos and the Branding of Authenticity

There is a parallelism between singers who, like Ortiz and Rivera, embody a narco-identity while claiming to be from Culiacán or Sinaloa, and *Billboard's* use of the term "regional Mexican" to classify and brand narcocorridos. The deployment of a narco-identity and place is essential to a "brand culture" that hides the deterritorialized character of the music industry today. As Sarah Banet-Weiser posits, brand culture refers to the process by which the converging relationships between marketing, a product, and consumers "become cultural contexts for everyday living, individual identity, and affective relationships"

(2012, 3). Claiming thus that embodiment and place are central to the branding of artists and media genres that give industrial meaning to the term "narcocorrido" is more than claiming that place has become commoditized. In our contemporary culture, branding is central to the meanings we give to cultural experiences; hence, branding is not only about capitalism but also, as Banet-Weiser notes, about identity. The claims of Mexicanity and the way performers like Ortiz and Rivera have embodied the narco-brand are thus not only commercial tactics. They are also the means by which Mexican American urban youth, who are the typical consumers of narcocorridos, reconfigure their marginalization through the tactical deployment of counterhegemonic fantasies that narcocorridos activate, even if these fantasies simultaneously stress the deterritorialized character of the music. Deterritorialization here is more than simply the lack of ground or locality; it is also the cultural ruse that underscores the music's lack of responsiveness to social conditions in Mexico and/or the United States and a tactic consumers use to connect to fantasies of power and sufficiency.

Connecting narcocorrido performers, urban Mexican American youth, and transnational music corporations like *Billboard* is a relatively simple truth: The narco-brand is all about authenticity, and this is not an oxymoron. Banet-Weiser (2012) notes the relevant connections that branding has with authenticity in contemporary culture. The "process of branding," she writes, "impacts the way we understand who we are, how we organize ourselves in the world, what stories we tell ourselves about ourselves" (5). Branding is thus essential to self-identity. Thus, branding becomes intertwined with the personal and social processes by which we define our authentic self, including the social practices, objects, and knowledges that can yield for us—and often give us—an aura of authenticity. Not all practices, objects, or knowledges do this, and part of the labor of being a functioning modern individual lies in learning to recognize the meaning of authenticity in practices, objects, and knowledges (7). One of the most significant lessons in Banet-Weiser's work is that the relationship of branding to capitalism does not preclude capitalism from being part of the social processes by which people legitimately construct authenticity, even if this authenticity is built through consumption (8). In a world where social relations are often commercial, the authentic and the commercial cannot be opposites.

This perplexing insight is well known by many musical performers, including those who perform in the gangsta rap genre. Similar to narcocorrido, and reacting against the mainstreaming of hip-hop, since the late 1980s gangsta rap has traditionally relied on autobiographical claims of place, class, hypermasculinity, and marginalization to position itself as a patriarchal counterhegemonic and popular music genre dedicated to narrating the living conditions of "the hood" (Oware 2011, 24). The critical and economic success of the genre and its anchoring on authenticity have attracted also middle-class performers who, like Vanilla Ice, were aware of the codes of authenticity and crafted a personal brand according to these codes, even if his claims were fictitious. As Katja Lee (2008) suggests, the Vanilla Ice scandal, which happened after critics and fans learned of his "vanilla" upbringing, simply underscores the audience's investment in the real and the expectation of an authentic "correlation between the lived experience of the artists and their art" (354).

A similar reliance on an authenticity crafted on place (Sinaloa, for instance) and marginalization is at the heart of narcocorrido branding. The question then is, How is the branding of authenticity achieved in narco-culture? And for whom is this branding useful?

Banet-Weiser points out that some categories of life are particularly susceptible to being conceived as authentic, and these categories include self-identity, politics, creativity, and religious experiences. As I show in this and the following sections, the narco-brand connects self-identity to politics, and this is possible because of the cultural labor of performers, consumers, and institutions. The use of culture as politics is a learned process that helps individuals interpret their lives in relationship to some social transactions that take meaning through the lens of power. Just like "the street" takes a politicized meaning in gangsta rap, drug trafficking becomes counterhegemonic in narcocorridos. These two genres are evidence that the political is not a pre-given category of life, but is the part of our lives that, through a particular optic, becomes subject to power. Because it is learned, the political is the result of social processes that rely on the semantic actions of institutions. Hence, the political underpinnings of the narco-brand are experienced in relationship to identity, but depend on broad institutional support and affirmation. It is this interrelation that defines the connection between narcocorrido performers, Mexican American urban youth, and *Billboard*. How is it that this connection came to depend on and be defined by experiences of power?

What Are Narcocorridos If Not Folklore?

The narcocorrido connects to power because it belongs to narrative traditions historically connected to a counterhegemonic stand. As such, it inherits cultural meanings that suggest that this musical genre is the proper narrative vehicle to use to speak against injustice and to do so from the position of the disenfranchised. This cultural baggage is the result of the meanings associated with the traditional folkloric music genre of the Mexican *corrido*. The corrido is one of the oldest and most enduring forms of musical folklore in Mexico. Reaching back centuries to Spanish narrative traditions, the corrido originated as an oral form for memorializing events and people. In simple poetic form, corridos told stories that mattered. Corridos are what Jesús Martín-Barbero (1993) would call a popular form of media: They originate among the popular classes and were meant to construct and reconstruct a version of reality from their standpoint. Unsurprisingly, corridos often have a counterhegemonic potential.

During the latter half of the nineteenth century, the Mexican corrido took a peculiar epic and counterhegemonic form. Instead of emphasizing events such as fiestas or battles, as early corridos did, the Mexican corrido has, for more than a century, emphasized the deeds of men and women in their struggles against power. As Guillermo Hernández notes, Mexican corridos were the preferred cultural form for narrating the deeds of rebels during the presidency of Porfirio Díaz in the last decade of the eighteenth century, and ever since, the corrido has retained a counterhegemonic aura (1992, 324).

Distribution technologies changed the narrative conventions of corridos. As an oral form, corridos were indebted to the values and interests of a geographical region. They were responsive to locality. But already in the nineteenth century corridos were published on sheets of paper and sold by the musicians who composed them. The publishing of corridos gave these narratives a new reach and cultural potential. Paper reaches farther than the singer's voice and lasts longer; publishing thus delinked the corrido from orality, locality, and the present time (Hernández 1992, 326). The record player engendered further transformations. Corridos became vehicles for stardom, and their narrative conventions multiplied. Instead of being narrowly defined by the local, as were early corridos, or the epic, a common style during wartime, corridos were also written to tell the lives and deeds of both common people and criminals in their struggles against the law. It is this particular type of counterhegemonic gesture, complexly bound to antisocial behavior and culture, that narcocorridos inherit.

Narcocorridos began to appear in the 1930s with titles like "Maldita droga" and "Por morfina y cocaína" (Ramírez-Pimienta 2011, 13). Always exploring the moral life and deeds of drug dealers, the narcocorrido portrays a world from the point of view of the outlaw, making it an ideal vehicle for counterhegemonic storytelling, including fantasies against traditional social mores and against the state. The subgenre did not immediately succeed commercially. It took a few decades for the music to become popular. It was not until the 1970s, a time in which Mexican drug cartels had grown and consolidated their influence around the growth, sale, and traffic of marijuana and heroin, that this lurid cultural genre gained broad popularity. In 1974, the little-known *norteño* band Los Tigres del Norte recorded *Contrabando y traición*, and the title track, also known as "La camelia," became one of the biggest hits in the history of *norteño* music. With this and other narcocorridos, Los Tigres del Norte became arguably the most influential Mexican regional band in history and redefined the narcocorrido genre, making it a cultural phenomenon that expanded from California, where they lived, worked, and recorded, to northern Mexico, where they became akin to matinee idols (Wald 2001).

Like Los Tigres' reach across national borders, the narcocorrido has always been a transnational cultural form (Ramírez-Pimienta 2011, 159). It geographically originated in northern Mexico and in the American Southwest. It is concerned with the drug trade, a social phenomenon that spans the world and importantly connects Mexico to the United States. And it is historically linked to transnational traditions that bind the music style to the US and German migrations. This influence is the clearest in the two polka-based music styles that are the aesthetic core of most contemporary narcocorridos: *norteño* and *banda* music.

In addition to being the two musical genres central to narcocorridos, *banda* and *norteño* music are the two leading music categories in the *Billboard* regional Mexican album category. They are also the leading genres in the regional Mexican radio format. Today, most of the playtime and most of the record sales in the regional Mexican music category are for *banda* and *norteño* music, with artists like Ortiz, La Arrolladora Banda El Limón, Roberto Tapia, and Grupo Pesado, who, as an example, on the week of December 15, 2012, dominated the top five spots in *Billboard*'s regional Mexican song category (La Arrolladora Banda El Limón had two songs in the top five). Rivera was in fourteenth place with her song "La misma gran señora." These artists dominate sales with romantic ballads like "Solo vine a despedirme" (Ortiz), "Mirando al cielo" (Roberto Tapia), "Mi promesa" (Grupo Pesado), and "Cabecita dura" and "El primer lugar" (La Arrolladora Banda El Limón) (*Billboard*'s website for the week of December 15, 2012). This may mean that the romantic ballad remains the most important subgenre of *banda* and *norteño*. But it also means that regional Mexican is dominated by artists whose personal brand is closely associated with narcocorridos. Except for Grupo Pesado, which has made a public rejection of narcocorridos, the rest of the top five have a musical repertory that includes narcocorridos (Contreras 2008). La Arrolladora Banda El Limón may have only a few, but Ortiz and Tapia are two of the most important narcocorrido singers today. Rivera's life is closely connected to the narco-imaginary. The appeal of these artists, even while singing romantic ballads, is undisputedly bound to a brand crafted through the performance of narcocorridos.

Today, narcocorridos, like all music, are distributed in CD and digital format; as it is for other musical genres, their online distribution increasingly accounts for the majority of the sales. Since 2008, the early recordings of Rivera have been distributed by the Orchard, a gigantic multinational that specializes in digital distribution (Ben-Yehuda 2008). The Orchard, which globally controls more than 1.3 million songs and 5,000 videos, locates, places, and markets songs in hundreds of digital stores like iTunes, eMusic, Google, Rhapsody, Rdio, Spotify, and V CAST. It also sells songs with potential to become ringtones to mobile carriers like Verizon, Vodafone, and Bell Canada. Although the Orchard also distributes to physical music stores, its digital distribution services are the central cog in its business model.

Digital technologies of circulation have again left an imprint on the corrido in general and the narcocorrido in particular, facilitating on the one hand the production and distribution of narcocorridos across nations, but also straining the ability of the genre to continue connecting to the counterhegemonic and the experiential. Thanks to direct sales as songs and albums, and CD distribution schemas based on websites rather than physical music stores, contemporary narcocorridos are less constrained than ever by place and nation than vinyl recordings, tapes, or CDs. This has meant that stars based in California, such as Ortiz and Rivera, can have instant access to the rest of the US territory, a feature key to Latino artists whose fans are increasingly located in cities and towns without a music store that specializes in Latinas/os. Just as important, digital distribution allows these artists to quickly reach the Mexican market, which constitutes a sizable portion of their music and concert sales. If in the 1970s the narcocorrido had to make the arduous trip from California, where it was often recorded, as in the case of Los Tigres del Norte, to the rest of the United States and northern Mexico, digital technologies and online distribution have made this process instantaneous. As relevant to the sale and radio playtime of narcocorridos, online distribution and Internet radio have meant that narcocorridos can bypass the censoring efforts of several Mexican states, including Sinaloa, Baja California Norte, and Chihuahua. Digital technologies hence allow the relatively unrestricted circulation of the music, in spite of efforts by the Mexican state to restrict it (Amaya 2013).

Although narcocorridos are not the only type of song played in *banda* and *norteño*, they are so important to regional Mexican that I argue that the narcocorrido is one of the most important musical forms for the 32 million Mexican Americans. It is because of narcocorridos that Los Tigres rose to the top of the Latino music world forty years ago; it is because of narcocorridos that Rivera had a shot at being the "diva of *banda* music"; and it is because of narcocorridos that Ortiz, very recently, skyrocketed to the top of the regional Mexican and Latin charts. Significant to this article, it is because of narcocorridos and digital music distribution that Rivera's last recording, the double-disc *Joyas prestadas*, skyrocketed to the top of the *Billboard* Latin albums chart days after her death. Marketed individually, on the week of December 22, *Joyas prestadas pop* sat at number two and *Joyas prestadas banda* sat at number four. Two of the top five spots in this coveted category were Rivera's.

Narcocorridos are central to the branding of some of the top stars in the regional Mexican and Latin categories, giving these singers and musical ensembles the branding of authenticity. After all, it is the narcocorrido, and not the romantic ballad, that connects music consumers to the present social realities of violence and power differentials that too commonly define the lives of Latinas/os. In addition, because narcocorridos continue the corrido tradition, they can be perceived as popular, not mass, music. Fans routinely argue that they like narcocorridos because they "tell the pure truth," and this truth-telling capacity connects back to the old corridos' role as a valid repository of a community's memory, a place for historicity and the creation of proper heroes (Villalobos and Ramírez-Pimienta 2004). This truth-telling capacity lends authenticity to contemporary narcocorridos, to the singers who use them for branding, and to *Billboard*, a transnational magazine and corporation that in using the moniker "regional Mexican" aims to classify *banda* and *norteño* as music connected to a place, Mexico, and to the flesh-and-blood communities of Mexicans, not simply to audiences. Given this, it is reasonable to stipulate the following: If, as Isabel Molina Guzmán and Angharad Valdivia (2005) argue, Latinas/os are the "it" category of consumers and audiences among marketers and advertisers in the United States, the "taste" for narcocorridos has to be seen as one of the most significant developments in Latino and US culture in the last decades.

A Place for Transnationalism and Deterritorialization

Today, many narcocorrido singers are based in northern Mexico, near the places where the influence of the drug cartels is greatest. In towns and cities like Ciudad Juárez, Culiacán, Tijuana, and Nuevo Laredo, the recurrence of drug-related events has inspired complex cultural responses, including cultural forms and practices that support the cartels, and others that reject them. Some narcocorridos are thus popular responses to these social conditions. Small, local *banda* or *norteño* ensembles in Sinaloa, for instance, are sometimes asked to compose a corrido in honor of someone killed in a drug-related event. The song is later performed during the funeral as a gesture of respect and a symbol of love for the deceased. Almost never recorded, these narcocorridos are an example of a folkloric, popular tradition.[1]

Today, these truly popular narcocorridos are in the minority. The majority of narcocorridos are the product of a cultural-industrial apparatus dominated by the interests and needs of capitalism and transnational music companies. The vinyl record facilitated the disconnection between corrido and place and initiated a process whereby the field of music became defined and dominated by stardom, commercialism, and branding. Digital distribution technologies have exacerbated this process, participating in the growing deterritorialization of the corrido and its contemporary and dominant subgenre, the narcocorrido. Just as Los Tigres del Norte managed to become the early stars of the narcocorrido from California, away from Mexico and the violence brought about by the drug cartels, today, an increasing number of narcocorrido stars are based in the United States. In addition to those already mentioned, narcocorrido megastars who live in the United States at least part of the year include Juan Gabriel, Marco Antonio Solís, Adolfo Ángel, Pepe Aguilar, Los Huracanes del Norte, Los Tucanes de Tijuana, Los Bravos del Norte, and many more (Ramírez-Pimienta 2011, 187). Just as importantly, the majority of narcocorridos are produced and recorded in the US Southwest, with most recorded in California and Texas (though a growing number come from cities like Chicago and Detroit). The careers of Rivera and Ortiz are examples of the process by which the narcocorrido brand can exist as a signifier of deterritorialization.

Rivera was born in a household marked by narcocorridos (Quinones 2012). In 1988 her father, Pedro Rivera, an immigrant from Mexico, founded the record label Cintas Acuario, which is credited with launching the career of the hugely famous narcocorrido singer and songwriter Chalino Sánchez. If musicians like Los Tigres have always represented the highly commercializable end of the narcocorrido, in the late 1980s and during the 1990s, Chalino (the moniker his fans prefer) represented the popular and the authentic. His lyrics seemed to have the proper amount of rural credibility that defined the original corrido, and his raspy, untrained voice added authenticity to a music career that ended in violence. He was born in Badiraguato, a small town in the Sinaloa mountains that is notorious for being the original home of several of the most powerful drug cartels, including the Sinaloa Cartel, the biggest crime organization in the world. In and around Badiraguato were born Pedro Áviles, the first Mexican drug kingpin, Ismael "El Mayo" Zambada, a boss in the Sinaloa Cartel, Ernesto Fonseca Carrillo, the leader of the Guadalajara Cartel, Rafael Caro Quintero, convicted for the death of the DEA agent Enrique Camarena, Joaquín "El Chapo" Guzmán Loera, the current head of the Sinaloa Cartel, and the Beltrán Leyva brothers, who initiated the Beltrán Leyva cartel. No other town this size in the world can be credited with a bigger effect on the world of crime around the globe. This rough town was the credible backdrop to Chalino's musical career, and his death cemented his fame. In 1992 he became famous in Mexico and the United States when, during a music concert, a patron neared the stage and began shooting at Chalino. Though hit on the side, Chalino, famously, took out his own gun and fired back, and by the end of the evening, two people were killed, including the would-be killer. His reputation grew, but the success lasted only a few months. In May 1992 Chalino was killed, execution-style, in Mexico after a concert. These events proved extremely profitable to the labels that recorded Chalino, including Cintas Acuarios. If Chalino was famous prior to his death, he became a rock star after, and his recordings continue to sell today.

The recording brand of Cintas Acuario is dependent on the narco-corrido as an authentic cultural product, and Pedro Rivera refers to himself on his website as "El Patriarca del Corrido" (the patriarch of the corrido). All his sons and his daughter, Jenni, became musicians, with Lupillo Rivera climbing to the pinnacle of the music world. Today, Lupillo is one of the biggest stars in narcocorridos and regularly appears in the *Billboard* rankings in the United States and in Mexico.

Lupillo notwithstanding, the most successful of the Rivera family was Jenni, who became a music star and who, over time, also became a star in the world of television in the United States and Mexico. Rivera began recording in 1994, and she released her first album in 1995 (*La chacalosa*, Capitol/EMI), which sold around one million copies. The title song, "La chacalosa," is the story of a drug queen-pin, and the song positioned Rivera as a singer branded by narco-culture. In this song, Rivera performs in the first person as the daughter of a trafficker ("soy hija de un traficante"), who was raised by and inherited the heroin business from her father ("conozco bien las movidas, me crié entre la mafia grande de la major mercancia"). The song describes her illegal poppy crops in Jalisco and her heroin labs in Sonora and declares, from a curious feminist standpoint that would be repeated in many of her songs, that women can also become narco-leaders ("y también las mujeres pueden"). *La chacalosa* included several other tracks that furthered Rivera's narco-brand, including "También las mujeres pueden," a song originally made popular by Los Tigres, and "La perra contrabandista," which literally translates as "The Trafficker Bitch." Like other narcocorrido singers, she also performed romantic ballads (*La chacalosa* included, for instance, "Libro abierto," a *ranchera* standard ballad), but her identity as a powerful woman willing to defy male-ruled society depended on her drug-related songs. Although in several albums she continued the tradition of other famous Mexican women singers (e.g., *Farewell to Selena* and *Joyas prestadas*), her work can also be described as an ongoing conversation with the great ones of the narcocorrido. This is particularly true in her 1999 album *Reyna de reynas*, in which she is in conversation with one of the greatest narcocorrido albums, *Jefe de jefes* (1997), by Los Tigres del Norte. This narco-album reasserted Rivera's complex gender performance, and invited listeners to, at least briefly, reflect on the sexism implied in the traditional, male-dominated narcocorrido subgenre.

In 2009 Ortiz was a little-known narcocorrido singer in Sinaloa, Mexico. To publicize himself, he would upload videos of his performance to youtube.com. He began having a following and, as a publicity stunt, in the fall of 2009 he travelled to Los Angeles, his home city, to do an underground performance that attracted three thousand people, including an executive of Del Records, who, impressed, took a chance and signed Ortiz. Practically all the musicians with Del Records are narco-singers, and from its origins in 2008, Del Records began developing a narco-brand identified as Corridos Enfermos (Sick Corridos) or Enfermedad Masiva (Massive Illness). This curious use of illness as metaphor in the branding of Del Records music compilations is reminiscent of the narco-brand El Movimiento Alterado (Altered Movement), developed by the brothers Adolfo and Omar Valenzuela Rivera, Los Twiins. Corridos Enfermos, like El Movimiento Alterado, brings together artists to record quite successful compilations of narcocorridos

(Amaya 2013). In Corridos Enfermos, Enfermedad Masiva, and El Movimiento Alterado, being out-of-health and being altered are metaphors that signal both the music's counterhegemonic identity and also the sense that the crime world the music glorifies is an unhealthy aspect of normal, sane society. Although not as successful as El Movimiento Alterado, Corridos Enfermos strengthens Del Records' narco-brand and introduces listeners to other singers working for the label. At this moment, Ortiz is Del Records' most successful artist, repeatedly reaching the top of the *Billboard* rankings.

Ortiz has no qualms about performing narcocorridos. A huge percentage of his songs deal with the drug world, and, although they are not always from the point of view of the *narcotraficante* ("Sangre azul," for instance, is from the point of view of a policeman), the majority depict the drug war from the perspective of the cartels. "La última sombra," "Aquí les afirmo," "Morir y existir," and many others speak of violence, drugs, revenge, and trafficking. In addition to these classic drug-related topics, Ortiz also composes and performs narcocorridos that are about the narco-lifestyle. "El trockero Locochon" and "Culiacán vs. Mazatlán," for instance, are about highly stylized pickup trucks (pimped, if you wish) and sports cars. "A la moda" is about fashion, jewelry, and consumption. These narco-lifestyle songs and the videos that publicize them are full of young women who seem to be the sexual reward for engaging in the proper display of excessive consumption. During the last three years, Ortiz has thus delivered a series of performances that, taken together, paint a fantastic type of masculinity bound to violence, wealth, rebellion, and traditional heteronormative sexuality. How can these fantasies connect to authenticity? Or, differently stated, What cultural labor do performers have to do in order to construct authenticity out of these deterritorialized fantasies? Why do fans believe that narcocorridos tell "the pure truth"?

Violent Identities as Brands

As a musical narrative form, the narcocorrido relies on two powerful sociocultural antecedents: the folkloric aura of the corrido, which I discussed above, and the narco-imaginary's connection to conspicuous consumption. These two combine to produce the most common narrative modality in contemporary narcocorridos and the central cog in the narco-brand: first-person narration, a trope also found in gangsta rap. Although first- and third-person narration have always been common in corridos, contemporary narcocorridos have all but eliminated third-person narration. Unlike old epic corridos, which often used third-person narration, as in "El corrido de Pancho Villa," most narcocorridos today are first-person narratives that connect the corrido to the experiential and that efficiently identify the singer(s) with the imaginary world the song creates. This is a contemporary phenomenon that relates to the way the narco-brand circulates among Mexican American urban youth. Like gangsta rap in other youth communities, narcocorridos have become hegemonic among urban Mexican American youth, who use these songs and performances to resignify the violence and poverty that too often surround them (Morrison 2008).

Old narcocorridos like "Contrabando y traición" or "La banda del carro rojo" were third-person narrations that placed the singer in the traditional position of memorializing events and people. Today, the form of address found in "La chacalosa" ("They look for me because I'm a *chacalosa*; I'm the daughter of a drug trafficker") is the norm, and the third-person narration is rarely used for new compositions. Artists like Ortiz, Rivera, and all of the members of Corridos Enfermos and El Movimiento Alterado do not typically sing descriptions of things that happen to others or moralize about the outcomes of illegal activity. They do not share the news or distribute local lore; they *are* the news and place themselves at the center of the stories. These singers, in song and performance, embody the narco-imaginary and present themselves as examples of drug-dealing success, as beneficiaries of the wealth found in drug trafficking, as those inflicting violence on others, or as those suffering the violence.

A first-person narration of violence implies that the singer is often singing from the position of those who survive the violence or those who inflicted it. Exceptions do exist, as in Ortiz's "Cara a la muerte," a first-person narration moralizing about a traitor being killed. The majority of today's songs, however, are told from the position of power, of survival. There is no moralizing, but only justifying the survivor's success, which, in narcocorridos, often comes down to arguing for or presenting a superior masculinity—or, as in Rivera's song, a superior femininity. For instance, in the frightening "14 guerras," Ortiz declares,

> I am the Taliban ghost of El Chapo . . .
> I have tortured, decapitated, assaulted and named
> And if fear crosses my path I connect
> With my intelligence
> That's how I do my job, with heart, I am a killer

Ortiz takes on the identity of an assassin and torturer who believes himself the ghostly presence of "El Chapo" Guzmán, the leader of the Sinaloa Cartel. The masculinity he presents is relatively complex, for it relies on intelligence to carry out the harshest violence on others. Yet this masculinity is unmistakably tied to masculine excess, for it is meant to inflict pain and wage war.

The first-person narration does more than brand the singer as the embodiment of strength and ruthlessness. The narcocorrido always seems to carry the specter of the popular, the real, and the authentic. Even as a massified form of culture, narcocorridos typically attempt to profit from the old-fashioned counterhegemonic spirit of old corridos. This means, among other things, that the narcocorrido brand is committed to a certain historicity and experiential validity that are constructed through references to place, to actual drug organizations, to real people involved in the drug trade, and, sometimes, to real events. Hence, the narcocorrido singer(s) must create brand authenticity by singing as if actual violence were part of their daily lives. Thus, narcostars sing as if they were "El Chapo" Guzmán, "El Mayo" Zambada, El M-1 (Manuel Torres Félix), or other famous capos.

The experiential is here a trope that forces facticity into fictional and nonfictional corridos. This includes claiming to be from a place where violence is common. Instead of placing themselves in "the hood," corrido singers place themselves in cities like Culiacán, the capital of Sinaloa; Badiraguato, the place that saw the beginning of the Sinaloa and other important cartels; Tijuana; Mazatlán; and Durango, to name a few. Predictably, the violent cities brand the singer, and this effect can be augmented by connecting the biography of the singer to the cities of violence. Ortiz, for instance, makes a huge deal of the fact that he lived for some time in Culiacán (Sinaloa, Mexico), Tijuana (Baja California, Mexico), and Bogotá (Colombia), three cities commonly linked to the drug trade and drug violence. Rivera commonly claims Mexican and Sinaloan roots, thanks to her father, and has many songs that refer to Sinaloa (e.g., "La pochita de Sinaloa" and "Sinaloa, princesa norteña").

The narcocorrido's connection to violence is central to the narco-brand, even if the violence is conjured up with managerial imagery, as in some of Rivera's lines. Yet experiences of violence are not the only common branding mechanism. Narco-lifestyle corridos engage the violence obliquely, as they tend to depict social interactions that are possible only as the aftermath of violent criminal activity. In corridos such as Ortiz's "Culiacán vs. Mazatlán," the protagonist, from Culiacán, races his highly altered Camaro against the Viper of someone from Mazatlán. Though the Camaro loses, they race again, this time the Viper against a Corvette, and the Corvette wins. In the current imaginary of Mexican American youth, these displays of conspicuous consumption exist because of illegal actions related to drugs; the cars and the scantily clad women who seem to always circle the vehicles in the music videos stand for the spoils of violence, the economic and sexual rewards for joining the cartels. The song "A la moda," a huge hit for Ortiz, is full of expensive brands that define the hyper-wealthy, including Ferrari, Dolce and Gabbana, Prada, and Rolex. In the music video that accompanies the song, Ortiz displays wealth and fashion trendiness by changing outfits every few seconds; by entering the hall of an expensive hotel after driving his Ferrari; by being followed by several bodyguards; and by surrounding himself with beautiful women in a club with a table full of expensive liquor bottles. In short, Ortiz embodies the consumption and immoral frankness of the narco-lord.

Violence and conspicuous consumption are the two key ways of performing authenticity and constructing the narco-brand. The first-person narration of violence and wealth allows fans to personally connect to these two very important categories of life, even if this connection exists in the fantasy world. Narcocorridos tell the pure truth and fans can, however briefly, hold on to the notion that they are the ones who can inflict pain, not only receive it. Fans, however briefly, can imagine the experience of obscene wealth, even if after the dance club closes they must go back to their decrepit reality.

Conclusion

Authenticity is a powerful and demanding brand. As if to ratify that his colorful biography is evidence of his intimate knowledge of the violence he sings about, Ortiz barely survived an attack on him on March 20, 2011, in Villa del Alvarez (Mexico). His manager and promoter, Ramiro Caro, was not that fortunate. Rivera died in a plane crash, but news outlets in Mexico and the United States were quick to report that the Drug Enforcement Administration was investigating the owner of the plane, implying that Rivera's death was somehow related to drugs. I doubt it.

The music this paper deals with is catchy and rhythmic; it gets to the hips. It is old and it is new. It originated in the luscious hills of the Sierra Madre of Mexico's Pacific Coast, the same hills that saw the origin of the cultivation of heroin at the beginning of the twentieth century. Sinaloa is known for its beaches, mountains, marijuana, heroin, and the Sinaloa Cartel. These elements combined with cultural traditions of music and violence that eventually, in the second half of the twentieth century, became the origin of narcocorridos. Although from Sinaloa, the music, the violence, and the cartels are all transnational forces that have a significant presence in the United States and Latin America. In this paper I have shown how these forces have become part of the Latino and music world, giving authenticity to musical expressions that depend on fantasies of place and of experience. The fantasy of place, which *Billboard* profits from, simplistically connects music written, performed, produced, and consumed in the United States to Mexico. Some regional Mexican is from Mexico, but the bulk of narcocorridos that are used to give authenticity to the category are not. Fantasies of experience underscore the performances that define narco-stars like Rivera and Ortiz, and this claim to the experiential lubricates the circulation of music among a population hungry for cultural experiences of power.

NOTE

1. Video cameras are now so common that you can find some videos of these emotional performances during funerals on youtube.com.

REFERENCES

Amaya, Hector. 2013. "Authorship and Death: Narco-Violence in Mexico and the New Aesthetics of Nation." In *A Companion to Media Authorship*, edited by Jonathan Gray and Derek Johnson. Malden, MA: Blackwell.

Appadurai, Arjun. 1996. *Modernity at Large: Cultural Dimensions of Globalization*. Minneapolis: University of Minnesota Press.

Banet-Weiser, Sarah. 2012. *Authentic: The Politics of Ambivalence in a Brand Culture*. New York: New York University Press.

Ben-Yehuda, Ayala. 2008. "Orchard Inks Key Regional Mexican Labels." *Billboard*, October 8, http://www.billboard.com/features/orchard-inks-key-regional-mexican-labels-1003872343.story#/features/orchard-inks-key-regional-mexican-labels-1003872343.story.

Cobo, Leila. 2008. "Regional Mexican Revival." *Billboard*, October 7, http://www.billboard.biz/bbbiz/genre/latin/regional-mexican-revival-1003871249.story.

———. 2011. "Inaugural Billboard Mexican Music Awards Deliver Strong Ratings on Telemundo." *Billboard*, October 31, http://www.billboard.biz/bbbiz/genre/latin/inaugural-billboard-mexican-music-awards-1005454952.story.

Contreras, Claudia. 2008. "Dice No a Narcocorridos." *El Universal*, February 29, http://www.eluniversal.com.mx/espectaculos/81871.html.

Hernández, Guillermo. 1992. "El corrido ayer y hoy." In *Entre la magia y la historia: Tradiciones, mitos y leyendas de la frontera*, edited by José Manuel Valenzuela Arce. Tijuana, Baja California, México: Programa Cultural de las Fronteras, El Colegio de la Frontera Norte.

Herrera-Sobek, Maria. 1990. *The Mexican Corrido: A Feminist Analysis*. Bloomington: Indiana University Press.

Lee, Katja. 2008. "Reconsidering Rap's 'I': Eminem's Autobiographical Postures and the Construction of Identity Authenticity." *Canadian Review of American Studies* 38, no. 3: 352–73.

Maciel, David, and María Herrera-Sobek. 1998. *Culture across Borders: Mexican Immigration and Popular Culture*. Tucson: University of Arizona Press.

Martín-Barbero, Jesús. 1993. *Communication, Culture and Hegemony: From the Media to Mediations*. Newbury Park: Sage.

Molina Guzmán, Isabel, and Angharad N. Valdivia. 2005. "Brain, Brow, and Booty: Latino Iconicity in U.S. Popular Culture." *Communication Review* 7: 205–21.

Morrison, Amanda Maria. 2008. "Musical Trafficking: Urban Youth and the Narcocorrido-Hardcore Rap Nexus." *Western Folklore* 67, no. 4: 379–97.

Oware, Matthew. 2011. "Brotherly Love: Homosociality and Black Masculinity in Gangsta Rap Music." *Journal of African American Studies* 15: 22–39.

Quinones, Sam. 2012. "Jenni Rivera's Musical Family Helped Popularize Mexican Narco-Ballads." *Los Angeles Times*, December 10, http://latimesblogs.latimes.com/lanow/2012/12/jenni-riveras-musical-family-helped-popularize-the-narco-ballad.html.

Ramírez-Pimienta, Juan Carlos. 2011. *Cantar a los narcos*. Mexico City: Temas de Hoy.

Valenzuela Arce, José Manuel. 1992. *Entre la magia y la historia: Tradiciones, mitos y leyendas de la frontera*. Tijuana, Baja California, México: Programa Cultural de las Fronteras, El Colegio de la Frontera Norte.

Villalobos, José Pablo, and Juan Carlos Ramírez-Pimienta. 2004. "Corridos and La Pura Verdad: Myths and Realities of the Mexican Ballad." *South Central Review* 21, no. 3: 129–49.

Wald, Elijah. 2001. *Narcocorrido: A Journey into the Music of Drugs, Guns, and Guerrillas*. New York: Rayo.

PART III

Cultural Politics

12

"No Papers, No Fear"

DREAM Activism, New Social Media, and
the Queering of Immigrant Rights

CRISTINA BELTRÁN

Introduction

For over a decade, heightened fears regarding terrorism and national
security have sanctioned an increasingly nativist, anti-immigrant climate that criminalizes noncitizens. These dynamics have stymied even
the most modest attempts at reform: Both George W. Bush and Barack
Obama have championed enforcement-driven immigration legislation
whose pathways to citizenship are as onerous as they are insufficient.
Yet even these limited efforts to address America's broken immigration
system have been difficult to achieve.

As comprehensive reform has run into repeated legislative road-
blocks, immigration rights activists have often focused on passage of the
Development, Relief, and Education for Alien Minors Act. Introduced
in 2001, the DREAM Act would extend a six-year conditional legal status to undocumented youth who meet several criteria, including

> entry into the United States before age 16; continuous presence in the United
> States for five years prior to the bill's enactment; receipt of a high school
> diploma or its equivalent (i.e., a GED); and demonstrated good moral char-
> acter. Qualifying youth would be authorized to work in the United States,
> go to school, or join the military. If during the six-year period they graduate

from a two-year college, complete at least two years of a four-year degree, or serve at least two years in the U.S. military, the beneficiary would be able to adjust from conditional to permanent residence status.[1]

As a discrete piece of legislation that applies to a particular segment of the population, the DREAM Act is far from comprehensive. Moreover, by focusing on children who did not "choose" to immigrate illegally and whose opportunities are limited through no fault of their own, the DREAM Act reinforces a good immigrant/bad immigrant account of migration that criminalizes undocumented parents as lawbreakers but labels their children "innocent," upstanding, and assimilated. Stories of young people who would qualify for the DREAM Act often emphasize their academic success, involvement in community and volunteer activities, and desire to engage in military service. Moreover, having come of age in the United States, these young people speak English; indeed, a number of Dreamers are English-dominant and therefore characterized as less "foreign" than other segments of the unauthorized populations.

Yet despite the many ways this population fits into liberal conceptions of the "good" immigrant whose success "gives" to the nation, congressional advocates have failed to pass the DREAM Act, as anti-immigrant legislation at the state level has actually grown more virulent since 2001.[2] In other words, despite pursuing a legislative strategy that emphasized the nonthreatening and innocent character of undocumented youth, hostility toward unauthorized immigrants (including Dreamers) has only grown in recent years. In response, DREAM activism has been notable for its increasingly confrontational and creative character. Drawing heavily on new social media platforms and open-source sites such as YouTube, Twitter, Tumblr, and Facebook, Dreamers have created an alternative public sphere, generating online content that speaks to an imagined public of both allies and adversaries; Facebook groups such as UndocuQueer and online video series such as "Undocumented and Awkward" and "UndocuCribs" show the many ways social media operate as spaces of confrontation, contemplation, and self-assertion.

One of this movement's most exciting elements involves the way that undocumented youth have been inspired by and appropriated the gay rights movement's strategies of visibility. Often LGBT youth themselves,

DREAM activists who choose to "come out" and openly declare their undocumented status emphasize the linkages that connect sexuality and migration. Posting their stories online and announcing their status at rallies, marches, and conferences, Dreamers show how such acts of self-disclosure and risk-taking are powerful enactments of political freedom that push us to rethink the meaning of citizenship—a status they both challenge and seek to inhabit. Moreover, by emphasizing peer-to-peer forms of communication that combine newer technologies with older forms of mobilization, the use of new social media has facilitated what I characterize as Dreamers' "queer" vision of democracy—a participatory politics that rejects secrecy in favor of more aggressive forms of nonconformist visibility, voice, and protest. Facebook, YouTube, and other forms of social media have made it possible for radical Dreamers to queer the movement, allowing them to express more complex and sophisticated conceptions of loyalty, legality, migration, sexuality, and patriotism than those typically offered by political elites. In its rejection of criminalization and defiant attitude toward state power, DREAM activism queers democracy. At the same time, by coming out, Dreamers put a human face on a neoliberal political system that seeks to create "a borderless economy and a barricaded border."[3]

Migrant Activism: Resistance, Publicity, and Risk

In the United States, the undocumented have a long history of political participation, particularly when it comes to engaging in protest and other forms of mass action. Throughout the twentieth century, fights for worker rights and against anti-immigrant legislation produced forms of undocumented resistance and activism; consider the mass protests in 1994 against the passage of California's Proposition 187.[4] But it was the immigrant rights protests of 2006 that inaugurated a *nationwide* movement of undocumented subjects claiming visibility and giving voice to their dreams and frustrations.

Demonstrating against harsh anti-immigrant congressional legislation, immigrants across the United States participated in hundreds of marches, rallies, and school and labor walkouts throughout the spring of 2006.[5] According to René Galindo, an estimated "3 to 5 million people participated, with approximately 1.5 million people marching in 108 locations around the country between April 8 and April 10 alone. . . . In some cities, the immigration reform marches were the largest street demonstrations ever recorded."[6]

The mega-marches of 2006 marked an important shift in immigrant rights politics and organizing. Unwilling to obey the strictures of illegality, with its demands of silence and secrecy, the undocumented resisted the state's injunction that they remain unknown and faceless. Rather than being a population spoken *for* and *about*, immigrants and their allies engaged in mass actions in order to influence policy and give voice to their political opinions and values.

Risking visibility and deportation in order to make their voices heard, undocumented protesters faced significant risk and, therefore, often sought to reduce the perils of publicity by mobilizing the power of the democratic crowd. Through large-scale mass actions, protesters managed to be politically visible while remaining obscure and hard to identify. For example, by gathering and intermingling their bodies in public acts of protest, mass demonstrations made it difficult to distinguish citizen from noncitizen. William Flores has characterized this sort of activism as "protection through collective action."[7] Similarly, while various undocumented individuals spoke onstage at the 2006 rallies (or spoke to journalists at the events), the views and voices of the vast majority of the undocumented were mostly articulated through signs and chants.

The 2006 protests saw little discussion of social media as a mobilizing force. With YouTube still a fledgling site and Facebook not yet available to the general public, efforts to mobilize the undocumented stressed more traditional organizations and media outlets. The organizations and media outlets most responsible for mobilizing immigrants (including the undocumented) included Spanish-language media, including television and (more particularly) talk radio, community-based organizations, Chicano/Latino student and community organizations, labor unions, the Catholic Church, immigrant hometown associations, and immigrant sports leagues.[8] In terms of the technology used to mobilize immigrant populations, organizers for the 2006 demonstrations were characterized as relying on "mass distribution of flyers, door-knocking, phone banking, and word of mouth." And while some encouraged the use of "web sites, e-mail, and faxes," activists used social media primarily to coordinate with those who were already members of community-based organizations.[9] In general, when trying to spread information about the rallies and mobilize a mass base of participants, activists used social media less than more traditional forms of outreach such as ethnic media, "press conferences, radio, television, and newspapers."[10]

While the 2006 protests were successful in putting a stop to H.R. 4437, anti-immigrant legislation actually grew more pernicious. Conditions for immigrants did not improve following the 2008 election—if anything, the situation worsened. Under President Obama, the number of deportations actually increased: Since 2009, the federal government has carried out far more deportations than during the *two* full presidential terms of George W. Bush.[11] This combination of increased animosity toward immigrants at the state and local level, impatience with the inability of the federal government to pass either comprehensive immigration reform or the DREAM Act, and widespread political inaction are some of the likely reasons that Dreamers' activism has become increasingly confrontational and creative.

Undocumented and Unafraid: Dreamers and the Politics of Coming Out

Seeking to call attention to and support for the DREAM Act, Dreamers in Chicago launched the "Coming Out of the Shadows" campaign in 2010. Modeled on the National Coming Out Day initiated in 1988, "Coming Out of the Shadows" was inspired by the struggle for LGBT rights and the idea of "coming out" as a political strategy.[12] The 2010 campaign included a march and rally featuring a group of students publicly proclaiming their undocumented status.[13] During these rallies, Dreamers declared themselves "undocumented and unafraid" (expanding the slogan in 2011 to "Undocumented, unafraid, and unapologetic"). Chanting, "No papers, no fear! Immigrants are marching here!," Chicago participants made it clear that this new phase of the movement would center on speaking out and publicly defying the rhetoric of criminalization. Following the Chicago actions, unauthorized youth are increasingly electing to come out, eschewing secrecy in favor of claiming membership through a more aggressive politics of visibility and protest that includes cross-state pilgrimages, hunger strikes, bus tours, rallies, sit-ins, and other forms of direct action. Often LGBT youth themselves, many DREAM activists emphasize the linkages that exist between coming out as queer and coming out as undocumented.

In using the term *queer*, I draw on Michael Warner's definition as the rejection of "a minoritizing logic of toleration or simple political-interest representation in favor of a more thorough resistance to regimes of the normal."[14] In characterizing Dreamers as queering the politics of migration, my analysis aligns with the work of Nicholas De Genova and his claim that the more militant elements of the 2006 marches reflect a "radically open-ended politics of migrant presence" that shares elements of the "destabilizing politics of queer presence."[15] According to De Genova, defiant chants such as, "¡Aquí estamos, y no nos vamos!" (Here we are, and we're not leaving!) are "remarkably analogous" to the slogan "We're here, we're queer, get used to it!"[16] By refusing the politics of innocence, questioning the state-centered logics of citizenship, and reconfiguring the criteria for political membership, Dreamers are queering the movement in ways that can't be "delimited in advance."

As Diana Fuss has written, the process of coming out can be understood as "a movement into a metaphysics of presence, speech and cultural visibility." In this way, to be out "is really to be in—inside the realm of the visible, the speakable, and culturally intelligible."[17] For undocumented youth, coming out represents a similar effort to become civically legible and politically speakable. Not surprisingly, the practice of coming out as undocumented quickly became a staple of immigrant youth politics—unauthorized youth began posting videos online telling their stories and openly naming themselves as undocumented.

The activism and energy of undocumented LGBT youth have been particularly significant. The National Immigrant Youth Alliance (NIYA), for example, established an UndocuQueer website on which queer undocumented youth can post their stories online. Drawing on their lived experience, the website seeks to build "visibility and explore the intersections between mainstream immigrant rights and queer rights organizing spaces." The emergence of such subjects was unexpected, particularly since, as Eithne Luibhéid and Lionel Cantú argue, the very presence of queer undocumented youth challenges the longstanding tendency "to presume either that all queers are legal citizens or that all immigrants are heterosexual."[18] In contesting this assumption, undocumented LGBT youth often frame their activism in terms of the intersections between a politics of migration and a politics of sexuality. Describing this dynamic on the NIYA website, activists identifying themselves as UndocuQueer wrote,

> We are queer undocumented youth. We cannot afford to be in either the queer or undocumented closet. We cannot and will not hide; we cannot and will not let those who haven't been in our shoes decide and tell us how to act, how to feel and that this isn't our home. We have the right to be whoever we want to be and love whoever we want to love. It is a shame that the only path we have to legalization is to lead a heterosexual lifestyle. We shouldn't and won't conform to such ideas. We have a right to live and love to the full extent of our capacity.
>
> We urge you to come out! Now is the time to come and proclaim that you're UndocuQueer, Unafraid and Unashamed![19]

In stating that they "shouldn't and won't conform" to the idea that "the only path to legalization is to lead a heterosexual lifestyle," queer Dreamers force the immigrant rights movement to consider how sexuality has served as grounds for controlling what sorts of newcomers are allowed to enter the country. In 1965, for example, revisions to immigration law "not only reaffirmed lesbian and gay exclusion but also further codified heterosexual, nuclear family relations as the primary basis for admission to the United States by reserving nearly three-quarters of all permanent immigration visas for people with those ties."[20] As scholars of migration and sexuality have noted, because the US government has historically refused to recognize lesbian and gay relationships as a legitimate basis for acquiring legal permanent resident status, lesbian/gay couples were denied access to one of the most common ways to become a legal permanent resident: through direct family ties.

The situation for same-sex couples changed on July 26, 2013, when the Supreme Court ruled that the federal Defense of Marriage Act (an act that defined marriage as a union between one man and one woman) was unconstitutional.[21] Yet despite an increase in same-sex couples applying for green cards, a majority of US states continue to prohibit same-sex civil marriage either by statute or in their constitutions. In other words, equal access to marriage is still not a viable option for most same-sex couples. A preference for nuclear, heterosexual families continues to fundamentally structure US immigration law. Yet by denaturalizing a limited and heteronormative logic of family, queer critiques of immigration expose how the US immigration control apparatus "significantly regulates sexuality and reproduces oppressive sexual norms that are gendered, racialized, and classed."[22]

Dreamers Online: Multiple Voices and New Affective Terrain

Regardless of their sexual orientation, Dreamers help queer the politics of migration in their refusal to accept liberal critiques of immigration that criminalize individuals while failing to address the economic factors that structure global practices of labor and migration. Social media sites such as YouTube, Facebook, and Twitter have facilitated the proliferation of undocumented voices and perspectives, making such queerings even more possible. According to the MacArthur Research Network on Youth and Participatory Politics (YPP) 2012 report "Participatory Politics: New Media and Youth Political Action," new social media are significant for their ability to facilitate forms of participation "not guided by deference to elites or formal institutions."[23] Instead, participation is often "peer based, focused on expression, interactive, nonhierarchical, and not guided by deference to elite driven institutions."[24] The ability to circumvent "traditional gatekeepers of information and influence" has been critical to DREAM activists' ability to pluralize the politics of immigration, moving beyond the liberal politics of representation that defined previous immigration debates. For example, many activists post videos on YouTube prior to committing acts of civil disobedience.

"If You're Watching This Video, I've Been Arrested": The Civil Disobedience of Georgina Perez

A significant aspect of civil disobedience videos has been the practice of giving one's full name and naming one's "taboo" status (as undocumented and/or queer). "Coming out" online often opens with a Dreamer stating his or her name, state of residence, and, "If you are watching this, it's because I've been arrested." The videos are typically built around first-person narratives regarding the speaker's status, why he or she feels that coming out is important, and urging others to come out and join the movement. Georgina Perez, a member of the Georgia Dreamers, posted a video online in April 2011, which states in full,

My name is Georgina Perez, I'm undocumented, and I am unafraid. I was brought to the U.S. when I was 3 years old. Currently I'm 21 years old. I'm ready to stand up and fight back for my community. Throughout the last five years, as undocumented youth, we have done everything in order to get open dialogue with elected officials and politicians. In good faith, we've waited and waited, and instead we've been given the runaround. We've done the petitions, we've done the flyering, the lobbying, the protests, the rallies, and instead of our voices being heard, we're just not seeing any change. We're seeing that our communities are being criminalized; we're seeing racist legislation; we're seeing family separation. And that's why today I'm coming out as undocumented and unafraid. I will no longer stand and wait for someone to come and save me. I will no longer wait for someone to come dictate and tell me what to do while I'm being denied the access to higher education. I'm tired of politicians always using us as a scapegoat, always criminalizing us, in order for them to win a seat. I'm tired of that. I'm not going to apologize for my mother bringing me here. I'm not going to apologize for speaking my native language. I'm a proud Georgian; I'm a proud Mexicana.

I was brought to this country by a very, very courageous woman. She's my hero, my mother. And she left everyone and everything she knew behind in order for her to give me a better life. So I'm not going to let anyone or anything stop me from getting my higher education; I'm not going to let her sacrifices be in vain. I'm not, 'cause she's my hero. And I'm not going to blame her—I thank her for bringing me here.

I'm tired of students like Jessica [Colotl, then a Kennesaw State University senior facing deportation] being persecuted for trying to get a basic education. When Jessica's case went public here in Georgia, a lot of us, a lot of us went deeper into the shadows. And we became scared. Many allies told us to be quiet, to take a step back, you know, because the environment is not good—just be quiet. But I've come to the realization that in order for us to beat this, we have to show them that we're more unafraid than ever before. I want to stand up and ask these legislators, Do you really, really want to be on the wrong side of history?

I want to . . . I stand here. I ask these legislators to stop criminalizing our communities, because the more you do this, we're not going to stay quiet anymore. We're tired of that. We're not going to stand back. We're not going to be silent. We're not going to be in the shadows. We're not going to let this happen any longer. We're going to step up and fight for our communities.

So I'm asking you—my ally, my friend, my fellow undocumented student, youth—are you going to be on our side? Or which side are you going to be on? Because me, as an undocumented youth, I know where I stand; I know on which side of history I'm going to be on. My name is Georgina Perez, I'm undocumented, and I am no longer afraid.[25]

The Perez video is powerful in its complex and audacious claims to membership and rights. She states that she is "not going to apologize for speaking my native language" and names herself as a "proud Georgian" as well as "a proud Mexicana." Claiming that elected officials and politicians have given petitioners "the runaround," Perez names herself as a southerner who has the authority to criticize and make demands on her elected representatives. In this way, her affective ties to the South also represent acts of resistance—she is asserting her rights as a deserving member of a polity that refuses to claim her. In her refusal to "apologize" for her actions, Perez resists the characterization of the undocumented as subjects who have engaged in unlawful acts. Instead, she names immigration policies, the US political process, and the misdeeds of politicians as the sites of wrongdoing and offense.

Civil disobedience testimonials refuse the criminalizing logic of unauthorized border crossings. For Perez, this refusal is tied to her identity as a daughter and her relationship to her mother. Rather than blaming her mother for her own status as undocumented, she tearfully expresses love, respect, and gratitude for her mother's choices, saying, "I'm not going to blame her for bringing me here" and calling her "a very, very courageous woman" and "my hero." Perez's speech regarding the structural and affective dynamics of immigration explodes the simplistic logic of "legal/illegal" and puts a human face on the complex dynamics of migration as the space of economic arrangements, human desire, and community building.

The Perez video works to destigmatize the status of undocumented immigrants while also demanding that her unique life story be seen and heard. Refusing to abide by nationalist scripts that demand that immigrants express only love and gratitude toward the United States, Perez expresses anger and frustration with the US political system, calling for an intensification of mass action and protest. Refusing allies' advice to "be quiet," she states that "I will no longer stand and wait for someone to come and save me." Calling on her fellow Dreamers and allies to join her, Perez asserts that "in order for us to beat this, we have to show them that we're more unafraid than ever before."

By going online and proclaiming themselves undocumented, activists such as Perez expose the limits of liberal notions of privacy. As David Phillips and Carolyn Cunningham note, as an antidote to surveillance, "privacy protects the autonomous individual," but practices of surveillance "are fundamentally about the creation of social knowledge, social positions, and social order."[26] Because of Dreamers' social position as "undocumented," the private realm serves as the site of a social order characterized by secrecy, exploitation, and fear. In this way, DREAM activists' use of the Internet highlights privacy's failure as a form of protection. At the same time, engaging the politics of surveillance is a dangerous and uncertain game. Publicly naming oneself online while engaging in acts of civil disobedience can easily lead to arrest, deportation, and other forms of state-sanctioned violence. Moreover, vulnerability is reenacted on the Internet: One's visibility now has a kind of permanence, as an online presence retains a life beyond the initial post.

Dreamer Diversity: From Soldiers to "Terror Babies"

Radical Dreamers such as Georgina Perez are not the only ones making themselves heard via social media. As noted earlier, new media allow for the proliferation of expressive practices and critiques produced by a diverse group of undocumented youth. The Internet provides a platform for agonistic critiques from activists like Perez as well as more liberal depictions of immigrant politics. Consider the testimony of Carlos Roa, posted on the website We Are America: Stories of Today's Immigrants. The posts presented on this site draw on more liberal narratives of service and membership:

My name is Carlos Roa, and I am America. My family and myself came
to the United States back in 1989. I was only 2 years old. . . . I graduated
in 2005 from high school, and I wanted to get into college; I wanted to
join the military. And those options weren't—I couldn't do any of that.
And so it's frustrating—the fact that I wanna give back and I'm willing
to serve this country in military service, and I don't even have the option
to do so. When you're shooting down people's dreams, that's bad. It's bad
for everyone—not just immigrants. . . .

If you work hard and if you try and you strive and you can realize
your potential and you can be a contributing member to society—that's
something that this country has prided itself on. And we've seen that—at
the turn of the century, we saw how immigrants changed this nation for
the better. Of Irish, of Polish, of Italian descent—how they were able to
shape . . . very much change this nation for the better and make this
country better. We are no different than the immigrants of the past.[27]

Roa, then a student studying architecture at Miami Dade College, was
one of four students who in 2010 walked 1,500 miles to Washington,
DC, as part of the "Trail of Dreams." Yet alongside his activism, Roa's
testimonial hews to a xenophilic narrative of the good and "giving" foreigner. Unlike Perez, who criticizes American policies and names herself "undocumented and unafraid," Roa chooses not to clarify his status.
Instead, he states that "I am America" and characterizes himself as a
patriotic subject willing to serve in the military during wartime.[28] In
speaking of the United States as a land of hard work and opportunity,
Roa tries to locate his own family's story in the larger story of European immigration in America ("We are no different than the immigrants of the past"). While such efforts are understandable, they sustain
the binary of "good immigrants" versus "bad immigrants"—those who
are worthy of "being folded (back) into life" and those whose lives are
understood to be of less value.[29]

Yet another genre of online testimony can be seen in posts created
by the group Dreamers Adrift. An online media project "by undocumented youth and for undocumented youth," Dreamers Adrift posts
skits, blogs, and raps that are more oppositional, angry, and funny than
traditional, familiar forms of immigrant testimony. In contrast to the
nationalist logic of Roa's liberal narrative, Dreamers Adrift articulates

a more agonistic approach that uses humor and irony to critique US immigration policy. Consider the posts by the cofounder Jesús Iñiguez, who uses rap to offer critique and create political community. His March 2011 rap "To All My DREAMheads," performed in his car, addresses allies and aims to create community among fellow activists across the state and nation:

> E.S.L. in the flesh comin' through
> With another fresh DREAM Act sesh for my cats and ladies
> Allies, undocumented folks, anchor and terror babies
> Like that senator from Texas said
> Too many conspiracy theories get into his head, y'all
> And he's in a position where he could be votin'
> On some pretty cool decisions
> Affecting our communities
> Acting without impunity
> But he ain't foolin' me
> 'Cause I grew to be
> Skeptical of politicians
> 'Cause lately they be actin' vicious and brainless and shameless
> The type of shit they be pullin' in Congress is heinous
> No taxation without representation
> They don't even know the type of shit that we be facin' on the day to day
> Livin' on a daily basis
> Havin' to deal with these elephant nutcases
> Makin' us out to be one of the main rivals
> Feelin' entitled 'cause they be skimmin' through the Bible
> But that's not what Jesús would do
> I gotta make a move 'cause I'm through payin' dues
> And I'm through being used and abused and refused
> This is the true here: Fuck Fox News
> I got nothin' to lose
> That's why I'm politickin'
> You're trippin' if you're thinkin' that I'm gonna shut my mouth
> Undocumented and proud and unafraid
> On a legal crusade to get paid
> Don't hate

I'm tryin' to get my paperwork straight
And get all my documents in order
I'm only gettin' older
And I'm tryin' to kick it on this side of the border
'Cause life expectancy on the other side is shorter
It's a sad reality but shit is crazy
But the threat of goin' back don't faze me
It makes me wanna organize
You best to recognize right propaganda lies
So I hope it opens your eyes and we can stick together
This endeavor bonded us forever
Remember: If we can stick together then we've already won
DREAM Act now two-zero-one-one
This goes out to DREAM Team L.A. and the O.C. DREAM Team,
    FUEL from Long Beach, and all the other DREAM Act organi-
    zations around this nation organizing around this legislation.[30]

In contrast to Roa's effort to create a narrative of immigration that links the undocumented to earlier waves of "good" immigration from Europe, Iñiguez uses phrases such as "anchor and terror babies" to mock those who would accuse the undocumented of being takers and terrorists. Aggressively criticizing politicians (who are characterized as vicious, brainless, and shameless), he is particularly harsh toward right-wing media and politicians, referring to "those elephant nutcases" and telling his listeners to "fuck Fox News." Yet despite its combative words, the rap maintains a playful and hopeful tone, telling Iñiguez's fellow Dreamers that "this endeavor bonded us forever" and that "if we can stick together then we've already won." Moreover, with its concluding shout-out to various Southern California DREAM organizations, the rap is clearly aimed not at skeptical citizens but at his fellow activists—undocumented youth who see themselves as part of the fight for immigrant rights. And finally, the fact that Iñiguez is rapping while driving is politically significant: Because California did not grant the undocumented driver's licenses in 2011, the act of driving in the video is a quotidian and unspoken act of defiance that frames the rap as a whole.

Conclusion: From Deferred Action to Comprehensive Immigration Reform

Refusing the demand that they identify themselves exclusively as patriotic, apologetic, and grateful, groups such as Dreamers Adrift are creating a space where the undocumented can also be sarcastic, angry, funny, ironic, enraged, and brash. Operating at the intersection of liberal inclusion and radical possibility, Dreamers have demonstrated an ability to successfully "queer" the politics of immigration, epitomized by their pressuring of President Obama to grant deferred action to DREAM Act–eligible youth in the summer of 2012. Referred to as Deferred Action for Childhood Arrivals (or DACA), the program provides certain undocumented youth with administrative relief from deportation. A year earlier, Dreamers began calling on Obama to issue an executive order to stop deportations and allow undocumented youth the opportunity to obtain work permits, driver's licenses, and other forms of documentation. This increasingly confrontational approach can be seen in a Dreamers Adrift video uploaded to YouTube on October 1, 2011:

Obama, the immigrant community is under attack.

You have shown no leadership in taking a strong, bold stand—

In the protection of our civil liberties and rights as immigrants in this country.

What happened to your promise of immigration reform?

Were you just pandering to the Latino vote, or was that real talk?

You claim you want the DREAM Act to pass through a democratic process.

But that has been an excuse for you to stand on the sidelines while a million undocumented folks are criminalized and deported under your administration.

Presidents in the past have signed executive orders that have positively affected society as a whole, so why can't you do the same for Dreamers?

As Dreamers, we have a duty to confront you and your administration regarding your lack of leadership.

Our demand is clear:

> You have the power to grant administrative relief to all DREAM Act–eligible youth through an executive order. Do it.[31]

Mainstream immigrant advocacy groups did not embrace the Dreamers' confrontational approach. "[W]orried about the effect of pushing Obama publicly on the contentious issue in the midst of his re-election campaign," traditional organizations were "angry at Obama, but terrified of Romney." Many advocates were afraid to lean on the White House publicly for fear of hurting the president's electoral chances and electing a challenger who had publicly stated that he would "veto any DREAM Act that reached his desk."[32] In the face of such electoral anxiety, it fell on Dreamers to take the lead on making demands of the White House. Dreamers were the first group to ask the president to take administrative action—a request that leaders of the Congressional Hispanic Congressional Caucus made only *after* Dreamers had made a similar request to the Obama administration senior adviser Valerie Jarrett earlier that year.[33]

Ultimately, it was DREAM activists outside Washington who developed their own plan to pressure Obama. In early June, Veronica Gomez and Javier Hernandez, undocumented representatives of the National Immigrant Youth Alliance, occupied the president's Denver campaign headquarters, staging a six-day hunger strike while camped inside the Obama for America offices.[34] Following the Denver action, activists pledged to carry out acts of civil disobedience in campaign offices across the country. Dreamers put out statements saying that if Obama refused to pass administrative relief, his campaign would face a summer of direct-action protests just as he was working to secure the Latino vote in swing states such as Colorado, Nevada, and Florida:

> Undocumented youth will be escalating in other actions. They are going to be arrested in some states, that's what youth decided to do. The message is: we want an executive order. . . . The President has clear legal authority to give our community relief, yet he continues to say he doesn't have the power. . . . Rest assured, we will . . . take our voices to the White House and to his campaign offices until we see Obama exercise leadership.[35]

Frustrated, angry, and savvy, DREAM activists echoed the political logic of groups such as ACT UP and Queer Nation that challenged the government's decision to view AIDS not as "an emergency" but as "merely a permanent disaster."[36] Refusing to wait until after the election to make their voices heard, Dreamers approached the ongoing attacks on the undocumented as an emergency rather than a permanent disaster.

On August 14, 2012, just two months after Obama's announcement of DACA, San Antonio Mayor Julián Castro became the first Latino to deliver a keynote address at the Democratic National Convention. That same day, a group of undocumented immigrants arrived at the DNC in Charlotte, North Carolina. Part of the "No Papers, No Fear" Ride for Justice, these activists had been on a cross-country tour since July, traveling on what they called the UndocuBus. Dissatisfied by the deferred-deportation order, riders criticized the Obama administration for what they characterized as the president's "flawed and unjust immigration record." Blocking an intersection leading to the convention, riders knelt on a colorful banner that read, "Sin Papeles, Sin Miedo" (No papers, no fear) and held up signs reading "Undocumented." After protesters ignored a bilingual dispersal order, ten protesters were handcuffed one at a time and placed in police vans, where they continued to chant, "Undocumented, unafraid!"[37] That same day, the DNC made history by inviting Dreamer Benita Veliz to address delegates.

This parallel story of party mobilization alongside radical political action speaks to the complexities of this current moment of immigrant civil rights. Here, Latino civic membership operates through concurrent narratives of gratitude and liberal inclusion spoken by a rising Latino politician and a Dreamer alongside direct actions by undocumented youth who speak of an attachment to the United States shaped by desire, hope, disappointment, and outrage. Despite the Obama administration's hopes, such subjects are more than a loyal and compliant segment of a future Democratic electorate—they are political actors with diverse and contentious views regarding both political parties.

The ongoing struggle for comprehensive immigration reform is far from over. Whether Congress and the Obama administration will be able to pass immigration reform anytime soon is far from certain.[38] And even if legislation passes, the results are likely to be less just and fair than these communities deserve. What offers reason for cheer is that no matter what happens, the undocumented are organizing, and their activism will continue to shape the discussion of immigration for years to come. And as their voices proliferate on the Internet, in the street, and in the halls of power, today's challenge lies in creating a civic culture capable of recognizing the value of such complex civic attachments. Dreamers articulate a passionate ambivalence—a queer optimism tempered by mistrust and loss. Such subjects deepen our conceptions of citizenship, reminding us that democratic membership is a fraught and spirited enterprise. And as the struggle for a just vision of political association continues, immigrants and their allies will need to continue to cultivate democratic sensibilities that are unrepentant, audacious, and fearless.[39]

NOTES

1. See Perez, *We Are Americans*, xxi-xxii.
2. In April 2010, Republican Governor Jan Brewer of Arizona signed into law SB 1070. SB 1070 expanded the powers of state police officers to ask about the immigration status of anyone they stop, and to hold those suspected of being illegal immigrants. The legislation requires police officers, "when practicable," to detain people they reasonably suspect are in the country without authorization and to verify their status with federal officials, unless doing so would hinder an investigation or emergency medical treatment. The law also makes it a state crime—a misdemeanor—to not carry immigration papers. In a similar vein, on June 2011, Alabama passed HB 56 (the Hammon-Beason Alabama Taxpayer and Citizen Protection Act). HB 56 requires public schools to collect the immigration status of new students and their parents and makes it a felony for anyone to transport or house an undocumented immigrant. HB 56 was signed into law by Republican Governor Robert Bentley on June 9, 2011. Both provisions are currently blocked by federal courts pending a ruling.
3. Nevins, "Searching for Security," 135.
4. See Garcia, *Mexican Americans*; Flores, "New Citizens, New Rights"; and Weber, *Dark Sweat, White Gold*.
5. The initial trigger for the protests was the US House of Representatives' December 2005 passage of H.R. 4437 (the Border Protection, Antiterrorism, and Illegal Immigration Control Act of 2005). Declaring that simply being undocumented constituted a felony, the bill criminalized anyone who offered nonemergency assistance to undocumented workers and their families.
6. Galindo, "Repartitioning the National Community," 37–38.
7. See Flores, "New Citizens, New Rights," 95. See also Beltrán, "Going Public," 609–10.

8. See Barreto et al., "Mobilization"; and Pallares and Flores-González, ¡Marcha!

9. One location where new social media *did* in fact play a more significant role during the 2006 protests was during the student walkouts that took place in Los Angeles in March of that year. According to Alfonso Gonzales, "most youth heard of the walkout through text messages and through the internet message system MySpace." See Gonzales, *Reform without Justice*, 102.

10. See Barreto et al., "Mobilization," 744.

11. See "Obama's Deportation Record Worse than Bush."

12. The movement was also inspired by the civil rights movement and its use of sit-ins, hunger strikes, freedom rides, and other forms of nonviolent civil disobedience. See http://www.hrc.org/ncod/.

13. To see videos from the "Coming Out of the Shadows Campaign" of 2010 and 2011, see http://www.youtube.com/watch?v=HS93wb_jpAg&feature=related and http://www.youtube.com/watch?v=MQOOvtn21_Q&feature=related.

14. Warner, *Fear of a Queer Planet*, xxvi.

15. De Genova, "The Queer Politics of Migration," 101.

16. Ibid.

17. Fuss, *Inside/Out*, 4.

18. Luibhéid and Cantú, *Queer Migrations*, xxxv.

19. See http://theniya.org/undocuqueer/.

20. Luibhéid and Cantú, *Queer Migrations*, xiii-xv. See also Cantú, *The Sexuality of Migration*. Lesbians and gays were barred for decades from entering the United States as legal immigrants. In 1990, exclusion based on sexual orientation was finally removed from immigration law.

21. See Preston, "For Gay Immigrants, Marriage Ruling Brings Relief."

22. Luibhéid and Cantú, *Queer Migrations*, x.

23. Cohen, Kahne et al., "Participatory Politics," vi. While not focused on undocumented youth per se, the YPP analysis and definitions are enormously helpful in thinking about how DREAM activists have used new social media in order to both engage *and* sidestep mainstream immigrant rights organizations.

24. Ibid., 9.

25. See http://www.youtube.com/watch?v=mTeh1moqiEU&feature=youtu.be.

26. Phillips and Cunningham, "Queering Surveillance Research," 33.

27. See http://weareamericastories.org/videos/carlos-the-story-of-an-undocumented-student/.

28. See http://www.trail2010.org/about/.

29. Puar, *Terrorist Assemblages*, 35.

30. See http://www.youtube.com/watch?v=SvVGLSgAHMU Or see Dreamers Adrift Channel: http://www.youtube.com/user/dreamersadrift?feature=results_main.

31. "President Obama: Administrative Relief NOW!!" See http://www.youtube.com/watch?v=ycK_j3MHGtA&feature=relmfu.

32. Ross, "How the Deferred Action Immigration Program Went from Dream to Reality."
33. Ibid.
34. Hing, "DREAMers Stage Sit-Ins."
35. Ibid.
36. Crimp, "Right On, Girlfriend!" 304.
37. Knefel, "No Papers, No Fear."
38. For more on the congressional effort to overhaul immigration in 2013, see chapter 6 of Gonzales, *Reform without Justice*.
39. Portions of this essay are drawn from my forthcoming article in *From Voice to Influence: Understanding Citizenship in a Digital Age*, edited by Danielle S. Allen and Jennifer S. Light. Chicago: University of Chicago Press.

REFERENCES

Arendt, Hannah. *The Human Condition*. Chicago: University of Chicago Press, 1958.

Barreto, Matt A., Sylvia Manzano, Ricardo Ramírez, and Kathy Rim. "Mobilization, Participation, and Solidaridad: Latino Participation in the 2006 Immigration Protest Rallies." *Urban Affairs Review* 44, no. 5 (2009): 736–64.

Beltrán, Cristina. "Going Public: Hannah Arendt, Immigrant Action, and the Space of Appearance." *Political Theory* 37 (2009): 595–622.

Cantú, Lionel. *The Sexuality of Migration: Border Crossings and Mexican Immigrant Men*. New York: New York University Press, 2009.

Chun, Wendy Hui Kyong. *Control and Freedom: Power and Paranoia in the Age of Fiber Optics*. Cambridge: MIT Press, 2006.

Cohen, Cathy, Joseph Kahne, et al. "Participatory Politics: New Media and Youth Political Action." MacArthur Research Network on Youth and Participatory Politics (YPP), 2012.

Crimp, Douglas. "Right On, Girlfriend!" In *Fear of a Queer Planet: Queer Politics and Social Theory*, edited by Michael Warner. Minneapolis: University of Minnesota Press, 1993.

Davilá, Arlene. *Latino Spin: Public Image and the Whitewashing of Race*. New York: New York University Press, 2008.

De Genova, Nicholas. "The Queer Politics of Migration: Reflections on 'Illegality' and Incorrigibility." *Studies in Social Justice* 4, no. 2 (2010): 101–26.

Flores, William V. "New Citizens, New Rights: Undocumented Immigrants and Latino Cultural Citizenship." *Latin American Perspectives* 30, no. 2 (March 2003): 87–100.

Fuss, Diana. *Inside/Out: Lesbian Theories, Gay Theories*. New York: Routledge, 1991.

Galindo, René. "Repartitioning the National Community: Political Visibility and Voice for Undocumented Immigrants in the Spring 2006 Immigration Rights Marches." *Aztlán: A Journal of Chicano Studies* 35, no. 2 (Fall 2010): 37–64.

García, Mario T. *Mexican Americans: Leadership, Ideology, and Identity, 1930–1960*. New Haven: Yale University Press, 1991.

Gonzales, Alfonso. *Reform without Justice: Latino Migrant Politics and the Homeland Security State*. New York: Oxford University Press, 2013.

Gray, Mary L. *Out in the Country: Youth, Media, and Queer Visibility in Rural America.* New York: New York University Press, 2009.

Gross, Larry. Foreword to *Queer Online: Media Technology and Sexuality,* edited by Kate O'Riordan and David Phillips. New York: Peter Lang, 2007.

Halperin, David. *Saint Foucault: Towards a Gay Hagiography.* New York: Oxford University Press, 1995.

Hing, Julianne. "DREAMers Stage Sit-Ins at Obama Office to Force Deportation Standoff." Colorlines, June 13, 2012, http://colorlines.com/archives/2012/06/dreamers_planned_obama_campaign_office_sit-ins_force_deportation_standoff.html.

Honig, Bonnie. *Democracy and the Foreigner.* Princeton: Princeton University Press, 2003.

Knefel, Molly. "No Papers, No Fear: Risking Deportation at the DNC." *Yes Magazine,* September 6, 2012, http://nopapersnofear.org/blog/post.php?s=2012-09-06-no-papers-no-fear-risking-deportation-at-the-dnc.

Luibhéid, Eithne, and Lionel Cantú. *Queer Migrations: Sexuality, U.S. Citizenship, and Border Crossings.* Minneapolis: University of Minnesota Press, 2005.

Nevins, Joseph. "Searching for Security: Boundary and Immigration Enforcement in an Age of Intensifying Globalization." *Social Justice* 28, no. 2 (Summer 2001): 132–48.

"Obama's Deportation Record Worse than Bush." *FilAm: A Magazine for Filipino Americans in New York,* March 14, 2012.

O'Riordan, Kate. "Queer Theories and Cybersubjects: Intersecting Figures." In *Queer Online: Media Technology and Sexuality,* edited by Kate O'Riordan and David Phillips. New York: Peter Lang, 2007.

O'Riordan, Kate, and David Phillips, eds. *Queer Online: Media Technology and Sexuality.* New York: Peter Lang, 2007.

Pallares, Amalia, and Nilda Flores-González, eds. *¡Marcha!: Latino Chicago and the Immigrant Rights Movement.* Champaign: University of Illinois Press, 2010.

Perez, William. *We Are Americans: Undocumented Students Pursuing the American Dream.* Sterling, VA: Stylus, 2009.

Phillips, David, and Carolyn Cunningham. "Queering Surveillance Research." In *Queer Online: Media Technology and Sexuality,* edited by Kate O'Riordan and David Phillips. New York: Peter Lang, 2007.

Preston, Julia. "For Gay Immigrants, Marriage Ruling Brings Relief and a Path to a Green Card." *New York Times,* June 27, 2013.

———. "Young Immigrant Activists Cast a Wider Net." *New York Times,* December 2, 2012.

Preston, Julia, and John H. Cushman. "Obama to Permit Young Migrants to Remain in the U.S." *New York Times,* June 15, 2012.

Puar, Jasbir. *Terrorist Assemblages: Homonationalism in Queer Times.* Durham: Duke University Press, 2007.

Ross, Janell. "How the Deferred Action Immigration Program Went from Dream to Reality." *Huffington Post,* August 19, 2012.

Vargas, Jose Antonio. "My Life as an Undocumented Immigrant." *New York Times Magazine*, June 22, 2011.

———. "Not Legal, Not Leaving." *Time*, June 25, 2012.

Warner, Michael. *Fear of a Queer Planet: Queer Politics and Social Theory*. Minneapolis: University of Minnesota Press, 1993.

Weber, Devra. *Dark Sweat, White Gold: California Farm Workers, Cotton, and the New Deal*. Berkeley: University of California Press, 1996.

13

Latina/o Audiences as Citizens

Bridging Culture, Media, and Politics

JILLIAN BÁEZ

"She looks so lonely and . . . I think it represents minorities.
Alone, dark, lost."
–Alejandra, nineteen-year-old Mexican American college
student, describing a Latina model in a Coca-Cola
advertisement

"It's good to see Latinas out there—that they're actually getting ahead."
–Monica, twenty-four-year-old Mexican college student,
referring to the Latina celebrities Jennifer Lopez and Salma
Hayek

"I think just having access to products that do meet our
needs is important. That's why I think media needs to realize that there is this [Latina/o] population out there. We are
consumers so if you're not giving us what we want then we're
forced to use something else, whatever's available."
–Elena, twenty-nine-year-old Puerto Rican occupational
therapist, commenting on Latina/o buying power

Between 2005 and 2012 I conducted ethnographic research in Chicago,
Illinois, with a diverse group of Latina media audiences in order to
understand how they perceived representations of the Latina body in
Latina/o-oriented media. Over the course of my research, I noticed that
discussions of the relationship between media, culture, and citizenship
were commonplace among my participants—adult Mexican, Puerto

Rican, and Colombian women living in Chicago. In studying Latinas in Chicago and their engagement with Latina representations in various media forms, I found that, as in the epigraphs above, their interactions with mainstream and ethnic media were very much about assessing their location within the US imaginary. I was struck to see that many of the women's responses to mainstream and ethnic media representations of Latina/os foregrounded issues of belonging, respect, recognition, and access to or denial of the "American Dream." The epigraphs above point to how notions of citizenship, or belonging to the nation culturally, politically, and economically, are tied to Latina/o audiences' engagement with mainstream and ethnic media. Indeed, citizenship was one of the main frames through which these audiences made sense of the media around and about them.[1]

While citizenship is a central concept explored in recent and important Latina/o studies scholarship (e.g., Chavez 2008; Coll 2010; Dávila 2012; De Genova 2005; Oboler 2006), it remains relatively undertheorized in studies of Latina/os and the media. In particular, few scholars have attempted to examine the intersections between Latina/o media audiences and citizenship, with the exception of the work of Arlene Dávila (2012), Vicki Mayer (2003), and Lucila Vargas (2009).[2] In this essay, I foreground citizenship as a theoretical concept to understand not only how Latina/o audiences interpret Latina/o-oriented media, but also why and how they are invested in media representation. More specifically, I tease out how Latina/o audiences draw from both symbolic and material notions of citizenship in their perceptions of media.

In the 1990s, Latina/o studies scholars such as Renato Rosaldo (1994) and William Flores and Rina Benmayor (1997) offered cultural citizenship as a way to remedy conventional ways of conceptualizing citizenship that ignored the contributions of Latina/os to the US civil society. The strength of this approach lies in its extension of citizenship beyond legal status to include contributions in the form of cultural production (i.e., theater, festivals, parades, and so on). Cultural citizenship, with its focus on the more symbolic aspects of citizenship such as feelings of belonging and recognition, has been critiqued for ignoring the more material experiences of citizenship, which most importantly include access to legal documentation (Anguiano and Chávez 2011; Dávila 2012; Ong 1996; Siu 2005). The empirical evidence I provide in this essay demonstrates that symbolic and material forms of citizenship operate in tandem with one another in the worldviews of Latina/o audiences. In other words, it is not that cultural citizenship is irrelevant to Latina/o audiences. Rather, cultural citizenship is still relevant to *some* Latina/o audiences, usually those who are documented and upwardly mobile, while material forms of citizenship are far more pressing to more marginalized and vulnerable Latina/o communities.

In order to understand the relationship between media representation and consumption, this audience study employs an ethnographic approach that combines multisited participant observation with in-depth interviews. The bulk of my research comes from sustained field-work in 2005–2007, with several post-fieldwork visits between 2008 and 2012. The project is locally situated in Chicago—a site chosen for its diverse Latina/o nationalities and history of Latina/o immigration dating to the nineteenth century. A focus on Chicago also serves to decenter the bicoastal focus of most Latina/o studies scholarship. I spent most of my fieldwork in predominately Latina/o neighborhoods such as Humboldt Park, Logan Square, Pilsen, and Little Village. My sample included nearly forty Latina participants of various ages, classes, nationalities, and sexualities, whom I observed at multiple sites in which participants referred to the Latina body implicitly or explicitly. These sites included beauty salons, Latina/o cultural parades and festivals, gyms, and community organizations in various neighborhoods throughout the city. I also spent time consuming television, radio, and film with key informants in their homes, cars, and movie theaters. To complement the participant observation, I conducted twenty semi-structured, individual interviews and five small-group interviews comprising four to five Latinas in peer groups (e.g., college students, mothers in their thirties).[3] The interviews and focus groups consisted of questions about specific media texts and participants' broader understandings of how Latinas and their bodies are depicted in mainstream and Latina/o media. The media texts included various advertisements, the film *Real Women Have Curves* (2002), and the first two seasons of the network television series *Ugly Betty* (2006–2010).[4]

There were numerous examples from my fieldwork of how Latina audiences see themselves in relation to media representation. In the next two sections, I discuss three ways that Latina/o audiences assess matters of belonging through media. The first example illustrates how Latina/o audiences view mainstream English-language media representation as a quest for respect and recognition. The second case demonstrates how Latina/o audiences cannot escape understanding media through a consumerist logic that ultimately reifies their role as consumer-citizens. The last example underscores the limitations of cultural citizenship by examining how the undocumented are viewed in relation to media. Ultimately, these three case studies suggest that notions of citizenship are crucial for understanding Latina/o audiences within shifting political and media industry landscapes. In doing so, I provide a framework for a broader and more systemic understanding of the crossroads of culture, media, and politics.

Respeto and Cultural Citizenship

It was minus 12 degrees Fahrenheit on Superbowl Sunday in February 2007. The Rivera family invited me to their small brick home in the Chicago suburb of Cicero to watch the Superbowl and partake in traditional football viewing snacks such as pizza, buffalo wings, and soda. The Rivera family consisted of Nina, a forty-seven-year-old homemaker, her husband, Mario, a fifty-year-old postal worker and musician, their twenty-seven-year-old son, Junior, a staff member at a local private university, and their daughter, Maribel, a twenty-four-year-old college student. Prior to this day I had been to the Rivera house a few times and had come to know the family fairly well.

Before moving to Cicero, the Riveras raised their children in Portage Park, a predominantly Polish area on the northwest side of Chicago. Nina and Mario were second-generation Puerto Ricans born and raised in the predominantly Puerto Rican Humboldt Park neighborhood. A few years after marrying and having their first child, they moved to Portage Park. They bought their first home in Cicero, a middle-class suburb home to many Mexican immigrants and Italian Americans, only two years before I had met them.

As we sat on the sofa in the Riveras' small living room, the family fell silent as the game opened with tropical Latin music playing on a speaker and mambo dancers wearing bright yellow, red, pink, and orange costumes. When the first commercial break began, Nina mentioned that the music during the opening was recorded and not a live band playing. Given the Superbowl's location in Miami and its large Latina/o population, she asked, "Why aren't there any Latin bands?"[5] She added, "That's our country for you." Here Nina was referring to what she perceived as the marginalization of Latina/os within media. Latin music was playing in the background, but actual Latina/o musicians were not in the spotlight. Mario then said that he wrote a "Cha-Cha for the Bears" jingle for a local radio contest, but was disappointed when he lost to a rap song by a Polish American rapper named "Pol." I never heard either song, so I cannot attest to the aesthetic quality of Mario's jingle, but he was convinced he did not win the contest because he is Puerto Rican. Overall, the family agreed that while tropical Latin music genres, especially salsa, are popular in mainstream media, Latin bands are not foregrounded in general.

After halftime, Nina again mentioned the lack of representation of Latina/os in the game opening and began to relate stories about the difficulties she faced with teachers and other parents in the public school system while raising her two children. She discussed how teachers thought Maribel was "slow" because she liked to mimic the cartoon character Bugs Bunny's voice. Nina was proud to point out that she advocated for her daughter despite Maribel's teacher's insistence that she had a learning disability. Nina then showed me photo albums of her children when they were school-aged. As Nina pointed out a young white girl in one of her son's elementary school class photos, Junior said that this girl told him he was a "dirty spic" who lived with roaches. Nina responded, "My house is clean," and said that she was involved in the PTA. In this instance, although Nina did not make the distinction between media representations and her children's racialized educational experiences, she did see these as connected issues about marginalization and racism. In this way, she read the erasure of Latina/os in the Superbowl musical sequence through a lens of recognition and belonging. For her, erasure from mainstream media was similar to the marginalization she and her children felt within the educational system. In this way, Nina related her personal stories to the media representations she watched.

Issues of representation and recognition continue to be paramount to underrepresented communities, but this case study suggests that we take a closer look at representation and recognition. In particular, it points to the continued saliency of cultural citizenship and the more symbolic aspects of belonging. Renato Rosaldo (1994) argues that there is a need for a vernacular notion of citizenship and offers the term *respeto* (respect), which his participants use in their claim for individual dignity, full citizenship, and social justice. This quest for *respeto* among one's neighbors, coworkers, and others can eventually bleed into a claim of rights in the public sphere. In this way, cultural citizenship is about a new kind of citizenry—one that is located on the ground level of everyday life and that demands rights from both one's fellow citizens and the state. Thus, cultural citizenship can be understood as a kind of "micro-politics" that has the potential to turn into macro-politics. For instance, in the above case, the Rivera family expressed frustration at media depictions that they found limiting.[6] In particular, Nina indicated that even though she identified as a member of the United States in her usage of the phrase "our country," she felt invisible in the mediated national imaginary. In this sense, this active reading of media can be considered an expression of cultural citizenship—a struggle over how they and their bodies are represented in the public sphere, in this instance, the media. In this case, Latina/o audiences talk about mainstream media as a way to express their sense of belongingness in the United States, and hence, are invested in the more symbolic aspects of citizenship.

Latinas as Consumer-Citizens

Most of the Latina audiences I observed and interviewed primarily read media through a consumerist logic. When I first began interviewing women about advertisements in particular, many of the women immediately responded to my questions by telling me whether or not they thought an ad was "effective." In other words, they assumed that I wanted to know whether the ad could persuade potential consumers to buy the product it was advertising. In this way, the women were not only interpellated by a marketing discourse where anything can be commodified, but also by the pervasiveness of marketing research. Indeed, many of the women made reference to having participated or wanting to participate in marketing research in the form of surveys and focus groups. They saw marketing research as not only a way to make extra money, but also to have their say about new products and media. It is also notable that for many of the women, the only other experience they had with research was in marketing focus groups in downtown Chicago. These women were often recruited by market researchers while picking up lunch during their work breaks or riding the train.

Marketing research heavily informed the women's engagements with media. Indeed, the way they made advertisements intelligible was by determining their marketability. Many women were surprised, and even some displayed discomfort, when I asked them to focus not so much on the effectiveness of the ad, as on how the ad made them think or feel. In other words, I was asking about affect, not effect.[7] Maribel (also described in the first case study) commented that she found her interview with me "very hard because it took a lot of thinking," precisely because she had never been asked about media from a non-marketing perspective. Maribel was an avid consumer of popular culture, particularly beauty products and fashion, and it was difficult for her to talk about ads without considering how she might or might not purchase those products. Her mother, Nina, also expressed difficulty with the interview, saying afterward that she wished she had time to "study" the ads, television programs, and films we discussed before the interview.[8]

I draw attention here to the consumerist logic used by Latina audiences not only to shed light on one dimension of their decoding strategies, but also to discuss some of the limitations inherent in viewing citizenship and consumption as synonymous. Performing cultural citizenship through consumption, though highly problematic because it limits our contributions to the economic realm, is inevitable in a consumer society. There is ample scholarly literature that contends that in consumer societies consumption and citizenship are conflated to the point that we all identify in some way as consumer-citizens (Dávila 2012; García Canclini 2001; Yúdice 1995). For example, it is through this consumer-citizen lens that Latina audiences make sense of Latina/o advertising. It is not only in audiences' preoccupation with reading the "effectiveness" of an ad to persuade consumers to buy a particular product, service, or lifestyle. Rather, this consumer-citizen interpretive strategy is also evident in their commonsense knowledge of advertising norms. For example, many of the women expressed the opinion that using women's bodies to sell commodities was a standard advertising practice. Other women demonstrated their commonsense knowledge of advertising norms, and media literacy, in identifying images that appeared to be digitized.[9]

Further emblematic of the consumer-citizen interpretive strategy was the women's constant mention of the "buying power" of Latina/os. Given the timeframe of the bulk of my fieldwork (2005–2007), this is not surprising, as the growing "buying power" of Latina/os was making the front pages of not only advertising trade magazines, but also mainstream publications. This "buying power" was read as a form of Latina/o agency through consumer choice.[10] For example, Jovita, a Mexican woman in her mid-thirties who worked as a midlevel university administrator, made the following observation:

> There's not even a real attempt on the media's part to look at the lives of a Latino and make their product applicable to that. The other side of the problem is that Latinos will still buy the damn product and allow that to happen. Allow the media through their purchasing power. Allow the media not to make any allowances for them and to disregard that. . . . So, it's problematic on both ends.

Here Jovita not only points to the media's superficiality in representing Latina/os, but also holds Latina/o audiences partially responsible. In this way, Latinas like Jovita viewed Latina/o consumers as agents because they wield the consumer choice that accompanies their "buying power." Arlene Dávila (2008, 2012) argues that Latina/os are increasingly mainstreamed and whitened by scholars, marketers, and politicians who locate their power in consumption. In other words, while Latina/os are more visible in mainstream discourses, it is as consumers, not as citizens. Jovita's comment points to these discourses that locate Latina/os as agents precisely because of their buying power—not their political power.

Furthermore, many women expressed excitement at being wooed as a market by transnational media conglomerates in both the English-language and Spanish-language industries. This excitement was in direct contrast to the Riveras, described in the first case study, who felt that they were not a part of mainstream media. Differences in media outlets are probably the reason for this discrepancy in audience perceptions. While Latina/os remain highly underrepresented in mainstream film and television, Latina/os are increasingly present in niche and general market advertising. In light of the increased presence in advertising media, the construction of Latina/os as a niche market was likened by some women to a "coming of age" for the Latina/o community. These women saw the mainstream interest in the Latina/o market as a precursor to more visibility and power in US society in general. For many of the women it was as if Latina/os' worthiness was validated by the increasing visibility of marketing to Latina/os. Dávila (2012, 2008) argues that this idea of "coming of age" is one of the most pervasive myths in dominant discourses that erase the realities that many Latina/os continue to face, such as poverty and lack of access to higher education and health care despite increased "buying power." As such, the danger lies not only in identifying with a consumerist discourse that commodifies Latinidad, but also in confusing mediated visibility with political power. While perceived "buying power" may indeed garner Latina/os more visibility in the public sphere, it does not guarantee social justice and equality for Latina/o communities. This is one of the ways—and perhaps the most important way—the conflation of a citizen-consumer identity serves to reproduce hegemony and limits the possibility for agency in privileging a symbolic form of citizenship.

Today the co-optation of Latina/o culture is rampant in political, academic, and media spheres. There is ample scholarship that demonstrates that Latinidad is co-opted in homogenized, essentialized, and ultimately disempowering ways. Thus, we need to remain hesitant about celebrating a commodified Latinidad, because it can mask the marginalized realities that many Latina/os face. Latina/os are implicated in a consumer-citizen subjectivity that emphasizes the so-called buying power of this pan-ethnic group without ensuring social rights and welfare. As Coco Fusco (1995), Alejandro Lugo (2000), and Stacy Takacs (1999) have argued, Latina/o commodities are more readily accepted (and celebrated) by dominant society than are actual Latina/o people. Like Arlene Dávila (2008, 2012), I am hesitant to uncritically accept that Latina/os are coming of age. More aptly, Latinidad continues to be commodified for an ever more broad audience, while the inequality that Latina/os experience is pushed below the surface of public discourse. To locate Latina audiences as citizens requires that we move away from viewing their contributions to US society as primarily through consumption (though certainly this is a way Latina/os themselves might perceive their own roles as citizens).

Overall, the categories of citizen and consumer can no longer be separated in a consumer society like the United States. This is clear in the women's reading of commercial media. There was no way for them to make sense of media without drawing from a consumerist logic, even in the few instances in which some critiqued consumer culture. However, this also illustrates that Latina audiences are very media-literate. They were able to make sense of texts through their commonsense knowledge of media production and market research. This distinguishes these women from earlier generations of audiences that did not experience the same level of access to how media is produced. For instance, consider the bonus features on DVDs and cable television shows like MTV's *Making of the Video* (1999–2009) and VH1's *Behind the Music* (1997–present) that expose audiences to the production process. Ultimately, the interpellation of Latina/o audiences as consumer-citizens behooves us to consider how the market increasingly mediates contemporary identities and power relations.

Claims to Material Citizenship

During the main part of my fieldwork, between 2006 and 2007, undocumented immigration was becoming a topic of heated debate in local and national news, underscoring the most recent immigration backlash in the United States. At the time, I had been working with a number of participants, but was seeking more immigrant women to include in my sample. I worked closely with a few women who migrated to the United States as teens, but very few participants migrated within the last five years. One of my key informants introduced me to Elvira Arellano, an undocumented woman from Michoacán, Mexico, taking sanctuary at the Adalberto Methodist Church in the historically Puerto Rican neighborhood of Humboldt Park in Chicago. When I met Arellano in late 2006, she had already been in sanctuary for a few months, and her story gained press coverage at both the local and national level. Indeed, at this point not only was she covered in news sources like the

Chicago Tribune, but she was also being regularly critiqued in conservative political shows like *Lou Dobbs Tonight* on CNN. I interviewed Arellano formally in February 2007 about representations of Latinas in mainstream and Spanish-language media, as I did the other participants, but I also talked to her about her own depiction in news media. This was a particularly opportune time to interview Arellano because being in sanctuary allowed her to reflect on all the media attention she was receiving.[11]

In her small apartment on the top floor of the church, Arellano began the interview by describing her current situation as an undocumented mother of a son with US citizenship. She displayed confident body language by sitting up straight and maintaining consistent eye contact. Perhaps given her extensive experience with the press, she had become somewhat of a professional interviewee, with long and detailed answers. In particular, her story sounded rehearsed and very similar to the language she used in media interviews. Unlike the participants who were well versed in responding to marketing research about consumer preferences and behaviors, Arellano was more familiar with being interviewed by media professionals regarding her legal status. Overall, the first half of our two-hour interview traced her journey from a largely invisible undocumented immigrant to a media icon.

After Arellano was arrested and processed in 2001 after working at Chicago's O'Hare Airport under a false Social Security number, she sought the help of Centro Sin Fronteras, a local community organization that advocates for immigrants. Despite being advised by her lawyer not to engage with the media, Arellano began talking to the mainstream and Spanish-language press, viewing news media as a vehicle for sharing her plight with the public. She also adds that it was not just her seeking out the press, but "los medios de comunicación estaban buscando la noticia."[12] Arellano stated that her impetus to engage with the media came after she was released from detention and watched other immigrants not able to reunite with their families:

Pues yo pensé por yo gracias a Dios pude pasar la noche con mi hijo. Que fue una noche muy difícil pero estamos juntos y esas familias aún no. Y fue en ese entonces que decidí pues hablar ante de los medios de comunicación y solamente lo que yo dijé salió del corazón. Lo que yo sentía en ese momento. La tristeza por como se nos estaba tratando. Como si fueramos criminales.[13]

Here, and in much of her rhetoric in general, Arellano countered one of the major archetypes of Latinos in media representations—that of the criminal, dating back to Hollywood images of the bandit in the early twentieth century. The criminalization of undocumented immigrants continues in the public sphere despite the shifting social and historical construction of legality (De Genova 2005). In particular, Arellano contested being called a fugitive (and hence criminal), contending that everyone knows exactly where she is taking sanctuary. She also added that undocumented immigrants primarily migrate to the United States for work and that Latina/os who commit crimes are usually citizens and/or residents.

During the second half of my interview with Arellano I asked her about her thoughts on broader media representations of Latinas in other media besides the news, but she seemed uninterested. Indeed, she was far more concerned with Latina/os being labeled as criminal and the dehumanizing representations of undocumented immigrants than the hypersexualization of Latinas in entertainment media. Her lack of a critique of hypersexualized images of Latinas differed greatly from the majority of the participants, who described hypersexualization as *the* most problematic media representation of Latinas (see Báez 2007, 2008). This may indicate Arellano's investment in more material politics of the body, given that she was facing deportation, and the other participants' concerns with more symbolic bodies in media representations. In other words, Arellano was interested in media as a vehicle for more than just representation. She wanted to use media to legalize her status, and later, for social change. Certainly, she did not want Latina/os to be depicted as criminals and undeserving of legal citizenship, but she more precisely wanted to use the press to strategically advocate for immigration reform. Ultimately, Arellano had a different relationship to media, whereby she served in a quasi-producer role as a conduit for information, while most of the other participants were largely consumers.[14]

In the end, Arellano had a fraught relationship with the media— some misconstrued her story and/or used it to discredit her, while other journalists used Arellano's story to shed a compassionate light on the plight of undocumented immigrants in calling for immigration reform. Reception of Arellano by other participants was also fraught with tensions. For example, during my fieldwork, several participants of Mexican origin expressed resentment and shame about Arellano's visibility in the press. Some participants claimed that Arellano "enjoys manipulating the media" and argued that Arellano fights for rights that she does not deserve. In other words, not only is Arellano perceived as manipulative, but she is deemed "unworthy" of not only citizenship, but even protest. One participant in particular, Jovita (the same participant described in the previous section), argued that Arellano was not competent to speak as a leader for the immigration movement, describing her as "not articulate." Jovita also critiques Arellano's claim to citizenship because it is partly based on her being a mother of a US citizen; Jovita contends that motherhood is not a legitimate claim to citizenship. Interestingly, in my interview with Arellano, she argued that the Puerto Rican community (including the working-class, historically Puerto Rican community in the Humboldt Park neighborhood, where she stayed in sanctuary, and the Puerto Rican Congressman Luis Gutiérrez) were more supportive than the Mexican (American) community. This case suggests that in some instances class lines are crossed less easily than ethnic boundaries. Reception of news coverage of Arellano also reveals Latina/o audiences' preferences for representations of Latina/os as documented residents and citizens who display normative, middle-class cultural capital (i.e., "articulate" language) at the expense of working-class and undocumented women, who are already largely invisible in media. Thus, Latina/o audiences remain steeply entrenched in a politics of respectability that values normativity.

Other participants, particularly Puerto Rican women and second- and third-generation Mexicans, were generally silent about Arellano even though they were very vocal about other national and local Latina media icons such as the actress Salma Hayek, the actress and singer Jennifer Lopez, the reggaetón artist Ivy Queen, and the recent addition of Marisol to Mattel's American Girl doll line.[15] I suspect this is partly because most of the participants were still processing the effects of the 1990s Latin boom and the recent emphasis in the news on Latino buying power. It was difficult for Latina audiences to register contradictory messages of being welcome and unwelcome by mainstream media. Instead, Latina/o audiences clearly favored more symbolic forms of citizenship such as celebrity culture and consumer culture than material aspects of citizenship such as legal status.

In sum, this snapshot of Arellano's engagement with the press demonstrates how Latina audiences use media representations to determine who is worthy and unworthy of legal citizenship. In this way, media are used as vehicles to determine inclusion and exclusion. Latina audiences use media not only to imagine their own place in the nation, as the first two case studies demonstrate, but also to police who gets to tell their stories in the press. Most of the participants privileged a representation of Latina/os as normative citizens (i.e., middle-class with legal citizenship) at the expense of working-class and undocumented Latina/os. Thus, this case study exemplifies how media can be a platform for competing notions of belonging among Latina/o audiences.

Conclusion

In today's mediated, globalized world, it is imperative for scholars to understand how media and citizenship intersect; more specifically, it is essential to engage in the interdisciplinary project of theorizing citizenship within audience studies. The above case studies of Latina audiences can inform our understanding of Latina/os and media in the following ways: (1) by demonstrating how people on the ground level might internalize, negotiate, and counter media representations; (2) by highlighting how mainstream and ethnic media serve to solidify imagined and real, local collective identities; and (3) by motivating subordinated groups to produce alternative media in instances when the resources are available. Furthermore, examining cultural citizenship and audience studies can also shed more light on how notions of "citizen" and "consumer" are becoming synonymous. Vicki Mayer (2003) begins to examine this in her ethnographic study of Mexican American media production and consumption in San Antonio, Texas, in which she finds that her participants felt that others saw them more as equal consumers, not citizens. In this way, it is also fruitful to deploy George Yúdice's concept of "private citizenship" to understand the ways Latina/o audiences might use their "buying power" to perform citizenry as individual consumers (Yúdice 1995).

It should be noted that I did not initially set out to explore issues of citizenship in this study. After analyzing data gathered from exploratory research in the summer of 2005, I began noticing that when I probed participants on why they took issue with most media representations of Latinas, many would respond that what was at stake was their worthiness. More specifically, they expressed concern over whether or not Latinas would be perceived as worthy citizens. This came about in the form of statements such as, "this [pattern of media representation] will influence how others [non-Latina/os] think of us," and "media determines whether anyone will take us seriously." Aside from the women's belief in strong media effects—an assertion most media scholars would complicate—what is important here is the salience audiences place on media. Indeed, as Nick Couldry (2001) asserts, people tend to naturalize the media's power through a belief in the media as an authority that legitimizes who and what is important. Latina/os' place within the nation is often thought to be not only imagined by media, but also secured by media. Another way of putting this is that media become the gauge for Latina audiences to measure their status in the United States. In this way, symbolic notions of citizenship were invoked by many Latina audience members. At the same time, the last case study also demonstrates how more material aspects of citizenship are also present in Latinas' relationship to media. Media are viewed by audiences as a way to not only express their place within the nation, but also to potentially gain access to legalization.

Ultimately, these case studies can help us to better understand how cultural citizenship is enacted in everyday life, often in the more informal, "hidden" practices of daily life such as representation and meaning making (Hermes 2005). This essay urges scholars and media workers to think of Latina/o audiences as not only consumers, but also publics. Given the immigration crisis and the many other issues confronting Latina/os today, such as housing, health, and education, it is imperative that we not forget that Latina/os are also part of the larger US public. Also, in keeping with the remarks of participants described in this essay, while Latina/os are framed as consumers and are readily able to make media intelligible through a consumerist logic, they also make demands for more dynamic media representations that reflect their desires to be acknowledged and respected as full citizens of the United

States. Some audiences also see media as a space to demand a pathway to legal citizenship. Overall, these case studies encourage us to treat Latina/os not merely as consumers, as most commercial media intend, but also as citizens who are engaging with media representations in the search for recognition, respect, and belonging to the nation on both the symbolic and material levels.

NOTES

1. This research is part of a larger book project that explores how Latina audiences engage with mediated representations of the Latina body in Latina/o-oriented media. While I focus here on citizenship and belonging, I examine issues of the body, gender, sexuality, race, ethnicity, class, age, and space in the book and other writing (see Báez 2007, 2008).

2. Kristin Moran's study of Latina/o family television viewing also indicates that Latina/o audiences are reading media through a lens of belonging, but Moran does not theorize this finding as a form of cultural citizenship.

3. All participants, with the exception of Elvira Arellano, were given pseudonyms to protect their anonymity. I chose to use Arellano's actual name, with her permission, because she is such an iconic figure in news outlets and the immigrant rights movement.

4. As a third-generation Puerto Rican woman with a working-class background and current middle-class status who is bilingual and has legal citizenship, I found my relationship to the participants oscillating between insider and outsider status. As such, I shift between using "I," "we," and "they" when referring to the participants, as appropriate to each situation. I provide more detail on my positionality as the researcher in my forthcoming book *The Latina Gaze: Latina Audiences and Citizenship*.

5. According to the US census, Latina/os are the majority of the population in Miami.

6. This is consistent with Angharad Valdivia's (2000) argument that audiences, particularly women of color, do not always experience pleasure when consuming film and other popular culture, as film theorists (particularly psychoanalysts) have suggested.

7. I thank Michael Mandiberg for clarifying this distinction between my desire for participants to respond in terms of *affect* and participants' insistence on discussing media in terms of effect.

8. Certainly, these instances also speak to how the participants perceived my authority as a media researcher. Thank you to María Elena Cepeda for making this important point.

9. Digital editing tools, such as airbrushing and cutting and pasting, are now commonplace in the publishing and advertising industries.

10. For another example of this sentiment, see María Elena Cepeda's chapter in this volume.
11. For an examination of the press coverage of Arellano, see McElmurry (2009).
12. The media were even *looking for* the news.
13. Well, I thought thank God I could spend the evening with my son. It was a difficult night, but we were together and those families still weren't. And it was from that moment that I decided then to talk in front of the media, and what I said came from my heart—what I felt in that moment. The sadness for how they were treating us. As if we were criminals.
14. After Arellano's deportation in August 2007, she took on the role of media producer more fully by engaging with social media (Facebook, Twitter, blogs) to advocate for immigration from Michoacán, Mexico. This is the subject of a project that I am currently developing about the use of social media in the immigration reform movement.
15. Please note that I explore these issues in other work (see Báez 2007 and 2008).

REFERENCES

Anguiano, Claudia A., and Karma R. Chávez. 2011. "DREAMers' Discourse: Young Latino/a Immigrants and the Naturalization of the American Dream." In *Latina/o Discourse in Vernacular Spaces: Somos de Una Voz?*, edited by Michelle A. Holling, 81–99. Lanham, MD: Lexington Books.

Báez, Jillian M. 2007. "Speaking of Jennifer Lopez: Discourses of Iconicity and Identity Formation among Latina Audiences." *Media Report to Women* 35 (1): 5–13.

———. 2008. "Mexican/Mexican American Women Talk Back: Audience Responses to Representations of Latinidad in U.S. Advertising." In *Latina/o Communication Studies Today*, edited by Angharad N. Valdivia, 257–81. New York: Peter Lang.

Chavez, Leo. 2008. *The Latino Threat: Constructing Immigrants, Citizens, and the Nation*. Stanford: Stanford University Press.

Coll, Kathleen. 2010. *Remaking Citizenship: Latina Immigrants and New American Politics*. Stanford: Stanford University Press.

Couldry, Nick. 2001. *The Place of Media Power: Pilgrims and Witnesses of the Media Age*. London: Routledge.

Dávila, Arlene. 2008. *Latino Spin: Public Image and the Whitewashing of Race*. New York: New York University Press.

———. 2012. *Latinos, Inc.: The Marketing and Making of a People*. 2nd ed. Berkeley: University of California Press.

De Genova, Nicholas. 2005. *Working the Boundaries: Race, Space, and Illegality in Mexican Chicago*. Durham: Duke University Press.

Flores, William V., and Rina Benmayor, eds. 1997. *Latino Cultural Citizenship: Claiming Identity, Space, and Rights*. Boston: Beacon.

Fusco, Coco. 1995. *English Is Broken Here: Notes on the Cultural Fusion in the Americas*. New York: New Press.

García Canclini, Néstor. 2001. *Consumers and Citizens: Globalization and Multicultural Conflicts*. Minneapolis: University of Minnesota Press.

Hermes, Joke. 2005. *Re-Reading Popular Culture*. Oxford: Blackwell.

Lugo, Alejandro. 2000. "Theorizing Border Inspections." *Cultural Dynamics* 12 (3): 353–73.

Mayer, Vicki. 2003. *Producing Dreams, Consuming Youth: Mexican Americans and Mass Media*. New Brunswick: Rutgers University Press.

McElmurry, Sara E. 2009. "Elvira Arellano: No Rosa Parks—Creation of 'Us' versus 'Them' in an Opinion Column." *Hispanic Journal of Behavioral Sciences* 31 (2): 182–203.

Moran, Kristin C. 2011. *Listening to Latina/o Youth: Television Consumption within Families*. New York: Peter Lang.

Oboler, Suzanne, ed. 2006. *Latinos and Citizenship: Dilemmas of Belonging*. New York: Palgrave Macmillan.

Ong, Aihwa. 1996. "Cultural Citizenship as Subject-Making: Immigrants Negotiate Racial and Cultural Boundaries in the United States." *Current Anthropology* 37 (5): 737–62.

Rosaldo, Renato. 1994. "Cultural Citizenship and Educational Democracy." *Cultural Anthropology* 9 (3): 402–11.

Sio, Lok C. D. 2005. *Memories of a Future Home: Diasporic Citizenship of Chinese in Panama*. Stanford: Stanford University Press.

Takacs, Stacy. 1999. "Alien-Nation: Immigration, National Identity and Transnationalism." *Cultural Studies* 13 (4): 591–620.

Valdivia, Angharad. 2000. *A Latina in the Land of Hollywood: And Other Essays on Media Culture*. Tucson: University of Arizona Press.

Vargas, Lucila. 2009. *Latina Teens, Migration, and Popular Culture*. New York: Peter Lang.

Yúdice, George. 1995. "Civil Society, Consumption and Governmentality in an Age of Global Restructuring." *Social Text* 45 (4).

14

Un Desmadre Positivo

Notes on How Jenni Rivera Played *Music*

DEBORAH R. VARGAS

Gerardo Rodriguez, a self-proclaimed Jenni Rivera fan, once wrote that "we, the fans, make her. Not the radio, not newspapers, not the TV—it was us."[1] What is insightful about Rodriguez's comment is that it breaks the normative construction of popular music as something that is created and produced by the music industry and the artist and is merely consumed by fans. Rodriguez's statement emphatically states that it was not simply the culture industry that created Jenni Rivera. Instead, Rodriguez's standpoint as fan and consumer charges Latino media scholars of music to reconsider analytic frameworks that too often are unidirectional and linear.[2] Within the context of hyper-globalized commodification, where it seems no form of cultural labor, especially music, is free from the drive of capitalist markets, Rodriguez's statement prompts us to pause, to reorient, and to shift meanings and concepts in media analysis. This prompt is especially critical when attempting to make sense of a *mexicana* pop icon such as Jenni Rivera, whose approach to playing music must be comprehended less through the mechanics of vocals, musicianship, or media players, but by reorienting the idea of "playing" to also include a consideration of the structural elements of the artist's life, a life propelled into music by her desires to escape, and by the necessity to trounce silence. In sum, in order to understand the cultural consumption of Rivera's music, we must understand how Rivera "played" music, that is, worked its normative standards of commercialization and production, the way working-class communities of color learn to "hustle" or "play" the system. This chapter is a Chicana/o Latina/o cultural studies approach to musical meaning and the possibilities that emerge, both problematic and potentially dissenting, of alternative meanings for playing music.

Angie Chabram-Dernersesian asserts that the concern of Chicano/ Latino cultural studies should be "cultural practices and productions from the point of view of their intrication with, and within, relations of power of capitalist societies that are structured in dominance and privilege and that still carry the imprints of earlier geopolitical legacies."[3] By extension, any analysis of Jenni Rivera must begin with the ways her immigrant experiential strategies acquired around labor came to bear on the cultivation of her music career—as a job, here distinct from art—and the ways her fans understood themselves as central to Rivera's musical production and iconicity. In fact, Rivera was often described as a "social singer" to emphasize the role her music played to raise awareness of social issues. This description simultaneously upholds the problematic binary between music as art and music as a means for social critique, and also points to Rivera's music as doing something unique compared to most *mexicana* singing artists of her generation.[4]

Two meanings of media transmission are critical for considering alternative meanings of *playing* music that I argue Rivera's iconicity cultivated: to allow to pass through a medium and being a medium for. A different understanding of the relationship between music making and consumption allows for a critical engagement with Jenni Rivera's musical labor and the ways *playing* her music by fans fostered alternative *mexicana* subjectivities and communities within a social world that continually challenges their endeavors for a quotidian existence.[5] Rivera played music to transmit *testimonios* of gender nonconformity. Rivera's fans played her music to transmit undisciplined desires, endorse immigrant civil rights, and protest women's abuse.[6] "She was the first Mexican American female singer from Southern California to achieve superstardom on both sides of the border, and that success inspired the legion of fans who shared her immigrant roots and humble working-class upbringing."[7]

Playing Music: "¡A Chambiar!"

Jenni Rivera's musical hustle actually disrupts the myth of music as a cultural art form. Instead, her approach to making music is anchored in the working-class epistemologies of informal economy entrepreneurship. In this way, consumers are rearticulated as dynamic communities through social media networks, and the artist's power as a popular icon becomes a conduit for publicizing social justice agendas. Such a consideration of music is what Angie Chabram-Dernersesian describes in her proposition for Chicana/o Latina/o cultural studies as the importance of difference, production, and positionality in the shifting terrains of Latin@ cultural productions.[8] Rivera cultivated a technology of *testimonio*, using music to play back the chorus of *chismes* about her personal life, publicly displaying nonnormative gender through *chusmerías*, and linking her iconicity to social justice issues, that constructed a fan base as more than simply receptors of musical commodities.

Jenni Rivera, born Dolores Janney Rivera Saavedra, was born July 2, 1969, in Long Beach, California, the third child and eldest daughter of six children, to Pedro and Rosa, immigrants from Sonora and Jalisco, Mexico, respectively. Rivera is what we may identify as a typical first-generation Chicana born to Mexican immigrant parents: growing up in a working-class, bilingual, and bicultural world and attending public schools. Like many working-class youth, Rivera desired to earn a better livelihood, taking business classes in order to open her own real estate agency, Divina Reality. During her sophomore year in high school Rivera gave birth to her first child, Janney, after becoming involved with an older man, José Trinidad Marín, who also fathered her next two children. This early relationship would leave traces of physical and emotional abuse that would frame much of Rivera's life and her eventual advocacy of survivors of domestic abuse. The immigrant labor ethic she was raised in, knowledge of the social world acquired as a young mother in an abusive relationship, and the strategies of cultivating ways to assure her own well-being came together to form the Jenni Rivera who would create a lasting impact on the *norteño*/Mexican music world.

In 1995 Rivera released her first album, *La Chacalosa*. Generally, the term *chacalosa* refers to a girl who likes to have fun, party, drink, and at times is known to be involved in some sort of illegal activity, especially associated with drugs. *Chacalosas*, in the context of Rivera's music, are thus represented as Mexican working-class/immigrant women who have survived bad relationships and who have little trust in men. *Chacalosas* are hard-living souls. It would become a nickname for Rivera herself, based on the popularity of her song and its aptness as a symbol for her life. In fact, an overview of her life includes some of the characteristics that defined *chacalosas*, including three divorces, overcoming domestic abuse, and strains on relationships with her elder brothers. Transmitted through Rivera's performance as well as through the narratives of her songs, *la chacalosa* would construct a powerful gendered representation of *mexicanas* that countered their containment in dominant projects that construct them as normative citizen-subjects. Rivera staged a nonnormative gender *mexicana* subjectivity by *playing* her music, often cultivating messages—in song and in her activism—about class warfare, immigrant xenophobia, and women's abuse.

Rivera staged her career by being savvy and assertive. Pepe Garza, the program director at 105.5 Que Buena, the Los Angeles regional Mexican radio station, one of the first stations to give airtime to Rivera's music, recalled having first come across Rivera while she was trying to shop airtime for her first song:

> It was a song called "Las Malandrinas." She asked me if she could perform [on an awards show called *Premios que buena* that Garza was producing]. I told her, "no, you're not that famous. But since your brother [Lupillo Rivera] is going to receive an award, why don't you present it to him?" She agreed. But when she got up on the podium to announce the award, she yelled, "dónde están mis malandrinas?" and she started singing the song. The crowd went crazy. I knew then that she had an audience.[9]

Jenni Rivera was offered an opportunity and she, in turn, made it her premiere. Rivera's savvy talent at *playing* music, or hustling the moment offered to her by Garza, is based on an immigrant epistemology of survival and persistence, or a working-class sensibility of finding any opportunity to create a different path for existence. Growing up, Rivera was surrounded by the *mexicano* immigrant/working class.

Rivera's parents' immigration was part of a significant demographic shift, whereby the Mexican-descent population of the greater Los Angeles area now became predominately immigrant, a huge presence that grew rapidly into the indispensible yet unacknowledged labor force that propelled Southern California's economic growth.[10] Rivera's approaches to music were based on what she witnessed growing up. In 1984, Pedro Rivera put out his first record, drawing from the $14,000 he had made selling buttons for the Los Angeles Olympics. Pedro Rivera recognized that "people wanted to hear their names in corridos"; eventually people hired him to write corridos for those in his neighborhood. Sadly, Pedro Rivera would one day write a corrido honoring the life and name of his late daughter.

Rivera's immigrant work ethic was one that required you to make your own way and create your own opportunities, a creative force that comes from knowing there is no steady work, only steady effort. Rivera once recalled that as a youngster she sold cans for scrap metal and hawked music records at her family's stand at a Los Angeles flea market.[11] This work ethic is expressed in the Mexican Spanish vernacular terms for labor or work: "Necesito jale" (I need a job) or "¡Quiero chambiar!" (I want to work!). As a young woman and as a young single mother, Rivera was skilled at seeking *chambas* and *jales* in a variety of venues; she began working as a teenager, attending Long Beach Poly High School, and by age fifteen she was pregnant with her first child, fathered by a much older Trino Marín. Rivera's parents reacted by kicking her out of the house, resulting in her complete dependence on Marín.

After an eight-year marriage to Marín—one filled with emotional and physical abuse, including two suicide attempts—Rivera gained enough courage to divorce him.[12] During her marriage Rivera worked secretly to obtain her high school diploma and eventually took college courses. She majored in business administration at California State University–Long Beach and headed into the real estate business. "Growing up in Long Beach, I learned to face the world. I also learned that I wanted more for myself and wanted to become something."[13] Rivera *played* music by bringing her life's *chamba* spirit with her. Rivera did not intend to produce music; she never wanted to become a singer. In fact, she entered the music scene through the mundane tasks of answering phones and handling sales at the family's "mom-and-pop" record label, Cintas Acuario.[14]

Rivera became keenly aware of the varied parts of the music industry machine, and therefore she purposefully *played* music, aware that this playing involved more than the mere sonic transmission of sound through voice or performance. Rivera understood that it was not merely managers, producers, and radio personalities who kept her music playing in circulation, but those who made T-shirts, created disc compilations, and even snapped pictures of her. In Miami to promote an album in 2005, Rivera's entire music team sat down to dinner after working all day. Carlos Pérez, a publicist at Fonovisa/Universal Music Latin Entertainment, recalled,

> The waiters and the people from the kitchen were taking her picture. Jenni said, "Carlos, tell them to come here and we'll pose for a picture," but the kitchen staff said they weren't allowed to do that. So Jenni said, "Okay, I'll come to the kitchen, then."[15]

After dinner they found themselves the target of paparazzi who were camped outside the restaurant waiting for Rivera to exit. Rivera was offered a way out through the back door to avoid them, but she refused, saying to Pérez, "'do you know what they have to go through to get paid for that one shot?' She then whistled at the paparazzi and yelled, 'muchachos! I'm just going to ask you one favor. When I say I'm done, let's call it a day.'"[16]

Playing Jenni Rivera

Jessica Quintana, executive director of Centro CHA, a nonprofit Latino social service agency formed in 1992 in Long Beach, recalled during a memorial held for Jenni Rivera days after her death, "we wanted to recognize her because she had done so much with her life despite her struggles. Jenni could always relate to the constituents we serve. There are a lot of people here that are still going through the same challenges that she went through."[17] Quintana continued, "she talked about her life in a very open way and really cared about the issues that affected women, like poverty, domestic violence and independence."[18] Certainly, comments such as "she was just like every-one else" have become staple phrases when a popular figure dies. Yet it would be difficult to find examples of Rivera's musical iconicity that did not align her popular representation and musical themes with the exploited subjects of labor and gender violence. Moreover, Rivera's representation never shied away from airing her dirty laundry. "People could relate to her struggles, that's why so many people loved her," said Quintana. "She captivated her audience by being herself at all times and being open with her life through her music and interviews with the press."[19]

Rivera's manner of *playing* music—her music industry *chamba*—provides an alternative meaning for the production and transmission of music. Moreover, Rivera *played* music in ways that created spaces for gender and sexual subjects that are often shunned in neoliberal projects of normative *mexicanidad*. As Rivera became more powerful in her iconicity, she became more emboldened to "act out" *lo de abajo* (the déclassé) or *chusmería*, a form of "behavior that refuses standards of bourgeois comportment" and to a significant degree is "linked to stigmatized class identity" through nonconformist performances or enactments.[20] Rivera's representation and music channeled nonnormative gender through song characterizations of *la malandrina* and *la chacolosa*, and thus her public testimony of personal life dramas enabled social network spaces of conversation, imitation, and contestation among her fans, the often self-proclaimed *malandrinas* and *chacalosas* often hailed by Rivera and curators of their own social network virtual communities. Rivera *played* music and her fans *played* Rivera. Rivera transmitted stories, scandal, and harsh lived realities. Rivera's *malandrinas* and *chacalosas* transmitted themselves as imperfect, contradictory, and empowered beings who so often face violent acts of contained normative womanhood. For example, a person identified as Christina Mex posted on a blog replying to another fan who had said that Rivera's passing was a sign that everyone should seek God as a savior. In her post, Mex writes that fans like her didn't see Rivera as superior to them:

> Just because we're in pain because of her death doesn't mean that we
> automatically put her on a pedestal. . . . some of us are hurting because

she represents strength and hope for us and was a voice for many of us. Jenni knew and understand [*sic*] the many types of issues that women have to go through because she has LIVED IT.²¹

Invisible, exploited, and nonnormative *mexicano* subjectivities are indecipherable within US state-sanctioned discourses of the heteronormative citizen-subject or the legal immigrant subject. Social networks become key sites for such communities otherwise expunged from privileged spaces of legal and class-based participation. Whereas I have argued—following two meanings of transmission—that Rivera channeled nonnormative *testimonios* of gender and immigrant civil rights through the medium of music, including recordings, video, and live performance, she too became a medium for the dialogues of her fans. Jenni Rivera was the impetus for many social network sites, including the Facebook pages "Las chacalosas de Jenni Rivera," "Cartel de Jenni Rivera," and "DivasParranderasYParranderos," among many others. One of the most powerful social networks was the Twitter group J-Unit (or as they referred to themselves in Spanish, "jota-unit"), whose membership was so integrated in Rivera's life that, during the days after her passing, Rivera's mother directed media to this Twitter site for details on Rivera's funeral and other breaking information.

Rivera's @jennirivera Twitter site and websites of her reality television show were also networks through which fans engaged not only with Rivera but also with each other, commenting on everything from music to social issues. Moreover, such media demonstrate that Jenni Rivera was *played* and not merely consumed by her fans. Specifically, her music provided a space for *mexicana* subjectivities that were in contradistinction to what Arlene Dávila has called Latino "corrective" images, "the commercial representation of Latinidad [that] brings to the forefront the pervasiveness of racial hierarchies in the very constitution of corrective images."²² Rivera's public antics, her racialized class representations through the *chacalosas, malandrinas,* and *narcotraficantes,* configured an iconicity irredeemable as a "corrected" or normative brown citizen. Such is the case with the reappropriated Corona beer brand label that plays on stereotypes of Mexicans as beer drinkers who, as "imports from Mexico," become the US public's greatest fear. In this contemporary US context, working-class *mexicanas* and undocumented immigrants are very familiar with the broken promises of the state to reward "good" and "appropriate" racial subjects. Thus, what I find significant about these social network virtual communities is how they *played* Rivera—as a medium, a musical conduit through which fans at times had access to alternative discourses of lived experiences, gender representations, and political agendas regarding domestic abuse and LGBT and immigrant civil rights. Rivera's *chacalosa* and *malandrina* representations were replayed by her fans as audacious and undaunted and as potential possibilities for empowerment within contexts of labor and gender oppression. Moreover, such representations through her live performance, reality television characters, and song lyrics bore witness to everyday brutalities expedited under globalization regimes, gender violence, and immigrant xenophobia.

Jenni Rivera was often described by fans and the media as *una mujerona*, a big woman. Rivera certainly enacted such bigness—as a woman who takes up too much space and as a big force to reckon with—through her brash public acts and public postings about her personal life. For example, it was quite common for Rivera to use her Twitter account as a means of conversation instead of merely posting her whereabouts or announcing her shows. She once posted on her @jennirivera Twitter site, quoting Tupac Shakur, a response to judgmental remarks in the media about her personal life choices: "'Only God can judge me . . . all you other motha fckrs need to say out of my business.' . . . Tupac." The themes of much of Rivera's music demonstrated how Rivera embodied the *chusmería* associated with aberrant femininities.[23] In this way, Rivera was known for recording *narcocorrido* songs that often featured narratives about the women partners, wives, or daughters of *narcotraficantes* (narco-traffickers). In the 1995 song "La Chacalosa," she sings of being the prideful daughter of a narco-trafficker:

> Me buscan por chacalosa soy hija de un traficante
> Conozco bien las movidas
> Me crié entre la mafia grande
>
> (They look for me because I'm a chacalosa, I'm the daughter of a
>   drug trafficker
> I know the moves well
> I was raised in a major mafia)

Figure 14.1. Cover of Jenni Rivera's album *La Chacalosa*.

"La Chacalosa" most certainly can be viewed as romanticizing and musically exploiting the violent circumstances surrounding the power-ful presence of narco-traffickers in cities and rural towns across Mexico. Yet, I propose that the song also transmits the devastating reality her *mexicana* fan base recognized and could therefore possibly process dif-ferently. As Mark Edberg stresses, there must be diligent effort not to homogenize narcocorrido music or the ways narratives or characters are interpreted; rather, we must "unpack the complex and multilayered context feeding the near mythical characters featured in narcocorridos," especially gender and class.[24] By extension, narrating the presence of women as connected to narco-trafficking violence potentially accom-plishes at least two things: it disrupts the idea of *mexicanas* as demure victims and complicates racialized, classed, dominant representations of *mexicanas* that circulate in the public sphere, as fair-skinned and middle-class or as brown domestic and agricultural servants.[25] "La Chacalosa" created such a huge following among Rivera's women fans that internet social groups sprang up, creating networks of those who identified with the themes of being a bad girl, a partier, and a troublemaker, including "Las chacalosas de Jenni Rivera," on Facebook and Myspace, that invited interested persons to join:

> K onda mi gente! Bienvenidos a la pagina oficial de las chacalosas. . . . para los que no nos conosen somos un grupo de amigas que nos gusta andar de party. . . . siempre nos gusta divertirnos y andar al 100! . . . pues como saben apenas andamos comensando nuestra clicka de puras muchachonas que les gusta la parranda so la que le entre solo manden un mensaje a nuestra pagina.

The interconnected ways Rivera *played* her career and the ways fans *played* new imaginaries outside the confinements of normativity and erasure were unique, and at times posed a significant counterweight to the business of music media. "I am the same as the public, as my fans," Rivera once said in an interview.[26]

"Las Malandrinas," recorded in 1999, was another example of this, and propelled another *mexicana* iconography her fans connected with.[27]

> Nos dicen las malandrinas
> porque hacemos mucho ruido
> porque tomamos cerveza
> y nos gusta el mejor vino
> En los salones de baile
> siempre pedimos corridos
> no somos como las popis
> que se paran mucho el cuello
>
> (They call us the delinquent women
> because we make lots of noise
> because we drink beer
> and we love the best wine

In the dancehalls
we always request corridos
we're not like the arrogant ones
who keep their collars upright)

The song and its representation became so popular that, in fact, Rivera would later commonly call out to her women fans, "¿Dónde están mis *malandrinas* y mis *chacalosas*?"

The unique characteristic about Rivera is that her personal life seemed to often align with the personas she sang about, such as the figures of the *malandrina* and the *chacalosa*. One example of this occurred during a concert performance in Puerto Vallarta. At one point during a song Rivera stops the music to confront an audience member who has just thrown beer at her from the front rows of the audience. Rivera brings the young woman on stage, where she directly confronts her. They stand face to face and Rivera says to her, "A ver, tíremelo. Tíremelo aquí donde estoy, tíremelo. Quien cree que tiene más huevos, usted o yo?" (Let's see, throw it at me. Throw it at me here where I am, throw it. Who do you think has more balls, you or me?) The crowd starts chanting "Jenni, Jenni, Jenni." Security then takes the woman off stage as Jenni addresses the audience:

> Les digo por favor, que si yo los respeto a ustedes, que también me den ese respeto a mí. Vengo a cantarles con todo mi corazón. Yo pudiera estar en mi casa, puedo estar en el hotel haciendo un niño. Pero aquí estoy con ustedes. Y si de veras tienen el rencor para tirarle algo a una persona que está trabajando, pues haganlo aquí de cerca, no hay problema. Es todo lo que les pido.

> (I ask you please, if I respect you, then please respect me. I come to sing for you with all of my heart. I could be at home, I could be in my hotel trying to make a baby. But I am here with you. If anyone really has the spite to throw something at someone who is working, then do it here, close to me, no problem. That's all I ask.)[28]

In this incident Rivera seems most offended by the disrespect of her performance, which she specifically refers to as "work." What is especially significant to convey to her audience is the exchange of respect, I argue here, as a mode of power not acquired through monetary or material capital but through loyalty to self-preservation. The respect Rivera demands in this scenario is a working-class cultural sensibility contextualized in the social world of immigrant *mexicano* Long Beach. Rivera's decision to personally confront the woman—rather than have her security simply remove her from the audience—is another way of displaying that she is capable of taking care of herself.

While most celebrities would steer clear of spectacles that might be cast as inappropriate femininity, Rivera turned away from silence and toward transparency. When she was a young married woman, Rivera often recalled in interviews, her first husband physically abused her, especially when she desired more than to be at home cooking and cleaning.[29] As a domestic abuse survivor, Rivera learned the first principle of fighting back—to speak out, because shame and silence endangered her survival. Rivera publicly displayed her shortcomings, failures, and flaws, I contend, because it meant undoing the violence of silence. Social networks of Rivera's fans too utilized virtual communities as ways to "act out" as brown bodies resistant to complacency and deference and as an alternative to the "Dreamer" citizen or *domesticana* acknowledged only as perpetual deferential labor.

Rivera was passionate about using her musical medium to speak out against domestic violence. Since she had experienced domestic abuse as a young wife, Rivera's words and actions meant a great deal to those who had experienced or were experiencing the same challenges to survive. The Los Angeles music journalist Fernando González stated that

> the secret to her fame was not that she had such an outstanding, gifted voice, because she didn't, it was that she poured her life story into her songs, with all her faults, downfalls and tragedies, including a teen pregnancy and domestic abuse. The fans made her a star because they saw themselves reflected in her.[30]

Many of the virtual communities established through Rivera's fandom were more than mere social sites, but social imaginaries bound by codes of promise and respect for the themes raised and performed by Rivera.[31] J-Unit's site stated as part of its group membership agreement, "Compromiso ser un J-unit," "Ser parte del J-Unit de Jenni Rivera. Es un compromiso y una responsabilidad. Es apoyarla y llevar con respeto su legado. J-Unit no es una moda. Es un Estilo de vida. Una entrega incondicional." (To be part of Jenni Rivera's J-Unit. It is a commitment and a responsibility. It is to support her and carry on her legacy with respect. J-Unit is not a style. It is a way of life. An unconditional surrender.) In 2010, she was named a celebrity spokesperson for the National Coalition Against Domestic Violence (NCADV) in Los Angeles. To further commemorate her dedication to battered women, the Los Angeles City Council officially named August 6 "Jenni Rivera Day."[32] Rivera also founded a charitable organization— the Jenni Rivera Love Foundation—that offered supportive services to single mothers and victims of both domestic and sexual abuse, especially undocumented immigrant women. Moreover, Rivera's advocacy for gender issues also included LGBT equality. In addition, Rivera was extremely passionate about undocumented immigrant civil rights. She was one of the first and the few major Latino celebrities to use the term "racist" in referring to Arizona's Senate Bill 1070.[33] In fact, a press release announcing her participation in the May 29, 2010, Arizona state capital rally admonished other Latino celebrities for not showing up: "While other artists have contributed their names, Jenni has offered to present herself." A few days prior to the rally she would tweet @jennirivera, "el sábado estaré marchando en Arizona en contra de la ley SB1070. La marcha será de seis millas a 10:30am." (On Saturday I'll be marching in Arizona to protest SB 1070. The march will be six miles, at 10:30 a.m.)

As Michelle González Maldonado put it, "Jenni Rivera did not just use her fame as a form of self-promotion, but as a platform for populations who are voiceless in the dominant discourse."[34] Rivera testified to social injustice, immigrant xenophobia, and gender violence while often performing the very violent realities her fans survived daily. For example, Rivera drew on narcocorrido terms to describe her fans' social networks: "es mi propia cartel" (it's my own cartel), she said of her fan base, describing its function as making "un gran desmadre positivo" (a great deal of positive disorderliness).

Jenni Rivera once tweeted out to her fans on J-Unit, "Dear J-Unit: When I die remember to please make sure I am buried upside down . . . so the haters can continue to kiss my ass, Jenni." Rivera never seemed interested in *playing* nice with other celebrities or members of the public who sometimes launched judgmental attacks on her public dramas, failures at multiple marriages, and songs about badly behaving women. Rivera seemed born to fight, and her tough street smarts or *malandrina* sensibility prompted her strategies for *playing* music. In a *Dallas Morning News* interview, Rivera once stated that when she was a child growing up in her immigrant community in Long Beach, "I wasn't allowed to have dolls." Raised among four brothers, she continued,

> my mom bought them for me, but they [her brothers] would tear them apart and get rid of them. They wanted to teach me karate and doing pop-wheelies in the street and playing baseball and playing marbles and being a great wrestler. It kind of made me tough. I got in trouble if I got into a fight and I came back crying.[35]

Rivera's fan Diana Reyes once described her in a Twitter post as "La Diva, La malandrina, La Gran Señora, La Socia, La Chacalosa, La Reina . . . Simplemente La Mejor" (The diva, the *malandrina*, the grand lady, the buddy, the *chacalosa*, the queen . . . simply the best).[36] The list is not merely an accounting of Rivera's nicknames. It also calls out the *mexicana* subjectivities *played* every day in attempts to voice dissent against the corrective systems of normative fictions of citizenship. Monikers of disobedient gender such as *la malandrina* and *la chacalosa*, among others cultivated by Rivera, created representations that—while controversial—formed musical spectacles that shamelessly shattered the violent myth that for undocumented and class-disenfranchised *mexicanas*, complaisant silence, hard work, and playing by the rules result in safety, well-being, and freedom from exploitation. Rivera was well aware of her power and status, and by extension the ways she *played* her power in the music industry, as a means to persist and to be a witness for those struggling to exist. As such, Jenni Rivera and the virtual communities of her fans offer us the chance to consider the possibilities that new musical meanings and cultural media consumption can sometimes cultivate for Latin@ publics.

NOTES

1. "Remembering Jenni," *Latina*, March 2013, 103.
2. See Stuart Hall, "Encoding/Decoding," in *Media and Cultural Studies: Keyworks*, ed. Meenakshi Gigi Durham and Douglas M. Kellner (Malden: Blackwell, 2001).
3. Angie Chabram-Dernersesian, "Introduction to Part 1," in *The Chicana/o Cultural Studies Reader*, ed. Angie Chabram-Dernersesian (New York: Routledge, 2006), 5. Chabram-Dernersesian draws from Tony Bennett, "Putting Policy into Cultural Studies," in *Cultural Studies*, ed. Lawrence Grossberg, Cary Nelson, and Paula Treichler (New York: Routledge, 1991), 33.
4. The word *mexicanas* is lowercase and italicized throughout; I use this style to disrupt the distinction between one of Mexican citizenship and those Mexican-descent US citizens residing in the United States.
5. When I italicize the words "playing" and "played" in this essay, I aim to signify the unique mode of engaging/producing/consuming music that pertains to Rivera and, at times, her fans.
6. See Michel de Certeau, *The Practice of Everyday Life* (Berkeley: University of California Press, 1984) and his meaning of "tactic."
7. Fernando González, "Jenni Rivera's Fame Built on Gut-Level Connection with Her Fans," *Miami Herald*, December 11, 2012, http://www.miamiherald.com/2012/12/10/3136089/jenni-riveras-fame-built-on-gut.html#storylink=cpy.
8. Chabram-Dernersesian, "Introduction to Part 1," 1–22.
9. "Remembering Jenni," 103. The vernacular term *malandrinas* is a play on the term *malandro*, meaning criminal or good-for-nothing.
10. Sam Quinones, "Jenni Rivera's Musical Family Helped Popularize Mexican Narco-Ballads," *Los Angeles Times*, December 10, 2012.
11. Cindy Y. Rodriguez, "Jenni Rivera Is Mourned, but Still Inspires," *CNN Entertainment*, December 11, 2012.
12. Mandy Fridmann, "Jenni Rivera: Mexican-American Singer's Tragic End Echoes Life of Hardship on Journey to Stardom," *Huffington Post*, December 10, 2012. Jenni Rivera and Trino Marín had three children: Janney, known as "Chiquis," Jacquelin, and Trino Angelo. Marín would eventually be charged with raping his daughters Janney and Jacquelin and Jenni Rivera's sister Rosie.
13. "Jenni Rivera Death: Long Beach Candlelight Vigil Planned as Hometown Mourns," *Long Beach Press-Telegram*, December 12, 2012, http://www.presstelegram.com/news/ci_22162201/jenni-rivera-death-long-beach-candlelight-vigil-planned.
14. Alejo Sierra, "Jenni Rivera: La Divina," *Open Your Eyes: Latino Magazine*, n.d.
15. "Remembering Jenni," 104.
16. Ibid.
17. "Jenni Rivera's Death."
18. Ibid.
19. Ibid.

20. José Esteban Muñoz, *Disidentifications: Queers of Color and the Performance of Politics* (Minneapolis: University of Minnesota Press, 1999), 182.

21. See https://thatwhoeverbelieves.wordpress.com/2012/12/11/ an-open-letter-to-jenni-rivera-fans/.

22. Arlene Dávila, *Latinos, Inc.: The Marketing and Making of a People* (New York: New York University Press, 2001), 90–91, 123.

23. Catherine Ramírez, *The Woman in the Zoot Suit: Nation and the Cultural Politics of Memory* (Durham: Duke University Press, 2009), xx.

24. Mark C. Edberg, "Narcocorridos: Narratives of a Cultural Persona and Power on the Border," in *Transnational Encounters: Music and Performance at the U.S.-Mexico Border*, ed. Alejandro L. Madrid (New York: Oxford University Press, 2011), 67.

25. For a significant analysis of the representation of the maid in mass culture, see Isabel Molina-Guzmán, "Maid in Hollywood: Producing Latina Labor in an Anti-Immigration Imaginary," in *Dangerous Curves: Latina Bodies in the Media* (New York: New York University Press, 2010), 151–74.

26. "Jenni Rivera: Teen Mom, Abused Wife, and Lonely Star on the Rise," *Fox News Latino*, December 10, 2012.

27. *Que Me Entierren con la Banda* (Fonovisa, 1999).

28. See http://www.youtube.com/watch?v=aoU6-6olSis. Rivera performs what Marie Keta Miranda refers to as a "code of respect" contextualized in a working-class claim to territory, the public sphere, and nonnormative gender. See Marie Keta Miranda, *Homegirls in the Public Sphere* (Austin: University of Texas Press, 2003).

29. Rodriguez, "Jenni Rivera Is Mourned, but Still Inspires."

30. González, "Jenni Rivera's Fame Built on Gut-Level Connection."

31. See Alicia Schmidt Camacho, *Migrant Imaginaries: Latino Cultural Politics in the US-Mexico Borderlands* (New York: New York University Press, 2008).

32. Nina Terrero, "Jenni Rivera: Advocate and Champion of Women," NBC Latino, December 12, 2012, http://nbclatino.com/2012/12/10/ jenni-rivera-advocate-and-champion-of-women/.

33. "Highest Grossing Female Mexican Regional Tour Artist, Jenni Rivera, Lends Voice to Defend the People of Arizona," press release, May 10, 2010. The press release included the following statement:
   (Phoenix, AZ) La Gran Señora, Jenni Rivera, joins the movement against SB 1070 with a live concert at the end of Saturday's march from Indian Steele Park to the State Capitol. The legendary winner of "Best Artist of the Year" in 2009 from Premios de la Radio and leader of the Regional Mexican genre, Jenni Rivera, answers the call of the people of Arizona for a leader and a voice to represent their struggles. Jenni Rivera chose to participate in the march because she shares the outrage of the tens of thousands of people who will march prior to the concert and who have been targeted by this

hateful law that views any Mexican American or anyone with brown skin as "reasonably suspicious."

34. Michelle González Maldonado, "Mourning Jenni Rivera: When a Lady Dies," *Religion Dispatches*, December 13, 2012. By the time of her passing, Jenni Rivera was a massive media icon, having appeared on the reality TV show *Chiquis & Raq-C*, featuring her oldest daughter, Janney "Chiquis" Marín; having produced and starred in *I Love Jenni*, a Spanish-language reality TV show on Telemundo's Mun2 network; and having served as a coach and judge on *La Voz* or *The Voice, Mexico.*

35. Ibid.

36. See https://twitter.com/jenniriverafans.

15

Marketing, Performing, and Interpreting Multiple Latinidades

Los Tigres del Norte and Calle 13's "América"

MARÍA ELENA CEPEDA

For well over a decade, mainstream US media outlets have persistently linked discussions of Latina/o demographic growth to commentaries regarding increased Latina/o buying power. Adhering to the capitalist logic that "Latinas/os can spend, therefore Latinas/os exist," the Latin(o) popular music industry has thus endeavored to cater to as well as shape Latina/o consumer behavior.[1] One such effort, the May 2011 *MTV Unplugged* concert DVD by the US-Mexican band Los Tigres del Norte, exemplifies industry attempts to expressly define Latinidad for mass consumption in the domestic, transnational, and international spheres. During the concert DVD performance of their hit single "América," Los Tigres del Norte, long known for their political commentary on pan-American identity and immigration, blend *norteño* and rap with the assistance of René Pérez Joglar of Calle 13, an eclectic Puerto Rican musical group and vocal supporters of Puerto Rican independence and other progressive causes.

This essay opens with a consideration of Los Tigres del Norte's place within the broader Latin(o) music sphere as well as the circumstances surrounding the marketing and production of their *MTV Unplugged* album and DVD. The second portion is dedicated to a textual analysis of Los Tigres' music video performance of the song "América" accompanied by Pérez Joglar. Drawing on semi-structured interviews conducted with a small sample of Springfield, Massachusetts, Latina/o youth ages eighteen to twenty-three during May and June 2012, the final section centers on audience responses to the music video. Specifically, this study asks, What particular discursive, visual, and musical strategies are utilized by the music video's producers and performers in order to craft a brand of Latinidad palatable to a broad array of consumers across borders? How do Latina/o youth interpret these signifiers, particularly with respect to notions of *familia* (family) and gender? How do individuals living in primarily Puerto Rican urban centers negotiate multiple (and specifically Mexican-centered) media Latinidades? Ultimately, this essay argues that a complex, contradictory dynamics of production, circulation, and consumption undergirds the usage of Latinidad as a transnational marketing strategy and site of identity performance, specifically with respect to dominant representations of Mexicans and Puerto Ricans. Furthermore, it underscores the manner in which Latinidad functions as an expansive ethno-racial and supranational concept in theory, yet frequently proves more narrowly construed in its media actualizations.

Los Tigres del Norte and the Transnational Latina/o
Market: We Spend, Therefore We Exist

The seminal *norteño* band Los Tigres del Norte, made up of the four Hernández brothers (Jorge, Hernán, Eduardo, and Luis) and their cousin Oscar Lara, was originally formed in Sinaloa, Mexico, in 1968. By the early 1970s, the band members had migrated north as unauthorized immigrants to San José, California, by way of Mexicali. In 1972, the band charted its first major hit, "Contrabando y traición" (Contraband and betrayal), and has since enjoyed a place among *norteño*'s most popular and influential intergenerational acts. While the band's work has been described as unequivocally pan–Latin American in nature and expressly directed at undocumented, immigrant Mexicans,[2] the aesthetic and thematic features of Los Tigres' music suggest a slightly different reading: they are above all a distinctly US-Mexican borderlands outfit whose fan base is both transnational *and* domestic in scope. With overtly politicized music and lyrics that speak to questions of ethno-racial identity, immigration, class, and national borders, Los Tigres' compositions and performances "don't glorify the band, they glorify the audience."[3]

With generations of fans on both sides of the US-Mexican border and throughout the Spanish-speaking world, by the spring of 2011 Los Tigres had sold 4.1 million albums in the United States alone, according to Nielsen SoundScan, and roughly 34 million albums worldwide. However, the US sales figures almost certainly represent a significant underestimation, as the cost of being added to the SoundScan database has proven prohibitively expensive for the family-run businesses that frequently sell Mexican regional titles. Moreover, Los Tigres del Norte derived a mere 2 percent of the total sales of their most recent album from digital downloads, a format that provides the major record labels with further input regarding sales figures.[4] This persistent undercounting has inevitably shaped the ways Los Tigres del Norte in particular and Mexican regional music in general are marketed within both Spanish-language and Latina/o-centered media. It is currently estimated that sales of Mexican regional music—a wide-ranging category that includes genres as diverse as *norteño*, *vallenato*, *cumbia*, *mariachi*, and *ranchera*—account for approximately 60 percent of all Latin(o) music sales in the United States. While even sales of Mexican regional music have lessened during the recent industry crisis, this decline pales in comparison to that of other Latin(o) music genres.[5] Relative sales stability aside, however, Mexican regional acts have long had to contend with a mainstream Latin(o) music industry that has downplayed if not openly ignored their predominance for a variety of factors, among them flawed assumptions regarding a lack of purchasing power among US-Mexican consumers. The historical association of Mexican regional music with working-class performers and consumers has not left those at the helm of institutions such as the Latin Grammys eager to claim these populations, either. As Arlene Dávila has demonstrated, the overrepresentation of elite Latin American interests in Spanish-language and Latina/o-centered marketing firms partially accounts for these sharp ethno-racial and class biases.[6] In the particular case of Mexican regional music, the current size and projected future expansion of the US-Mexican population, its hybrid character, and a profoundly entrenched sense of a historical legacy of conflict on both sides of the border have also rendered the promotion of all things Mexican (and certainly anything working-class, non-bilingual, and ostensibly brown) largely unworthy of the current, Miami-based music industry's attentions.

As Deborah Paredez has observed in the case of the slain Tejana performer Selena, industry attitudes toward *norteño* ultimately reflect recognition of the Latina/o population's increasing economic, cultural, and political clout, heavily tempered by mainstream apprehensions.[7] These industry prejudices simultaneously played a singular role in the privileging of white or light-skinned bilingual *caribeño* acts as the literal face of the so-called Latin music boom of the late 1990s and early twenty-first century.[8] Given the vexed position of *norteño* music within the media and marketing structures of the current Latin(o) music industry, Los Tigres del Norte's February 2011 *MTV Unplugged* concert album and accompanying DVD (simply titled *Tr3s Presents: MTV Unplugged, Los Tigres del Norte and Friends*) offer evidence of a potential shift in marketing tactics, if not underlying attitudes. Taped at the Hollywood Palladium in Los Angeles, Los Tigres' concert was the inaugural *Unplugged* concert produced by US-based Tr3s, a bicultural, Latina/o-centered channel launched in September 2006 as part of the MTV conglomerate. It also represented the very first time that any Mexican regional act had been featured as part of the *Unplugged* series, a popular MTV flagship program that began airing during the 1989–90 television season.[9] The concert DVD featured Los Tigres playing many of their most beloved songs accompanied by carefully selected Latina/o and Latin American performers such as Paulina Rubio, Zack de la Rocha, Juanes, and René Pérez Joglar of Calle 13, among others. Conceived in an effort to draw a broad range of younger, transnational consumers beyond what is widely assumed to be an older Mexican and US-Mexican fan base, the concert and album were also aired and released in Spain, an untraditional market for Mexican regional music.

As Eddie Gutiérrez, Tr3s's current marketing coordinator, explained, efforts to market the album in Europe were the responsibility of Fonovisa Inc., a Spanish-language record label that primarily focuses on Mexican music under the auspices of the California-based Universal Music Latin Entertainment. Latin American promotional efforts were managed by MTV Latinoamérica. Given that it solely markets within the United States, Tr3s was therefore not involved in the international marketing of Los Tigres' album and DVD. Nevertheless, MTV's primary (and very public) stated goal was to appeal to the US-based Latina/o market.[10]

Ultimately, *Los Tigres del Norte and Friends* became Los Tigres del Norte's twenty-third number one album on the *Billboard* regional Mexican albums chart. It also debuted and peaked at number three on *Billboard*'s list of top Latin albums, and rose to number one on the Mexican albums chart, where it became the best-selling album of 2011. At the twelfth annual Latin Grammys, the album was named best *norteño* album of 2011, and also earned the honor of best *banda* or *norteño* album at the mainstream (English-language) Grammys. Despite the overwhelming triumph of *Los Tigres del Norte and Friends*, Los Tigres del Norte in many ways still embody the paradoxical location of Mexican regional musics vis-à-vis other Latin(o) genres, in which robust sales do not necessarily translate into comparable mainstream Latina/o media visibility or prominent corporate sponsorships. Relative to their sales success, Los Tigres are thus rendered quasi-invisible, due in part to the marginalization of Mexican regional genres. In this context, the Mexican-centered brand of Latinidad privileged in the group's video for "América," and audience reactions to it, enhance our comprehension of the contradictory dynamics underlying the usage and performance of multiple Latinidades as an element of transnational marketing strategy.

Los Tigres del Norte and Calle 13's "América": Performing Multiple Latinidades

As a traditional performance clip, "América" attempts to re-create the ambiance of Los Tigres del Norte's renowned live concerts (which are famously long and performed without a set list), albeit in much more slickly produced fashion. The video's camera work, which features straightforward close-ups and circular panning shots, highlights the band's musical skills and the connection that they enjoy with their audience, which is presented as overwhelmingly Latina/o, under forty, and stylishly attired in nightclub wear. The band's surprise guest for the song, René Pérez Joglar of Calle 13, is best known to fans as "Residente"

(Resident). As Calle 13's lead singer and songwriter, Residente appears without the group's other two performers, his stepbrother Eduardo José Cabra Martínez ("Visitante"/Visitor), vocalist, instrumentalist, and beat producer, and his sister Ileana Cabra Joglar ("PG-13"), backup vocalist. Natives of the San Juan, Puerto Rico, suburbs, Calle 13 rose to prominence in 2005 with the Internet release of its hit "Querido FBI" (Dear FBI), and has since won a record-breaking nineteen Latin Grammys. While the band's members are frequently classified as reggaetón performers (a label that they reject as too confining), Calle 13's music actually incorporates multiple genres, ranging from jazz to *cumbia* to hip-hop.[11] Like Los Tigres del Norte, Calle 13 is known for the political content of its songs: band members are fervent supporters of the Puerto Rican independence movement, and their music, as exemplified by the group's 2011 Latin Grammy–winning hit "Latinoamérica," clearly identifies Puerto Rico as a distinctly Latin American space, thereby contesting its long-standing colonial ties to the United States.

"América" opens with an affirmative declaration of Latin(o) Americans' claims to "American" identity. Through the forthright language of possession ("De América, yo soy"), the category of "American" is effectively expanded to encompass not just Anglo-Americans, but *americanas/os* as well:

> Haber nacido en América, es como una bendición
> Llena de bellas imágenes que alegran el corazón
> Mosaico de mil colores, bellas mujeres y flores
> Para los pueblos de América, les canto mi canción
> De América, yo soy, de América, yo soy.[12]

The brief chorus ("De América, yo soy, de América, yo soy" [I am from America, I am from America]) is quickly punctuated by the sudden appearance of Calle 13's Residente, who immediately begins to rap an abridged version of "Latinoamérica":

> Tengo los lagos, tengo los ríos
> Tengo mis dientes pa' cuando me sonrío
> La nieve que maquilla mis montañas
> Tengo el sol que me seca y la lluvia que me baña . . .

Trabajo en bruto pero con orgullo
Aquí se comparte, lo mío es tuyo
Este pueblo no se ahoga con marullos
Y si se derrumba yo lo reconstruyo.[13]

Los Tigres' lead singer, Jorge Hernández, then interjects with a brief spoken stanza, declaring,

Norteamérica es todo el continente
Quien nace aquí es americano
El color podrá ser diferente
Mas como hijos de Dios
Somos hermanos.[14]

Following a chorus listing the various Latin American and Caribbean nations, Residente again begins to rap, this time in a more assertive tone that simultaneously references the region's colonial past and its present status:

Todo lo comparto con mis hermanos
Soy la pesadilla del sueño americano
Soy América
Soy lo que dejaron
Todas las sobras
De lo que se robaron.[15]

The inter-Latina/o performance of "América" by Residente and Los Tigres del Norte thus offers a sweeping lesson in Latin American geography, social history, and political critique, creating what Patricia Zavella terms "repertoires of memory," or "social practices that present alternative histories" that ultimately foment the construction of counterpublics.[16] Underscoring a masculinist ("Somos hermanos" [We are brothers]), racialized ("El color podrá ser diferente" [The color may be different]), and Spanish-language–centered vision of the collective ethos that separates North from South, "América" foregrounds the contested character of what is commonly understood as "American" identity. Notably, in Los Tigres del Norte and Residente's intent to (re)insert

Latin America into the United States' political and historical topography (or, to paraphrase Michelle Habell-Pallán, to remind us that "[Latin(o) American] history is American history, and vice versa"),[17] the performers fail to account for those other hybrid individuals whose claims to Americanness (be it to Latin America *and/or* the United States) are so often questioned: namely, US-based Latinas/os. Despite their stated desire for a more expansive notion of "American" identity, and marketers' intentions to reach a broader Latina/o audience, Los Tigres and Residente privilege the Latin American and promote Latin American "authenticity" in a fashion that ultimately erases the over 53 million Latinas/os living in the United States. This result is particularly ironic for two reasons: one, the fact that the very musical genres that Los Tigres and Residente perform (*norteño* and rap) are themselves epic products of cultural and ethno-racial *mestizaje* across borders; and two, *norteño's* own marginal location not only outside the parameters of industry-accepted "Latin" music, but beyond the boundaries of mainstream US popular music as a whole. Nevertheless, in one phrase that contests Latin America's long-standing commodification by the North, Residente does invoke the ongoing (im)migratory pulse that consistently challenges dominant notions of what it means to be "American": "Soy la pesadilla del sueño americano" (I am the nightmare of the American Dream).[18] This is the sole aperture at which he explicitly frames the Latina/o, the Latin American, and the "American" in hemispheric terms, as he spins a stock phrase from the grand narrative of U.S immigration.

Throughout "América," *norteño's* symbols and the sense of *mexicanidad* (however monological) to which they are intimately connected foreground the US-Mexican and Mexican experiences, underscoring their uniqueness in comparison to those of other Latina/o populations. In this context, the musical and visual cues employed to reference both non-Mexican (in this case, Puerto Rican) and Mexican identity prove of particular interest, due in part to the fact that the live performance itself takes place in Los Angeles, the world's largest Mexican metropolis outside Mexico City. During the performance, Puerto Rican identity is visually signified by the T-shirt and baseball cap worn by Residente during part of the performance. Caribbean Spanish and rap similarly function as sonic markers of Puerto Rico, and perhaps more importantly, as strategically selected elements in the effort to broaden Los Tigres' market base.

Figure 15.1. Residente of Calle 13 performs Mexican identity by dressing in the familiar *tejana* (ten-gallon cowboy hat) and a red, white, and green Mexican soccer warm-up suit. From MTV's *Unplugged*. © 2011 Viacom International Inc. All rights reserved.

In comparison to the easy, practiced motions of his onstage companions, Residente's physical presence serves as a restless counterpoint to Los Tigres del Norte, echoing the ways movement both reflects and produces ethno-racial, class, and national identities.[19] On his Puerto Rican body, Mexicanness is symbolized by a black ten-gallon cowboy hat, and a soccer warm-up jacket fashioned from the colors of the Mexican flag (figure 15.1). Nevertheless, while *mexicanidad* is privileged in this particular instance, at the same time the brand of Puerto Rican identity performed by Calle 13 is not entirely subsumed, either. Notably, the juncture at which he (re)asserts his Puerto Rican identity—the moment when Residente removes his Mexican jacket to reveal a T-shirt with the words "Puerto Rico" emblazoned across it—coincides with the precise moment at which the Los Angeles audience is chanting "¡México! ¡México!" (figure 15.2). In response, Jorge Hernández of Los Tigres del Norte alters the chant to "¡Puerto Rico! ¡Puerto Rico!"[20] Such gestures underscore the frequently conflicting character of pan-Latina/o identity. As Cristina Beltrán asserts, they also remind us that Latinidad and Latina/o political mobilization in general are mindfully constructed, as opposed to preexisting, entities.[21]

The divergent symbols of media Latinidad offered here ultimately reinscribe the simplistic, yet meaningfully tangible, vehicles through which everyday Latina/o identity is frequently understood by Latinas/os and non-Latinas/os alike, as well as dominant renderings of Latinidad. However, Latinidad, while most frequently gendered as female within transnational media circuits, is not necessarily limited to such constructions.[22] Perhaps most significantly, within the national mainstream media it is largely if not at times solely through these and other visual and sonic vectors of Mexicanness that non-*mexicano* Latina/o identities are rendered quasi-coherent—or at worst, a burgeoning threat in need of containment—to many non-Latinas/os. Thus, at this political moment, being Latina/o frequently means being Mexican, a point that speaks to the particular location of Latin(o) Americans within the US national imaginary.

In a larger sense, Los Tigres del Norte and their musical project also offer a commentary on the multifaceted, at times conflicting, ways the specific (Mexican national and transnational identities) and the general (Latinidad writ large) interact within Latina/o-centered and Spanish-language media structures in a manner that underscores the ongoing saliency of *both* frameworks of identification, regardless of their underlying problematics. Both within and beyond major Latina/o urban centers, local ethno-racial identities continue to enjoy great political, economic, and symbolic significance, just as the nation-state has not lost its everyday primacy. The latter perhaps rings most true for those individuals who must cross geopolitical borders on a regular basis, above all the undocumented. This performance of "América" therefore does not mark a strictly "borderless" or post-national moment, as some analyses of Los Tigres' music would suggest.[23]

Media Producers and Cultural Readers: Latina/o Youth in Springfield, Massachusetts

With a population of just over 153,000, the city of Springfield is located in western Massachusetts's Pioneer Valley. It is the third-largest city in the commonwealth of Massachusetts, following Boston and Worcester. According to the 2010 census, 38.8 percent of Springfield residents self-identified as "Hispanic or Latino," with the overwhelming majority

Figure 15.2. Residente visually emphasizes his Puerto Rican roots near the close of "América." From MTV's *Unplugged.* © 2011 Viacom International Inc. All rights reserved.

claiming Puerto Rican ancestry (33.2 percent), followed by "Other Hispanic or Latino" descent (4.4 percent), Mexican ancestry (1 percent), and Cuban descent (0.3 percent).[24] Significantly, the majority of the city's Latina/o residents have arrived in the area within the last two decades. Just south of smaller cities of relatively high Latina/o (largely Puerto Rican) population density such as Holyoke, Springfield exists in close proximity to what is at times locally referred to as the "tofu curtain," or the socioeconomic, educational, and ethno-racial divide that separates the city from other wealthier (and whiter) communities just to the north, particularly Northampton and Amherst.

With the exception of two informants, all of the Springfield youth interviewed were of Puerto Rican ancestry. Barring one recent graduate, all had taken college-level courses or were about to begin pursuing a college degree. The two interviewees who did not strictly self-identify as Puerto Rican labeled themselves "Puerto Rican and Black" and "Hispanic" (further discussion revealed that the latter informant was specifically of Afro-Panamanian descent). In this regard, the small sample of individuals interviewed loosely reflected Springfield's present Latina/o demographics. Informants were recruited through their ties to the Latino Youth Media Institute, a project funded through WGBY, the public television station for western New England. Youth interviews were conducted at the Latino Youth Media Institute's space in the WGBY building, and additional information about the informants was later solicited via e-mail and during other less formal contexts such as meals. Each interview lasted approximately forty-five minutes to an hour, and included a brief handout aimed at gathering basic demographic data, a portion dedicated to viewing the five-minute video performance clip of "América," and a follow-up set of semi-structured questions.

Designed to increase the Latina/o community's engagement with WGBY, the Latino Youth Media Institute supports internships for local Latina/o youth interested in gaining communications-related training. Indeed, the Latino Youth Media Institute's emphasis on community engagement and building interns' production skills clearly colored individual responses both during and outside the interviews. All of the youth with whom I spoke approached their responses from the perspective of popular music consumers (which is undeniably a form of production in and of itself), but mostly notably from the stance of individuals literate in various types of media production, ranging from television camera operation to audio/video editing to deejay-ing and vocal performance, among others. In this vein, part-time DJ Héctor, nineteen, repeatedly cited the critical nature of the relationship between performers and audience in his comments. Similarly, Alejandro, twenty-one, who has experience as an audio engineer, noted the unique features defining *norteño* instrumentation and vocal delivery.

As Tr3s's domestic marketing strategy for *Los Tigres del Norte and Friends* had anticipated, few of the college-age informants were acquainted with *norteño* music or Los Tigres in particular. (They did, however, note the ways MTV treated Latinas/os as a highly segregated niche market; as Alejandro remarked, "They [Latina/o artists] don't get the props that they deserve. . . . everything is pretty separate"). In contrast, Residente represented a familiar face and sound to most. Furthermore, all displayed a keen awareness of the power of popular music as a purveyor of sociocultural norms and values, even when divorced from the music video's strong visuals. Markedly gendered, unity-centered notions of Latinidad, the song's primary message about what it means to be "American," and the discrepancies between Puerto Rican and

Mexican identities ultimately emerged as key overriding themes during the interviews.

Much like "América's" emphasis on brotherhood as the gendered tie that binds Latin(o) Americans, the language of *familia* (family) dominated informants' discussions of Latinidad. As Héctor interpreted the song's central message, "it's kind of, be proud of where you're from. No matter where you're from, no matter if you come from South America or you come from Mexico or Puerto Rico it's like . . . we're still a big family together." Moreover, for Héctor, "América" exemplified the performative, dynamic dimensions of Latinidad, as he noted the intricate "back and forth, back and forth" that characterized the onstage interactions between Los Tigres and Residente. Expressing a gendered understanding of Latinidad as a unity based in "brotherhood," Shayla, eighteen, highlighted the ways in which for her, the performance transcended everyday inter-Latina/o conflicts and hierarchies: "And when Calle 13 came on stage it wasn't like, 'Oh, he's performing now, just backup,' they were all performing as one and it wasn't about him, and it wasn't about Los Tigres del Norte—it was about all of them, and it was like one unity. . . . they're like brothers, brothers in America." Significantly, most of the informants articulated an identical understanding of Latinidad as distinctly rooted in a sense of brotherhood, regardless of their own gendered subject locations.[25] However, this interpretation proves quite plausible if one takes into account the frequent absence of women from Latin(o) musical performances such as "América," particularly as instrumentalists.

Aside from the interpretation of Latinidad as a gendered, unifying force, virtually all of the Springfield Latina/o youth interviewed commented on "América's" central message with respect to the hemispheric nature of American identity. Zydalis, twenty-two, reflected upon a more expansive, and at times inherently conflictive, notion of Americanness:

ZYDALIS: I feel like a lot of the time we feel almost ashamed to be Latinos and, and I think that hurts us, it hurts us a lot. . . . I think that they make us feel that we have to be so American—and what is "American"?

MARÍA ELENA: That was my next question.

ZYDALIS: Yeah. (*Laughs.*)

MARÍA ELENA: (*Laughs.*) What does "American" mean to you?

ZYDALIS: It's different because you can't—"American" is not just speaking English . . .

MARÍA ELENA: . . . and being white.

ZYDALIS: . . . and being white. . . . I think the media kind of makes being American seem like you have to be white, and you have to speak English and that's not what it's all about.

John, twenty-three, confessed to not having devoted much previous thought to the issue of national or hemispheric labels. After watching the video clip, however, he remarked,

> I think when people say "American" they mean "United States of America" American. They're not thinking that you're [Latinas/os are] on the North American continent, the South American continent—they are American. So, it's more of like, what are you really trying to say by saying that we [Latinas/os] are Americans?

In short, for informants, "América" provoked a stark and at times transgressive recognition of the ways Latinas/os and Latin Americans are encompassed (or not) within the signifier "American," regardless of one's primary cultural, linguistic, and/or geographic affiliations. As geo-cultural designators, "America" and "American" therefore proved rife with domestic interethnic tensions and hierarchies, in addition to reflecting greater hemispheric geopolitical struggles.

With few exceptions, the distinctions that informants largely bypassed within their conceptualizations of Latinidad yet foregrounded in their discussions of American identity repeatedly emerged in our conversations regarding the key differences between Mexicans and Puerto Ricans. The Puerto Rican youths interviewed largely framed Mexicans in terms of their location within the US labor market. As John, a Puerto Rican who was raised by a Mexican stepfather, noted, "what I've picked up is like they're very hardworking people, that they're [Mexicans] just like, listen—all we're trying to do is make money here in America to possibly send it back home." Shayla, who has a Mexican grandmother, voiced a similar sentiment: "I see my grandmother works

with a lot of Mexicans and she helps them find jobs, and they're willing to do everything and anything." Mexicans' citizenship status vis-à-
vis that of Puerto Ricans marked another key site of their difference.
This disparity was communicated in two ways: first, under the implicit
assumption that all Mexicans were in fact unauthorized immigrants;
and second, via an explicit comparison to the citizenship rights pos-
sessed by Puerto Ricans. As Zydalis observed,

> I think maybe with the Mexicans . . . they get . . . looked down upon
> because they're not like US citizens. A lot of people think that if you're
> Mexican and live in America you kind of like came illegally, and that's
> not always the case. And then like for Puerto Ricans we're already citi-
> zens, you know what I'm saying, even if we're born in Puerto Rico.

Notably, these specific frameworks of inter-Latina/o recognition echoed
the politics of citizenship enacted among Puerto Ricans and Mexicans
in spaces such as pan-Latina/o Chicago, despite the considerable population imbalance between the two communities.[26] Moreover, they also
signaled the power of media representations to mold individual and
communal out-group perceptions, despite consumer agency. At the
same time, most respondents also expressed a painful awareness of the
negative stereotypes attached to Puerto Ricans (both in the media and
in their daily lives),[27] in addition to the tendency for the historical and
cultural specificities of Puerto Rican identity to be collapsed into Mexicanness, even within spaces such as Springfield, where Puerto Ricans
numerically predominate. (As Shayla succinctly stated, "I think there's
this big assumption that all, like, Spanish people are Mexican.")[28]

The preceding audience research, textual analysis, and discussion of
the production/marking contexts regarding "América" by Los Tigres del
Norte and Residente of Calle 13 highlight the often carefully choreo-
graphed character of inter-Latina/o media representations. Simultaneously, this essay illustrates the ways Latina/o consumers at times disrupt
such sanitized renderings of Latinidad, particularly in their willingness
to challenge restrictive conceptualizations of "American" identity.[29] Via
a focus on the markedly understudied Latina/o population of Springfield, Massachusetts, we are also witness to the highly gendered, *familia*-
centric frameworks frequently attached to in-group understandings of

Latinidad, as well as Latina/o consumers' stark awareness of the manner in which multiple Latinidades can operate in both concert and conflict. In the case of Los Tigres del Norte and Calle 13's "América," Latinidad clearly functions as a potent transnational marketing tool as well as a category that gains much of its fluidity from its performative dimensions. While we cannot deny the fundamental impacts of regional location, citizenship status, and other elements of individual subjectivity in the quotidian context, the above research further suggests that in some respects *all* Latinas/os are rendered Mexican in a political climate in which prescriptive notions of media Latinidad remain uncontested, proposals such as Arizona's SB 1070 can emerge, and comprehensive immigration reform has yet to materialize. This environment perhaps provides an even more urgent rationale, as Frances Aparicio has suggested, for reframing Latinidad—and particularly its representations in media and popular culture—as a mechanism that does not overtly ignore, yet at times selectively and mindfully looks beyond, its own flattening potential in the service of political mobilization and mutual understanding.[30]

NOTES

Muchísimas gracias to my research assistant, Ofelia Carrillo Dorado, for her many vital contributions to this study. I am also grateful to Arlene Dávila of New York University; Jaime Rhemrev and Ramona Field of the University of Wisconsin–Madison; and the Crossing Borders conference at Williams College for opportunities to present earlier drafts of this essay. Warm thanks are also due to Jillian Báez, Dolores Inés Casillas, and the editors and reviewers of this volume for their insightful editorial comments. Finally, I would like to express my very sincere gratitude to Vanessa Pabón, Rogelio Miñana, and the interns of WGBY Springfield's Latino Youth Media Institute for their invaluable participation in this project.

1. The term "Latin(o)" music is intended to emphasize the tensions between the designators "Latin" (the label that much of the mainstream media employ) and "Latina/o" (a grassroots term utilized by many Latinas/os), without privileging either. As Aparicio and Jáquez assert, we must consider the symbolic gaps between the category of "Latin music" and the social groups that presumably produce and consume these forms. See Aparicio, Jáquez, and Cepeda, *Musical Migrations*, 1–10.

2. Tatar, "Latin American Immigrants," 34.

3. Wilkinson, "Immigration Blues"; Ratliff, "Singing Stories." Also see Saldívar, *Border Matters*; and Zavella, *I'm Neither Here nor There*.

4. Wilkinson, "Immigration Blues"; Cantor-Navas, "Tiger Beat." The infrequency of digital downloads in this case most likely points to the digital divide separating Latina/o and white consumers, as well as the older demographic that tends to purchase Los Tigres' music.

5. Cobo, "Against the Odds."

6. Dávila, *Latinos, Inc.*

7. Paredez, *Selenidad*, 8.

8. Cepeda, *Musical ImagiNation*; Aparicio, "Jennifer as Selena," 92.

9. Cantor-Navas, "Tiger Beat."

10. Eddie Gutiérrez, personal communication, October 1, 2012; Cantor-Navas, "Tiger Beat."

11. Nieves Moreno, "A Man Lives Here," 256–57.

12. To have been born in America is like a blessing
 Full of beautiful images that make the heart happy
 Mosaic of a thousand colors, beautiful women and flowers
 For the people of America I sing my song
 I am from America, I am from America.
 Los Tigres del Norte featuring Calle 13, "América," Disc 2, *Tr3s Presents MTV Unplugged: Los Tigres del Norte and Friends*, deluxe edition CD/DVD (Woodland Hills, CA: Fonovisa, 2011).

13. I have the lakes, I have the rivers
 I have my teeth for when I smile
 The snow that dresses up my mountains
 I have the sun that dries me and the rain that bathes me . . .
 I work hard but with pride
 Here we share, what's mine is yours
 These people don't drown under large waves
 And if it collapses I'll rebuild it.

14. North America is all of the continent / Those born here are American / The color may be different / But as children of God / We are brothers.

15. I share everything with my brothers / I'm the nightmare of the American Dream / I am America / I'm what they left behind / All of the leftovers / Of what they robbed.

16. Zavella, *I'm Neither Here nor There*, 191.

17. Habell-Pallán, *Loca Motion*, 187.

18. Los Tigres del Norte featuring Calle 13, "América."

19. Desmond, "Embodying Difference," 36.

20. *Muchísimas gracias* to Juana Suárez for pointing out this small, yet significant gesture to me.

21. Beltrán, *The Trouble with Unity*, 127.

22. See Valdivia, "The Gendered Face of Latinidad," 53–67.

23. See Tatar, "Latin American Immigrants," 45, as well as Smith and Guarnizo, "The Locations of Transnationalism," 23.

24. White-identified residents form the bulk of the city's population (55.3 percent), with African American (25 percent) and Asian American, Pacific Islander, and American Indian or Alaska Native (a combined 5 percent) communities existing in smaller numbers. US Census Bureau, "Profile of General Population."
25. Interestingly, none of the interviewees ever employed the term "Latinidad," which reinforces the notion that while the concept of Latinidad is broadly referenced and understood on the ground, the terminology attached to it largely remains within the purview of academia.
26. See De Genova and Ramos-Zayas, *Latino Crossings*; and Pérez, "Puertorriqueñas rencorosas."
27. In this respect, Zydalis remarked, "They [non-Latinas/os] are kind of surprised when they see me, I've graduated college and they're like, 'Oh but you're Puerto Rican, you were supposed to have kids.'"
28. Here the term "Spanish" is colloquially employed to refer to those of Latin(o) American descent, as is often done in the US Northeast.
29. For additional commentary regarding the transgressive nature of some Latina/o audience readings of Latinidad, see Dávila, *Latinos, Inc.*, as well as the chapter by Jillian Báez in this volume.
30. Aparicio, "Jennifer as Selena," 90–91.

REFERENCES

Aparicio, Frances R. "Jennifer as Selena: Rethinking Latinidad in Media and Popular Culture." *Latino Studies* 1, no. 1 (2003): 90–105.

Aparicio, Frances R., and Cándida Jáquez with María Elena Cepeda. *Musical Migrations: Transnationalism and Cultural Hybridity in Latin(o) America*. New York: St. Martin's, 2003.

Beltrán, Cristina. *The Trouble with Unity: Latino Politics and the Creation of Identity*. New York: Oxford University Press, 2010.

Cantor-Navas, Judy. "Tiger Beat: Los Tigres del Norte to Hit *MTV Unplugged* This Spring." *Billboard*, March 19, 2001, 10.

Cepeda, María Elena. *Musical ImagiNation: U.S.-Colombian Identity and the Latin Music Boom*. New York: New York University Press, 2010.

Cobo, Leila. "Against the Odds: Regional Mexican Dominant Latin Genre despite Market Adversity." *Billboard*, June 28, 2008, 51.

Dávila, Arlene. *Latinos, Inc.: The Marketing and Making of a People*. Berkeley: University of California Press, 2001.

De Genova, Nicholas, and Ana Y. Ramos-Zayas. *Latino Crossings: Mexicans, Puerto Ricans, and the Politics of Race and Citizenship*. New York: Routledge, 2003.

Desmond, Jane. "Embodying Difference: Issues in Dance and Cultural Studies." In *Everynight Life: Culture and Dance in Latin/o America*, edited by Celeste Fraser Delgado and José Esteban Muñoz, 33–64. Durham: Duke University Press, 1997.

Habell-Pallán, Michelle. *Loca Motion: The Travels of Latina and Chicana Popular Culture*. New York: New York University Press, 2005.

Nieves Moreno, Alfredo. "A Man Lives Here: Reggaeton's Hypermasculine Resident." Translated by Héctor Fernández L'Hoeste. In *Reggaeton*, edited by Raquel Z. Rivera, Wayne Marshall, and Deborah Pacini Hernandez, 252–79. Durham: Duke University Press, 2009.

Paredez, Deborah. *Selenidad: Selena, Latina/os, and the Performance of Memory*. Durham: Duke University Press, 2009.

Pérez, Gina. "Puertorriqueñas rencorosas y mejicanas sufridas: Gendered Ethnic Identity Formation in Chicago's Latino Communities." *Journal of Latin American Anthropology* 8, no. 2 (2003): 96–124.

Ratliff, Ben. "Singing Stories from Lives Lived Far Away from Home." *New York Times*, February 19, 2007, E1(L).

Saldívar, José David. *Border Matters: Remapping American Cultural Studies*. Berkeley: University of California Press, 1997.

Smith, Michael Peter, and Luis Eduardo Guarnizo. "The Locations of Transnationalism." Introduction to *Transnationalism from Below*, edited by Luis Eduardo Guarnizo and Michael Peter Smith, 3–34. New Brunswick: Transaction, 1998.

Tatar, Bradley S. "Latin American Immigrants, Identity and Nationalism in the Music of *Los Tigres del Norte*." *Journal of Latino-Latin American Studies* 1, no. 3 (2004): 33–64.

Los Tigres del Norte featuring Calle 13. "América." Disc 2. *Tr3s Presents MTV Unplugged: Los Tigres del Norte and Friends*, deluxe edition CD/DVD. Woodland Hills, CA: Fonovisa, 2011.

US Census Bureau. "Profile of General Population and Housing Characteristics: 2010, Springfield city, Massachusetts." Table. US Census Bureau, DP-1, http://www.factfinder.census.gov.

Valdivia, Angharad N. "The Gendered Face of Latinidad: Global Circulation of Hybridity." In *Circuits of Visibility: Gender and Transnational Media Cultures*, edited by Radha Sarma Hegde. New York: New York University Press, 2011.

Wilkinson, Alec. "Immigration Blues." *New Yorker*, May 24, 2010, 34.

Zavella, Patricia. *I'm Neither Here nor There: Mexicans' Quotidian Struggles with Migration and Poverty*. Durham: Duke University Press, 2011.

16

Latinos in Alternative Media

Latinos as an Alternative Media Paradigm

ED MORALES

"Alternative media, which are situated outside of the mainstream, have been said to articulate a "social order different from and often opposed to the dominant." The point of
distinction aims to celebrate diversity within society and
increase our shared understanding of one another."
—Linda Jean Kenix, introduction to *Alternative and
Mainstream Media* (2011)

While it is the goal of many Latin@ activists to demonstrate that Latin@s
are very much like mainstream Americans in order to smooth the way
for immigration reform, the fact is that Latin@s, and the hybrid cultures
we represent, are very much an "alternative" to mainstream American
culture. The stories of Latin@s in the United States, whether told by
Latin@ journalists or not, were, during the era of progressive cultural
and nationalist movements of the 1960s and 1970s, often an integral part
of alternative journalism and formed part of a general alternative journalism narrative that also included other marginalized groups. But over
the last thirty years, the paradigm has changed, often excluding the stories of Latin@s as alternative journalism came to mean something else.

Any discussion of Latin@s and alternative media should first examine the current state of alternative media, and how we can conceive
of Latin@ involvement in media production as something that constitutes an alternative to mainstream media production. While most
definitions of alternative media characterize them as generally "outside"
mainstream media conventions, there is apparently an increasing convergence, or sharing in method and practice, between the two, making
it hard to conceive of mainstream and alternative media as mutually

exclusive. The history of alternative media suggests that they have operated outside the world of large media corporations, producing content that is more locally based, providing a perspective for a marginalized group or area. But as alternative media have grown, they have increasingly become the subject of corporate mergers, and the dreaded concentration of media that has affected the mainstream media. Consequently much of alternative media's critique of, say, capitalism, consumerism, and patriarchy has become muted over the years.[1]

The convergence of alternative and mainstream media has been greatly enhanced with the advent of rapidly evolving new technologies. With the shift to online reading, both mainstream and alternative media have begun to use the same kinds of techniques to attract reader attention, including using video, repeat-motion GIF images, and hyperlinks that connect the reader to both mainstream and alternative publications. Younger journalists are more prone to begin their careers in alternative media as a stepping-stone toward eventually working in the mainstream, rather than work in alternative media as a kind of prolonged commitment to alternative reporting.

In this way, alternative media have shirked some of their responsibility to challenge hegemony, or what Gramsci or Chomsky alike would call the "manufacture of consent." Another less obvious way that alternative media do not challenge hegemony is to slowly abandon their role of allowing voices from nonwhite communities to emerge. This is particularly a challenge to Latino alternative journalists, whose focus on their own communities is a challenge to established societal notions such as presenting the issue of race in America as a black/white binary.

Going back to its origins in the wake of countercultural and national liberation movements of the 1960s and 1970s, the Latin@ community's status as an underserved and marginalized community made Latin@ issues and Latin@ media producers an excellent fit for alternative media production in the United States. This seeming journalistic mandate is even more valid in the current climate, as predictions of an increasing Latin@ population continue to mount. Institutional research suggests that by the third generation, English becomes the dominant language used by US Latin@s, and since the vast majority of alternative journalism in this country is produced in English, there doesn't seem to be a language barrier involved.[2] Yet the alternative media's "alternative" focus does not seem to include Latin@s in a systematic way, and in fact Latin@ issues and Latin@ media producers have demonstrably less representation in the alternative media than in the mainstream.

One way to explain the lack of Latin@s and other minorities in alternative journalism is the conflict between "alternative" culture and the cultures of people of color, one parallel to what feminists have theorized as "intersectionality." Alternative culture has its roots in the literature and cultural practices of countercultural critics and journalists who see themselves as an alternative to mainstream perspectives and mainstream journalists and commentators. For a time, this meant that the counterculture was consistently critiquing the concentration of capital, consumerism, and patriarchy. But the shift to the right has greatly eroded the counterculture, and alternative media have become less about these critiques and more about an alternative lifestyle and its attendant consumerism. Or, at times, when alternative media have focused on left critiques of an increasingly conservative streak in American politics, they focus more on white middle-class activism than the struggles of poor people of color.

While alternative lifestyles can still be a welcome critique of mainstream conventions, America's racial and ethnic minorities, as long as they remain unincorporated into mainstream mores and aspirations, have taken on more of the identity of a permanent counterculture. One could argue that African Americans, who as the most consistent opposition to the conservative policies of the Republican Party at the ballot box, have been more consistently "countercultural" critics of mainstream politics of culture, but have also become less important as the subjects of alternative media. In other words, it has become even more central to African American and Latin@ political identity to oppose the status quo.

Throughout its early history, alternative journalism featured several writers who came out of politically conscious Latin@ communities across the country. Writers like Pablo Guzmán at the *Village Voice* and Rubén Martínez at the *LA Weekly* gave voice to Latino issues the way their African American counterparts covered issues relevant to African Americans. Although they wrote for mainstream publications like the *New York Daily News* and the *Chicago Tribune*, writers like

Juan González and Achy Obejas have committed much of their career to alternative radio programs like *Democracy Now!* and the gay rights magazine the *Advocate* respectively. Maria Hinojosa has been a long-time contributor to PBS news programs for a couple of decades.

But as alternative journalism has been converging with mainstream journalism, it has left much of the subject material Latino journalists have covered to the so-called ethnic media, whether smaller regional publications directed at recent immigrants or corporate giants like Univision and Telemundo. Alternative journalism, unless it is entirely steeped in the premise of class analysis—as in the case of journalistic institutions conceived of entirely in the service of labor unions or of popular people's movements or immigrant communities—has essentially become a journalism for an elite, highly educated class whose politics are left of center but who are most often not part of a minority or marginalized group. This reality has become more exacerbated as the income distribution gap widens and fewer minorities are given access to an educational level that would make them likely consumers of alternative journalism.

A cursory examination of the mastheads of the major alternative newspapers in the United States, which are published weekly and whose ownership has been increasingly concentrated in fewer hands (most notably Voice Media Group, which owns New York's *Village Voice* and ten other weeklies in Miami, Seattle, San Francisco, Dallas, Houston, and Orange County, California, among others),[3] reveals typically minuscule numbers of Latino and minority editorial staffers.[4] The *Village Voice* features one senior associate editor who is Latina and no staff writers, the *Phoenix New Times* one Latina staff writer, and the *SF Weekly* two Latino contributors, although one is Gustavo Arellano, whose humor-driven "Ask a Mexican" is reproduced in several Voice Media Group properties.[5]

Alternative newspapers not owned by Voice Media Group tell a similar tale. Neither the *Washington City Paper*, the *Chicago Reader*, nor the *Boston Phoenix* feature Latinos on their editorial mastheads, and the *LA Weekly*, which serves Los Angeles County, where there are over 4.5 million Latinos, has one Latino staff writer besides the columnist Arellano. The only real exception to this pattern is the *Miami New Times*, which features seven Latinos on its editorial masthead, most likely because of the dominance of middle-class Latinos in that city's institutions and government.

As a former *Village Voice* staff writer, I can testify that I worked with one "fully identified" Latino editor and four African American editors in the thirteen years I was a contributor to the weekly, and that I was the only Latino staff writer during that time period. In my early years, the editorial staffers of color were often organized in a "minority caucus," and we did our own informal studies of the numbers of minority writers used and the number of cover stories and cover lines that were given to minority writers and minority subjects, and they were roughly parallel to the figures produced by countless studies by institutions like ASNE, Poynter, and the Pew Hispanic Center, showing that these figures represented about half of the percentage of minority population in the New York metropolitan area.

A similar imbalance exists in the institutions of public television and public radio, media whose content, although not specifically countercultural, represent an "alternative" analogous to that of alternative weeklies. "Taking the Public Out of Public TV," an October 2010 cover story in FAIR's (Fairness in Accuracy and Reporting) magazine *Extra*, claimed that "'public television' features guest lists strongly dominated by white, male, and elite sources, who are far more likely to represent corporations and war makers than environmentalists or peace advocates." The article also contends that there is an increasing penetration of corporate ownership and agenda in public television—ostensibly as the result of relentless pressure from conservative ideologues who criticized what they felt was a liberal bias. It also states that there has also been a marginalization of the voices of women and people of color in PBS's flagship news program, *The News Hour*, and a gradual decline of programs focused on and hosted by people of color.

The story revealed that the "for-profit conglomerate Liberty Media has held a controlling stake in *The News Hour* since 1994," that guests tended to defend the oil industry after a major oil spill in the Gulf of Mexico, and that no antiwar group or person with antiwar views was allowed to speak during segments focusing on the war in Afghanistan. Latinos represented only 1 percent of US sources. While Ray Suarez is a strong presence on the program, he is one of the few Latin@ faces seen on PBS—another has been Maria Hinojosa, who in 2010 started her own media group called Futuro Media Group.[6] The *Charlie Rose* show was criticized for featuring just two guests in one year who "represented the public interest voices that public television is supposed to highlight." In November 2013, Ray Suarez left his position as chief national correspondent at the *PBS NewsHour*, apparently because he felt passed over when Gwen Ifill and Judy Woodruff were named co-anchors, ending a rotation at the anchor desk that included Suarez. He quickly became anchor of a news show at Al Jazeera America.

Another program that was criticized was *Need to Know*, which was created to succeed *Bill Moyers Journal*, one of PBS's best investigative programs. WNET New York's vice president of content, Stephen Segaller, responded to FAIR's criticism in this way:

> By providing only a cursory overview of *Need to Know*'s extremely varied and balanced content, but a detailed assessment of the racial profile of our on-air guests, FAIR seems to equate racial and gender representation in the stories with balance or diversity in reporting. This nose-counting exercise is at its core an inaccurate representation of our commitment to balanced and enterprising journalism, but at the very least it should be complete.

This sort of rhetoric is at the core of the problem of minority and Latin@ representation in media—the principles of journalistic objectivity and "balance" in journalism, which minority and Latin@ journalists and their advocates do not deviate from, trump the importance of minority/Latin@ presence or absence regardless of how that presence represents the point of view of a community. "Nose-counting," a practice the *Village Voice* minority caucus and countless other studies administered by minority professional journalist associations rely on as a baseline critique of hiring and representational policies, is trivialized as a "quantity over quality" argument, and there is no acknowledgment that notions of objectivity can vary from observer to observer. But of course the quest for "objectivity" has always been journalism's greatest dilemma, the discipline's central conceit that, when challenged, can cause the whole enterprise to collapse from within. When Latinos are proportionally represented on news broadcasts, "objectivity" is enhanced by the introduction of more varied points of view.

The situation at NPR is somewhat more ambiguous than at PBS and alternative weeklies. An ombudsman report released in April 2012 made the claim that the percentage of editorial workers of color at NPR was 23 percent, which easily exceeded the percentage of people of color in mainstream, and as we have seen, alternative weekly editorial staffs. However in August 2012, NPR announced it was using a $1.5 million grant from the Corporation for Public Broadcasting to "put together a six-person team to report stories on race, ethnicity, and culture." Ironically, some of the pressure that led to this resulted from NPR's 2010 firing of the moderate conservative commentator Juan Williams, who had said on a Fox News program that he did not feel comfortable traveling on a plane with visibly identified Muslims, a statement that many if not most people of color would find offensive. Such logic about the "nose-counting" of people of color in the media leads to the need for minorities to assess whether they are just interested in increasing numbers of their group regardless of their political orientation.

At any rate, just weeks later, an article in the *LA Weekly* (written by a white journalist) chronicled an awkward effort by the southern California station KPCC to address the issue of minority—and in this case Latin@—listenership.[7] The story focused on the failed attempt to attract Latino listenership by pairing A Martinez, an on-air personality with "virtually no hard-news experience," with Madeline Brand, who the writer identifies as someone southern California NPR listeners regarded as a breath of fresh air. Brand's show, which had been on the air for almost two years, "was a departure from the stuffy *BBC Newshour* she replaced" (ostensibly a hard-news program), and delighted southern Californians by playing music from the contemporary electro-DJ star Skrillex between segments.

A Martinez's arrival was signaled by the use of "the trilling pan flute of 'Oye Mi Amore [sic]' by Maná" (an admittedly uninspired choice), and "a segment about the death of a tortilla magnate" replaced reports on Brooklyn co-ops. To the audience targeted by the *LA Weekly*, this would seem to be a substitution of pressing matters (co-ops and Brooklyn are markers for moneyed progressives) with questionable puff pieces. What is more superficial and irrelevant than tortillas? One comment posted on the show's website even found it "a bad, vaguely racist joke." Of course this is an attitude that both liberal whites and Latin@ NPR listeners might share.

The problem here was the $1.5 million grant from CPB, designed to not only serve a more diverse community, but lift ratings, despite the fact, the writer points out, that the previously Latino-free *Madeline Brand Show* earned a 2.6 percent market share, "the highest rated show produced by KPCC." Martinez was criticized for talking too much about sports, and that the move was "affirmative action gone amok." Even worse, Martinez, as host of an ESPN show earlier in his career, has been an advocate for steroid use.

To be fair, the article did come to the conclusion that it was questionable whether "three older white guys—Bill Davis, Russ Santon, and Crag Curtis [KPCC managers]—are the right people to decide what Southern California diversity should sound like." And it did make an important, if somewhat obvious observation about the US Latino market. A five-year study of Latino audience potential by the CPB found that second- and third-generation listeners were well within the grasp of NPR programming, possessing a "strong desire for news programming that represents multiple perspectives of an issue."

To say that Latinos have a strong desire for news that represents multiple perspectives of an issue is an understatement. One of the reasons marketers and media programmers have failed to solve the puzzle of attracting and serving Latin@ audiences is an inability to understand basic aspects of the core of Latin@ identity—that is, the multiplicity of perspectives and identities that Latin@s have, and the practical activity that is used to resolve these perspectives into a coherent worldview. For about fifteen years, since the first revelations about the emergence of Latin@s as the country's largest minority were manifested by phenomena like the Latin pop explosion and new advertising and media strategies to reach Latin@s in television, film, and the book industry, marketers and media producers have for the most part not been able to grasp the essential nature of Latin@ identity and how it influences them as consumers.

As Latin@s migrate to the United States and produce succeeding generations, their experience is unlike that of other European ethnic groups in that although language acquisition eventually displaces the dominance of their home country's Spanish, various aspects of their identity remain intact, "folded into" their new "American" identities.[8] Latin@s cannot merely be perceived as a conglomeration of ethnic or racial groups. Some scholars have called for understanding the formation of Latin@ identity through the prism of "ethno-race," that is, accounting for phenomena and experiences associated with both ethnic and racial groups.[9] These multiple levels of experience, added to the complicating factors of language—while English becomes predominant, Spanish does not disappear entirely, and hybrid slanguages like Spanglish come into play—make marketing to Latinos an almost incomprehensible task for marketers and media producers with no academic or business school understanding of how to grasp these complexities.

The irony here, as expressed earlier in this essay, is that alternatives to the mainstream media and mainstream marketing are conceived of through the prism of "alternative culture," or its concomitant much-less complex conception of alternatives to mainstream discourse. The way "alternative" is postulated in fields such as journalism and public TV and radio is drawn from notions of an alternative culture based on the experiences of whites who draw from a surface understanding of African American and marginalized cultures in a way that tends to obscure the source of their "alternative" extrapolations. Alternative journalism, or broadcast news for an educated elite, draws its alternative-ness from an off-center perspective and a series of coded languages that are not alternative enough to address America's permanent alternative constituencies: African Americans, Latinos, Asians, women, and the LGBT community.

The issue of language is central to understanding the way media producers and marketers fail to communicate effectively with Latino consumers. While the era of the 1998 Latin pop explosion, which saw the sudden popularity of musical entertainers like Ricky Martin, Marc Anthony, Shakira, Enrique Iglesias, and Jennifer Lopez, provided an impetus for exploration by various media conglomerates to prioritize the production and distribution of entertainment commodities for Latinos and Anglo Latinophiles, the efforts faded for several reasons:

1. Most of the Latin pop explosion artists are Spanish-dominant, so their work in English had limited efficacy and staying power.
2. The impact of the World Trade Center attacks created an anti-foreign sentiment that at first became an obstacle to the promotion of "difference," and eventually manifested itself in the anti-immigration reform movement's increased hostility toward Spanish-speaking immigrants.

3. The inability of marketers and media producers to understand how to use bilingual strategies or frameworks resulted in an across-the-board agreement that the use of Spanish-language media—television, books, and musical entertainment—was the most effective way to reach Latino consumers, despite the existence of countless studies that asserted that most Latinos in the United States are not immigrants, and a very high percentage are English-dominant by the third generation.[10]

So, although Shakira and Lopez continue to have success as English-language recording artists, Latin pop experiments in English (including collaborations with US acts, like the Alejandro Sanz–Alicia Keys duets) failed commercially. Chain bookstores like Barnes and Noble that featured Latino-themed sections in stores abandoned them in favor of a Libros en Español section online, and the Latin Grammy Awards—specifically created to try to break Latin music into the mainstream in a way that hadn't been done since the mambo era—were permanently moved from English-language CBS to Spanish-language Univision in response to low ratings.

While it is true that later generations of bilingual Latinos constitute a portion of the Spanish-language TV audience, the relegation of Latinos to being an object of marketing and media production in a language that gradually diminishes in importance for the group is an astoundingly irrational development in a culture dominated by the discourse that the profit motive is the bottom line in the guiding economic philosophy of the society. To address a group in a language that a majority does not prefer as its dominant parlance is extraordinarily inefficient in terms of maximizing profit. It is a glaring example of how marketing can clearly be affected by an extra-economic ideology that perceives the world in racial (and in some ways ethnic) binaries.

This illogical strategy resulted in the overdetermining of Spanish-language media, which in the United States are not Latino-owned, and the creation of a fresh set of stereotypes about Latinos as being English-deficient, conditions that allowed for Sofia Vergara's fractured-English spitfire act—nuanced or not—to become one of the iconic Latino television figures of the last decade. As the last decade progressed, stereotypical English-deficient representations on shows like *Saturday Night Live* replaced the more balanced characterizations of the *George Lopez*

Show, even slowing down a bit the trend of depicting Latinos as hardened English-proficient gangsters and criminals.[11] After all, how can you be gangsta if you can't speak English?

In 2012, a constellation of new factors has created a new and more hopeful atmosphere for Latinos in media, at least in staffing and representation, if not media ownership, which studies like Juan González's reveal to be bleak.[12] The distance from the 9/11 attacks and the relatively embarrassing failures of the wars in Iraq and Afghanistan as democracy-building experiments have diminished the air of jingoistic anti-foreign rhetoric that held sway at the turn of the century. Perhaps more importantly, the humiliating defeat of the Republican Party platform in the national election has made bankrupt the relentlessly anti-Latino drumbeat against immigration reform—in fact, the party's failure to appeal to Latinos is increasingly seen as key to the conservative right's failure in national politics.

Interestingly, the pro-immigration reform agenda has been strongly driven by Spanish-language networks not necessarily driven by political agendas but motivated by enhancing the legal status of a rapidly growing consumer group, recent immigrants and their children. In 2006, the year that some observers cite as the birth of a new Latino politics, radio DJs at Univision-owned stations were crucial in helping to draw huge crowds to immigration reform rallies in Los Angeles, Chicago, and other cities.[13] At the time Univision was owned by Jerrold Perenchio, who is not only not Latino but a major Republican donor. The momentum created by Univision's high-profile endorsement of immigration reform not only shored up its bottom line but allowed it to act as a practical example of "alternative" journalism, focusing on issues that affect not only recent immigrants but even Latino citizens who either had relatives subject to racial profiling or were disturbed by the increasingly anti-immigrant tone adopted by the mainstream media.

This constellation of events seems to have prompted newer, less stilted strategies by media producers and marketers in their approach to the Latino consumer, perhaps grasping Latin@s' potential as the subject of an alternative form of media. There is also a degree of opportunity afforded by the increasing fragmentation of media audiences, which has resulted in the availability of more "specialized" or "niche" programming. So far, bilingual networks like Mun2 and MTV TR3s and websites like remezcla.com have recognized the emerging market of young bilingual Latinos. Advertising strategies have followed suit: recent ads for wireless cell phone companies and fast food giants depict Latinos less as English-handicapped foreigners and more and more like multi-hued families with subtle assimilative tendencies who march to a slightly different bilingual drummer.

In 2011, large media conglomerates suddenly initiated new websites and channels that address the multilayered, ambivalent identities that are inevitably constructed in twenty-first-century America. NBC, *Huffington Post*/AOL, ABC-Univision, and Fox (whose Fox and Fox Latino sites were accused of duplicity in covering immigration reform from hard-right and pro-Latin@ perspectives)[14] have all begun new ventures in English that do a reasonably good job of covering issues important to Latin@s both in the United States and in Latin America. The staff at these sites is overwhelmingly Latin@, from assigning editors to reporters, a situation never seen at any major English-language media outlets in the United States except the *Miami Herald*. While these sites have generated some momentum, it was announced in late 2013 that NBC Latino would be shut down at the end of the year, and Latin@-themed news would be folded in to the mainstream NBC News site.

However, some of the material conditions of today's media world affect and/or inhibit the quality of the journalism at these new sites. Many blog sites, most notably the *Huffington Post*, have made it a practice not to pay most if not all non-staff contributors, which can tend to diminish the quality of the work. It can be more difficult for a young writer today to make a serious commitment to media or journalism because of this lack of remuneration than it was for someone publishing an occasional article in an alternative newspaper fifteen or twenty years ago. And since there have been historically fewer established journalists who have sustained careers since minorities began to join the media in significant numbers in the 1970s, there are fewer who can command remuneration comparable to the earnings of established white journalists. Not only is this a burden to those seeking a media or journalism career, but it also has the effect of diminishing the quality of material available to communities who are the target of such "alternative" journalism and media.

Another problem is that the liberal use of "Latino" in these new media ventures as a catchall label for both US Latinos and Latin Americans leads to inaccuracies in perceptions of both communities. One glaring side effect of this convergence of terms over the last ten years has been the depiction of Latinos in the United States as recent immigrants, indistinguishable from Latin Americans. This conflation also can exacerbate troubling issues of privileging Latin Americans at the expense of US Latinos through the use of these inaccurate labelings and representations.

These new media ventures are allowing news to be gathered, assigned, and edited in a way that has never been done by either the established or alternative media, perhaps making the case that many of the inaccuracies in mainstream media coverage of the Latin@ community can potentially be solved by the employment of editors and writers who, as Latin@s, understand the complexities of Latin@ identity and issues that I have just outlined. Despite skepticism about past failures of niche programming, the faster-growing youth demographic suggests that innovative programming and print and web media will inevitably become as profitable as the emerging consumer market allows it to be. The launch of the Fusion network in September 2013 represented an attempt by ABC/Disney and Univision to combine forces to create a television network directed at both Latino and general market millennials. Seduced by the potential of the new Latin@ media figure Selena Gomez, a creation of the Disney Channel, the network hoped to appeal to millennial-generation bicultural Latinos and "color-blind" Anglos, but was criticized for not featuring enough Latin@s of color. It also failed to make a commitment to bilingual programming. While largely unexplored by major media, code-switching bilingualism, multiracial awareness, and the subtle impact of America's demographic shift away from white majorities and racial binaries should pave the way for a future that actually institutionalizes bilingualism in concert with content in both languages.

The challenges faced by such new media are considerable, particularly if they expect to engage in the kind of antihegemonic opposition to the manufacture of consent that alternative journalism holds as its hallmark. Just as in the field of politics, where cultural nationalist movements sometimes ignored the concerns of its citizens about class- and gender-based discrimination, media created by and for Latin@s face similar paradoxes. That is why there is a need for such media to reflect honestly the concerns of the community they purport to cover and serve. In order to fulfill their potential as "alternative" media, Latin@-directed media must challenge internal hierarchical structures as well as their own methodologies and philosophical approaches to journalism. They must not "borrow" the same kind of binary models of race and gender, or hegemonic worldviews that excluded us from alternative journalism as it converged with mainstream journalism. They must continually find ways to present voices and concerns that truly reflect our community.

Then we'd really see some alternative journalism.

NOTES

1. See Linda Jean Kenix, introduction to *Alternative and Mainstream Media: The Converging Spectrum* (Bloomsbury Academic, 2011), 2–3.
2. "A Growing Share of Latinos Get Their News in English," Pew Hispanic Center, July 23, 2013.
3. In January 2013, the Voice Media Group sold the *Seattle Weekly* and the *SF Weekly* to local buyers in Seattle and San Francisco, respectively.
4. I examined the websites of ten alternative weekly websites in January 2013.
5. It is significant that the only syndicated column by a Latin@ regularly appearing in alternative weeklies is humor-driven and relies on "subverting" crass stereotyping.
6. Hinojosa has also had a presence on CNN. Interestingly, Hinojosa's venture is not the only new Latin@ group to use the idea of "the future" to brand itself. The year 2012 marked the birth of the Futuro Fund, a group of Latin@ fundraisers and lobbyists spearheaded by media figures like Eva Longoria to affect national immigration policy.
7. Tessa Stuart, "How KPCC's Quest for Latino Listeners Doomed *The Madeleine Brand Show*," *LA Weekly*, November 1, 2012.
8. This phenomenon need not be limited to Latin@s, and there is already evidence that it may be occurring with various Asian groups in their attempts to construct a pan-Asian identity and political advocacy. W. E. B. Du Bois's assertion of African Americans' "double consciousness" is an earlier expression of this idea.
9. Linda Martín Alcoff has advocated for this point of view in her essay "Latinos beyond the Binary," *Southern Journal of Philosophy* 47, no. 1 (Spring 2009): 112—28.
10. See Paul Taylor, Mark Hugo Lopez, Jessica Hamar Martínez, and Gabriel Velasco, "When Labels Don't Fit: Hispanics and Their Views of Identity," Pew Hispanic Center, April 4, 2012.
11. One embarrassing return to criminal stereotypes occurred in January 2012, when the sitcom *Work It* made a joke that implied a Puerto Rican character

would be qualified to become a pharmaceutical drug salesperson since his ethnicity had a natural knack for selling drugs. The show was cancelled after protests a few weeks later.

12. See Juan González and Joseph Torres, *News for All the People: The Epic Story of Race and the American Media* (Verso, 2011).

13. See Ed Morales, "The Media Is the Mensaje," *Nation*, May 15, 2006.

14. See Hilary Tone, "Fox Nation v. Fox News Latino on Obama's New Immigration Rule," Media Matters, January 3, 2013.

17

On History and Strategies for Activism

JUAN GONZÁLEZ

Good evening to all of you.[1] As someone who has devoted more than thirty years to chronicling day-to-day events in the areas of politics, economics, crime and law enforcement, and labor and race relations—what we journalists typically refer to as "hard news"—I've rarely paid much attention to the world of entertainment media, except to occasionally reflect on how it has shaped, or at times distorted, national consciousness, national identity, and the broader culture. Today, however, I share some historical trends that have contributed to our contemporary media system, as well as some ideas for contemporary activism and advocacy.

The news and entertainment media, of course, have evolved side by side over the past two hundreds years as interrelated wings of our mass communications system. At each stage of that system's development, however, government leaders who devised communications policies sought to emphasize how such policies promoted free speech and a more informed citizenry. Unfortunately, there have been repeated examples throughout US history where the entertainment wing of the media morphed into or gained dominance over the news wing, with the result being more distraction and disinformation for the public than facts and context.

Important social and political issues do get reflected at times in the entertainment media, but on a day-to-day basis the media's essential commercial goal—attracting the greatest number of eyeballs in order to peddle a product—creates an inevitable bias against and seeks to eliminate dissent, conflicting ideas, and marginal viewpoints.

Throughout my career, I have personally witnessed the relentless encroachment of entertainment into the realm of "hard news." A few years ago, I realized I had no idea how to reverse that trend because I did not fully understand how it had developed. Nor did I understand why the media continue to engender so much disdain, even anger and resentment, from broad swaths of the American people. Or why, despite all the progress in civil rights and equal opportunity over the past fifty years, the news media keep depicting racial and ethnic minorities in such a one-sided, stereotypical, and negative manner.

So I embarked on my own attempt to unravel and analyze how the US news media system was created, how it evolved from colonial times to the present, how it shaped the nature of American democracy, and especially the crucial role it played in the nation's ethnic and racial conflicts. The result of my research can be found in *News for All the People: The Epic Story of Race and the American Media*.

Among my most surprising discoveries was that the transnational influence of the US news media, something most of us take for granted today, goes back to the country's earliest days, when immigrant editors and publishers used the press freedoms guaranteed in the US Constitution to promote radical ideas of liberty in their own homelands. As far back as 1824, for instance, the Cuban Catholic priest Félix Valera founded the newspaper *El Habanero* in Philadelphia to help organize his countrymen's resistance to Spanish colonialism. Varela, who was being hunted by the Spanish Crown for his antislavery views, would print the paper here and smuggle copies back to Cuba. Likewise, the Mexican journalists and revolutionaries Catarino Garza and Ricardo Flores Magón published papers in El Paso, San Antonio, St. Louis, and other US cities around the turn of the twentieth century to stir up opposition to the Mexican dictator Porfirio Díaz. And Sun Yat-Sen, the founding father of modern China, headed the *Hawaiian Chinese News* in Honolulu in 1895 and later worked on the staff of San Francisco's *Chinese Free Press*. Through both papers, he sought to stoke opposition among overseas Chinese to imperial rule back home.

The extraordinary proliferation and influence of this early immigrant press are still not fully understood today. The city of New Orleans, for instance, was the great center of the Spanish-language press in nineteenth-century America, with more than twenty-five Spanish-language newspapers printed there before the Civil War, including the country's first Spanish daily, *Patria*, founded by Eusebio Juan Gómez and Victoriano Alemán in 1846. *Patria*'s masthead displayed the flags of Spain, Mexico, and the United States and proclaimed it the "organo de la población española de los estados unidos" (organ of the Spanish population of the United States). *Patria* boasted correspondents throughout the Caribbean region, and its articles were often quoted in mainstream English-language papers.

But my goal was not simply to resurrect the heroic and largely untold story of Hispanic, African American, Native American, and Asian American journalists who created a vibrant wing of the US press, although that in itself is a worthy and necessary endeavor. Along with my coauthor, Joseph Torres, I also was determined to chronicle just how the news media came to be such a colossal institution in our modern lives.

We gradually pieced together several key dynamics that laid the basis for our modern system:

First is the historic role of technology. The US media system has experienced repeated waves of technological change in mass communication, but each new technology has overturned or destabilized the existing order of information delivery.

Second is government policy. As each new technology undermined the existing communications system, government leaders were called upon to fashion new laws and regulations for the smooth functioning of media. Those leaders often had to respond to competing demands from old and new media owners, other business interests, and the needs of labor, ordinary citizens, and racial minorities, to balance private interests and public good.

Third is the question of how information is best disseminated in a democracy. We found that the hallmark of each new media policy debate throughout US history has been the issue of whether a centralized or decentralized system of mass communications best strengthens democratic institutions.

Fourth is the news media's role in shaping a national narrative and a national identity. Debates over mass communications policy in the United States have always been, when everything else is stripped away, a battle over control of that narrative, over what sectors of society are able to utilize freedom of the press to contribute to the collective story.

These four aspects of media evolution have been with us from colonial times to the present. The first great advance in our communications system and the first great policy decision, for example, was over creation of our first rudimentary Internet, better known as the US Post Office. In 1792 in Congress a great debate erupted between the founders over how information would flow within the new republic. Congress eventually decided that the free flow of news was so important to maintaining our fledgling democracy that the government would subsidize the delivery of newspapers to the American people, through something called the second-class mail system, and that the government would build postal roads throughout our vast territory to deliver that mail. By the early nineteenth century, more newspapers were circulating per person in the United States than in any country in the world; in both the biggest cities and the smallest towns, many people subscribed to two or three newspapers per day. This led to a highly decentralized and autonomous communications system. In fact, the main job of our postal system throughout the nineteenth century was not to deliver mail; only about 10 percent of its traffic was private mail, while 90 percent was newspapers. And until the Civil War, the postal system was the largest employer in the federal government. There were more postal employees than there were soldiers in the army until the Civil War. So you could make the argument that the main job of the federal government until the Civil War was the delivery of newspapers to the American people at discounted rates.

Then a new technology comes along, the telegraph. For the first time, you could get instant communication across telegraph lines, an advance that upset the existing order marked by hundreds of local, independently owned newspapers. The government had to step in and decide what to do with the telegraph. Would it be federally owned, like the post office, or privately run? Congress eventually rejected federal ownership, and as a result you had the emergence at first of hundreds of telegraph companies, but by the late 1860s one company began buying up all the smaller ones, and that led to the first industrial monopoly in the United States, a company by the name of Western Union. Western Union soon cemented an alliance with the Associated Press, the first great cooperative of newspaper owners in New York City, and together the AP and Western Union became the dominant information gate-keepers of the United States during the late nineteenth century. The AP/Western Union alliance reversed the previous fifty years of decentralized news flow in America. Their alliance centralized news and information delivery in a cartel that included the AP newspapers and the Western Union telegraph lines.

But a few decades later a new technology came along. The development of radio in the early twentieth century undermined the stranglehold of Western Union and the Associated Press over the news media. Suddenly, thousands of radio stations came on the air, very much like the early days of the Internet. Everyone was building radio transmitters, and many of their programs started to interfere with each other's signals. Once again, the government had to step in. In 1927, Congress created the Federal Radio Commission, and in 1934 the Federal Communications Commission. Those agencies organized the new media order and recentralized the new system of broadcasting. A couple of newly created networks, NBC and CBS, were handed the bulk of the best radio licenses by government regulators. The same networks that dominated radio later dominated television.

Eventually, however, a new technology emerged, cable television. It made possible many more channels than the broadcast stations were able to produce. Hundreds of independent cable systems sprang up all around the United States offering commercial-free stations at first (because with many cable networks you were paying a monthly fee, so the cable operators promised commercial-free channels). But gradually, as had happened in the nineteenth century with the telegraph, a few cable systems gobbled up all the small ones, so that today two cable giants, Comcast and Time Warner, effectively control the US cable market.

By the end of the twentieth century, however, the fifth great technological revolution in mass media had matured, the Internet. Among other things, it marked the merger into one of all previous mediums—voice, print, and video.

Each one of these technological advances revolutionized information delivery and required the government to step in with new rules. But each attempt to rewrite the rules provoked furious policy battles. The old media moguls, after all, didn't want the new media moguls to supplant them. Citizen groups, educators, racial minorities all wanted to be heard in those debates. One of the things we discovered in our research is that racial minorities gained greater access to news media and better representation of their lives and their conditions precisely in those moments when the government opted for a more decentralized system of media. And conversely, during those periods when a more centralized system held sway, racial minorities were shut out.

How can that be, some might say, given, for example, the explosive growth in Spanish-language media in the United States over the past fifty years? Well, appearances can be deceiving. US Anglo companies or foreign capital largely own the major Spanish-language media in the United States. With the exception of the Alarcón family's Spanish Broadcasting System, there are virtually no US Latinos who own major media companies. Very few African-American owners of major media outlets are left, especially in radio and television, the biggest being the Radio One and TV One cable networks owned by Cathy Hughes.

Even as the minority population of the country mushrooms past 35 percent, minority ownership of the media system has declined. This is largely a result of policy decisions in Washington made in the late 1990s, especially the enormous centralization of media after the Telecommunications Act of 1996.

The Internet, in the view of many, offers unprecedented potential to democratize media ownership and media access. After all, anyone today can be a publisher, radio, or TV station owner on the Internet. The flip side is that the Internet also provides unparalleled opportunity for each of us to be watched and subjected to surveillance. George Orwell could never have dreamed of what the government and corporations can do today in tracking everything that Americans do on the Internet. Everything. So you have this huge contradiction of greater access, yet greater potential for control, for monitoring what you do.

This is especially true given the transnational character of the Internet. I'd like to refer to another historical parallel, the emergence of the first great transnational-wired networks during the late nineteenth century. In 1893, the Associated Press quietly joined a little-known European communications cartel, which included Britain's Reuters, France's Havaz, and Germany's Wolff news agencies. The cartel had begun as early as 1869 to divide amongst its members the responsibility for disseminating news dispatches for Asia, Africa, and the Western Hemisphere. Once AP joined the group, Reuters and the other agencies agreed to stay out of the United States, and AP agreed, in return, to exclusively supply the European members with news from the United States and Latin America. The wire services thus carved up the world's information footprint in the same way that the European colonial powers carved up the world's resources and peoples.

Much of this story is presented in a 1980 book by the British historian Anthony Long, *The Geopolitics of Information*, and though Long's book is now more than thirty years old, it remains a brilliant and enduring analysis of the international battles over information flows between rich and poor in the world. To quote Long,

> It is no accident then that the same nations that controlled physical transportation around the globe, and which thereby maintained contact with their centres of trade and their colonies, also constructed the first news networks, to sell information to the world's newspapers. The traders and overseas administrators, like the explorers before them, were in themselves the basic sources of knowledge of the world. And it was their view which was implicit in imperial society's creation of the political realities of the globe.

Thus, the battle over information flow is really a battle over controlling a narrative, controlling people's perceptions of themselves, and it doesn't matter which company is where, or what parts of media they control, although it's certainly a good idea to keep track of the major players. The important thing to understand is that the flow of news always reflects political realities. The news media at once inform the masses of people, helping them keep their rulers in check, but also provide ways for the rulers to control their populations. That's why I have always believed that political leaders seek to control the news media even more in a democracy than in a dictatorship. In a democracy, "one person, one vote" is a dangerous principle. After all, the masses can always vote in ways the elite don't want them to. It is hardly an accident, in my view, that the mass-circulation newspaper developed in the United States during the 1830s, just as urban workers began to acquire the right to vote. Until that time, newspapers had been addressed to a tiny elite—landowners, clergymen, and businessmen, the only ones who could afford paying a year's subscription in advance to have their paper delivered at home. But once workers could vote, it became necessary to create penny papers that were sold on the streets of the major cities—a mass media to influence *how* those workers voted.

Our contemporary news media now face a great demographic transformation of their audience, the same demographic change faced by the political establishment of all the industrial nations of the West. For decades now, the people of the Third World have been immigrating to the West. Britain doesn't know what to do about all its Indian, Pakistani, and Jamaican immigrants; France doesn't know what to do about all its Algerians, Tunisians, and Moroccans. Germany doesn't know what to do about all the Turks. And the United States doesn't know what to do with all the Latin Americans and the Caribbean immigrants now within its borders. The people of the former colonial nations have migrated to the metropolises of their former colonial masters in such numbers that they are reshaping the very composition of those nations. In that context, the media systems become so much more important for coping with this demographic upheaval—that is, for controlling the narrative. But it's not simply a question of displaying greater diversity in the faces on the TV screen's evening news programs. More important is the question of *who owns the institutions that disseminate news and information.* The more decentralized and democratic media ownership is, the more democratic any nation is. And that is perhaps the biggest lesson I learned in my effort to unravel the amazing story of how our media system came to be.

In discussing how to safeguard access and democracy, I will start by addressing the contemporary moment of downsizing and downscaling. I work in both the commercial media and the alternative media, with *Democracy Now!*, so I have my feet in both worlds. In the commercial media, if you are a journalist today there is nothing but depression. You see newsrooms shrinking everywhere. Whether it's print, radio, or television, more and more people are getting laid off. More and more information is being regurgitated from the Internet, where few entrepreneurs want to pay a living wage to produce decent, original news reporting, unless you are at one of the major television networks. So many journalists in America today are totally demoralized. On the other hand, in shows like *Democracy Now!* and "alternative" or community media, there is an enormous sense of possibility, that the revolution created by the Internet has unleashed powers, and nobody knows where this will end up.

The key thing to keep in mind is that the center of power in the media world has shifted, from the content providers to the people who control the pipes. The power in media in the world today is not with the *New York Times*, not with ABC, it's not with those who produce the entertainment and news content, it is with those who transmit that content to your cell phone, to your cable box. It is with those who provide the navigation instruments to acquire content.

In America, we do not have to worry about censorship, we have to worry about the jumble of news and information being thrown at us, and we must figure out how to separate the nonsense and the garbage from what is important and what is real. So we must depend on navigation tools. That means that the power has shifted from the content providers, the newspaper chains and the broadcast networks, to the Googles, the Apples, the Time Warners, the Verizons, and the Comcasts.

A perfect example is NBC. Who purchased it recently? Comcast—a cable giant. Those who control the pipes bought the content. And then there is *Newsday*. Who bought it? Cablevision. The folks who provide you the service, bought the content. And those who control the Internet pipes want unfettered control of them. They want to determine how their pipes are going to provide you with all that entertainment and news. Will you be able to download a Netflix film at the same speed as Javier Castaño's Queens news website, or can Netflix pay more to get a faster download? And if Javier can't pay more, his website will download at a slower speed. So net neutrality becomes the fundamental issue right now in preserving democracy in terms of news and information flow. That's one issue.

Another big issue that people pay very little attention to is public access. A lot of public access programs are mediocre, but some are excellent. Sometimes some crazy person gets a show on a public access channel and people actually watch it because it provides stuff they don't get anywhere else. And certainly it provides great opportunity for minorities to have shows and to produce original material. When cable started, there were sixteen or seventeen channels and cable systems, and they had to provide a minimum of four public channels—local, state, university, and some public access channel. They provided all that as part of their public responsibility for having a monopoly on the right to string their lines along city streets. Now some cable systems have a thousand channels, and the number of public access channels is still very small. Once cable ownership became concentrated in a few dominant companies, those companies pressured the politicians to rewrite their franchise contracts, and the public gradually lost a battle to keep the same percentage of public access channels on local cable stations that had previously been required. In Illinois, AT&T operates its video system called U-verse. Now, in the entire state of Illinois, there's one public access channel, Channel 99. When you go to channel 99, you then download a menu, to find the AT&T public access channels in your town or your county.

So you have to hunt down one of a thousand channels to find public access in that state. That happened because AT&T essentially bought the Illinois state legislators to do that for them. Meanwhile, you can find multiple NBA Pass channels and scores of music channels on any cable system. But public access—the people's access to the media—is being decimated. You could be using interactive cable to promote great democracy and localism, but it's not being done because the movement is not organizing itself to demand these changes. So there's the public access issue.

I've already mentioned the surveillance issue. Everything you do on the Internet is being tracked. And nobody is saying, "Hey, we got to have some privacy on the Internet." There have to be better safeguards against surveillance.

And finally, there's minority ownership. And I don't think about minority ownership just in terms of owning sites. Something has to be done to assure racial and ethnic equity in the investment community, to bring about greater access to start-up capital for African-Americans and US Latinos seeking to transform the old narratives.

There are all kinds of things that can be done by government policy to ensure that there is an equitable and diverse media system in the country, but you have to work at it, and you have to grasp the historical lesson that media policy in America isn't determined by some abstract free market. It has always been fashioned by government leaders in response to technological change and public pressure.

NOTE

1. This piece was originally a speech delivered during the first Contemporary Latin@ Media conference, held at New York University, spring 2012.

Hector Amaya is Associate Professor of Media Studies at the University of Virginia and specializes in North American transnationalism, including Mexico, Cuba, and the United States. He writes on the cultural production of political identities and the complex manner in which cultural flows and immigration are transforming the nation-state. His most recent publication, *Citizenship Excess: Latino/as, Media, and the Nation*, was published by New York University Press (2013).

Jillian Báez is Assistant Professor of Media Culture at the College of Staten Island–City University of New York (CUNY) and an affiliate professor at the CUNY Mexican Studies Institute. She specializes in Latina/o media, audience studies, and transnational feminisms, and has published her work in the *Journal of Popular Communication, Centro: Journal of the Center for Puerto Rican Studies, Critical Studies in Media Communication*, and *Women's Studies Quarterly*.

Cristina Beltrán is Associate Professor in the Department of Social and Cultural Analysis at New York University and is the author of *The Trouble with Unity: Latino Politics and the Creation of Identity* (2010). Her work has appeared in *Political Theory, Aztlán, Politics & Gender, Political Research Quarterly, Du Bois Review*, and various edited volumes.

Dolores Inés Casillas is Assistant Professor in the Department of Chicana and Chicano Studies, and a faculty affiliate of Latin American Studies and Film and Media Studies, at the University of California–Santa Barbara. Her manuscript, *Sounds of Belonging: Public Advocacy on Spanish-Language Radio, 1922–2006* (forthcoming from New York University Press), examines how immigration politics throughout the twentieth century has shaped US Spanish-language radio.

Mari Castañeda is Associate Professor in the Department of Communication and the Center for Latin American, Caribbean and Latino

Studies at the University of Massachusetts–Amherst, and director of diversity advancement for the College of Social and Behavioral Sciences. Her fields of study include new media and communication policy, transcultural political economy, and Latino/Chicano media studies. She recently coedited *Telenovelas and Soap Operas in the Digital Age: Global Industries and New Audiences* (2011), and *Mothers in Academia* (2013).

María Elena Cepeda is Associate Professor of Latina/o Studies at Williams College, with a focus on transnational Latina/o media and popular culture. She is the author of *Musical ImagiNation: U.S.-Colombian Identity and the Latin Music Boom* (New York University Press, 2010), and coeditor with Dolores Inés Casillas of the forthcoming *Routledge Companion to Latina/o Media Studies*.

Arlene Dávila is Professor of Anthropology and American Studies at New York University and researches on Latino/Latin American cultural politics, political economy, and media. Her most recent publication, *Culture Works: Space, Value, and Mobility across the Neoliberal Americas*, was published by New York University Press (2012).

Vanessa Díaz is a journalist, filmmaker, and PhD candidate in Anthropology at the University of Michigan. A Ford Foundation and Smithsonian Institute Fellow, she is currently completing her dissertation, "Manufacturing Celebrity, Marketing Fame: An Ethnographic Study of Celebrity Media Production"; she also wrote and produced the independent feature-length documentary *Cuban HipHop: Desde el Principio*.

André Dorcé is Lecturer-Researcher in Communication Sciences at the Universidad Autónoma Metropolitana in Mexico City. He has worked as Founding Ombudsman at Public Broadcasting Station Canal 22, and his research focuses on the role of both material and symbolic communication technologies as expressions—and constitutive elements—of contemporary subjectivities and social power relations.

Rodrigo Gómez is Senior Lecturer in Communication and Cultural Policies at the Universidad Autónoma Metropolitana in Mexico City. He is the former president of the Mexican Association of Communication Research and is currently the vice-chair of the Political Economy Section of the International Association of Media Communication

Research (IAMCR), and serves on the editorial advisory board of the IAMCR journal *Political Economy of Communication.*

Juan González has been a professional journalist for more than thirty years and a staff columnist at the *New York Daily News* since 1987. He is a two-time recipient of the George Polk Award for commentary (1998 and 2010); a founder and past president of the National Association of Hispanic Journalists, and a member of NAHJ's Hall of Fame. A founding member of the Young Lords Party in the 1970s and of the National Congress for Puerto Rican Rights in the 1980s, González has received Lifetime Achievement Awards from the Hispanic Heritage Foundation, the National Council of La Raza, and the National Puerto Rican Coalition. González is the author of *Harvest of Empire: A History of Latinos in America,* and *Roll Down Your Window: Stories of a Forgotten America,* and coauthor with Joseph Torres of *News for All the People: The Epic Story of Race and the American Media.*

María Paula Martínez is Professor and Director of the M.A. in Journalism at Universidad de los Andes in Colombia. She is the coauthor of Mapping Digital Media: Colombia, an international research project led by the Open Society Foundation, and is currently developing the Colombian version of "The State of News Media."

Toby Miller is Distinguished Professor of Media and Cultural Studies at the University of California–Riverside. He is the author and editor of over thirty books that have been translated into many languages. You can follow his adventures at tobymiller.org.

Ed Morales is a lecturer at Columbia University's Center for the Study of Ethnicity and Race and a New York–based journalist who has written for the *Village Voice,* the *Nation,* the *New York Times,* the *Los Angeles Times, Rolling Stone,* the *Progressive Media Project,* and *Newsday.* Morales is also the author of two books, *Living in Spanglish* (2003) and *The Latin Beat* (2003), and the codirector of *Whose Barrio?* (2009), a documentary about the gentrification of East Harlem.

Frances Negrón-Muntaner is a filmmaker, scholar, and author of *Boricua Pop: Puerto Ricans and the Latinization of American Culture* (CHOICE Award, New York University Press, 2004), and *Sovereign Acts* (forthcoming). She is the Director of the Center for the Study of

Ethnicity and Race and cofounder of the Latino Arts and Activism Archive at Columbia University.

Juan Piñón is Assistant Professor of Media, Culture, and Communication at New York University and is the US coordinator of the Ibero-American Television Fiction Observatory (OBITEL), an international research project on television fiction. His work has been published in numerous journals, including *Communication Theory*, *Global Media and Communication*, *Television and New Media*, and the *International Journal of Cultural Studies*.

Henry Puente is Associate Professor at California State University–Fullerton. He has extensive entertainment industry experience, is a former film distribution executive, and is the author of *The Promotion and Distribution of U.S. Latino Films* (2011).

Omar Rincón is Program Director of the MA in Journalism and Associate Professor at Universidad de los Andes in Colombia. He is a journalist and analyst of media, culture, politics, and technology, and a TV critic for the newspaper *El Tiempo*.

Yeidy M. Rivero is Associate Professor in the Department of Screen Arts and Culture at the University of Michigan, and her research centers on television history, media and globalization, and race and ethnic representation in media. She is the author of *Tuning Out Blackness: Race and Nation in the History of Puerto Rican Television* (2005) and *Broadcasting Modernity: Cuban Commercial Television, 1950–1960* (forthcoming).

Deborah R. Vargas is Associate Professor in the Department of Ethnic Studies at the University of California–Riverside, and the author of *Dissonant Divas in Chicana Music: The Limits of La Onda* (2012). Her research areas include critical race feminisms, queer studies, Chicano studies, Latino studies, and cultural studies. She has published in *Feminist Studies*, *Women and Performance: A Journal of Feminist Theory*, *Aztlán: A Journal of Chicano Studies*, and *Social Text*.

Christopher Joseph Westgate is an Assistant Professor in the English Department at Johnson and Wales University. His articles and reviews have been published in *Media, Culture & Society*; *Communication, Culture & Critique*; the *Journal of Communication*; and the *Journal of Popular Music Studies*.

INDEX

ABC, 29, 39n1, 82, 108, 109, 113, 119. *See also Grey's Anatomy*

ABC-Univision, 82, 83–84, 89, 90. *See also* Fusion

Academy of Motion Picture Arts and Sciences, 13, 110

Access, to media, 6, 9, 118, 191, 219–20, 342; civil rights movement and, 10–11, 117; Latin@ radio and, 194–202; safeguarding, 344–47

Activism, 13, 116–21; advertising and, 118–19; goals, 322; immigration rights, 245–46; media-rated campaigns, *117, 118. See also* Afro-Colombian organizations; DREAM activists; Migrant activism; *specific campaigns*

Advertising, 104, 210; activism and, 118–19; affect versus effect, 273, 282n7; audience evaluation companies and, 208–9; bilingual, 333; industry, 51, 282n9; Latinas as consumer-citizens and, 272–76; Latin@ TV, *53;* NuvoTV, 67, 68, 71–72; Spanish-language media and, 51; spending and markets of interest, *53;* telenovelas and, 54. *See also* Marketing

Advocacy, media, 11, 110, 113, 116–21, 260, 337; Latin@ radio and, 200–202, 203. *See also* Activism

Advocate, 325

African Americans, 112–13; alternative media and, 324; Arbitron and, 210–11, 212, 215–16; ethnic radio and, 188–92; Latin@s compared to, 111; representation, 151

African Diaspora, 157–58

Afro-Colombian organizations, 164, 165; African Diaspora and, 157–58; casting expectations, 150, 151; "horizon of expectation" and, 154, 156; RCN and, 149–50. *See also* Cimarrón Nacional

Alarcón, Raúl, Jr., 211–12, 219

Alliance, 47–51, 55, 171–72, 181; enterprise, 180; NuvoTV, 67–68. *See also specific alliances*

Alternative media, 322, 335, 344–45; African Americans and, 324; inaccurate labeling, 334; language and, 323–24, 330–31, 332–34; marketing and, 329–30; NPR and, 328–29; ownership, 325; PBS and, 325, 326–27; production, 322–23; representation, 324, 325–27

Amas de casa desesperadas, 153–54

Amaya, Hector, 12

"América" (Los Tigres del Norte and Calle 13), 303, 304, 307–12, *311, 313;* cultural reading of, 314–18

América Móvil, 56n6

"American" identity, 303, 308, 310, 314–16, 317, 329–30

Andrade, Amelia, 178

Anti-immigration discourse, 4, 330; on *Lou Dobbs Tonight,* 119–21; underrepresentation and, 10

Appadurai, Arjun, 225

Arbitron Inc., 207–9, 219–20; African Americans and, 210–11, 212, 215–16; assimilating to practices of, 214–16; fees, 212–13; language preference and, 216–18; measurement transitions, 210–14. *See also* Portable People Meter; *specific technologies*

Arellano, Elvira, 276–78, 283n14